PAUL ROBINSON

AFTER SURVIVAL

A TEACHER'S GUIDE TO CANADIAN RESOURCES

PETER MARTIN ASSOCIATES LIMITED

Canadian Cataloguing in Publication Data

Robinson, Paul, 1938—
  After survival

Bibliography: p.
ISBN 0-88778-147-0 bd.   ISBN 0-88778-150-0 pa.
1. Canadian studies. I. Title.

FC95.4.R62   971   C77-001024-5
F1025.R62

Design: Michael Solomon

PETER MARTIN ASSOCIATES LIMITED
280 Bloor Street West, Toronto, Ontario M5S 1W1

United Kingdom: Books Canada, 1 Bedford Road, London N2, England
United States: Books Canada, 33 East Tupper St., Buffalo, N.Y. 14203

For Dale, Evan and Lindsay
and the young Canadians
of their generation

Acknowledgements

My continuing gratitude is expressed to: my mother and father for
the influence of a fine home; friends in education and related endeavours throughout Canada for the opportunities to work and
learn more about this country and its peoples; The Atlantic Institute
of Education in Halifax for the opportunity to engage in teaching,
research and community-based education activities; Joseph Lauwerys,
William Hamilton and Gary Anderson of the Atlantic Institute of
Education for advice and generosity in permitting me the time to
work on this book; Judy Publicover, also of the Institute, for understanding, skill and good spirits in transposing my scribbles to a readable manuscript; Carol and Peter Martin for taking a chance on a
novice writer; Kay Repka for patience, thoroughness and efficiency
in editing and re-writing; Marjorie Fee for her stamina in the monumental task of checking the bibliography; my children, Dale, Evan
and Lindsay for good humour, toleration and counsel during the
ups and downs of my working experience; Elaine Robinson, wife,
mother and partner for sharing and participating in my life and
work.

A simple "thank you" is inadequate. I hope that friends from
the Labrador coast to the Queen Charlotte Islands; and from the
Annapolis Valley of Nova Scotia to Grise Fiord, Northwest Territories will accept what is of value in these pages as a token of my
respect and affection for them and their children.

Contents

Chapter 1

INTRODUCTION

"Have we survived?
If so, what happens AFTER survival?"

Margaret Atwood, *Survival*

The acclamation which followed the publication of Margaret Atwood's *Survival: A Thematic Study of Canadian Literature* (Toronto: Anansi, 1972) is a devastating comment on the Canadian psyche. One hundred and five years after Confederation Canada's literary heritage has arrived. "CanLit" is of topical, best-selling interest.

In the 1960's Bernard Hodgetts and his associates kindled a fire which, if not yet blazing, continues to smoulder through the underbrush of education. He investigated and analyzed the extent and effectiveness of the teaching of Canadian studies (history, in particular) in the schools. His book, *What Culture? What Heritage?: A Study of Civic Education in Canada* (Toronto: O.I.S.E., 1968) is, like *Survival,* a must for anyone wishing to have in-depth information at his fingertips. His research findings were not encouraging.

Edmonton publisher Mel Hurtig instigated a nationwide "Canadian Awareness Survey" in 1975. Throughout the ten provinces, the Yukon, and Northwest Territories, a cross-section of students in their last year of high school were requested to complete a questionnaire. Tabulation of the results provided a dismaying picture of students' knowledge of their own country. Some of the more striking results included:

About 70% had little or no idea what percentage of Canada's population is French-Canadian.

61% were unable to name the B.N.A. Act as Canada's constitution.

About half had no idea why the War Measures Act was proclaimed in 1970.

92% could not identify Norman Bethune.

Hurtig, M., *Never Heard of Them . . . They Must Be Canadian,* (Toronto: Canadabooks, 1975)

And there have been others. Robin Matthews and James Steele in their book, *The Struggle for Canadian Universities* (Toronto: New,

1

1969), created a flurry of anxiety among the academics when they surveyed the staffing procedures in the universities. Non-Canadian influence over education does not cease when the textbook writers silence the click-clack of their typewriters. The lecturer, the professor, the department chairperson, may well be foreign too. Nearly a decade before Matthews' and Steele's revelations, Robertson Davies noted the dependency of Canadian universities on teachers from Great Britain and the United States.

> . . . in 1962, only 62% of the staff members engaged by Canadian universities were Canadian, trained wholly or in part in Canada. (*Atlantic Month,* November 1962)

In retrospect, 62% may have been the high water mark in terms of Canadian staffing at the university level.

George Martell and the staff of *This Magazine* have hammered away with consistency and regularity at the theme of Canadian control, be it applied to education or to other pursuits. Other education journalists pale by comparison with *This Magazine*'s efforts to arouse educators from their inertia.

Finally, almost from another era it seems, there have been those like Walter Gordon, Eric Kierans, and Mel Watkins, whose concerns, though not directed specifically to education, are basic to the issue of Canadian survival.

Mentioning this random collection of respected writers, academics, and political theorists is not merely a name-dropping exercise designed to get the reader's attention. Rather, it is a matter of underscoring the severity of the education crisis which confronts the nation's schools directly, and the minds of students indirectly. Canadians control education in the same fashion they control the economy—hardly at all.

It is within the scope of this book to look at one aspect of this crisis—the learning materials: text books, library books, film materials, recorded material, games and toys, picture sets, periodicals, maps and charts—which are used to direct the learning of children and young people from kindergarten through high school graduation. Teachers excepted, these constitute the single most influential factor in determining what the student learns in school. From the domination of the magazine industry for young readers by *Jack and Jill, Humpty-Dumpty, Children's Hi-Lites*; to the Scholastic monopoly of the paperback industry for the pre-teen years; to the *Time* magazine current events program for high school students, American influence bestrides Canadian education like the ancient Colossus.

The enormity and the gravity of the situation can be illustrated readily by examining the practices and products of major book distributors and publishers who have cornered the education market.

Bro-Dart of Canada Ltd. provides an interesting case study, particularly with respect to the library books which students are most likely to encounter. Before plunging into the details, one irritant must be mentioned. That insidious little phrase, "of Canada Ltd.", is as symbolic of this industry as it is of the breakfast cereals consumed in the morning, or the sheets between which Canadians crawl at night. The most influential distributors and publishers are branch plants—subsidiaries of Xerox, I.B.M., or other American-based parent firms.

The Canadian subsidiary of Bro-Dart, like almost all major firms of this type, is located in or near Toronto—in this instance Brantford, Ontario. Its 1975 catalogue of books for secondary schools (grades 7-12) lists a staggering total of 57 500 titles—obviously an immense quantity of books, and the catalogue is a very handy reference. Teachers, librarians, and school administrators, who have the responsibility for ordering books, are saved the time and trouble of sorting through an apparently limitless array of individual publishers' catalogues in their search for materials. Bro-Dart has performed admirably this detailed, time-consuming task. Nevertheless, before anyone strikes a librarian's best friend award for this company, a query or two about the sources which influenced Bro-Dart's selections is in order. Two prime categories of sources were employed: the shelf lists (i.e. the library collections) of selected high schools and the recommendations of book reviewers. In the words of Bro-Dart:

" . . . Bro-Dart conducted a research study of the shelf lists of six high-school libraries believed to be typical of the best secondary school libraries in the country. The six schools were chosen for their excellent library collections, nationally respected personnel, geographical location, community characteristics and curriculum."

Books For Secondary School Libraries Grades 7-12 (Brantford: Bro-Dart, 1975, p. 1)

Fair enough. But, it may be asked, in what geographic locations, employing which curricula, are these six high schools found? The answers are:

East Hanover, New Jersey   Oak Park, Illinois
Rochester, New York   Plantation, Florida
Oakland, California   Bethesda, Maryland

Apparently Canadian high school libraries are not a priority concern of Bro Dart.

What about the book reviews cited in the catalogue? Can one expect at least a doff of the hat in the direction of Canada? Not at all. Exclusive attention is given to American periodicals:

School Library Journal
Booklist
The McNaughton Young Adult Plan
The New York Times Book Review

Admittedly, even with the absolute lack of interest in Canadian sources, it is possible to find a tiny percentage of Canadiana in the catalogue IF you have the memory of a computer. Bro-Dart, like numerous other companies, does not indicate to the reader which titles are Canadian. The only way this can be determined is by trying to identify the writers and/or the publishers. To say that this is not easy to do is to understate the case. Practically speaking, trying to select Canadian books from Bro-Dart's listings is impossible. The end result is that the potential purchaser is on the horns of a dilemma.

It speaks well of the company's business acumen that not only is an exhaustive array of books available but, should it be desired, a pre-packaged library can be bought within an attractive price range:

The Basic Book Collection for Junior High Schools—398 titles (recommended by the American Library Association):$1 900.00

The Vocational-Technical Learning Materials Library—4 360 titles (published by Bro-Dart): $42 700.00

For a relatively small additional cost the package comes processed—library indexing, card cataloguing, etc. are all included. The fact that the customer is buying a "pig-in-a poke" may be of relatively little concern. Bro-Dart makes it all so terribly easy. In a perverse sort of way, the nourishment of the body provided by the instant T.V. dinner has been supplemented by the nourishment of the mind through instant libraries.

A clue as to why most Bro-Dart materials are not suitable for Canadian schools is found in the fact that two percent or less of all the publishers mentioned are Canadian (including foreign subsidiaries operating in Canada). This may explain why the books on Abraham Lincoln outnumber the titles pertaining to Sir Wilfred Laurier by a margin of twenty-two to zero. As for Sir John A. Macdonald, he is of no great importance compared to Marilyn Monroe, if the listed book titles are any indication.

Let it not be concluded, however, that Bro-Dart is the villain of the piece. Far from it. An examination of the 1975 catalogue of Canadian Book Wholesale, "the fastest growing wholesale book inventory in Canada", is equally instructive.

The inclusion of the word 'Canadian' in the firm's name implies that this is a distributor of Canadian books.

The sources of information which guided the selection of the 5300 titles do include school authorities in Edmonton and Toronto.

The book reviews consulted include basic Canadian references: *Books In Canada, In Review, The Ontario Library Journal.*

Specific reference is made to the publications issued by the Ontario Ministry of Education and the British Columbia Department of Education.

It may come as a surprise, then, to realize that Canadian Book Wholesale's merchandise differs little from that of Bro-Dart. Canadian Book Wholesale does not indicate to its catalogue readers which of its titles are Canadian. The annotated bibliography may afford a clue—if a Canadian reference point is mentioned. Failing this, the only recourse is to try to identify writers and/or publishers. For example, McCLELLAND AND STEWART, in block print, is a fairly safe bet. "The Canadian Publishers", the slogan of McClelland and Stewart, would probably ring bells in the minds of those responsible for buying learning materials for the schools. The question is, can the same thing be said for Petheric, Coach House, and Mitchell, which are equally Canadian, but certainly less well known nationally? Similarly, the names of writers such as Farley Mowat, Sheila Burnford, Thomas Raddall and Mordecai Richler, if not household words, are at least reasonably well known. Can the same be said for Christie Harris, William Kurelek, and Ann Blades? Unless the reader possesses the encyclopedic knowledge of an ardent Canadian bibliophile, the chances are excellent that the few Canadian books which are listed will go unnoticed or, at best, will be purchased only by chance.

With the exception of the history section, the probability of finding any Canadian materials at all is remote. Ignoring important considerations like the quality and usefulness of the items, and assuming the problem is simply one of purchasing books written by Canadians, the percentages of Canadian books available from Canadian Book Wholesale in specific subject fields are as follows:

Music	3%	Literature	42%
The Arts	20%	History	62%
Biography	24%		

These areas of learning were deliberately selected on the assumption that if Canadian material is available, then it will more likely be found in the humanities and fine arts rather than in mathematics and the physical sciences. In other words, the odds were stacked in favour of Canadian Book Wholesale. In the combined fields of physics, chemistry and allied sciences, and earth sciences, not quite two per cent of the books listed are Canadian. The agricultural section is slightly better—five per cent of the books are Canadian. One must stretch the definition of agriculture to include Farley Mowat's *A Whale For The Killing* (Toronto: McClelland, 1972), and *The Eastern Panther* (Toronto: Clarke, Irwin, 1972).

At the risk of overkill, a parting glance can be taken at the fiction section of the catalogue. Part and parcel of the educational process in any school is the encouragement given to "leisure" or "free reading periods", as they are sometimes called. The student who makes a selection of a novel or a book of poetry as provided by Canadian Book Wholesale would have one chance in sixteen of finding anything written by a Canadian—discounting again the quality and/or the relevance to Canada. It is interesting to note that the books of two writers, Lucy Maud Montgomery and Lyn Cook, comprise thirteen per cent of the available Canadiana. Mordecai Richler, W.O. Mitchell, and Margaret Atwood get one mention apiece. Margaret Laurence, Leonard Cohen, and Ernest Buckler are excluded entirely. By contrast, Alfred Hitchcock is worthy of four titles. The literary quality of his writing vis-à-vis that of any half dozen Canadian writers who come to mind, is not a moot point. The name of Canadian Book Wholesale grossly misrepresents its function as a distributor of Canadian learning materials.

Similarly with the Co-operative Book Centre of Canada Ltd.; the discrepancy between its advertising copy and the content of the catalogue, *Co-op '76 Checklist,* is prodigious. Casual reading of the promotional brochure, *New Directions in Canadian Wholesale Book Distribution,* could suggest that here is one distributor willing to confront unequivocally the foreign-domination issue. In the words of the Co-op:

> If any of us in this challenging, exciting industry does anything to damage the profits of Canadian publishers, thus reducing the number of Canadian books published, the American and British publishers will quickly fill the void with foreign material. (*New Directions In Canadian Wholesale Book Distribution,* Cooperative Book Centre of Canada Ltd., Toronto).

On the topic of "foreign material" used to "fill the void" in Canadian publishing, the Co-op can speak with authority. The 1976 K-13 catalogue lists approximately 22 500 titles. In the same curriculum subjects noted for Canadian Book Wholesale, the percentages of Canadiana are:

Music	6%	Literature	27%
The Arts	8%	History	23%
Biography	27%		

The explanation lies in the sources of information the Co-op used in making its recommendations; 75 per cent of the review journals consulted are American. Only *In Review* and the *Ontario Library Review* were evidently worthy of consideration from a Canadian perspective.

Scholar's Choice, "The Preferred Canadian Company For Learning Materials and Equipment", provides a department store service to the educational consumer. Filmstrips, music supplies, playground equipment, maps, globes, and imaginative programs are a few of the advertised product lines. Books, too, are available. The *Library Book Catalogue* lists 8500 titles conveniently grouped by subject and age level. The "Preferred Canadian Company" makes one-stop shopping a classroom reality. Only when the search for Canadian content comes to the fore does the slogan begin to grate. Less than 7 per cent of the library materials are Canadian—using a very liberal definition of that term. ("Books by Canadian authors and publishers, or books having a Canadian setting have been identified by an asterisk. . . ." Scholar's Choice Library Book Catalogue No. 302.)

By this point it may appear that the problem of finding Canadian books and other materials for schools is insoluble. Certainly the major distributing companies help to create that impression. In turn, scrutiny of the catalogues of the vast majority of publishing firms would seem to confirm this pessimistic view. Logically, it would be expected that the multi-national corporations, which control the lion's share of the publishing industry, would put into print proportionately more foreign-developed items than Canadian titles. In this respect the practice of including some Canadian material in the vain hope of appearing to be concerned with the national interest is typical. Gage Educational Publishing is an example. The 1975 catalogue of elementary (kindergarten through grade 6) materials lists 2870 items, including duplicate listings (materials listed under "social studies" reappear under "language arts" and vice versa). Of these, 28 per cent (797 items) may be either of Canadian origin or Canadianized versions of American materials. Employing the same yardstick as applied to Canadian Book Wholesale, namely, making the assumption that Canadian materials are most likely to be found in the social studies (history, geography) field, if they are to be found at all, it is unnerving to realize that only 26 per cent of the materials are in fact Canadian. In the health section the percentage of Canadiana is straightforward—it is zero.

Subject to the incessant indoctrination which leads many Canadians to accept the inevitability of foreign control over their lives, few people are likely to react strongly to the branch plant economy as applied to publishing. It is the way things have always been. But what of the Canadian-owned publishing houses themselves? Surely, they are the last bastion of defence. Regrettably, Canadian-owned publishing cannot be equated in every instance with Canadian-written books. Possibly the most vivid example of what the teacher or librarian is up against in trying to find Canadiana is provided by the parent firm of that national institution, *Maclean's Magazine.* Maclean-Hunter, which publishes "Canada's Newsmagazine", *Chatelaine,* and various other periodicals, has launched into the learning materials industry extensively in the past five years. Maclean-Hunter has made this move independently, but also under the prestigious label of Macmillan of Canada, which they now control. A superficial perusal of the 1975 catalogue reveals what might appear to be a continual thorn in the flesh—the absence of any Canadian designation. Could it be that Maclean-Hunter, seeing itself as Canadian as "Hockey Night in Canada", does not sense any obligation to indicate that less than 20 per cent of their material is Canadian? Excluding the math materials, the origin of which cannot be determined by the description provided, 87 per cent of the other items are imports from the United States or elsewhere. The percentages with respect to Macmillan of Canada are comparable.

Where does this leave the education system when it comes to giving Canadian students the opportunity to learn and to grow in their understanding of their own country? From books to periodicals, films to recordings, the foreign saturation of the Canadian mind is almost complete. But there remains a glimmer of hope. Two vital steps are required to alter the incredible imbalance which presently exists.

1. Such quality Canadian materials as are available from the multinational distributors and publishers can be identified and evaluated.

2. The few large Canadian-owned publishers and the many small independent firms can become the focus of attention for those responsible for locating useful Canadiana.

It is the intent of the following chapters to demonstrate how these steps can be taken. Twenty-five curriculum subjects ranging alphabetically from Art, Biology, and Business to Social Studies, minority cultures and ethnic groups ("Ukrainians and Other Unknown Canadians") have been examined with a view to locating and utilizing Canadian developed materials. Within each subject area materials were sought for the appropriate grade levels from kindergarten through high school graduation. The approximately three thousand titles have been arranged thematically, both to encourage their use and to provide a convenient method of integrating resource materials among the curriculum subjects.

Two limitations of this book must be stressed. In Chapter 2 the guidelines used by the author for evaluating the various materials are detailed. These criteria reflect the bias of the writer in two ways. Materials were selected because of their quality and not simply because they were prepared by Canadians. Once the choices were made, themes were established to provide each curriculum subject with a focus. The possibility of arriving at unanimity on either the definition of quality, or the determination of significant themes is remote at best.

A second major limitation is found in Chapter 3, "Getting Started is Half the Fun". *The Canadian Publishers' Directory* (Toronto: Greey de Pencier, 1975) lists in excess of three thousand book publishers, wholesalers, French language publishers, and audio-visual suppliers. No attempt was made to evaluate the Canadian materials from all these firms. For this reason alone, some excellent resources have undoubtedly been overlooked.

In fairness to readers and publishers alike, it is suggested that the bibliographic information be viewed as departure points. If nothing else, it is hoped the various chapters will indicate that the time and effort required to provide a Canadian foundation for each learning opportunity are justifiable.

To this end the ideas, topics, textbooks, and reference materials have been assembled.

Chapter 2

GUIDELINES FOR SELECTION OF MATERIALS

Criteria for evaluating and selecting learning materials are abundant in education research. In large part their presence reflects the search for the technologically sound measuring device that will do for textbooks what the Ottawa Centre of the Consumers' Association of Canada does for laundry detergents. Through readability scales, word-count formulae, and measuring devices of advanced sophistication, the educational technologist seeks solutions to the complex question: "How do children learn?"

The merit in these approaches to evaluating the effectiveness of books, audio-visual materials, and science apparatus is not now in question. What must be emphasized is that there is another aspect to materials evaluation and selection which traditionally has been overlooked. Canadian educators have not been accustomed to searching for those items which mirror the social imperatives of the nation, and in turn, the international community in which we live. In a practical sense Canadian classrooms are devoid of items that clearly suggest to the student the language implications of a bilingual nation; the ethnic and cultural pluralism within and without Canada; or the socio-economic realities of society.

In this chapter six broad categories of criteria are mentioned as these influenced the selection of materials for each chapter bibliography. Primary emphasis is placed on those guidelines which underline the realities of Canadian society. Particular mention is made of evaluating materials for prejudice, a criterion which has been thoroughly researched and documented in *Teaching Prejudice* (McDiarmid and Pratt, Toronto: O.I.S.E., 1971); *Textbook Analysis* (Halifax: Nova Scotia Human Rights Commission, 1974) and *The Shocking Truth: Indians In Textbooks* (Winnipeg: Manitoba Indian Brotherhood, 1974). The learning methodology inherent in materials is also addressed. The type of structured/unstructured learning situation

10

the teacher is attempting to establish is influenced by the philosophical bias of the textbook writer. The practical aspects of deciding what to buy and how much accessory equipment is required cannot be dismissed at a time of budgeting restraints and financial accountability.

Although on the surface the guidelines may appear to be complicated, essentially when taken together they underline one basic premise. Learning materials can be chosen which will provide a social purpose and a sense of direction to the child's educational experience.

A

Materials prepared in both official languages (English and French) are needed in every learning situation. Typically, the English-speaking student who has the opportunity is taught French as an isolated subject which he "takes" 40 minutes a day, three days a week (or 80 minutes every day for half of the school year, if a semester system is employed). The inherent weakness in this approach is that the study of the language becomes an end in itself. Mastery of French, like the memorization of the Pythagorian theorem, is something that is "done". It may be good for high school credits; it may be useful for university entrance requirements; it may even be a status symbol for the academic "stream". Seldom is the language viewed not just as an end in itself, but as a means, a tool, which can be used to facilitate better understanding in any subject area. In an officially bilingual country, a monumental mistake is being perpetuated so long as French (or English, as the case may be) is treated in this fragmentary fashion. *The Two Histories* (Toronto: C.B.C. Learning Systems, 1972), a half-hour cassette tape of dialogue between French-speaking and English-speaking college students, depicts an on-going problem in the schools. English language history books provide their particular version of Canada while French language materials provide a quite different interpretation.

One can only speculate on the benefits to be derived by making it possible for Alberta students to study history from a Quebec perspective, or for Gaspésie students to see the history of New Brunswick through the eyes of Acadian historians. Through this utilitarian approach, the interweaving of viewpoints and ideas throughout the school curriculum could become a reality. Languages would be employed in their intended fashion—as a means of improving communication and facilitating understanding.

Similarly, languages could become integral features of fine arts and literature. What is Pauline Julien saying in her music to English-speaking Canada, or what do W.O. Mitchell and Wallace Stegner have to say in their novels about life on the prairies which could develop greater understanding in Quebec? In mathematics, the genius of Zolten Dienes (Université de Sherbrooke) should be utilized in both French and English. Such bilingual mathematical materials are available.

B

Within the broad bilingual framework there exists a pluralistic society, representative of many cultural and ethnic groups. Materials reflecting this diversity are necessary on two counts. First, children of minority groups are entitled equally to the opportunity to learn about their particular customs, traditions, languages, and contributions to the nation's history. Secondly, beside this particular need is the broader necessity of providing every student with the chance to grow in awareness and understanding of all the peoples which comprise the Canadian populace.

Cultural appreciation must be viewed as a two-way street. Pursuing multi-cultural understanding will reinforce the individual's cultural pride and enhance the growth of respect among all groups. Token approaches, whereby a grade three child spends a couple of weeks in October "studying Indians" after which the "real" story of Canada (i.e. the coming of the   white man) can be studied in earnest, must be halted. Multi-cultural understanding must become an integral part of education.

C

Learning materials which reflect the social and economic realities of society are a necessity. Much of what is presently in use in schools reflects a middle-class, sexist bias, particularly in reading. Although the prose style of many such materials is dull, even mind-deadening, the more subtle evil is the inculcation of stereotypes. The indoctrination process commences early in the child's school life. The "good life" consists of such items as:

—mommy, daddy, and two kids (one of each)
—a pet (mischievous)
—split-level bungalow (on Daffodil Drive)
—a non-white pal (middle class, too)
—a granny (on the farm)

Given the cast of characters and the setting, the plot is not thick.

Neither are the attitudes and values conveyed obscure. Happiness is:
  —a white-collar job for dad
  —a frilly apron for mom
  —family planning
  —a two-car garage and similar manifestations of economic well-
    being
  —a fresh-from-the-pages-of-the-mail-order-catalogue look on all
    concerned.

The fact that these images have little, if anything, to do with the
society in which children live has been of limited concern to the
educators responsible for such items. The realities of poverty, unemployment, pollution, discrimination, exploitation, and racism
apparently have no place in learning materials. It is little wonder,
therefore, that children of the mass-media age, particularly as influenced by television, have some difficulty becoming "turned-on" to
reading, and more in seeing the school as relevant to their experiences
after the 3:30 dismissal bell has rung.

   At the junior high levels, the problem increases. Standardized textbooks, as authorized by Departments of Education, often reinforce
the artificial atmosphere. Issues of social, economic, and political
concern are emasculated of any controversy. Anything which might
quicken the pulse and generate some enthusiasm is either ignored
or written in a style which would do justice to a senatorial report on
postage stamps. It can be safely assumed that any resemblance which
the student sees between textbook social studies courses and current
affairs television programming is accidental.

D

Prejudice is the spectre which haunts many widely used materials.
Before leaping to the conclusion that burning books is the answer,
it is important to note that materials which have been deliberately
contrived to teach about prejudice are valuable. Similarly, in the
hands of a knowledgeable, sensitive teacher, materials characterized
by bias can be used to advantage. An example is the 1969 Information Canada publication, *Fur Trade Canoe Routes of Canada / Then
and Now*. Recommended in the 1974 Circular 15 of the Ontario
Ministry of Education, this book does have considerable potential in
a variety of curriculum subjects, including environmental studies,
recreation, and history. For catching a glimpse of the era of the
voyageur and the excitement of white-water canoeing, *Fur Trade
Canoe Routes* is difficult to equal. It is therefore disappointing to

read carefully the section entitled "The Contribution of the Indian" (p. 18-19) and to realize the clarity with which the author perceived the historical niche of native peoples. In rapid succession the reader is informed of the "partnership" that native and non-native peoples shared in the wilderness economy; the "special rapport" between the Indian and the fur trader; the unique role of the "chief's daughter"; the "fair dealing" of the Hudson's Bay Company, and the resounding conclusion to the effect that once the Iroquois were "pacified" business went on as usual.

Setting aside the unwarranted assumption that teachers always know what to do with prejudiced material, the concern has to be for those items which masquerade under the guise of objectivity. In effect, the messages conveyed in too many materials can serve to reinforce ignorance, intensify negative feelings toward minority groups, and confirm unfounded suspicions. Evaluating materials in terms of bias can be performed readily by considering two categories— sins of omission, and sins of commission. The sins of omission provide the greater challenge. It is necessary to ask continuously: What sides of the story are being left out? Are there aspects of the subject being taught to the students which should be included but are not? The odds favour the application of this criterion to history materials, but what about all the other areas of learning? Art is one example. It is by no means a certainty that in studying art a student will be exposed to even the Group of Seven. The best that can be said is that Tom Thomson, A.Y. Jackson, and Lawren Harris are more likely to receive attention than the Saskatchewan Emma Lake School of Painting, the Quebec Automatistes, or the Maritime artists Alex Colville and Tom Forrestall. Parallel examples can be illustrated in literature. Textbook anthologies focus on English-speaking Canada in general and on Ontario contributors in particular. Writers from other parts of Canada get sporadic mention, if any. As for history and the social sciences, the omissions are of mammoth proportions. (Elaboration is provided in the appropriate chapters.) One indication of the dimension of the problem is found in the highly respected and widely used book, *Dominion of the North* by Donald Creighton (Toronto: Macmillan, 1958). Out of 581 pages of text, the settlement of the Canadian West by Eastern European peoples receives less than one page. Needless to say, Indian peoples have no history after the treaties were signed, and women, like other oppressed segments of the population, are seldom seen and even more rarely heard.

Sins of commission are in most instances easier to detect. Things to watch for include:

1. *Value laden terminology.* "Primitive", "savage", and "uncivilized" are applied frequently to native peoples. "Squaw" and "redskins" persist as well. "Massacre" is the result of "Indians on the warpath." Unblemished "victories" in combat are the province of white people. "Medicine men" believed in "spirits" while "Christians" believed in "God". "Savages" used tomahawks and bows and arrows, while "civilized" people used repeating rifles and biological warfare (e.g. blankets infected with smallpox bacteria.)

2. *Stereotypes.* When Pierre Vallières described Québécois as the *White Niggers of America* (Toronto: McClelland, 1971), the analogy was perhaps closer than he realized. Whereas black peoples dine on fried chicken and execute a fast shuffle on the dance floor, Québécois are partial to maple syrup and the singing of folksy lumberjack songs. Quite a jolly, if innocuous bunch! Scots, by contrast are stern, frugal, and hard-working—the veritable backbone of the nation. Methodists provide spiritual strength. Roman Catholics, being somewhat more adventuresome, tend to be suspect. The Métis provided brawn—the voyageur image, but not brains—the legacy of Louis Riel. For women, there was always the butter to churn.

3. *Illustrations, Layout, Design.* The assembly of pictures and text often grossly distorts the content. A non-textbook example is the 1975 McGraw-Hill catalogue for elementary schools. The pictorial layout might create the impression that 90 per cent of the titles listed are Canadian. In effect, a count of the items will indicate almost the opposite. The vast majority of books are American. Similar techniques can be used in the textbooks themselves. The illustrations often imply that Russians glower (that's Communism for you); the French smile (imbibing too much of the grape?); Latin Americans are happy-go-lucky, if down at the heels (ignorance is bliss?); Chinese are regimented (the "Red" Chinese, that is); and Americans are industrious and wealthy (well, what did you expect?)! Closer to home, the visual imagery can be no less striking and inaccurate: British Columbians spend much time chopping down trees; Maritimers peer out of the fog on occasion; prairie citizens surely suffer from eye strain and sunburn standing around squinting at the limitless horizon; while the big city dwellers of the east refine their sophisticated lifestyles. As for the North, it is the home of God's Frozen People.

Lighthearted though this may appear, the degree of bias and bigotry that pervades far too many learning materials has serious implications for Canadian society as a whole. It is as trite as it is true to state that, as a nation, Canada defies logic. Its size, the regional diversity and disparities, the composition of the population, the

pull of geography against the lines of transportation and communication—all place heavy strains on the federal state. At the same time, if
one more cliché can be tolerated, the goal of unity amid diversity is
pertinent to the future not only of Canada, but of the planet itself.
One seemingly small but valuable step in the pursuit of that goal is
to provide learning experiences for young and old alike which will
create better understanding, develop human awareness, and contribute to mutual appreciation and respect. To this end a dramatic
change in the quality and quantity of books and other materials
which are made available in schools is required.

E

Learning methodology is a contentious issue in education circles.
How does an individual learn in the most effective, efficient manner?
Supposedly, if it could be determined absolutely that students learn
best in a given way, then learning materials could be developed which
would put the science of learning into practice. Even if *one* right way
could not be pinpointed for every individual, then maybe three, five,
or a dozen ways could be plotted. Once the limits of possibilities
were known, it would be a matter of grouping the students accord-
ingly and providing the appropriate learning experiences. (First you
diagnose the problem, then administer the remedy—a process remi-
niscent of the categorizing of grade one children into robins, starlings,
and crows for the purpose of teaching them to read. To be six years
old and a "crow" was to bear a stigma of considerable proportions.
Not only did the child have to contend with being in the "slow reading group", but the connotation of the label was difficult to ignore.)

Like a pack of huskies worrying a beleaguered polar bear, many
influential educators are persistent and tenacious in their pursuit of
the elusive solutions. Broadly speaking, their energies are dispersed
along the spectrum ranging from the ideas of the American behaviour-
ist psychologist B.F. Skinner, to those of the British open-school
advocate A.S. Neill. (Canadian education is almost completely dominated by the influence of foreign philosophers, psychologists, and
researchers.) Lying between the extremes are all manner of schools
of thought, the identification of which can prove challenging. In
attempting to understand the jargon, as applied to learning materials,
a glossary of terms is useful. Publishers' catalogues are strewn with
terms such as:

1. *Controlled vocabulary.* A predetermined limit is placed on the
number of words used in a reading series. Presumably, if the twelve

hundred (or is it the 1329?) most commonly used words are learned, then a blow will have been struck for basic literacy.

2. *Phonetics.* In language arts rules have been developed to help pupils "sound out" difficult words.

3. *Sight method.* Perhaps the shape of the letters provides a clue helpful in learning to read: "h" is tall like an "l" with a hump on it while "q" is actually a "c" with a tail attached.

4. *Linguistics.* The science of language could transform bilingual education, if only the research evidence were available to all teachers.

5. *Kinesic linguistics.* Body language, or, for the pre-reader, an opportunity to "feel" the sound and shape of "f" by tracing with a finger the letter flocked in felt.

6. *Programmed learning.* The vocabulary of the computer has been plagiarized. "In-puts", "out-puts" and "information retrieval" are required for the "client recipients" (i.e. students) who work at "levels." For example, using a "measuring device" (i.e., a standardized test), it is possible to determine that a student is at the 2.8 level of reading difficulty, meaning the individual is somewhat better than a "normal" grade two student, but not quite reading at the standard of a grade three pupil. With this knowledge, books can be presumably selected which fit the ability indicated by 2.8.

7. *Behavioural objectives.* To develop materials implies a sense of purpose—what objectives are to be met? Thus the body of knowledge to be learned can be fractured into concepts, (i.e. generalizations) both major and minor, and labelled as cognitive. How the knowledge might influence the attitudes, values (i.e. feelings and beliefs) of the individual can be termed the affective domain. In order to make effective use of books, films and the like, learning skills are required. And so on.

8. *Sciencing.* Believe it or not, this is becoming an "in" word similar to "hands-on". These terms can be thought of as semantic variations of "experience is the best teacher" or learning by doing. (Can you guess what *mathematizing* means?)

9. *Learning packages.* Combining some, all, or none of the foregoing, learning materials can be developed in a package or kit which might include: reading materials, pictures, manipulative objects (things to touch and feel), cassette recordings, and film strips. The intent is not necessarily to provide something for everybody, but more to assail all of the senses, leaving little to mere chance. The degree of

structuring (how detailed the objectives are), which characterizes the package, will determine the freedom of the learner to speculate or follow a hunch.

Expressions of similar calibre could be added to the glossary. The important point to realize is the complexity of the task. Without question strides have been made in understanding how people learn, and for that reason alone ridicule of educational psychologists and other specialists is not entirely justified. However, educators do become mesmerized by terminology of their own making. Human concerns can then be lost, not necessarily deliberately, through the abundant use of pedagogical gobbledegook. Rather than providing clarification, the end result is confusion, with the big loser being the student. What may be good for young people in a specific instance can often be determined more by common sense than by wrestling with the meaning of the modular development of discovery units in science, or similar convoluted phraseology.

F

A checklist of the less mysterious properties of learning materials can be helpful. Look for:

1. *The size of the print.* Apart from visual impairment, the size of the print for young readers is important. Typically, major reading series have this concern well in hand. Problems are more likely to be encountered in selecting individual reference and library books. *The Mountain Goats of Temlaham* and *How Summer Came To Canada* (Toronto: Oxford, 1969) are beautiful productions. The full colour illustrations by Elizabeth Cleaver and the text by William Toye are exemplary. For the elementary-age child the effectiveness of the books might have been increased if a larger type had been chosen, and if the text were more readily distinguishable from the illustrations. Small concerns possibly, but important for children.

2. *Size of the book.* An unusual characteristic on the surface, but for the kindergarten and primary-age child, books which little hands can manage are important. If the book is meant for use at a table or desk, then it should lie flat when opened. The child's strength can be a related factor. Stubby, thick books tend to spring together when opened. The use of force only succeeds in cracking the binding and loosening the pages.

3. *Variety.* The format of any number of materials amounts to little more than "Read the following pages and answer the questions".

The teacher's handbooks which accompany unimaginative materials of this type can be deadly, too. Both children and teacher suffer— the child because of the ensuing boredom and the teacher because of the automaton-like text: "Open the book to page 2; tell the pupils to . . . ; ask the following questions; have the children . . . ." The spontaneity and creativity of the teacher are denied. The teaching machine moves closer to reality.

4. *Inter-relationships.* Traditionally, competent primary teachers have followed the practice of relating the child's learning experiences around a common theme. Through this project method, the study of a particular topic will call upon understandings and skills which can be labelled as reading, language arts, history, geography, art, science. The essence of this approach is to develop relationships in order that the pursuit of knowledge can be perceived as an integrated whole rather than as a series of isolated experiences. Finding learning materials which will extend the logical learning methodology of kindergarten to grade three classrooms into the following years is difficult. At approximately the grade four level, curriculum designers begin the process of fragmenting learning into bits and pieces (i.e. subjects) which serve to destroy the connecting links between what takes place in the first period of the school day (e.g. literature) and the fifth period (e.g. music). Predictably, the catalogues of publishing companies reflect this situation. A solution lies in teachers working cooperatively on the development of mutually acceptable themes and then choosing appropriate materials from whatever sources are available. For example, within an environmental theme students might study the peoples and regions of Canada emphasizing:

—feeling for the land through poetry;
—interpreting the environment through painting;
—expressing ecological concerns through songs of protest;
—comprehending government action/inaction through history and political science;
—determining hereditary concerns through anthropology;
—altering the environment through science.

5. *Economics.* The lyrics of Stompin' Tom Connors' popular song "The Consumer" also apply to the merchandizing of learning materials. Frequently, the method is based on the existence of a guaranteed market. A language arts series for grades one to six can be priced proportionately lower for the first couple of years of the program. The assumption is that once students have become locked into the sequence, the materials for the later years, regardless of price, will

be purchased as well. Examining the cost escalation of a series can be valuable.

Similarly a sharp knife should be used to eliminate the attractive but needless supplementary items which place a strain on the learning materials budget. Consumable workbooks in the *Project Mathematics Series* (Toronto: Holt) for example, not only are an expensive addition but can ruin the effectiveness of what should be an activity-centred mathematics program. Teacher guidebooks often do little more than repeat the material found in the student's text, with the addition of the type of information teachers should have received in their professional training. Spirit duplicator sheets, overhead transparencies, and answer books may be time-saving, but the dollars involved are better spent on the students.

Superficially it might appear that a diabolical scheme has been hatched by the publishers to extract the last nickel from the educational purse. Such an accusation is not always warranted. Publishers, like soap powder manufacturers, market essentially what their particular public wants. Through surveys of the opinions of teachers and other educators, the publisher knows what will sell. And notice that the emphasis is not on what is good for children, although that may be a happy by-product. If the people responsible for buying materials are susceptible to the latest in gimmickry and gadgetry, then publishers would be foolish not to capitalize on this gullibility. Comparison shopping and a discriminating eye are as necessary in this arena as they are on a weekly jaunt to the supermarket.

The list of things to weigh in the balance when trying to make intelligent choices of materials may appear to be discouragingly lengthy. Students are deserving of the best—not what is expedient, nor what happens to catch the fancy of adults, but the best in terms of the individual pupil's aptitudes, interests, and needs. One last point—educators should not lose sight of the pleasure that can come from the interaction among children, teachers, and learning materials.

Chapter 3

GETTING STARTED IS HALF THE FUN

In the search for educational materials developed in Canada, a para-
dox appeared repeatedly. Foreign control and domination of the
learning materials industry do pose serious problems for the understanding students have of their own country. However, there is available an increasing variety of sources and resources to which the concerned individual can turn for assistance. The assembly of information upon which this book is based demonstrates vividly that realistic
alternatives to non-Canadian materials are accessible in many instances.

A cross-section of examples of published material and organiza-
tional activities bears out this contention.

Canadian Materials For Schools (Kathleen Snow and Philomena
Hauck, Toronto: McClelland, 1970) was prepared for the convenience of curriculum specialists and teachers with an emphasis
on those items prepared in the English language.)

Communique (Willowdale, Ontario: Association of Canadian Community Colleges) is an on-going publication providing in-depth
bibliographic information on specific topics (e.g. Canadian Military, Native Studies, Museums, and Canadian Studies).

Canadian Books For Children / Livres Canadiens Pour Enfants
(McDonough, editor, Toronto: UTP, 1976) provides an annotated
catalogue of books for younger readers in both official languages.

Contact (Toronto: The Canada Studies Foundation) is a monthly
publication designed to facilitate the exchange of ideas and information among teachers of Canadian studies.

A Centre For Canadian Children's Books (Toronto: Books and
Periodical Development Council) has been established to promote the writing, publishing, selling and reading of Canadian children's books.

The examples can be extended and expanded. (The "Items For
Teachers" section in each chapter bibliography highlights many

21

of these, as does the concluding chapter.) The "problem" in Canadian education is not having few available resources to draw upon. Rather, it is how to give the teacher, the librarian, the administrator, and the curriculum specialist access to the necessary source information.

One of the prime motives in preparing this book was to attempt to gather as much of this knowledge as was possible within the limitations of a single publication. The objective was not to supplant the excellent contributions made by numerous writers and groups throughout the country, but to bring together the sources in one convenient reference handbook. The influence of *Whole Earth Catalogue*-type publications was strong. Educators need to know where and how to get the materials and ideas which can significantly improve classroom learning opportunities.

A five part process was used as a means of establishing contact with publishers, distributors, evaluation and review periodicals, departments of education, and teacher organizations. Something more than a casual examination of educational publishing was pursued which may help to dispel the notion that there is no one to turn to and nothing to work with in Canada.

A

The Association of Canadian Publishers was a valuable ally. This organization represents many of the Canadian-owned publishing houses. One of its many functions is to provide an articulate defence of the proposition that a vigorous publishing industry, owned and controlled by Canadians, is a necessity. As a service to its members, the Association distributes a *Directory of Canadian Publishers* (Toronto: Greey de Pencier). Included in it are not only the names and addresses of the member companies, but also the multi-national firms, French language publishers, book wholesalers, and distributors. It was through this *Directory* that contact was established with one hundred publishers of learning materials. A deliberate attempt was made to secure catalogue information on a representative basis. Publishing firms were categorized as follows:

1. Multi-national Corporations
   (a) American subsidiaries   27
   (b) British subsidiaries   5
   (c) French subsidiaries   2
                     Total   34

N.B. Several of the multi-national companies erect signposts in their catalogues which save some time, if nothing else. The sign of the maple leaf is employed frequently to denote Canadiana. Whether or not this indicates an item prepared by Canadians, or simply that the material was printed in Canada, is not always indicated. Neither is the meaning of the phrase "Canadian revised edition" self-evident. Beyond the use of the maple leaf, other symbols employed include printing *Canada* in italics, or using different coloured printing inks.

2. Canadian-owned Publishers

(a)	located in Ontario	29
(b)	Quebec	10
(c)	British Columbia	8
(d)	New Brunswick	3
(e)	Nova Scotia	3
(f)	Alberta	2
(g)	Manitoba	7
(h)	Newfoundland	2
(i)	Saskatchewan	1
(j)	Prince Edward Island	1
	Total	66

N.B. The Directory did not list any publishers in Newfoundland. Both Breakwater Books in Portugal Cove, and Memorial University, St. John's were added to the Directory's sources. Similarly, the Prince Edward Island Heritage Foundation in Charlottetown and the Nova Scotia Museum in Halifax were worthy additions in terms of broadening the coverage given to Maritime sources of materials.

3. Canadian-owned Distributors

Seven companies which distribute Canadian books, and materials from elsewhere, primarily the United States, were contacted. These major distributing companies list not only books but in certain instances a comprehensive range of education products from jigsaw puzzles to pre-packaged science laboratories.

4. Within the list of Canadian publishing houses, an effort was made to ensure coverage of unique learning materials needs.
   (a) One company, the Canadian Women's Education Press, Toronto, publishes non-sexist children's literature.
   (b) Les Éditions d'Acadie, Moncton, N.B. is a source for Acadian French materials.
   (c) Three companies, Black Rose Books, Montreal, Progress Books and NC Press, Toronto, publish Marxist-Leninist items.
   (d) Eight publishers located in the province of Quebec publish French Canadian writers.
   (e) Nine university publishers were included.

(f) Specialty publishers such as International Self-Counsel Press (law materials) and the Canadian Education Association (professional materials for educators) have items which suit particular needs.

N.B. Addresses of all publishers and distributors are found in the Appendix.

B

For film sources, four companies (Moreland-Latchford, Viking, International Tele-Film Enterprises, and Canadian F.D.S. Audio-Visual), and two federal government organizations (the National Film Board and the Canadian Film Development Corporation) were contacted for their respective catalogues. Other businesses, notably Scholar's Choice, have Canadian filmstrips available.

C

The possibility always exists, despite the best of intentions, that something of value has been overlooked. One check was to wade through the abundance of publications emanating from the ten provincial and one territorial departments of education. Annually, a veritable flood of curriculum guidebooks, brochures,and materials catalogues surges forth from the government curriculum agencies. A study of the recommended lists of learning materials reveals that only in the social studies and possibly literature curricula has much attention been given to Canadian content. Of the eleven educational jurisdictions, the province of Ontario has provided the most notable service to its teachers in terms of promoting an awareness of Canadian materials in all subjects.

D

It would be heartening if it could be stated that professional teachers' organizations compensate for the indifference shown by many government bureaucracies. But such is not the case. Although almost all teachers belong to provincial or territorial associations, federations, or unions, their organizations often take a very feeble position on the question of education for Canadians. Scrutinizing their newspapers and professional journals, the reader will seldom find mention of anything, Canadian or otherwise, that might be beneficial to students. It is through the curriculum specialist councils, established by the associations, that the more useful information is likely to be unearthed.

E

Canadian periodicals, in expanding numbers, are providing valuable services to education. A ramble through book review columns, advertisements, and news items can disclose sources of information and provide critiques useful in evaluating books, in particular. Five periodicals were extensively relied upon for guidance:

Quill and Quire
Books in Canada
The Canadian Reader
In Review
Canadian Materials

Quill and Quire is a must for keeping informed on Canadian publishing in its entirety. At regular intervals an educational supplement is published which provides comprehensive coverage of the learning materials industry.

Books in Canada confines its attention to the review of trade editions and is considerably less exhaustive in its coverage than is *Quill and Quire.*

The Canadian Reader, the monthly publication of The Readers' Club of Canada, is similarly useful for keeping abreast of recent trade books. Only sporadically is there comment on school materials.

In Review: Canadian Books For Children is published quarterly by the Ontario Provincial Library Service. It provides excellent reviews of fiction and non-fiction and, as well, provides profiles of authors, reviews of titles no longer in print, and evaluations of professional books of interest to teachers and librarians.

Canadian Materials: An Annotated Critical Bibliography For Canadian Schools and Libraries is published three times a year by the Canadian Library Association. It covers material in all media formats produced in Canada for elementary and secondary schools. The reviewers are teachers and librarians from throughout Canada.

The availability of these periodicals in each school will diminish appreciably the problem of knowing where to find items appropriate to each subject and grade.

The collation of information for each individual chapter was based on these sources and an ever-widening circle of contacts. The concluding chapter, "Ruminations and Projections", provides a list of these resources and attempts to extract some of the lessons learned. Future travellers through the field of Canadiana may wish to employ these lessons as signposts to guide their own particular odyssey.

Chapter 4

ART

"What the hell is the matter with them in Montreal?" was how the painter J.W. Morrice expressed his contempt for the failure of Canadians to support the Canadian artistic endeavour of the 1920s. His words are echoed on a national scale in the classrooms of the 1970s. The study of Canadian art receives little attention in the nation's schools.

The reasons are varied. In the minds of curriculum designers, the study of art is something of an afterthought, interesting and even enjoyable, but not of sufficient importance to receive much emphasis. Evidently, art must not interfere with what school is really about—namely, reading, writing, and arithmetic. The lowly status accorded to art is reflected in curriculum handbooks issued to teachers by Departments of Education that state that art for elementary age children must not exceed a specified percentage of time per week. By contrasting this time with that accorded the language arts, teachers quickly become aware of the practical meaning of those progressive education phrases, "open-education" and "individualized learning". The teacher can have all the freedom in the world as long as "you teach 'em good"—in the basics. Reinforcing the curriculum's orientation to areas of learning other than art (also music and drama) is the organizing of learning experiences through time-tables. Most schools would not be schools were it not possible to pigeon-hole subject matter into neat compartments. The principal, working independently or in concert with the superintendent and teachers, typically slots literature, language, mathematics, science, and social studies into the time-table well in advance of the "non-essentials". Art will be relegated to those twin categories of indecision, *if* and *when*; *if* there is a teacher available, and *when* there is time. The end result is to fit in this subject toward the end of the school day, or on Friday afternoon when students are presumably restless and the

26

time cannot be otherwise better spent studying the causes of the
Punic Wars, or making a papier-mâché model of the Panama Canal.
In the junior-senior high grades the situation deteriorates. If available at all, art is more likely to be scheduled in such a manner as to
be only available to the "not-so-bright". Apparently students who
cannot cut the mustard in algebra are automatically "good with their
hands". What could be better than to fill those hands with paint
brushes and scissors?

The lack of importance attached to art is to a large degree a reflection of public opinion. Art is a frill, something that in times of
plenty might be tossed a crumb or two in the form of hiring an art
teacher and buying some supplies—paints, brushes, paper, but not
necessarily books and films about art. In times of stress, art is close
to the head of the procession awaiting the axe. When teacher-pupil
ratios decline—lop off the art teacher. When budgets are restricted—
cancel the order for art supplies. When standards of academic excellence slide—beef up the 3R's and eliminate the "fun subjects". When
discipline relaxes, the fault lies in the permissive atmosphere of subjects like art. After all, how can serious learning take place when
students are moving about, rummaging through materials, talking
and laughing? Never let it be said that society's problems cannot be
solved through the education system. A dose of essay writing on
imaginative topics such as "What A Buttercup Thinks of Spring"
will straighten out a lot of problems in a hurry.

The pity is that art could be the heart of the learning process.
Through art, students can be stimulated to inquiry into every facet
of humanity. More than this, visual-artistic literacy is as vital and
valid a means of communication as is the printed word, a message
lost on many educators but not on advertisers, the layout and design artists of mass circulation periodicals, or television producers.

To elevate Canadian art in the classroom above the level of tem-
pera paints, plaster of Paris, and glue is a herculean task. Changing
the attitudes and understandings of people is difficult in itself. The
fact that there is virtually nothing to help either teachers or students
to learn about the development of art in Canada may be the most
crushing indictment of all. The available books and audio-visual materials have been prepared almost exclusively with public tastes in
mind, not the needs of schools. Conversely, the few existing Canadian titles in art for teachers are how-to-do-it publications and not
materials about art. The point need not be belaboured. In Canadian
education the individual must grow accustomed (or immune) to the
absence of materials and of any sense of direction.

To the novice student of Canadian art it may be startling to realize the numerous possibilities which could enrich every aspect of the curriculum.

Assume for the moment that a junior high student in Medicine Hat is studying in social studies the various regions of Canada. Combined with the textbook and library resources in history and geography, would it not be feasible to examine how painters have perceived and interpreted their local environment? A non-definitive list of artists might include:

from British Columbia:	B.C. Binning
	Gordon Smith
	Jack Shadbolt
	Claude Breeze
	Frederick Whymper
from the prairies:	Lionel leMoine FitzGerald
	William Kurelek
	The Regina Five (Ronald Bloore,
	Kenneth Lochhead, Arthur McKay,
	Douglas Martin and Ted Godwin)
from Ontario:	David Milne
	Harold Town
	Michael Snow
	Leonard Hutchinson
from Quebec:	Ozias Leduc
	Joseph Legaré
	Jean-Paul Riopelle
	Alfred Pellan
	Arthur Villeneuve
from the Atlantic Provinces:	Christopher Pratt
	Maurice Cullen
	Miller Brittain
	Alex Colville
	Tom Forrestal
from the North:	Kenojuak
	Kalvak
	Pitseolak
	Nanogak

At the elementary grade levels every child has to labour through the interminable voyages of Jacques Cartier and other explorers. The drudgery of "Discovering the West" or unravelling the intri-

cacies of the Treaty of Utrecht would be relieved if the panorama of
the pre-confederation years were viewed through the sweep of the
painter's brush. The travels across Canada of William G.R. Hind; the
portrayal of peasant society in Quebec by Cornelius Kreighoff; Paul
Kane's records on canvas of aspects of Indian life on the prairies
could all be incorporated. Questions about the artist's concept of
his subject material would follow logically. What stereotypes did the
painters reinforce? Contrast the interpretative paintings of native
life, as composed by white artists, with the more recent works of
George Clutesi, Norval Morriseau, and Daphne Beavon ("Odjig"), who
are themselves Indian artists from British Columbia, Ontario, and
Manitoba respectively. Approaching art in this way encourages students to deepen their social and political awareness.

The contributions of women could be related to the pressing
social concern for equality between the sexes. Interestingly enough,
the best known Northern painters and print makers (as mentioned
above) are all women. Emily Carr ranks among the most outstanding artists, male or female. Rita Letendre and Marcelle Ferron are
recognized far beyond their native province of Quebec, as is Joyce
Wieland of Ontario. In Atlantic Canada Ruth Wainwright, Jeanne
Arsenault, Alma Lorenzen and Mary Pratt are representative of Nova
Scotia, Prince Edward Island, New Brunswick and Newfoundland
respectively.

The Group of Seven can be a study in itself, given its fundamental
role in establishing a uniquely Canadian artistic impression. For the
vast majority of students, who have no opportunity to experience
life in Northern Ontario or the high Arctic, there is no substitute
for the feeling captured in the paintings of Jackson, Lismer, Mac-
Donald, Harris, Varley, Carmichael, and Thomson. In turn, their
environmental interpretations can be related to the science classroom
where, in combination with the wildlife paintings of Martin Glen
Loates, the study of ecological problems such as the James Bay
hydroelectric project can be given an additional dimension.

Political science in the high school grades might appear to be hopelessly divorced from art. In English-speaking Canada, it is safe to say
that the contributions of Paul-Emile Borduas and his Québecois contemporaries pass virtually unnoticed. The political manifesto "Re-
fus Global", prepared by Borduas and signed by fifteen of his
colleagues, is a significant document in aiding understanding not
only the cultural ferment in Quebec but also the growing impatience
of a people too long submerged within a colonial system. More recently, Barry Lord has attempted to redefine Canadian art in terms

of Marxist ideology. His efforts indicate a changing mood on the part of some Canadians who no longer wish to tolerate imperialism of the mind or the economy.

Students who have the opportunity to grapple with "foreign ownership" can extend their studies into an evaluation of the impact of European and American artistic techniques on people like Horatio Walker (Barbizon style), Homer Watson (labelled the 'Canadian Constable' by Oscar Wilde), J.W. Morrice (glowingly referred to by Matisse), or the influence of the United States on Saskatchewan painters.

On a different tangent, a study of the financial support of government, industry and wealthy, influential individuals will bring into view the historical and current concern for sustaining artistic development in Canada, with possible contrasts drawn from other countries. From airport terminal art to the support of the Canada Council, the long arm of government involvement can be detected and appreciated. Similarly, conglomerates such as the C.P.R., banks, oil companies, retail chain stores such as the Hudson's Bay Company, have become the latter day Medicis without whose patronage Canadian art would have an even harder struggle for survival. For many students who do not have access to private or public galleries, the Seagram collection or similar movable feasts may provide an opportunity to see and to enjoy first hand.

For a change of pace, learning about art through stamp and coin collecting affords interesting, informative possibilities. Both the Philatelic Service of the Post Office Department and the Canadian Mint have useful and economical brochures, booklets, and starter-kits available which will help to get things going in the classroom. Some ideas to consider can be illustrated as follows:

> The Centennial coinage of 1967 was designed by the "magic realist", Alex Colville.

> The 1970 Centennial of the Northwest Territories was commemorated through the issuing of The Enchanted Owl stamp, the best known work of Cape Dorset artist, Kenojuak.

> Reproduction of paintings by Aurèle de Foy, Suzor-Côté, Paul Kane, and the Group of Seven have been popularized on stamp issues of varying denominations.

> Christmas stamps have been designed by school children from across the country.

What about facets of the art curriculum other than painting? Inuit sculpture is internationally recognized, perhaps even seen as synonymous with Canadian art. In the classroom it is often neglected, if not rejected. This is difficult to explain in view of the possibilities.

The medium of the carver is a study in itself. Whale bone is the material used by Karoo Ashevak in Spence Bay. In nearby Pelly Bay (as the plane flies) Lee Arluk works wonders with the ivory teeth of the polar bear. Off the east coast of Baffin Island, Pauloosie uses the magnificently spiralled tusk of the narwhal. Soap stone of various colours and hues simplifies the identification of the works of such artists as Tiktak of Rankin Inlet (grey), Kanoyok of Baker Lake (black), Takeoloo of Lake Harbour (lime green), and Panelak of Pond Inlet (dark green flecked with gold).

The subject matter creates a deepening awareness of the Arctic environment. Traditional beliefs regarding people, animals, and the land are evoked through the ability of the carver to release the hidden shapes and designs embedded in bone and stone alike. By chisels, coping saws, and power hand tools, the supernatural powers of the angogok are recaptured and relived. The whale, seal, seabirds, and caribou are essential to survival. Many artists preserve them in ivory miniatures or impressive blocks of soap stone.

The history of these art forms, like all others, is fascinating. James Houston has received little recognition for his efforts. His name, if mentioned in schools at all, is more likely associated with the books he has written. One of these, *The White Dawn* (Toronto: Longman, 1971) has become a popular feature film. His efforts to encourage, organize, and publicize the artistry of the Cape Dorset peoples should be known to students, as should the efforts of Oblate priests such as Rousselière (Pond Inlet), Fournier (Igloolik), and Tardy (Holman Island). An awareness of the Eskimo Museum in Churchill, Manitoba, and the Manitoba Museum of Man in Winnipeg are variations on the same theme. George Swinton, University of Manitoba, is a recognized authority on Inuit art. His knowledge, like that of many other individuals and organizations (for instance, the Eskimo Arts Council), should not be ignored.

Mention of the economics of art may irk people who wish to overlook the harsher realities of native life. The arts and crafts industry is basic to the economy of many Northern settlements. Analyzing the economics will require study of federal government involvement (e.g. Canadian Arctic Producers), the growth of cooperatives, and the development of different art forms. Wall hangings, animal hide tapestries, weaving, engraving in silver and copper, pottery, and embroidery are some of the techniques which have been introduced. Concurrently, attempts are being made to inject new life into art forms which are in danger of vanishing. Particularly is this true among Northern Indian peoples. Some Slavey peoples of the Fort

Providence area still embroider on velvet with moose hair dyed in various bright colours. Porcupine quill work is another art form that only the elderly remember. When it is recognized that it is through the sale of these items that many Northern peoples receive their only cash income besides government assistance, then appreciation of their efforts becomes less a topic of amusing curiosity among the frequenters of galleries and more a subject to be understood in depth by as many people as possible.

Outside of the Arctic, the St. Lawrence river valley community of St. Jean-Port Joli provides a contrasting and vivid example of artistic development. Wood carving, ceramics, and pottery flourish, as do crafts like toy making and model ship building, not to mention the culinary arts. Indeed, St. Jean-Port Joli may be the only place in Canada, outside of the North, where the individual can sense the creativity of distinctive design. The flavour and the substance of the talents of the ceramist Louis Archambault, as one example, should be conveyed to all students.

Unrealistic though it may now be, one cannot help wondering what it would do for Canadian education as a whole if children and young people were given the chance to view people, places, and things through the perceptions of artists. Regardless of technique (paints, brushes, chisels, the welder's torch . . .), is it not possible that present and future generations might see in Canada something more than a reflection of the supermarket culture imported from elsewhere? A faint hope perhaps; but materials like the following would help to get on the threshold if not through the door of change itself. In the words of four Inuit artists from Rankin Inlet:

> "If we cannot come together ourselves, our works will speak for us."
>
> (Tiktak, Ukalik, Ujkuk, and Hakaluk, *Sculpture,* Ottawa, Canadian Eskimo Arts Council, 1971)

♦ ♦ ♦ ♦

Techniques for Teachers

The few items available will do little to create an understanding of Canadian art. They are primarily useful for the teacher who has had a minimum of art training and who has been saddled with the responsibility of filling out the time-table by teaching rudimentary techniques.

General

   Art is . . . , John C. Lindsay (G.L.C., 1975), $13.95. Practical handbook for the non-specialist teacher.

   Painting and Drawing

   Self-Expression through Art, 2nd ed. E.E. Harrison (Gage, 1960), $8.75.

   Art Starts Outdoors, Vancouver Environmental Education Project (B.C. Teachers' Federation, 1976), $1.70. Ideas for art in outdoor camps and day excursions.

   An Introduction to Art (film). 9 min, 16mm, English or French, Moreland-Latchford.

Arts and Crafts

   Weaving for Beginners, M.E. Black (Information Canada, 1975), 75¢ pa.

   You Can Weave, M.E. Black (McClelland, 1974), $4.95 pa.

   The Art of Preserving Flowers, E. MacDermot (James Lorimer, 1973), $4.95 pa.

   Fun and Profit with Screen Printing, Nick and Helma Mika (Mika, 1969), $15.00.

   Experiments with Film in the Art Classroom, (O.I.S.E., 1970), $2.40 pa. Grades 9—13.

   The Warp and Weft of Outdoor Weaving, Vancouver Environmental Education Project (B.C. Teachers' Federation, 1976), $1.65 pa.

   The Art of Aluminum Foil, Jane Hinton and Hugh Oliver (General, 1974), $4.95 pa.

   Merton Chambers Batik (film). 5 min, 16mm, col, English or French, International Tele-film Enterprises, $65.00 or $10.00 rental per day.

General Reference Library

Expensive colour printing, high quality paper and limited editions combine to make many items costly. Systematically over a period of years a comprehensive library can be established. Materials to choose from have been grouped in the following categories:

Painting, Drawing and Prints

   Three Hundred Years of Canadian Art, R.H. Hubbard (National Gallery, 1967), $8.00. Bilingual text.

   Eight Artists from Canada, Pierre Théberge (National Gallery, 1970),

$2.00 pa. A bilingual catalogue of an art exhibition representative of the years 1950 to 1969.

Canadian Watercolours and Drawings in the Royal Ontario Museum, M. Allodi (Royal Ontario Museum, 1974), 2 vols, $30.00. Two thousand drawings and watercolours of the mid-1700s to the 1930s, brief biographies of each artist included.

Canadian Watercolours of the 19th Century, Danielle Corbeil (National Gallery, 1970), $1.00 pa.

A Concise History of Canadian Painting, D. Reid (Oxford, 1973), $6.50 pa. Includes material up to the 1960s.

Painters in a New Land, M. Bell (McClelland, 1973), $15.95. Emphasis is on the frontier period.

Contemporary Canadian Painting, W. Withrow (McClelland, 1973), $25.00. The period from 1945 to the 1970s.

A Vision of Canada: The McMichael Canadian Collection, Paul Duval (Clarke, Irwin, 1973), $13.50. Reproductions from the McMichael Gallery, Kleinburg, Ont.

Four Decades: The Canadian Group of Painters and their Contemporaries, Paul Duval (Clarke, Irwin, 1973), $24.95. The era from the 1930s to the 1960s.

The History of Painting in Canada: Toward a People's Art, Barry Lord (N.C. Press, 1974), $6.95 pa.

Canadian Painting in the Thirties, Charles C. Hill (National Gallery, 1975), $12.00. Available in English or French.

A People's Art: Native, Provincial and Folk Painting in Canada, J. Russell Harper (U.T.P., 1975), $7.50 pa. Available in English or French.

Artists of Canada (filmstrip). col, N.F.B. set of 10, $5.00 each; b&w, one filmstrip, $4.00. Eleven representations of artists from Kreighoff to Borduas.

Artists of Pacific Canada (filmstrip). col, N.F.B., $5.00. The period 1920-1970.

Early Painters of British Columbia (filmslides). col, N.F.B., set of 10, $4.50. Includes examples of E. Richardson, William Hind, F. Whymper and Lucius R. O'Brien.

Architecture

The Ancestral Roof: Domestic Architecture of Upper Canada, M. McCrae and A. Adamson (Clarke, Irwin, 1963), $13.95. Bilingual text.

Canadian Architecture 1960/70, C. Ede (Burns, 1971), $35.00.

Encyclopédie de la maison québecoise, Michel Lessard and Michel and Hughette Marquis (Homme), $6.00.

For Everyone a Garden, Safdie (Tundra), $25.00. The architect of Habitat at Expo '67 provides an insight into his architectural designs in words and pictures.

Maisons et églises du Québec, Bedard (Ed. Officiel), 50¢ br.

Photography

Canada, Lorraine Monk and others (Clarke, Irwin, 1973), $17.50. Bilingual text.

Indian and Inuit Art

Inunnit: the Art of the Inuit (Information Canada, 1970), $3.25 pa. Bilingual text.

Masterpieces of Indian and Eskimo Art from Canada (National Gallery, 1969), $10.00 pa.

Indian Arts in Canada (Information Canada, 1974), $7.50.

'Ksan: Breath of our Grandfathers (Information Canada, 1974), $2.50 pa. The art of the Indian peoples of Northern British Columbia.

Artifacts of the North Coast Indians, Hilary Stewart (General, 1973), $12.95. Six Indian nations of the Pacific coast are represented.

Those Born at Koona, John and Carolyn Smyly (General, 1973), $12.95. The totem pole art of the Queen Charlotte Islands, B.C.

Indian Rock Carvings of the Pacific Northwest, Edward Meade (Gray, 1971), $5.95 pa.

Sculpture of the Eskimo, G. Swinton (McClelland, 1972), $22.50.

Eskimo Prints, James Houston (Longman, 1971), $7.50 pa.

Rock Drawings of the Micmac Indians, M. Robertson (Nova Scotia Museum, 1973), $2.50 pa.

Haida Argellite Carvings (filmstrip). b&w, N.F.B., $4.00.

Illustrations by Indian and Inuit Artists

Tales from the Igloo, M. Metayer (Hurtig, 1972), $4.85. Colour plates by Agnes Nanogak; end papers by H. Kalvak, Holman Island, N.W.T.

Windigo and Other Tales of the Ojibway, H. Schwarz (McClelland, 1972), $6.95. Illustrations by Norval Morriseau.

Sepass Tales, E. Street (Mitchell, 1974), $4.95. Illustrations by
B.C. artist George Clutesi.

Of Particular Interest
Odjig Print Gallery and Gift Shop, 331 Donald Street, Winnipeg, is
a good source for Indian prints. Catalogues of Inuit prints are
available from Cape Dorset Co-op, Cape Dorset, N.W.T.; Baker
Lake Co-op, Baker Lake, N.W.T.; and Holman Island Co-op, Holman Island, N.W.T.

Artists and their Works

The Group of Seven

There is no Finality: A Story of the Group of Seven,   Hunkin
(Burns, 19   ), $6.95 pa.

The Group of Seven, Peter Mellen (McClelland, 1970), $29.50.

A Canadian Art Movement: A Story of the Group of Seven, F.B.
Housser (Macmillan, 1974), $11.95. First published in 1926.

Lawren Harris, ed. B. Harris and R.G.P. Colgrove (Macmillan,
1969), $50.00.

Tom Thomson: The Algonquin Years, O. Addison (McGraw,
1975), $5.95.

A Painter's Country: The Autobiography of A.Y. Jackson, A.Y.
Jackson (Clarke, Irwin, 1967), $1.90 pa.

A.Y.'s Canada, N. Groves (Clarke, Irwin, 1968), $21.00.

Emily Carr

Growing Pains: The Autobiography of Emily Carr, Emily Carr
(Clarke, Irwin, 1966), $2.50 pa.

Fresh Seeing, Emily Carr (Clarke Irwin, 1967), $2.50 pa.

House of All Sorts, Emily Carr (Clarke, Irwin, 1967), $2.25 pa.

Hundreds and Thousands: The Journal of Emily Carr, Emily Carr
(Clarke, Irwin, 1966), $10.00.

Emily Carr, D. Shadbolt (J.J. Douglas), $5.00 pa.

Emily Carr and David Milne (filmslides). col, N.F.B., set of 10,
$4.50.

Early Canadian

James Wilson Morrice, K. Pepper (Clarke, Irwin, 1966), $4.50.

William Hind, J. Russell Harper (National Gallery, 1976), $3.50

pa. Biography of an early painter of western Canada. Canadian Artists Series No. 3.

Cornelius Kreighoff, H. de Dejouvancourt (Musson, 1973), $29.95. An illustrated biography.

Kreighoff Prints from the Canadiana Collection (prints). col, 14" x 17", Royal Ontario Museum, set of 4, $5.95.

A Journey through Early Canada with W.H. Bartlett (filmstrip). col, sound, Cinemedia, set of 3, $47.50. Paintings of 19th century Quebec, Ontario and the Maritimes by the landscape artist W.H. Bartlett.

Indian and Inuit

The Colours of Pride (film). 16mm, col, N.F.B., $220. The four Indian artists, Daphne Odjig, Allen Sapp, Alex Janvier and Norval Morriseau.

Kalvak (film). 20 min, 16mm, col, International Tele-Film Enterprises, $175 or $17.00 rental per day. The artistic excellence of Holman Island, N.W.T. resident, Helen Kalvak.

Morriseau: Ojibway Artist (film). 28 min, 16mm, col, English or French, International Tele-Film Enterprises, $360 or $30.00 rental per day.

Quebec

Painters of Quebec, R.H. Hubbard (National Gallery, 1973), $7.50. Bilingual text.

Panorama de la peinture au Québec, 1940-1966, Musée d'art contemporain (Ed. Officiel, 1967), $3.00 br.

Titles from the series Un Artiste Canadien-français, L'Editeur Officiel du Québec:

Napoléon Bourassa, 1827-1916, Anne Bourassa (Ed. Officiel, 1968), $1.50 br.

Hartung, Musée d'art contemporain et Musée du Québec, (Ed. Officiel, 1969), $2.50 br.

Marcelle Ferron, Musée du Québec (Ed. Officiel, 1970), $1.50 br.

Pellan, G. Lefebvre (McClelland, 1973), $18.95.

Paul-Emile Borduas, François-Marc Gagnon (National Gallery, 1976), $3.50 pa. A biographical monograph on the pioneer of automatism. Canadian Artists Series, No. 2.

Borduas et les automatistes, Musée d'art contemporain (Ed. Officiel, 1971), $3.00 br. Illustrations en noir et blanc et en couleur, reproduction de lithographie originale en hors-texte.

Exposition Riopelle 1967, Musée du Québec (Ed. Officiel, 1967), $1.50 br.

Riopelle, Guy Robert (Homme), $3.50.

Ozias Leduc: Religious and Symbolist Painting, Jean-René Ostiguy (National Gallery, 1974), $9.00. Bilingual text.

Two Painters from Quebec: Plamandon et Hamel, R.H. Hubbard (National Gallery, 1970), $5.00 pa.

Jacques de Tonnancour, J. Folch-Riban (P.U.Q., 1971), $4.00.

The Sleighs of my Childhood: Sleighs of Montreal 1820-1940, Carlo Italiana (Tundra, 1974), $9.95. Bilingual text.

Two Centuries of Ceramics in the Richelieu Valley: A Documentary History, H.H. Lambart (National Museum, 1970), $1.00 pa.

Encyclopédie des antiquités du Québec, Michel Lessard et Hughette Marquis (Homme), $6.00.

La poterie de Cap-Rouge, Michel Gaumond (Ed. Officiel, 1971), 50¢ br.

Paul-Emile Borduas and Alfred Pellan (filmslides). col, N.F.B., set of 10, $4.50.

De Niverville (film). 8 min, 16mm, col, English or French, International Tele-Film Enterprises, $90.00 or $10.00 rental per day.

Affiches couleurs symbolisant diverses activités culturelles; 24″ x 36″, L'Editeur Officiel du Québec.

 no. 1: Littérature, 50¢
 no. 2: Théâtre
 no. 3: Rencontre animation théâtre
 no. 4: Exposition
 no. 5: Musée du Québec
 no. 6: Musique
 no. 7: Cinéma
 no. 8: Civilisation du Québec

Atlantic Provinces

The Art of Alex Colville, Helen J. Dow (McGraw, 1972), $35.00.

Robert Harris, 1849-1919: The Man and His Work, Moncrieff Williamson (McClelland, 1971), $15.00. The artist who painted the Fathers of Confederation.

Robert Harris, Moncrieff Williamson (National Gallery, 1973), $5.00. Bilingual text.

Shaped by this Land, Tom Forrestall and Alden Nowlan (Brunswick, 1974), $27.50. The paintings of Forrestall and the poetry of Nowlan.

The Prairies

Sky Painter: The Story of Robert Newton Hurley, Jean Swanson (Western Producer, 1974), $12.50.

Braves and Buffalo: Plains Indian Life in 1837, Alfred J. Miller (U.T.P., 1973), $15.00.

Sculpture

The Girls, R. Sisler (Clarke, Irwin, 1973), $7.95. The biographies of Frances Loring and Florence Wyle.

Sculpture traditionnelle du Québec, Musée du Québec (Ed. Officiel, 1967), $2.00 br. Presentation de Jean Trudel, conservateur de l'art traditionnel.

Colour reproductions of paintings from Information Canada:

> *Bas de fleuve* by Marcel Barbeau, $16.00.
>
> *Convoy at Rendez-vous* by B.C. Binning, $14.00.
>
> *Maligne Lake, Jasper Park* by Lawren Harris, $12.00.
>
> *Katia* by Jacques Hurtubise, $14.00.
>
> *Algoma, November* by A.Y. Jackson, $12.00.
>
> *Blue Extension* by Kenneth Lochhead, $16.00.
>
> *Au clair de la lune* by Alfred Pellan, $14.00.
>
> *Red Leaves* by Tom Thomson, $15.00.
>
> *Stormy Weather, Georgian Bay* by Frederick Varley, $12.00.
>
> *Captain* by Joyce Wieland, $16.00.

Reproductions de chefs-d'oeuvre du Musée du Québec, 28¾″ x 40¾″; commande de l'Editeur Officiel du Québec:

> no. 3: *Le capitaine John Walker visite sa nouvelle maison de campagne* par Cornelius Kreighoff, $1.50.
>
> no. 4: *Structure rouge violet* par Guido Molinari, $1.50.
>
> no. 5: *Quatre enfants et un chien* par Théophile Hamel, $1.50.
>
> no. 6: *Les chutes de Saint-Ferréol* par Joseph Légaré, $1.50.
>
> no. 7: *Isabelle* par Jacques Hurtubise, $1.50.
>
> no. 13: *Québec vu du Bassin Louis* par Charles Huot, col, 22½″ x 29″, $2.50.

Collections des cartes postales sur l'art traditionnel du Québec (cartes postales). Ed. Officiel, la série complète, $2.00.

Stamp Collecting

Canada Stamps and Stories, Harvey Warm (Philatelic Service, Canada Post office, Crown Copyright, 1975), $2.50.

Stamp Starter Kit (kit). Philatelic Service, Canada Post Office, $2.00.

Postage Stamps Tell Canada's Story (filmstrips). col, sound, English or French, Cinemedia, set of 4, $59.00.

Specimens, Samples and Artifacts

write: National Museum of Canada
Information and Education Division
Victoria Memorial Building
McLeod and Metcalfe Streets
Ottawa.

Cartoons

Duncan MacPherson's 1970 Cartoon Book, Duncan MacPherson Toronto *Star,* 1970), $2.25.

Duncan MacPherson's 1972 Cartoon Book, Duncan MacPherson (Toronto *Star,* 1972), $3.00.

Periodicals

Artscanada, Artscanada, 3 Church Street, Toronto M5E 1M2. 6 issues annually, $18.00. An essential publication not only for the quality of the writing and illustrations but as a reference source for galleries, materials exhibitions. Special issues are collector's items.

Art Magazine, Art Magazine, 2498 Yonge Street, Suites 18 & 19, Toronto M4P 2H0. Quarterly, $7.00 annually. An equally important periodical.

Canadian Antiques Collector, Canadian Periodical Publishers' Association. 6 issues annually $18.00. Text and illustrations on such categories as furniture, silver, ceramics and glass.

Chapter 5

BIOLOGY and BOTANY

A capsule biography: Name: Michel Sarrazin
Year of Birth: 1659
Year of Death: 1735
Place of Residence: New France
Career: Surgeon
      Scientist
      Physiologist
      Anatomist
      Botanist
Comment: an unknown Canadian

M. Sarrazin is in good company. Canada does not have a scientific heritage as far as learning materials are concerned. American and British books have this field to themselves with few exceptions. The science student has to pursue studies which refer almost exclusively to foreign developments, individuals, research, and organization. The conventional wisdom of education on this point can be summed up briefly: scientific thought knows no national boundaries; therefore, the use of foreign materials in the classroom is of no concern. Agreed, the study of science should be international in the sense that theories and applications from wherever they can be found should be at the disposal of students. However, is it not possible to relate all of this to the Canadian context? Is it not feasible to allow young people to learn about their country's contributions to scientific advancement, as well as to learn something about the potential Canada has for making even greater contributions in the future? Or is it taken for granted that the science-minded individual must look elsewhere for information, as well as for opportunities?

41

Commencing with Sarrazin, who was responsible for the identification of many plants and animals in what is now Quebec, a skeleton outline of a Canadian-oriented biology-botany curriculum can be established. Broad categories for examination are plant genetics, food-science and medicine. In the initial instance, William Saunders and his son Charles were responsible for developing the Marquis strain of wheat which revolutionized prairie agriculture. J.H. Craigie and Margaret Newton investigated rust fungi and mutations in rust which were of crucial importance to the wheat farmer. Francis Peabody Sharp, a native of New Brunswick, was a nineteenth century horticulturist. Among his accomplishments were the cross-breeding of two thousand varieties of apples; the development from seed of apples which could be conveniently grown under New Brunswick climatic conditions; and the hybridization of apples and pears.

Of related importance in the food-science field has been the work of Archibald Huntsman, who, while working for the Fisheries Research Board in Halifax, became the first person in North America to develop a frozen food process with commercial applications. W.H. Cook of the National Research Council was responsible for the process required in the preparation of frozen, dried foods. An employee of the Department of Agriculture, E.A. Asselbergs, is given credit for the development of the "instant" potato flakes industry. If Canadian contributions are recognized at all, perhaps the invention of "Pablum" is the best known. F. Tisdall, T. Drake and A. Brown, all of whom were medical doctors, devised the formula for precooked infant cereal.

In the medical field, Sir William Osler was an early advocate of compulsory smallpox vaccination. While teaching in Montreal, he was one of the first doctors in North America to instruct students in the microbiology techniques of diagnosis. William MacCallum discovered the role of the parathyroid gland in tetany. Using birds as his subject material, he researched the sexual cycle of the malarial parasite in the bloodstream. His brother, J.B. MacCallum, researched the development of the spiral muscles making up the wall of the heart. Frederick Banting is the one Canadian who regularly gets passing reference in textbooks. Along with his student assistant, Charles Best, and with the help of J.J. Macleod, he discovered insulin. In 1923, Banting and Macleod received the Nobel Prize in medicine as recognition for the significance of their discovery. Dr. M. Barr is undoubtedly less well known. Yet his discovery of a distinct and constant difference between the cells of male and female animals is of no less consequence. Wilder Penfield was a world renowned neurosurgeon. His research included work on decompression sickness and on increased intracranial pressure resulting from concussion, development of blood substitutes during World War I, and surgical techniques for the removal of brain scars resulting from injuries at birth.

An alternative approach to the study of the contributions of individuals is to examine the variety of institutions, organizations, and agencies which have aided the quest for scientific understanding. The Connaught Laboratories of the University of Toronto have developed methods of producing a variety of biological products: insulin, herapin, injectable liver preparations, tetanus toxoid, and human blood serum. The development at these laboratories of a synthetic medium for the artificial cultivation of tissue cells in order to grow the poliomyelitis virus was instrumental in the development and testing of the Salk polio vaccine. In Quebec, botanical studies at the Université de Laval were stimulated by Abbé Leon Provancher and Abbé Ovide Brunet. Henry Marshall Tory was a pioneer advocate of scientific advancement in Alberta and is duly recognized on the Edmonton campus of the University of Alberta. The involvement of government has been extensive. The National Research Council, the Defence Research Board and the Department of Agriculture's Experimental Farm in Ottawa have contributed to all branches of scientific inquiry. The College of Fisheries in St. John's, Newfoundland, the Bedford Institute of Oceanography in Halifax, and the Mackenzie Research Laboratory in Inuvik, N.W.T., are three examples of specialized research centres which operate wholly or in part through public financial assistance. One other specialized agency deserves mention. The Arctic Institute of North America is a research and educational organization with headquarters in Calgary. The Institute's activities embrace many scientific disciplines, both natural and social, with a focus on polar regions.

A cursory glance at Canadian science is valuable only as it emphasizes the variety of directions which should be open to the inquiring minds of students. Of all the curriculum areas, substantial change in present science teaching practices can least be expected in the near future. Materials of benefit to teachers and students alike are embarrassingly scarce, with the exception of items on the flora and fauna of Canada, which are included in the chapter on Environment.

Biology

Biological Conservation, Ehrenfeld (Holt, 1970), $5.25 pa.
Pollution, pollution control, hunting and predator elimination,
characteristics of endangered species, population, political, economic and social policies are topics included.

Biological Science: Principles and Patterns of Life, rev. ed., D.I.
Galbraith and D.G. Wilson (Holt, 1960-66), $10.25.
Structure, chemistry and physiology of the cell; animal and plant
organisms; reproduction, development, heredity and genetics are
topics included.

Biology, Reimer and Wilson (Heath, 1976) $9.00. Grade 10.

Watchers at the Pond, F. Russell (McClelland, 1961), $7.95. The
general reader who wants to know more about the life cycles of
animals living in and around the wilderness pond will find this
interesting.

Un biologiste canadien: Michel Sarrazin, Valée (Ed. Officiel,
1927) $2.00 br.

Metabo: the Energy Game (game). (Vancouver Environmental
Education Project, B.C. Teachers' Federation) $6.50.

Chance: the DNA Game (game). (Vancouver Environmental Education Project, B.C. Teachers' Federation) $5.00.

Periodical

Arctic, The Arctic Institute of North America, 1020 Pine Ave. W.,
Montreal H3A 1A2.

Chapter 6

BUSINESS EDUCATION

Teaching about business practices, as opposed to instructing in
the skills of the office (typing, shorthand, bookkeeping) is an
often neglected aspect of the learning program. Students are
denied the opportunity to investigate the full range of business
endeavours: from private capitalist endeavors such as corporations,
conglomerates, and small businesses, to crown corporations, public
utilities, government development financing, and public-private
joint undertakings. Cooperatives, whether studied from the perspective of the Coady Institute at St. Francis Xavier University,
Antigonish, Nova Scotia, or the Saskatchewan Wheat Pool are also
often ignored.

What little attention is given to business practices suffers from
two defects.

A

Information about business tends to be concentrated on free enterprise, a situation reflected in available learning materials. This in
itself is surprising given the increasingly prominent roles played by
governments—federal, provincial, territorial, and municipal. The
movement away from unfettered free enterprise, as this can be
observed in pragmatic politics over the past three decades, has
made little impact on the business classroom. The learning materials too frequently reflect an economic-social system which either
no longer exists, or is of such questionable utility as to be devoid
of practical application. Except for the historical value of portraying a business philosophy appropriate to an era of unspoiled simplicity, it is probable that for many students the teaching of business concepts, strategies, and procedures is of little consequence.

B

Magnifying these problems is the reinforcement of social-economic class structures. The high school business curriculum tends to be a three to four year program somewhat less respectable than the academic matriculation stream; a bit higher on the scale than pre-employment programs; about on a par with industrial arts, technical-vocational subjects. Business courses are the female counterpart to the male preserve of machine shop, power mechanics, and drafting. If the counselling of students into business courses along mental ability-sexist lines is less than commendable, the differentiation in course content through learning materials is also a cause for concern. The clerk-typists, stenographers, and business machine operators of tomorrow may well acquire considerable mechanical skills: typing, taking dictation, and filing. Making provision for teaching the same students the why's and wherefore's of various types of businesses is another matter. It is the student in the academic program, the manager of the future who is more likely to get some exposure to the economics, politics, and sociology of the business community. (Parallel examples are found in the technical-vocational side of the curriculum where the "workers" are provided with the "tools", and the university-bound student with the insights and ideas.) Such classroom practices underline and strengthen the division of society into a hierarchy of social castes.

Revamping the business program requires, in part, the careful selection of learning materials from such disciplines as history, political science, and sociology. It must be noted that the items mentioned in the bibliography will not be found exclusively in business education catalogues. These catalogues tend to confine their attention to the skills areas and are listed following the books which will help the individual to understand how businesses operate in Canada.

◆ ◆ ◆ ◆

Canadian Business

Capitalism

An Introduction to Canadian Business, 2nd ed., M. Archer (McGraw, 1974), $10.95. Provides a comprehensive picture of various organizations and operations.

The Canadian Corporate Elite, Wallace Clement (McClelland, 1975), $5.95 pa. A study of the power-brokers who wield vast influence over Canadian business and political life.

The Canadian Establishment, vol. I, Peter C. Newman (McClelland, 1975), $14.95.

Canadian Business Strategies, John G. Sayers and R.W. Thornbury (Holt, 1972), $5.95 pa.

Canadian Business Concepts, John G. Sayers (Holt, 1972), $5.95 pa.

Canadian Banking, John A. Galbraith (McGraw, 1970), $10.25.

The Financial System of Canada, E.P. Neufeld (Macmillan, 1972), $33.00.

Canadian Business Studies Series (kit). MacLean-Hunter, set of 7 card sets plus teacher's guide, $20.00. Prepared by the *Financial Post,* the series provides case studies of conglomerates, communications, finance, industrials, real estate, multi-nationals and merchandizing. Among major Canadian corporations analysed are: Bell Canada, Bank of Nova Scotia, Imperial Oil, Block Brothers, International Nickel, Dominion Stores and Molson Industries.

Biographies of Capitalists

Robert McLaughlin: Carriage Builder, D. McLaughlin Henderson (Griffin, 1972), $4.95. The life of the founder of the McLaughlin Carriage Company and later the founder of General Motors of Canada.

Bush Pilot with a Briefcase, R. Keith (General, 1973), $1.95 pa. The biography of Grant McConachie, founder of Canadian Pacific Airlines.

K.C. Irving: Portrait of an Industrialist, R. Campbell and Russell Hunt (McClelland, 1973), $8.95. The life and times of the most powerful individual in the economic life of New Brunswick.

Lord Beaverbrook: A Profile (cassette tape). A.J.P. Taylor and people of New Brunswick, 60 min, C.B.C. Learning Systems, $15.00. About the Canadian-born business tycoon.

Canadian Business — The Socialist Viewpoint
Study of two biographies will give an awareness of arguments in opposition to the growth and spread of capitalism.

J.S. Woodsworth: A Man to Remember, G. MacInnis (Macmillan, 1974), $4.95 pa. The life of the founder of the Canadian socialist party, the C.C.F., later the N.D.P.

Tommy Douglas, Doris Shackleton (McClelland, 1975), $12.50.

Cooperatives

The Man from Margaree: Selections from the Writings of M.M. Coady, eds. M.M. Coady and A. Laidlaw (McClelland, 1975) $3.95 pa. The founder of the internationally recognized Coady Institute, Antigonish, Nova Scotia.

Government-Private Enterprise Joint Ventures

Pipeline, W. Kilbourn (Clarke, Irwin, 1970), $7.95. History of the C.D. Howe era of involving the federal government with corporations in constructing the Trans-Canada pipeline.

Forced Growth: Five studies of Government Involvement in the Development of Canada, P. Mathias (James Lorimer, 1971), $3.50 pa.

The National Dream/The Last Spike, Pierre Berton (McClelland, 1974), $4.95 pa. Set of two books relating the history of the building of the C.P.R. and the shenanigans of the government of Sir John A. Macdonald.

James Bay, B. Richardson (Clarke, Irwin, 1973), $2.75 pa.

James Bay, Robert Bourassa (Harvest), $3.00 pa. (In French *La baie James,* Robert Bourassa (Jour, 1973), $3.00 br.) The last two titles could be studied jointly. Boyce Richardson writes in defence of the concerns of the native people who live in the James Bay area, and the ecological-environmental considerations surrounding this immense hydro-electric power development. Robert Bourassa, Premier of Quebec, defends the project as conceived by his Liberal government.

Business versus the Individual

Land Grab; Oliver Buerge vs. the authority, D. Waterfield (Clarke, Irwin, 1973), $7.95. An account of one man's struggle against the powerful influence of British Columbia Hydro.

Selling Out (film).   28 min,   16 mm, col,   E.B., $299.00. A P.E.I. farmer is caught in the dilemma of wanting to sell his farm in a marketplace dominated by American investment.

Working People

The Anatomy of Poverty: The Condition of the Working Class in Montreal, 1879-1929, Terry Copp (McClelland, 1974), $3.95 pa.

On Strike!, Christine Sylvester and Marion Harris (O.I.S.E., 1973), $1.25 pa. One in the series on Canadian Critical Issues.

Charbonneau and le Chef, J.T. McDonough (McClelland, 1968), $2.50 pa.

Canada's Unions, Robert M. Laxer (James Lorimer, 1976), $6.95 pa. A reference item.

The Story of Unions in Canada, Jack Williams (Dent, 1975), $4.50 pa.

Dying Hard: The Ravages of Industrial Carnage, Leyton (McClelland, 1976), $3.95 pa. Edited autobiographies of nine miners from the Newfoundland communities of St. Lawrence and Lawn.

British Columbia: The People's Early Story, Harold Griffin (Commonwealth, 1958), $1.95 pa. The story of the early labour movement in British Columbia.

Miners and Steelworkers: Labour Unions in Cape Breton, Paul MacEwen (Hakkert, 1975), $12.50. A penetrating examination of the Cape Breton, Nova Scotia steel and coal industries.

Working People, J. Lorimer and M. Phillips (James Lorimer, 1971), $4.95 pa. Description of life in a working class Toronto neighbourhood.

The Winnipeg General Strike, D.C. Masters (U.T.P., 1971) $3.50 pa. Originally published 1950.

Winnipeg, 1919, new ed. N. Penner (James Lorimer, 1975), $3.95 pa. The strikers' own history of the General Strike.

On Strike, I. Abella (James Lorimer, 1974), $4.95 pa. An account of six important strikes in the history of the labour movement: Winnipeg, 1919: Estevan, 1931; Stratford, 1933; Oshawa, 1937; Ford-Windsor, 1945; and Asbestos, 1949.

Essays in Canadian Working Class History, ed. Gregory S. Kealey and Peter Warrean (McClelland, 1976), $5.95 pa.

Doctors' Strike, Robin F. Badgley and Samuel Wolfe (Macmillan, 1967), $3.75 pa. A history of the Saskatchewan doctors' strike.

Charbonneau et le Chef (record). J.T. McDonough. C.B.C. Publications Branch, 2 l.p. records, $7.50. A drama of the strike in Asbestos, P.Q. in 1949.

Buying and Selling

Marketing: A Canadian Profile, R. Picard (Pitman, 1972), $7.95. A history and analysis of marketing practices. Transparencies, $95.00.

Practical Marketing in Canada, W. Craig (Burns, 1969) $6.95.

Marketing Research in Canada: Principles, Reading and Cases, W. Mahatoo (Nelson, 1968) $8.95 pa.

Marketing in the Canadian Environment, B. Mallen and V. Kirplani and G. Lane. (Prentice, 1973) $4.95 pa.

Consumer Education, rev. ed., N.E. Brown (Macmillan, 1967), $1.50 pa.

The Consumer's Handbook: 99 Commercial Rip-offs and How to Spot Them, L. Gordon (McClelland, 1975), $3.95 pa.

The Big Sell, Pierre Berton (McClelland, 1963), 95¢ pa. An assessment of common business practices.

Hard to Swallow, W. Stewart (Macmillan, 1975), $5.95 pa. The food industry in Canada and its effects on the consumer.

The Darlings: The Mystique of the Supermarket, R. Chisholm (McClelland, 1969), $10.00. A study of consumers, i.e. 'the darlings' vis-à-vis bureaucracy, business, advertising.

Consumerism and the Youth Market (cassette tape) 30 min. C.B.C. Learning Systems, $8.00. About exploitation of youth by corporations, advertising etc.

What is money? (film); *Planning the use of Money* (film); *What do I receive for my Money?* (film); and *When I need More Money* (film). 9–11 min, 16mm, col, English or French, Moreland-Latchford, $140 each.

Skills

Typing

20th Century Typing, Cdn. 9th ed. (Gage, 1968), $16.40. A comprehensive four-part course; teacher's manual and working papers available.

Dicta-Typing: A Short Course, Geraldine Farmer and M.J. Brown (Gage, 1974), $1.50.

Typewriting Office Practice, Cdn. ed., P.S. Atkinson (Gage, 1974), $5.95.

Elementary Typing (film). 16mm, col, set of 5, $787 or rental.

Shorthand

Forkner Shorthand, H.L. Forkner and F. Brown (Gage, 1972), $5.20 pa.

Forkner Shorthand Outlines for the Business Vocabulary, Geraldine Farmer and M.L. Lore (Gage, 1972), $5.20 pa.

Bookkeeping and Office Practice

Debit equals Credit, Alec Taylor (Gage, 1962), $8.00. A three year course.

20th Century Bookkeeping and Accounting, L.D. Boynton (Gage, 1969), $9.60. Introductory course.

20th Century Bookkeeping and Accounting, Thomas Ferguson (Gage, 1970), $9.60. Advanced course.

Business Filing and Records Control, E.D. Bassett (Gage, 1966), $6.45.

Business Writing: Letters, Barbara Butchart (Gage, 1970), $1.95 pa.

Business Writing: Reports, D.W. Dashwood-Jones (Gage, 1971), $2.20 pa.

Creative Communication for Career Students, Dorothy Farmiloe (Holt, 1974), $4.95 pa.

Business Transcription Tape Library (cassette or reel-to-reel tape). Gage, each of three, $80.00. A complete library of taped dictation.

Accounting

Introduction to Accounting, rev. ed., F.E.V. Pilcher (General, 1972), $5.35.

Essential Accounting Concepts, rev. ed., David Haddon and John Sayers (Holt, 1975), $8.95.

Accounting Principles: A Canadian Viewpoint, R.M. Skinner (Canadian Institute of Chartered Accountants, 1972), $15.95.

Canadian Accounts Handbook, 2nd ed., W.G. Leonard (McGraw, 1972), $22.50.

Payroll Accounting, M.R. Tague (Pitman, 1973), $1.95 pa.

Canadian Business Handbook, 2nd ed., Dorothy M. Newman and others (McGraw, 1967), $16.95.

Money and Business, K.J. MacDonald and K.D. Dixon (Gage, 1969), $6.75.

Business Office Simulation System (kit). McGraw, $69.50. Three hundred and sixty office problems.

Accounting Concepts (filmstrips with accompanying cassette tapes). Holt. Set of 6, $90.00.

Using Computers and Calculators

Computer Science with FORTRAN, John R. Abrahams (Griffin, 1972), $4.95 pa.

Computers in Business, 2nd ed., M.K. Mackle and I.D. Ross (Gage, 1970), $1.90.

Information Processing in BASIC, J.A. Douglas (Griffin, 1972), $2.95 pa.

Introductory Computor Language, John E. Walsh (Pitman, 1971), $9.25.

Introductory Data Processing Projects, H.R. Furneaux and G.E. Joice (Dent, 1969), $1.25 pa.

Collator, Calculator, Accounting Machine (film). 14 min, 16mm, col, Moreland-Latchford, $175 or rental.

Data Processing (film). 16mm, col, Moreland-Latchford, set of 7, $1102.50 or rental.

A Matter of Survival (film). 25 min, 16mm, col, N.F.B. $220. What transpires when computors threaten job security.

Dictionaries

The Dictionary of Canadian English: The Senior Dictionary, Walter S. Avis and others (Gage, 1967), $9.50 pa. Ninety thousand entries.

Canadian Business Word Division, Geraldine Farmer (Gage, n.d.), $4.95 pa. A basic word list including metric terms, commonly misspelled words and words that differ according to the parts of speech.

Newspapers

Financial Post 1907-1970 (microfilm), 16mm, b&w, MacLean-Hunter.

Financial Post, subscription $15 annually, 52 issues. Box 9100, Postal Station A, Toronto M5W 1V5.

Financial Times, subscription $12 annually, 52 issues. 10 Arundel St., Place Bonaventure, Montreal, P.Q.

Periodical

Canadian Consumer, Consumer's Association of Canada, 251 Laurier Ave. W., Room 801, Ottawa K1P 5Z7. $5.00, six issues per year.

Teachers

CABET 1973: An Emerging Profile, Canadian Association of Business Education Teachers (Gage, 1974), $8.00. Conference reports on trends, issues, techniques.

Will that be Cash or . . . ?: A Look at Consumer Studies in Canada, Louise Beaugrand-Champagne (Canadian Education Association, 1975), $2.00 pa.

Chapter 7

CHEMISTRY

Chemistry, like Biology and Botany, does not have a Canadian base. The small number of Canadian-prepared learning materials found at the end of this chapter validates the point. From the viewpoint of a student it is almost impossible to receive any grounding whatever in the development of Canadian chemistry. To make matters worse, the few available learning materials relate exclusively to the learning of the science, and do not provide any orientation to the Canadian setting. It is not hard to understand why generations of graduating students tend to look elsewhere for careers in chemistry rather than in their own country. Three to four years of high school science instruction in which every example, model, experiment, or observation is drawn from foreign sources (primarily the United States) can only fortify the notion that opportunities lie outside Canada.

The complexion of Canadian chemistry instruction could be altered. Initially, one mental barrier must be demolished. Chemistry, like the other physical sciences, did not develop in Canada after the arrival of the European immigrants. One of the easiest traps for colonizing people, and their historians, is to assume that elements of "civilization", of which science is one, were imported to this country. Seldom is due recognition given to the scientific contributions of Indian and Inuit peoples. Viewed another way, human progress tends to be portrayed very unevenly, particularly in those areas of the world where Western Europeans settled, colonized, and expanded their empires. In Canada, students of the history of science would most probably begin their inquiries into the period following the settlement of New France. The thousands of years of Indian-Inuit civilizations preceding the seventeenth century are completely ignored, or else only examined from an anthropological viewpoint. No attempt is made to understand the scientific advances of native peoples; rather their contributions are regarded as a curiosity, something intriguing, but not to be confused with the achievements of civilization. Clearly, everyone in society is the loser. The Indian or Inuit student readily recognizes that his heritage is of no consequence, while the non-native affirms that everything worth knowing happened after 1604 (the settlement of Port Royal) or some other arbitrary date. Admittedly, labels such as chemistry, biology, and physics were of no consequence to people who viewed humanity and nature as one interrelated entity. That in itself is instructive, particularly now when non-native people are trying to acquire the understandings and skills necessary for survival in an imperilled environment. In a more tangible fashion, it is useful to review a limited sample of those native practices which rightfully fall into the general category of science.

Developments in chemistry in Canada were stimulated by the accessibility of rich and varied natural resources. Advances made by Indian peoples were no exception. The story of the beaver, in relation to the fur trade, is well known. Less widely acknowledged is the Indians' understanding of the medicinal qualities of the secretions of the scent glands. Located in sacs near the reproductive organs of the beaver, castorum was used as a remedy for earache, an historical fact known at least as early as 1685. The same oily substance was known for its ability to attract the unsuspecting beaver to traps.

The arrival of colonial settlers accentuated the native peoples' dependency upon the animal kingdom for their survival. Trade in hides, skins, and furs provided the trinkets of civilization that in turn whetted the appetite for more manufactured goods. Only seldom is any attention paid to the tanning-smoking process developed by the Indians, which helped to make this lucrative trade possible. Chipewyan people, for example, used a mixture of water combined with the brain of a moose as a tanning solution. Repeated soaking of the hide, followed by twisting and stretching, were required before the material was ready for curing over a slow-burning, smoky fire.

Colourful beads and bolts of calico cloth were integral features of the barter system. Prior to the importation of these European products, clothing, and the body itself, were decorated with natural dyes developed from berries, flowers, mosses, and lichens. Sea shells, bone fragments, animal claws, quills, hides, wood and stone were dipped, etched, or painted with these original colours to provide family totems, jewellery, or sacred symbols.

"Sugaring-off" is an early spring ritual in many parts of eastern

Canada. As early as 1703, explorers learned from Indian peoples the technique of evaporating the sap of the maple tree for the purpose of making various products (sugar, cream, syrup, water). Peter Pond's Journals (1765-1775) recount how he and his companions traded with the Indians for these delicacies that could be used as a sweetener for another Indian developed product, hemlock tea.

Romantic tales abound in Canadian history about the adventures of the coureur de bois, the voyageurs, and explorers in general. At another time and place in the nation's history, the invention of pemmican would have been heralded as the greatest thing since sliced bread. In today's idiom, pemmican would be considered in the same breath as quick dried foods and most likely merchandized as "Survival Meal in A Pouch!" From an historical perspective the fact that pemmican was a remarkable native development, necessary for both exploration and subsistence, is glossed over.

Non-native people are more likely to attribute Indian or Inuit knowledge of various food properties to a form of primitive understanding. It is amusing to speculate today on the honours that would be bestowed on someone who recognized the hallucinogenic properties of kinnikinik, the roughage value of hydrophyllum virginianum (water leaf), or the balanced diet provided by wild rice, the edible bulb of the Jack-in-the-pulpit, rhubarb, corn, potatoes, Labrador tea, and varieties of fish, wild game, and the like. The fact that Indian and Inuit people knew these things, taught them to the newcomers to their land, and practiced, rather than preached, a waste-not, want-not social system would now entitle them to at least an invitation to the latest Rome Conference on World Starvation, or a Stockholm Environmental Colloquium! In learning materials their contributions have gone unnoticed. It has been convenient to ignore these developments and to investigate the beginnings of Canadian chemistry along these lines:

1674 —Nicholas Follin in New France was granted the first chemical commercial license to produce soap.

1838 —Charles Fenerty of Halifax claimed to have invented a process for making paper from wood pulp.

1842 —H.H. Croft was appointed the first full time professor of chemistry in Canada at the University of Toronto.

1896 —W.T. Gibbs, at Buckingham, P.Q. developed a new type of furnace to produce phosphorous, using hydro-power from the nearby Lièvre River.

1925 —a process for extracting sulphuric acid from smelter gas

was developed, and the method of making viscose rayon
from wood pulp.

1929 — G.H.W Lucas, at the University of Toronto, introduced
cyclopropane, a new form of anaesthetic.

1930 — H.R. Griffith of Montreal, who was working in the area
of anaesthesia, introduced curare, a muscle-relaxant.

And so on down to the present time. Surely new directions in
the teaching of chemistry should include the complete range of
human endeavours.

A different approach to the study of chemistry can be taken
through the eyes of the geographer, beginning in British Columbia and working eastward.

Trail, B.C., is the centre of a mammoth COMINCO mining and
smelting industry. The gasses given off in the various stages of
the smelting process are converted into sulphuric acid which is
used in the manufacture of fertilizer.

At Fort Saskatchewan, outside of Edmonton, a method of
making synthetic ammonia is used for the leaching of nickel ore
mined at Lynn Lake, Saskatchewan.

T. Thorvaldson, at the University of Saskatchewan, Saskatoon,
studied the chemistry of cement. At the same university, J.W.T.
Spinks investigated radioactive tracers. To the south of Saskatoon,
near the community of Lanigan, the potash industry is of major
consequence.

Copper Cliff, Ontario, is the location of one of the world's largest
sulphur dioxide plants. The hydro-electric power of Niagara Falls
is chiefly responsible for the extensive production of calcium
cyanamide and sodium cyanide in that location. In 1925 the first
contact plant for the production of sulphuric acid was established
at Corneston. At Belleville, H.H. Dow, founder of Dow Chemical
Co., pioneered work in electrolytic cells.

Research into bauxite and the manufacture of aluminum was
carried on at Arvida, Quebec. Sources of hydro-power at Shawin-
igan Falls lent impetus to the electro-chemical industry.

A third approach to chemistry is to examine the impact of World
Wars I and II on inquiry, experimentation, and developments. The
need for synthetic materials to replace diminished and/or expensive
natural products led to the development of rubber at Sarnia, Ontario;
the production of nylon yarn at Kingston; the manufacture of ace-
tone, acetic acid, and acetic anhydride required by Britain in the
1914-1918 period; and the use of wood-pulp cellulose as a raw
material for propellants in place of cotton cellulose. The chemical
properties of materials used in explosives were of obvious importance. At the beginning of World War II, Canadian Industries Ltd.

developed a reverse-nitration process for making the explosive T.N.T. Other spheres of work included the manufacture of the explosive RDX and the use of nitroquanidine. Between the two wars exploratory work took place on the refinement cf pitchblende for radium development, and later, research into uranium with subsequent experimentation at Chalk River, Ontario.

Furthering this thematic study, it is practical to look at the contributions of individual Canadian chemists. A sprinkling of names to be considered include:

T.L. Wilson (investigations into calcium carbide, acetylene gas)

E.A. Le Sueur (diaphragm type of cell which is used in the production of caustic soda and chlorine from salt)

H.G. Thode (chemistry of isotopes)

R.F. Rutten and J.B. Collip (biochemistry)

J.A. Anderson and R.K. Larmour (cereal chemistry)

F.E. Beamish (analytical chemistry)

C.B. Thorne and J.S. Bates (pulp and paper research into high density bleaching and kraft green liquor clarification)

G.H. Tomlinson, Sr. (magnesium-base sulphate cooking process)

P.E. Gagnon and C.F.H. Allen (organic chemistry)

Some of the diverse products that have come from the initiatives of Canadian chemists are: cellophane, coal-tar acids, linseed oil (from flax), vinyl resins, pharmaceutical products (e.g. female sex hormone to be taken orally), synthetic fibres, plastics (e.g. Bakelite products), conversion of waste pyrite into sulphur, sulphur dioxide and iron dioxide.

As formidable as these Canadian accomplishments may appear to be, there is a less pleasant side to the story of chemistry in Canada. Students will find it revealing to explore the effect of foreign ownership on Canadian industry in terms of scientific advancement. Given Canada's position as a satellite in the American economic empire, it is not surprising to find that research is much more likely to take place at the site of parent companies in the United States. If public awareness is to be increased, students should be given the chance to analyze the implications of the economics of science. As a counterpoint to the study of foreign influence, study of a question such as "The Future of Canadian Science Activities" could lead to an examination of the contributions of the National Research Council (e.g. the work of F.E. Lathe on the development of refractories for lining high-temperature industrial furnaces, and the process developed by L.M. Pidgeon for making magnesium metal); the National Defence Board and federal and provincial departments such as Agriculture.

The brevity of the bibliography following surely indicates the need for expanded governmental and publishing involvement in this field of learning.

◆ ◆ ◆ ◆

Senior High School Materials

Titles from the Action Chemistry Series, Book Society:

Action Chemistry, K. Ashcroft (Book Society, 1974), $6.45.

Chemistry of Man and Molecules, L. Birenbaum (Book Society, 1975) $2.10 pa.

Water, Chemistry and Ecology, J. Hammill (Book Society, 1974), $2.10 pa.

Chemistry of the Car, K. Ashcroft and J. Hammill (Book Society, 1974), $2.10 pa.

Chemistry of Photography, K. Ashcroft (Book Society, 1974), $2.10 pa.

Chemistry: A Search for Understanding, H.D. Webber, R.A. Hill and G.R. Billings (Holt, 1970), $8.95. Lab manual, $3.95. An introductory text.

Chemistry: An Introductory Study, A. Allen, J.A. Page and K.R. Bonneymen (Gage, 1967), $6.50. Teacher's Commentary, $1.45 pa. A one year course.

Basic Modern Chemistry, 2nd ed., Jean-Paul Gravel and Gordon Hall (McGraw, 1969), $7.75. Laboratory experiments, $3.25. Objective tests, $2.35. An introductory text.

The Development of Bio-Chemistry in Canada, E.G. Young (U.T.P., 1976), $15.00. A reference for historical information.

Production of Sodium by Electrolysis (filmloop). 4 min, super 8mm, col, N.F.B., $21.00.

Spectrum and Rays (filmslides), col, N.F.B., set of 10, $4.00.

Chapter 8

COUNSELLING

The term "counselling" defies precise definition. In effect, as used in particular schools, it is an omnibus category covering either a multitude of sins or a shower of blessings, depending upon one's point of view.

The counselling, or guidance program (the labels are often used interchangeably) has the potential for wreaking almost irrevocable havoc in the life of the student, through lack of sensitivity and understanding. Or, conversely, counselling services can be the critical factor in helping the student to gain the maximum benefit and enjoyment through the crucial junior and senior high school years, in particular.

Because of the many uncertainties in deciding the nature and extent of the counselling program, it is useful to isolate five of its more obvious components. In turn, these can be used to guide the selection of appropriate materials.

A

Attitudes and Values. Unlike their counterparts of even a generation ago, young people today live in a society characterized by rapidly shifting patterns of attitudes and values. They are increasingly aware of the multiplicity of value systems of diverse cultural groups, and of conflicting attitudes and values within specific cultures. In particular instances, the emerging conflicts strike very close to the foundation upon which North American society has been developed. In helping young people to prepare themselves for living in the latter part of the twentieth century, the educator cannot ignore these changes. Consider the following examples.

"Searching for alternatives" may be the phrase that best describes the attitudes of many young and some older people. Implicit is a dissatisfaction with the perceived sterility of the assembly line, mass

production society. The notion that people are born to exist as
neatly processed products in a packaged consumer society is seen
to be hollow. Practical alternatives to this approach to life can include returning to the land, communal living, and, in extreme cases,
individual withdrawal from society itself.

Closely allied to this "people movement" has been the growth
in interest in the "old ways", with particular emphasis given to religious understanding and expression. The quest is in the direction
of combining elements of various religious persuasions in the hope
of developing a philosophy which has meaning for the individual.

On a broader scale, the cornerstone of North American "progress"
is itself under severe re-examination, if not attack. The pursuit of
an ever-increasing gross national product (G.N.P.) appears to be a
shallow raîson d'étre at a time when the very existence of humanity
is subject to searching analysis. In the not-so-distant past, natural
resources were regarded as limitless. The conventional wisdom was,
"What is good for General Motors is good for society as a whole."
Now the premises upon which the growth ethic is based are being
challenged as many people find the emphasis on materialism to be
not only limiting in scope, but self-defeating in its consequences.

The value of an "education" is open to debate. Increasing numbers of young people no longer concur that the logical progression
to follow is elementary-junior-senior high school, followed by university. Again the question of alternatives looms large. The technical
school, the junior college, the community college often bring greater
personal satisfaction than the more impersonal academic atmosphere
of the university. As well, options such as free schools, experiencing
life first hand, or opting completely out of the system, cannot be
overlooked.

For those who are involved in planning and developing learning
experiences, these and other attitudinal changes imply a need for
re-evaluating the role of the school and what takes place there, as
it affects the lives of people. Schools have to become open to allow-
ing young people to question and analyze alternatives. Ways of thinking that may be at odds with the purely scientific method must not
be squelched out of hand. Feelings, opinions, and beliefs that defy
a logical A to Z progression can be as important as objective data
that lends itself to microscopic analysis. Schools must become places
where students can find themselves and come to know and appreciate
the unique, as well as the similar, qualities of members of the human
family.

B

Survival. If learning experiences are to have effective meaning in the lives of people, then these experiences must provide the understandings and skills that are basic to surviving in societies—local, national, global—of increasing complexity and interdependency. People must be able not only to cope with the present, but perhaps more importantly, to be prepared to contend with the unforeseen, the improbable, the unpredictable—in a word, the "future". In a generalized way, one can contrast the growth of big government, business, and labour unions in the past twenty years with that of the first half of this century. The question is: "How do Mary and John Doe come to understand the multiplicity of agencies that influence or dominate their existence?" Dramatic illustrations of this problem can be found in any corner of Canada. From the municipal level to the provincial government, to the federal scene itself, the individual is confronted with a complex, often confusing assortment of officials, offices, policies, and programs which supposedly have something to do with the lives of people. To find out just who is responsible for what under these circumstances can be far from simple. It can only be speculated how much more difficult it is to know what is going on if you happen to come from a background where English or French is not your native language; where, culturally speaking, the asking of incessant questions to find answers is not done; where the trappings of status and bureaucracy are unfamiliar, or where people do not feel comfortable walking through a maze of offices in search of officialdom. Learning opportunities must include the chance for the individual to understand how the system can be made to work in the interests of people. Similar information with respect to the business world and unions must be forthcoming as well. Life in a consumer-oriented, credit card society requires knowledge and skills which cannot be left to chance. People's mental and physical health depends in large measure on being able to tolerate the stresses and strains imposed by "organized" society.

Similarly, survival in an increasingly urbanized society poses its own peculiar problems. The change from living in rural areas to high rise apartments, town houses, low-cost row housing, and suburban crescents, entails a remarkable shift in the living habits of many citizens. These factors, combined with the ready availability of alcohol and drugs and the potential spread of communicable diseases can add up to a social atmosphere bordering on the chaotic if not catastrophic.

The school simply cannot ignore these realities, using such dubious excuses as "there isn't time, and besides we must get on with the quadratic equations!" The facts of life today strongly suggest that unless people are given "life skills" to enable their survival in the present and the future, the other aspects of the learning program will be of interest only to the middle-class group of students who have relative control over their existence.

C

Freedom. Freedom to learn is a matter of responsible, individual choice. There is no 'one way' that can be prescribed as being appropriate to the needs of each student. Possibilities range from a relatively structured group learning environment to personal study and investigation on the part of the individual. It is the school's obligation to make provision for the realization of these possibilities through access to materials, supplies, and equipment; adequate time in which to seek out information, make assumptions, and draw conclusions; and the encouragement and guidance of responsive teachers. Freedom implies that individuals and groups of young people should have the opportunity to explore, to wrestle with, and eventually to solve, problems that have meaning for them. The latitude of choice should permit the individual to capitalize upon his particular strengths. Involvement in the power mechanics course might lead to an interest in reading about automotive inventions, interest in the out-of-doors might lead to photography or other forms of artistic expression; an aptitude for design might evolve into a study of geometrical concepts. The essence of this approach is to provide opportunities for all students to pursue their aptitudes and interests to the fullest extent.

D

Awareness—Personal and Social. Sexuality (including family life education and physiology), drug use and abuse (tobacco, alcohol, soft and hard drugs), venereal disease, as well as nutrition, dental care, general body needs and maturation are widely acknowledged aspects of the counselling services. Often less attention is paid to other equally important considerations.

The feelings of inferiority which can stem from being a member of a minority ethnic or cultural group. To be of Indian, Inuit, Eastern European, Asian, Latin American, or African origin in a society that is almost completely dominated by Western Euro-Canadians, means that for the young, who are searching for models of identification, there are very few if any available. The message may well come through that "making it" is synonomous with assimilation into the mainstream, coupled with a denial of self-worth, loss of cultural pride and identity and, most serious of all, a turning aside from one's own people. The alternative to the process of assimilation may be the other extreme, the development of an attitude of "Since I can't make it on my terms, I might just as well drop out."

To be a young person who has acquired English or French as a second language poses related problems. The individual must have considerable oral skills and a high degree of comprehension of the spoken and written word. To lack these skills is to jeopardize one's chances when opportunities become available. A person who feels insecure in a second language may well hesitate to advance his own needs and interests for fear of the condescension, if not outright rejection, of the listener. In a practical sense the second language speaker receives one more signal that his skills are deficient. Meanwhile, the native speaker of English or French can develop the attitude of equating language inadequacies with shyness, insecurity, even stupidity. Almost from the outset of a child's school experience, the individual's knowledge of, and pride in, his mother tongue can be destroyed through the prevalence of the common equation:

Language deficiencies in English (French) = ignorance.

(A child cannot learn anything until he speaks and understands the language of the teacher.)

Young people grow up in a society of stereotypes. Through the printed page and the mass media, an individual can become conditioned to a view of life totally at variance with reality. This process begins early in the child's school experience through exposure to biased learning materials, as mentioned previously. By the time an individual has reached adolescence, conflicts can develop as his growing awareness of the facts of life runs counter to the indoctrinated stereotypes of earlier years. Separating fact from fancy can be difficult. Children from minority groups (racial or socio-economic) can confront an even more trying situation as the harsher realities—poverty, prejudice, double standards—are not only seen, but experienced personally.

Learning experiences that will help youth to bridge these credibility chasms and indicate ways of coping with society as it is and bring about changes that will improve conditions in the future are badly needed.

The designation of 1975 as "International Women's Year" publicized many sexist practices that have been taken for granted. Schools are no exception, particularly with regard to vocational guidance procedures. Too commonly, career designation has been on the basis of sex rather than the individual's interests and abilities. Certain facets of the school curriculum have been considered appropriate for female students, for instance, business and commercial courses, while males are more likely to be plugged into automotives and/or electronics. Possibly more insidious has been the implication that science, particularly physics, is somehow a male preserve, while literature and the fine arts have feminine appeal. Granted, there is increasing awareness of this discrimination, but sexist thinking and practices are far from being eradicated.

E

School. It is useful to examine certain widely held beliefs regarding the nature and functions of schools. The implications of these views have a direct bearing on the quality of counselling services.

Frequently "school" and "education" are regarded as identical. The implication is that the school has a monopoly on whatever it is that constitutes "education." In reality, the role of the school must be viewed in a people-community perspective. The school is a community learning space that functions jointly with the home, the church, and community organizations that provide opportunities for learning experiences. The efforts of those associated with the school, administrators and counselling staff, in particular, must be directed towards providing learning opportunities that will complement rather than supplant the programs and experiences available in the community as a whole.

Children are sent to school because it is "good for them"—such is the widely accepted notion. More pragmatically, young people go to school because school makes it possible to get jobs, and jobs mean money. Unfortunately, going to school, getting an "education", does not ensure employment. In fact, there is much to suggest that such things as the home environment into which one is born, as well as luck, have more to do with finding a job and raising the socio-economic level than does the formal process of education. Moreover, the job marketplace is not what it used to be a generation ago. Technology and international finance, as well as changing attitudes toward the work ethic, are making their presence felt in a society that inches ever closer to a guaranteed annual income for substantial numbers of people. However, the myth of what education can do for people still flourishes and cannot be ignored.

What actually goes on inside the school is often even further removed from the experience of large segments of the public. Attempting to comprehend the "curriculum" is a chore in itself,

as is trying to understand evaluation procedures and the recording of individual student progress. Standardized test scores (intel-
ligence quotients and achievement levels) combined with aptitude
inventories may indeed satisfy the statisticians' concern for bell
curves, stanines, and standard deviations. Whether such measuring devices assist the student in understanding his own strengths
and weaknesses, or help parents to understand the educational
process is at best doubtful. At worst, any belief by students or
parents that "schools know best" can be destroyed through the
realization that objective student data is of major consequence.
Thanks to cumulative record cards, such information can become
the unseen hand guiding the student through his educational
career. Unknown to student and parent, an almost automated
approach can be devised to record the individual's progress. Tidy
categories of skills, attitudes, interests, mastery of content information, have been created in such a manner as to develop a checklist mentality toward evaluating each individual on a five-point
scale ranging from excellent to awful. The approach is chillingly
close to that used to evaluate the mass-produced products of an
assembly line. The school system is not in the business of manufacturing automatons that can be neatly categorized on a finite
scale. Rather the goal must be one of assisting the individual to
realize his potential to the fullest extent. The following list of
materials may prove useful.

♦ ♦ ♦ ♦

General References for Teachers

Introduction to Guidance, A. Herman (Holt, 1972), $5.50. A
book of readings.

Blueprint for Guidance in Canadian Schools, M.D. Parmenter
(Guidance Centre, University of Toronto, 1967-72) $1.60 pa.

Humanistic Psychology and Personalized Teaching, S.L. Kong
(Holt, 1970), $4.50 pa.

Intrinsic Motivation: A New Direction In Education, ed. H.I.
Day, D.E. Berlyne and D.E. Hunt (Holt, 1971), $5.40 pa.

Guidelines for Ethical Behaviour, Canadian Guidance and Counselling Association (Guidance Centre, University of Toronto),
45¢ pa.

Developmental Group Counselling, P. McDermott (Nelson, 1971),
$1.90 pa.

Educational Opportunity in Canada: The Pursuit of Equality, W.G. Fleming (Prentice, 1975), $3.75 pa.

Problems In The Teaching of Young Children, Andrew J. Biemiller (O.I.S.E, 1970), $3.50 pa.

The Learning Environment in Early Childhood, Christine Nash (Methuen, 1975), $7.95 pa.

Yes They Can!: A Practical Guide to the Teaching of Adolescent Slow Learners. K.J. Weber (Methuen, 1974), $7.95.

The Elementary School Counsellor in the Decade Ahead, H.W. Zingle and E.E. Fox (Holt, 1972) $3.95. A collection of papers delivered at a conference on counselling in the elementary school.

The Canadian Family in Comparative Perspective, L. Larson (Prentice, 1975), $10.95 pa. Useful as a teacher reference.

Hospitals are for Learning, Elizabeth Crocker (Atlantic Institute of Education, 1976), $1.00 pa. Ideas and resources to help teachers relate hospitals and health care to a variety of curriculum subjects.

General Reference Textbooks for High School Students

Guidance, H.L. Stein and W.H. Auld (Gage, 1961), $5.50. Introductory text for high school.

Health, Science and You, E. Chant and others (Holt, 1969), Book 3 — Grade 9 — $4.95. Teacher's edition, $4.95. Book 4 — Grade 10 — $4.95. Teacher's edition, $1.75.

Infection, John S. Prichard and M. Steele (Holt, 1970), $1.10 pa. A study of the defence of the body against infection and the role of these defences in the rejection of organ transplants.

Attitudes and Values

L'Arche Journal: A Family's Experiences in Jean Vanier's Community, J.H. Clarke (Griffin, 1973), $4.95 pa.

Tears of Silence, Jean Vanier (Griffin, 1970), $2.95 pa.

Jean Vanier (cassette tape). 60 min, C.B.C. Learning Systems, $15.00.

Inner Space (cassette tape). Jean Vanier, 30 min, C.B.C. Learning Systems, $8.00.

Hug Me Please, I Need It (cassette tape). 60 min, C.B.C. Learning Systems, $15.00. Deals with mental retardation and includes a conversation with Jean Vanier.

Moral Decision Making: Integrity / Honesty / Guilt / Hostility / Generosity (filmstrips with accompanying cassette tapes) col,

Moreland-Latchford, set of 5, $65.00 or $14.50 each. Teacher's handbook included.

Your Emotions: Your Fears / Your Anger / Your Envy / Your Frustrations (filmstrips with accompanying cassette tapes). col, Moreland-Latchford, set of 4, $55.00 or $14.50 each. Teacher's handbook included.

Maturity— Options and Consequences: Teenage Mother / Teenage Father / Growing Up / Trouble with Alcohol / Love and Marriage / Values— Yours and Theirs (filmstrips with accompanying cassette tapes). col, Moreland-Latchford, set of 6, $75.00 or $14.50 each. Teacher's handbook included.

Character Awareness: Courage / Deceit / Vanity / Perseverance / Jealousy / Loyalty (filmstrips with accompanying cassette tapes). col, Moreland-Latchford, set of 6, $75.00 or $14.50 each. Teacher's handbook included.

Emotions (film set). 16mm, col, English or French, Moreland-Latchford, 3 day rental, $16.95 or purchase.

Moral Decisions (film set). 16mm, col, English or French, Moreland-Latchford, 3 day rental, $16.95 or purchase.

Survival

Youth and the Law, 2nd ed., W.T. McGrath (Gage, 1973), $2.95 pa.

The Law and You, M.J. Arpin (C.B.C. Publications Branch, 1966), $1.00 pa.

The Teenage World, Philip Manuel (Nelson, 1970), $1.20 pa.

Adolescence: Some Critical Issues, J.J. Mitchell (Holt, 1971), $3.50 pa.

Living and Working, D.W. Jackson (Nelson, 1970), $1.20 pa.

Freedom To Learn

Alternatives in Education, ed. B. Rusk (O.I.S.E., 1971), $2.35 pa.

The Horn and the Beanstalk: Problems and Possibilities in Canadian Education, A. Burton; (Holt, 1972), $2.75 pa.

Thornlea: a case study of an innovative secondary school, M. Fullan and others (O.I.S.E., 1972), $2.15 pa.

Living and Learning In the Free School, Mark Novak (McClelland, 1975), $3.95 pa.

About Schools: What Every Canadian Parent Should Know, R.M. Stamp (New, 1975), $8.95. Useful as an overview of the community school movement in Canada.

You Can't Take A Bathtub on A Subway: A Personal History of SEED, Beverly and Murray Shukyn (Holt, 1973), $3.85 pa. The history of a community initiated alternative for secondary school education.

Options: Reforms and Alternatives for Canadian Education, T. Morrison and A.P. Burton (Holt, 1973), $7.25 pa.

The Learning Machine: A Hard Look at Toronto Schools, Loren Lind (Anansi, 1974), $4.75 pa.

You and Your Work Ways, M.D. Parmenter (Guidance Centre, University of Toronto, 1968-72), $2.50 pa.

Studying For Understanding, D.R. LaMarsh (Nelson, 1970), $1.20 pa.

The Learning Process, Donald LaMarsh (Nelson, 1970), $1.20 pa.

The Canadian Student's Guide To Research, S.S. Campbell and N. Luptin (General, 1974), $1.95 pa.

Form and Substance: A Canadian Guide to Format for the Research Paper, W.K. Thomas; (Gage, 1963), $5.20 pa.

Awareness: Personal and Social

Sexuality, Marriage and Children

Human Life: The First Ten Years, John J. Mitchell (Holt, 1973), $4.95 pa.

Discovery, Jean Elder, John Brewer and Elmer Huff (McGraw, 1970), $2.55 pa.

Growing Up, rev. ed. M.D. Parmenter (Guidance Centre, University of Toronto, 1972), $3.75 pa.

In Search of You, John Gilpin (Nelson, 1970), $1.20 pa.

As Others See Us, Donald R. LaMarsh (Nelson, 1971), $1.20 pa.

A Time of Change, R. Kinch (Holt, 1967) 50¢ pa. A pamphlet on menstruation.

Birth: The Story of How You Come To Be, Lionel Gendron (Harvest, 1970), $3.50 pa.

L'Adolescente veut savoir, Lionel Gendron (Homme, n.d.), $2.00 br.

Family Planning in Canada, ed. Benjamin Schlesinger (U.T.P., 1974), $3.95 pa.

Contraception, Lionel Gendron (Harvest), $1.95 pa.

La Contraception, Lionel Gendron (Homme), $3.00.

Today You are Pregnant, E. Findlay and Margaret Capes (McClelland, 1967), $4.95.

Preparing for Parenthood, R. Kinch (Holt, 1967), 95¢ pa.

Everything You Should Know about Law and Marriage, 2nd rev. ed., F. Chapman (Pagurian, 1974), $2.95 pa.

Canadian Mother and Child, 3rd ed., (Information Canada, 1968), 75¢ pa.

En attendant mon enfant, Yvette Pratte Marchessault (Homme, 1972), $3.00.

Up the Years from One to Six (Information Canada, 1973). $1.00 pa.

Understanding Young Children, Dorothy Burr (McGraw, 1966), $3.95.

Guide medical de mon medecin de famille, Lauzon (Homme), $3.00.

The Battered Child in Canada, M. Van Stolk (McClelland, 1972), $3.95.

The Slaughter of the Innocents, David Bakan (C.B.C. Publications Branch, 1971), $2.00 pa. A study of the 'battered child' phenomenon.

House without Windows, Gloria Sewell and Renate Wilson (Peter Martin, 1974), $8.95. An autobiography of a couple who cope with their particular handicap—blindness.

One Parent Families in Canada, B. Schlesinger (Guidance Centre, University of Toronto, 1974), 85¢ pa.

Kids Today: Sex Education and Family Life (cassette tape). 30 min, C.B.C. Learning Systems, set of 3, $8.00 each.

Venereal Disease (cassette tape). 60 min, C.B.C. Learning Systems, $15.00.

V.D.: Name Your Contacts (film). 22 min, 16mm, col, English or French, Moreland-Latchford, 3 day rental, $16.95 or purchase, $255.00. Additional films are available under major topics of Family Relations, Family Living and Sex Education.

Abortion (cassette tape). 60 min, C.B.C. Learning Systems, $15.00.

Deafness in Children (cassette tape). 30 min, C.B.C. Learning Systems, $8.00.

No Room at the Inn (cassette tape). 60 min, C.B.C. Learning Systems, $15.00. Case study of an unwed mother.

Minorities and Prejudice

What About Poverty in Canada?, B. Schlesinger (Guidance Centre, University of Toronto, 1972), 85¢ pa.

Immigrants in Canada, E. Ferguson (Guidance Centre, University of Toronto, 1974), 85¢ pa.

The Way of the Indian, (C.B.C. Publications Branch, 1963), $1.50 pa.

The Unjust Society, Harold Cardinal (Hurtig, 1969), $2.75 pa.

Textbook Analysis, Nova Scotia Human Rights Commission (Nova Scotia Government Book Store, 1974) 50¢ pa. A study of prejudice in learning materials.

Bilingual Schooling: Some experiences in Canada and the United States, Merrill Sevain (O.I.S.E., 1972), $4.00 pa.

Le langage de votre enfant, Claude Langevin (Homme, 1970), $2.50 br.

L'Avenir des étudiants et les étudiants de l'avenir, Le Centre Recherche Prospective en Education, Université du Québec, Trois Rivières (H.M.H.), $4.50.

Un minorité s'explique: les attitudes de la population francophone du nord-est Ontarien envers l'education de la langue française, (O.I.S.E., 1974), $4.95.

Language and Communication (cassette tape). 60 min, C.B.C. Learning Systems, $15.00. Various aspects of the problem of communication in a multi-language society are discussed.

Women

On Being a Woman: The Modern Woman's Guide to Gynecology, rev. ed., W. Gifford-Jones (McClelland, 1973), $3.95.

The Two-Thirds Minority, Sybil Shack (Guidance Centre, University of Toronto, 1973), $2.75 pa. A view of the roles of women in Canadian education.

Titles from the Women at Work series, by Beverley Allison and Judith Lawrence (Heath, 1975), $1.95 each, pa. Grade 3 reading level, illustrated.

Doctor Mary's Animals. Veterinarian.

Ellie Sells Fish. Fish market.

Let's take a Vote. Community politics.

Myra Builds a House.

Maryon makes Shapes. Sculptor.

Take One. Television production.

Ready for Take-Off. Aviation.

Open Wide. Dentistry.

Women in the Law In Nova Scotia, Halifax Women's Bureau (Canadian Women's Educational Press), 25¢ pa.

Women at Work In Nova Scotia, Halifax Women's Bureau (Canadian Women's Educational Press) 25¢ pa.

I Presume You Can Type, Sonja Sinclair (C.B.C. Publications Branch, 1969), $2.00 pa. Careers open to women.

Addiction

How We Quit Smoking (Information Canada, 1974), $1.00 pa.

The Forgotten Children, R. Margaret Cork (General, 1969), 95¢ pa. The effects of alcoholism on the family.

Final Report Of The Commission Of Inquiry Into The Non-Medical Use of Drugs, Information Canada), $7.95 pa.

Cannabis, (Information Canada, 1972), $3.00 pa.

Drugs, Society and Personal Choice, Harold Kalant and Oriana Kalant (General, 1971), $1.95 pa.

The Pursuit of Intoxication, A.I. Malcolm (General, 1972), $1.25 pa. Information on marijauna, L.S.D., speed and mescaline.

Learning About Drugs (filmstrips with accompanying l.p. records), McGraw, col, set of 4, $57.75.

Changes In The Lung Associated With Cigarette Smoking (film slides). N.F.B., col, set of 20, $9.00.

Alcoholism (cassette tape). 60 min, C.B.C. Learning Systems, $15.00.

School

Students and Schools, Barry Riddell and others (Maclean-Hunter, 1972), $1.00 pa. Students, parents, teachers express their views on school.

You and Your Career, M.D. Parmenter (Guidance Centre, University of Toronto, 1967-72), $2.65 pa.

Student Subject and Careers Series, gen. ed. H.O. Barrett (Guidance Centre, University of Toronto). Booklets on English, Biology, Chemistry, Mathematics, Geography, Music, French.

Community Colleges In Canada, G. Campbell (McGraw, 1971), $6.30.

Community Education in Canada: An Annotated Bibliography,

Linda Corman (O.I.S.E., 1975), $2.25 pa. Two hundred and nineteen items dealing with community education.

The Guide to Canadian Universities, J. Mitchell (Simon & Schuster, 19   ), $2.95 pa.

You and University, M.D. Parmenter (Guidance Centre, University of Toronto, 1968-72), $2.75 pa.

Your Further Education, rev. ed., M.D. Parmenter (Guidance Centre, University of Toronto, 1972), $3.25 pa.

Spectrum 77: A Handbook of 1977-78 entrance requirements for post-secondary education and training in Ontario, ed. Daryl Cook and others (Guidance Centre, University of Toronto, 1976), $2.00 pa.

Atlantic Spectrum 77: Post Secondary Education and Training in the Atlantic Region, ed. George London (Guidance Centre, University of Toronto, 1976), $1.80 pa.

Western Spectrum 77: Post Secondary Education and Training in Western Canada, ed. A. Herman and others(Guidance Centre, University of Toronto, 1976), $1.80 pa.

The World of Work, Donald W. Jackson (Nelson, 1970), $1.20 pa.

Le/La secretaire bilingual, Wilfred Lebel (Homme, 1968), $2.50 br.

Success in The World of Work, rev. ed. M.D. Parmenter (Guidance Centre, University of Toronto, 1972), $2.75 pa.

What Can I Do This Summer, C. Bedal (Guidance Centre, University of Toronto, 1976), 75¢ pa. Forthcoming, 1977 edition.

Useful Addresses

Guidance Centre Mailing Service
Guidance Centre
University of Toronto
(six mailings a year including: *The School Guidance Worker* (magazine); *Comment on Education* (magazine); Occupational Information Monographs; copies of books, posters, booklets)
Cost: $35.75 per year for complete service.

Canadian Health Education Specialist Society
Box 2305, Station "D"
Ottawa
K1P 5K0

Information Directorate
Health and Welfare Canada
Brooke Claxton Building
Ottawa
K1A 0K9

Addiction Research Foundation of Ontario
33 Russell Street
Toronto 179, Ontario

Department of Manpower and Immigration
Ottawa
(Bibliography of career information publications is available)

Periodicals

Involvement, The Family Resource Journal, Canadian Periodical Publishers' Association, six issues per year, $5.00. Covers normal growth and development, problems of emotional disturbance and issues that affect the well-being of children and families with children.

Miss Chatelaine, a monthly publication of Maclean-Hunter. Its utility for anything other than reinforcement of middle American attitudes and values is limited.

Tests

The Guidance Centre, University of Toronto and Nelson and Sons (Canada) Ltd. are two major sources. The tests in many cases are dated and normed on Ontario school population only. Their value is open to question.

Chapter 9

DRAMA

Much of what is written above about art in the schools is applicable
to drama. Except for large schools with specialist teachers, facilities,
and budgets, most schools have to struggle to provide much more
than an annual Christmas or variety concert, and possibly a spring-
time dramatic presentation. Drama is usually defined in terms of
performing, not as a subject of study that could enrich appreciation
of our cultural heritage. This is not to deny the importance of becoming involved in a theatrical production from an acting, producing, or staging perspective. Rather the lengthy, varied, often chequer-
ed history of Canadian drama, warrants much more comprehensive
attention than it is given.

The first dramatic presentation in North America took place in
the harbour of Port Royal, Nova Scotia, on November 14, 1606. *Le
Théâtre de Neptune* by Marc Lescarbot was performed by a company of Micmac Indian and French voyageur artists. Over a half-
century later a tri-lingual performance took place at the Jesuit
College in Quebec. Indian (Huron and Algonkian) and French languages were integral features of this 1658 drama by Fr. Ragueneau.

The Quebec Act of 1774 is just one of the often tiresome constitutional developments that dot the pages of Canadian history textbooks.
The tedium might be reduced if students also were given the chance
to expand their cultural horizons. The first drama performed in the
English language, *Acadius, or Love in a Calm*, was presented in Halifax in 1774. Youthful imaginations might be pricked through the
realization that the development of Canada was indeed something
more than a series of skirmishes and decent acts of a benevolent,
imperial government.

The nineteenth century saw the involvement of the Molson Breweries family in the development of the Théâtre Royal in Montreal;
the opening of a log theatre in Victoria in 1862; and the founding

74

of the Garrick Club in Hamilton from which developed the Players'
Guild. In the World War I era roadshows that travelled the country
playing in places like the Walker Theatre, Winnipeg, were common.
Vaudeville was in its heyday. Undoubtedly the most famous troupe
was the "Dumbells", a group of eighteen men who entertained military personnel both in Europe and in Canada, making a unique contribution to humour and to wartime morale.

Between the two World Wars live theatre appeared to have been
struck a lethal blow by radio and movies. Students of the mass
media age may find it entertaining and enlightening to try to reconstruct the impact of the silent screen and the wireless receiver on
the leisure habits of people who were living in the heady euphoria
of the "Twenties" and later "the Dirty Thirties".

The impact of Governors General on drama gets little attention
in schools. The Earl of Bessborough is in the same league as the Earl
of Stanley, though the latter receives greater acclaim through his
donation of the Stanley Cup, emblem of North American hockey
supremacy. It was Governor General Bessborough who organized
the Dominion Drama Festival in 1932. In large part through this
Festival, local dramatic productions were stimulated throughout the
nation. Seventeen years later the man who was to become Canada's
first native-born Governor General, Vincent Massey, chaired a Royal
Commission which was to have a remarkable influence on the performing arts. The Massey Commission on National Development in
the Arts, Letters, and Sciences (1949-1951) recommended direct
federal government financial assistance as one means of ensuring
artistic growth and development. The Commission recognized what
was soon to become an all-too-evident Canadian problem: without
vigorous attention and support, artistic development could be easily
arrested in the face of American competition. A continuing delicate
balancing act was required if cultural assimilation on the one hand,
or self-defeating parochialism on the other, were to be avoided. Six
years after the tabling of the Commission's recommendations, on
October 11, 1957, royal assent was given to the legislation establishing the Canada Council.

It would be reassuring to state that since the advent of the Canada Council drama has experienced nothing but encores. It would
also be incorrect. Students could profit through an analysis of the
efforts of the Council to sustain the arts. Through study of artistic
struggles for survival, an informed opinion might generate an aroused,
vigilant awareness which is essential if drama is to thrive.

One feature of the struggle is:
                    The Lure of Yankee Dollars!
Identifying the Canadian performers, producers, and directors who
made quick exits to the more lucrative opportunities to be found
outside of Canada constitutes a trip down memory lane:

Mary Pickford and Deanna Durbin were stars of the silent movies.

Yvonne de Carlo conjures up images of an early talent hunt to
locate "the most beautiful woman in the world".

Walter Pidgeon left his native New Brunswick at an early age.

Walter Huston and Glenn Ford likewise quickly departed.

Shirley Douglas Sutherland is of interest as the daughter of T.C.
Douglas, former premier of Saskatchewan.

Donald Sutherland is a Nova Scotian expatriate and one-time
spouse of Shirley Douglas.

Geneviève Bujold received international acclaim for her performance in *Anne of a Thousand Days*.

John Vernon and Margot Kidder are two relatively recent additions to the American television industry.

For comparison purposes, the careers of artists who have man-
aged to pursue their livelihoods successfully on both sides of the
49th parallel can be examined: Kate Reid, Francis Hyland, Raymond Massey, Barry Morse, and John Colicos are a representative
handful.

Ignoring personalities for the moment, an examination of theatrical companies and centres will involve the student not only in
drama, but in such seemingly diverse fields of learning as history,
politics, economics, and geography.

The Golden Jubilee of Alberta's status as a province was com-
memorated by the building of two magnificent and identical
auditoria in Calgary and Edmonton—the Jubilee Auditoria.

Canada's Centennial celebrations took many forms, not the least
of which were the opening of the National Arts Centre in Ottawa
and the Confederation Centre in Charlottetown.

In the Northwest Territories, Yellowknife has supported theatrical
companies, including Dramarctic and The Singing North. Their efforts are shared periodically with other Northern communities such
as Inuvik. Complementing made-in-the-North productions, are the
efforts of southern drama groups. The Edmonton-based Citadel
Theatre is well known in Alberta for its mobile troupe, "Citadel on
Wheels", which travels to rural centres. In the North, where roads

can be few and far between, the Citadel Theatre is known appropriately as "Citadel On Wings". Travelling in the venerable workhorse of Northern aviation, the DC 3, a company of actors and actresses has performed in the small, remote Inuit settlements of Gjoa Haven, Pelly Bay and Holman Island, among others.

The Mummers of Newfoundland not only have injected vitality into the artistic life of that province but, as importantly, have brought to the stage relevant events in the history of Newfoundland. The *I.W.A.*, an interpretation of the 1959 International Woodworkers of America Strike and *Buchans: Company Town* are two examples. A significant contribution of this group has been its interpretation of Newfoundland given in other parts of Canada.

It is difficult to develop any degree of personal empathy for foundations and corporations. By definition such bodies tend to be aloof from public affection. Their contributions are nonetheless important. The Beaverbrook Foundation was largely responsible for financing the Playhouse in Fredericton, while the O'Keefe Breweries are forever enshrined in the O'Keefe Centre of Toronto.

Urban renewal projects can play a role in furthering the growth of the performing arts. Place Des Arts in Montreal symbolizes attempts to rejuvenate the inner cities. Such centres serve to draw people into the downtown areas as opposed to furthering suburban sprawl.

History weighs heavily on Maritime life. The Neptune Theatre in Halifax draws its name from the original performance mentioned at the opening of this chapter. In Vancouver, historical links with England are reforged through the Queen Elizabeth Theatre.

Drama would not exist were it not for the leadership which has been given by individuals in the various centres. In this respect, Canada has been fortunate not only in providing an opportunity for native-born Canadians to take the necessary initiative, but also in attracting many European directors and producers, particularly following World War II. Among them have been: Sir Tyrone Guthrie and Michael Langham (Stratford Shakespearian Festival, initiated in 1953), Malcolm Black (Vancouver), Jean Gascon and Jean Louis Roux (Théâtre du Nouveau Monde, Quebec), Leon Major (Halifax), Murray Davis and Mavor Moore (Toronto), Yvette Brend'Amour and Mercedes Palomino (Montreal), John Hirsch (Winnipeg), and Christopher Brookes (St. John's).

Increasingly, the material at the disposal of the directors is written by Canadians. A profitable analysis can be made of the contributions of various playwrights. From British Columbia to Newfoundland, a selected list includes: Eric Nicol, George Ryga, W.O. Mitchell, Len Peterson, Joseph Schull, Roger Auger, Guy Gauthier, Morley Callaghan, Robertson Davies, Gratien Gélinas, Marcel Dubé, Yvette Gouin, Leopold Houlé, Lister Sinclair, Grace Butt, Ted Russell, Michael Cook, and Al Pittman.

Providing the spice, without which no artistic form can long remain palatable, is the function of the critics. B.K. Sandwell (editor of *Saturday Night* magazine from 1932-1951), Nathan Cohen (*Toronto Star,* originally from Cape Breton), Herbert Whittaker (*Globe and Mail*) and Hector Charlesworth (Toronto *Mail and Empire,* 1904-10, *Saturday Night* 1925-32, *Canadian Radio Broadcasting Commission*), and S. Morgan-Powell (*Montreal Star*), are a sample of the respected critics whose incisive coverage of the theatre should be available to drama students.

To facilitate dramatic study beyond the high school level, the efforts of Senator Donald Cameron in establishing the Banff School of Fine Arts are of marked consequence. In drama as well as other aspects of artistic endeavour, this school provides the facilities, professional staff, and setting for summer sessions which strengthen the conventional initiatives of colleges and universities.

Students can learn more about drama as well as dramatic techniques through materials like those listed below.

♦ ♦ ♦ ♦

About Canadian Drama

Creative Canada, (U.T.P., 1971, 1972), 2 vols, $15.00 each. Part of a projected biographical dictionary series covering all aspects of the performing arts.

Titles from the series Profiles in Canadian Drama, Gage:

George Ryga; Gratien Gélinas; James Reaney, and *Robertson Davies.* $2.95 each pa. Brief studies of major playwrights, their backgrounds, the characteristics of their works and their contributions to the development of drama in Canada.

Dramatists in Canada: Selected Essays, ed. William New (U.B.C. Press, 1972), $5.50 pa. Designed to introduce the reader to major Canadian plays and playwrights, and to trace the development of drama in Canada.

Drama Canada: Trends in Drama in Education during the Past 25 Years, Esmé Crampton (Guidance Centre, University of Toronto, 1972), $1.50 pa. Includes discussions of play-acting, drama festivals, theatre schools and professional companies.

Love and Whiskey: The Story of the Dominion Drama Festival, Betty Lee (McClelland, 1973), $8.95. A review of the heyday of the Festival between 1933 and 1969.

Renown at Stratford, 2nd ed., Tyrone Guthrie and Robertson Davies (Clarke, Irwin, 1953), $9.50. A review of the early years in the life of the Stratford, Ontario Shakespearian Festival.

Dictionnaire critique du théâtre québécois, Alain Pontaut (Lemeac) $3.95.

Le théâtre québécois, Jean-Cleo Godin and Laurent Mailhot (H.M.H.), $5.95.

Canada at 8:30 (film). 28 min, 16mm, col, Crawley Films, $172.00. A review of developments in theatre arts, ballet, and music.

Stratford, Canada (Jackdaw kit). Clarke, Irwin, $3.50.

Planning, Producing, Staging Techniques

Theatre on a Shoestring, Adrian Waller (Clarke, Irwin, 1973), $4.95 pa. A guide for staging productions.

A Theatre Happening, ed. Gordon Maurer and Sheila McLeod (Nelson, 1968), $1.50 pa. Provides information on all facets of production.

A Handbook of the Theatre, 2nd ed. Esmé Crampton (Gage, 1964), $9.25. Source book for producing a play.

Look Both Ways: Theatre Experiences, ed. Herman Voaden (Macmillan, 1975), $6.95 pa. A source book of creative drama for senior high.

Course of Study in Theatre Arts, (O.I.S.E., 1969), $3.30. Useful in the junior and senior high years as a basic course for students.

Child Drama in Action, Bill Tyas (Gage, 1971), $7.95. Twenty-two lessons for classroom use.

Play Acting in the Schools, Dorothy-Jane Goulding (McGraw, 1969), $3.15. Techniques for using play acting in any aspect of the curriculum.

Titles from the Methuen Drama Guides series, ed. Ken Weber (Methuen, 1972), $2.50 pa. Notes and suggestions for six dramas: *Hedda Gabler; Becket; The Lark; A Taste of Honey; In the Matter of J. Robert Oppenheimer; Oh What a Lovely War!.*

Educational Drama, Grace Layman (Methuen, 1975), $4.95 pa.
A teacher's guide to assist the development of a drama program
in the elementary grades.

Taking Off, Betty Keller (November, 1975), $3.75 pa. A handbook
for the teaching of creative drama.

Trick Doors and Other Dramatic Sketches, Betty Keller (November, 1974), $2.75 pa. Fourteen sketches afford the opportunity to
develop particular acting skills and techniques.

Opening Trick Doors, Betty Keller (November, 1975), $2.75 pa.
A guide to the use of material in *Trick Doors.*

A Different Drummer, David Kemp (McClelland, 1972), $3.50 pa.

Collections of Plays
Unless otherwise noted these collections are suitable for senior high
school grades.

We're Doing a Play, Dorothy-Jane Goulding (McGraw, 1969),
$3.15. Eight short plays accompanied by stage instructions and
production notes, grades three to five.

Invitation to Drama, rev. ed., Andrew A. Orr (Macmillan, 1967),
$2.95 pa. Includes *The Education of Phyllistine,* junior high.

Four Favourite Plays, Robertson Davies (Clarke, Irwin, 1968),
$2.25 pa. Three one-act plays; one three-act play.

Hunting Stuart and Other Plays, Robertson Davies (New, 1972),
Three comedies.

At my Heart's Core/Overlaid, Robertson Davies (Clarke, Irwin,
1966), $1.50 pa. A one-act play and a three-act play.

*Three Plays by Eric Nicol: Like Father, Like Fun; The Fourth
Monkey; Pillars of Sand,* Eric Nicol (Talonbooks, 1975), $4.95
pa.

A Collection of Canadian Plays, ed. Rolf Kottman (Simon &
Pierre, 4 vols, vol. I-III, $9.75 each; vol. IV $14.95. Twenty-five
plays. Volume IV contains ten plays for K-13.

The Play's the Thing, ed. T. Gifford (Macmillan, 1975). Includes
television dramas by Hugh Hood, Alice Munro, Eric Nicol and
F.R. Scott).

Masks of Childhood, James Reaney (New, 1972), $3.00 pa. Three
plays: *Easter Egg, Three Desks, The Killdeer.*

Encounter: Canadian Drama in Four Media, ed. Eugene Benson
(Methuen, 1973), $4.75 pa. An anthology of seven dramas representative of stage, television, radio and film productions.

A Thematic Approach to Drama

Attitudes and Values

Colours in the Dark, James Reaney (Talonbooks, 1969), $2.95 pa. The search for individual identity.

Bousille and the Just, Gratien Gélinas (Clarke, Irwin, 1966), $1.50 pa. A drama dealing with the loss of values in the modern world.

Tit-coq, Gratien Gélinas (Clarke, Irwin, 1967), $1.85 pa. A man's search for a family.

Shelter, Carol Bolt (Playwrights' Co-op, 1975), $2.50 pa. An entertaining look at life and politics in Saskatchewan and the role of women in private and public life.

Bonjour là, Bonjour, Michel Tremblay (Talonbooks, 1975), $3.50 pa. English translation of a drama set in rural Quebec involving a brother and his sisters.

Nobody Waved Good-bye, Don Owen (Macmillan, 1971), $1.10 pa.

Historical

The End of a Dream, Joan Forman (Holt, 1969), $2.75. Grades 6-10; Henry Hudson's last voyage.

The Turning Tide, Joan Forman (Holt, 1971), $2.25. Grades 6-10; Captain George Vancouver, 1792.

The Freedom of the House, Joan Forman (Holt, 1971), $1.50. Grades 6-10; French Canada and the American Revolution, 1775-76.

Westward to Canaan, Joan Forman (Holt, 1972), $1.75. Grades 9 and 10. Settlement of the Prairies by Ukrainian peoples, 1936.

The Photographic Moment, Mary Humphrey Baldridge (Playwrights' Co-op, 1975), $2.00 pa. A drama set in Alberta during the Depression years of the thirties.

The Rainmaker, Gwen Pharis Ringwood (Playwrights' Co-op, 1975), $1.50 pa. A drama set in Medicine Hat, Alberta when the town hired a rainmaker to help break the prairie drought.

Fifteen Miles of Broken Glass, Tom Hendry (Talonbooks, 1975). The life of a boy growing up in Winnipeg after World War II.

Maurice, Carol Bolt (Playwrights' Co-op, 1975), $2.50 pa. An historical drama based on the Duplessis era in Quebec.

Cyclone Jack by Carol Bolt and Billy Bishop and the Red Baron by Len Peterson, Carol Bolt and Len Peterson (Simon & Pierre,

1975), $3.75 pa. *Cyclone Jack* is based on the life of long distance runner Tom Longboat. *Billy Bishop and the Red Baron* is based on the World War I encounter between Bishop and the German aviator, Baron von Richthofen.

Bethune, Rod Langley (Talonbooks, 1975), $3.50 pa. Based on events in the life of Dr. Norman Bethune.

Handcuffs, James Reaney (Porcépic, 1975), $5.95; *Sticks and Stones,* James Reaney (Porcépic, 1975), $5.95 and *The St. Nicholas Hotel,* James Reaney (Porcépic, 1975), $5.95. A trilogy based on the life of the notorious Donnellys.

The Blood is Strong, Lister Sinclair (Book Society, 1956), $1.25. The settlement of Nova Scotia by Scots.

The Great Hunger, Len Peterson (Book Society, 1967), $1.50 pa. Ancient Inuit life in the Arctic.

Newfoundland

The Holdin' Ground, Ted Russell (McClelland, 1972), $1.25 pa.

The Head, Guts and Soundbone Dance, Michael Cook (Breakwater, 1975), $3.95 pa.

A Rope against the Sun, A. Pittman (Breakwater, 1975), $3.95 pa.

Jacob's Walk, Michael Cook (Talonbooks, 1976), $3.50 pa.

Indian Peoples

Almighty Voice, Len Peterson (Book Society, 1974), $1.50 pa. A drama set in the post-Riel period.

Indian, George Ryga (Book Society, 1967), 20¢ pa. An Alberta setting for the portrayal of racial injustice.

The Ecstasy of Rita Joe and Other Plays, George Ryga (New, 1970), $2.95 pa. Includes two other plays, *Indian* (see above) and *Grass and Wild Strawberries,* a drama about young people at odds with society.

Sister Balonika, Paul St. Pierre (Book Society, 1973), $2.25 pa. A Yukon setting for a drama based on life in an Indian residential school.

Political—Separatism in Quebec

Yesterday the Children Were Dancing, Gratien Gélinas (Clarke, Irwin, 1967), $1.75.

Captives of the Faceless Drummer, George Ryga (Talonbooks, 1972), $3.00 pa. Drama influenced by the F.L.Q. events of 1970).

Mental Health

The Labyrinth, Charles Israel (Macmillan, 1969), $1.20 pa. The struggle by a young woman to regain her mental health.

For Young Children

The Dandy Lion, Dodi Robb and Pat Patterson (New, 1972), $4.05.

The Popcorn Man, Dodi Robb and Pat Patterson (New, 1972), $4.05.

Les Éléphants de Tante Louise, Roger Auger (Landry, 1975), $3.00.

Professor Fuddle's Fantastic Fairy-Tale Machine, Alan Egerton Ball, Paul Bradbury; *King Grumbletum and the Magic Pie,* David Kemp (Simon & Pierre, 1975), $3.75 pa. Two dramas for the elementary grades.

Apple Butter and Other Plays For Children, James Reaney (Talonbooks, 1973), $4.00 pa. A collection of four plays.

Land of Magic Spell, by Larry Zacharko; *Which Witch is Which?* by Beth McMaster (Simon & Pierre, 1975), $3.75 pa. Two dramas for the primary grades.

Periodicals

Performing Arts in Canada, Canadian Periodical Publishers' Association, $3.00 Quarterly, student subscriptions, $2.00.

Canadian Theatre Review, Canadian Periodical Publishers' Association, $8.00 Quarterly.

Chapter 10

ECONOMICS

Economics, as portrayed here, is not defined as a set of objective principles which can be arbitrarily applied, poultice fashion, to the wounds of society. On the contrary, it is the art of drawing upon sociological, historical, political, and geographical information and combining these with economic theory and practice which should be the focus of the students' study.

A case can be made for making economics the core of the high school curriculum. The resolution of complex problems upon which national and international survival predominately rests underscores this need. Appropriate introductory courses made available no later than the junior high years should be provided as well.

Elevating economics from its present, almost incidental, status in the curriculum would serve two related purposes: a sense of direction would be realized in the learning program, and learning experiences, with the possible exception of theoretical mathematics and the physical sciences, could be integrated, to the mutual advantage of each contributing element.

How this might be accomplished can be illustrated through seven alternatives.

A

Students should have the opportunity to confront and demolish *the* Canadian myth. McGill University economist B.F. Keirstead stated this myth succinctly:

> "There is no more a Canadian economics than there is a Canadian chemistry."
>
> *Encyclopedia Canadiana* (Toronto: Grolier, 1963, Vol. III, p. 362)

Students readily could draw the conclusion that the implications of this unqualified statement are at the root of present and past economic problems. It does seem to indicate that economics, like the laws of nature, knows no national boundaries. Fruitful as pursuit of this notion may be, it is in trying to understand why this comment could be made that the greater challenge is found. What reasons can be documented in support of Keirstead's contention? An examination of Canada's apparent enchantment with economic theories and programs imported from other countries is a useful place to begin. Study of the successes and/or failures of past and present practices might shed further light as well.

Commencing in the late nineteenth century, university departments of economics were staffed by immigrants from England and Scotland whose academic baggage bore the imprint summed-up in the old chestnut—the sun never sets on the British Empire. Economists such as W.J. Ashley (University of Toronto), J. Watson (Queen's), J. Davidson (University of New Brunswick), and A.W. Flux (McGill), were in the vanguard of those who saw Canada as a legitimate offspring of the mother country. The colonial child was perceived as being little more than an extension of old England—an assessment which conveniently ignored the French Canadian population and its heritage. If it were possible to ignore French Canadians from the ivied towers of downtown Montreal (i.e., McGill University), how much easier was it to dismiss the concerns of prairie farmers or west coast residents who were a few thousand miles distant from the axis of high Canadian finance on Bay and St. James streets in Toronto and Montreal respectively! Undoubtedly, the paper credentials of the early economists, whether in academia, government, or business, were impressive, if not impeccable. On the other hand, their awareness and understanding of Canadian needs from sea to sea to sea was only marginal. Students may wish to examine the economics of building the C.P.R., negotiating land deals with the Hudson's Bay Co., or the treaties made with western and northern Indian peoples. Closer to the Toronto-Ottawa-Montreal triangle of financial power, it is helpful to review the economics of confederation vis-à-vis the Maritimes. Clearly, the geography of Canada alone dictated that economic theories must be developed within a Canadian context. Unfortunately this observation was lost on all parties concerned. In turn, this ignorance helped to ease the transition from one economic empire to another.

The setting sun of Britain was effectively replaced by the even

more powerful glare from the south. Comparing Canada's respective
positions as initially a British colony and later, as a fiefdom in the
American industrial estate is an exercise designed to energize the
mind and the spirit. Students could muster their attention around
the axiom: economics follows the economy. In a nation whose economy is largely controlled by foreign interest, the theories taught
in schools and universities, or otherwise generally disseminated, reflect the character of the economy. A branch plant economy breeds
branch plant thinking. A study of the learning materials used and
the staffing procedures of university departments of economics
yields useful evidence. A more intensive study could then examine
the nearly incestuous relationship which can exist among academic
economists, multi-national corporate board rooms, and federal-
provincial government bureaucracies.

Anticipated pessimism as to Canada's control over its economy
might be dissipated by turning to the next alternative: the theories
and views of Canadian economists.

B

The interval between World Wars I and II can be regarded as the
time when Canadian economics first flowered. The contributions of
Harold Innis were instrumental in this regard. His Staple Theory,
arising from an examination of primary resource industries (e.g., the
fur trade, the cod fisheries), is regarded as the initial significant
contribution to economic study within a Canadian perspective.
(Students may wish to compare the work of Innis with that of one
of his contemporaries, Stephen Leacock at McGill. More familiar
as a humorist, Leacock was a professor of economics who contributed profound as well as light-hearted writings to the study of "the
dismal science"). With the clarity of hindsight, it is possible to view
the career of Innis as only an interlude. One liberal-nationalist beach-
head buttressed by the reputation of the University of Toronto is
seemingly insufficient to stem the inevitable Canadian drift into
total American dependency. The influence of Innis did transcend
the boundaries of economics itself. Respected historians like Arthur
Lower and Donald Creighton came under his influence. Through
their academic and literary efforts the seeds sown by Innis, if not
vigorously cultivated, were at least permitted to germinate—ever so
slowly.

By the early 1960's the fusion of economic-political thinking
gradually moved into the forefront of the public's consciousness.
The careers of Walter Gordon and Eric Kierans are instructive. As

cabinet ministers they confronted one of the major dilemmas of the democratic system of government. How does the elected politician cope with an entrenched bureaucracy? How do progressive nationalists survive within the confines of a reactionary political party structure? Students could read short snatches from the biographies of Lester Pearson (Liberal Prime Minister) and Walter Gordon (a Pearson cabinet minister) for information on this point.

The contributions of Mel Watkins and Cy Gonick which come from outside the formal setting of party politics, should be studied. A professor of economics at the University of Toronto, Watkins was the principal author of the mid-sixties federal government report on foreign ownership and the structure of Canadian industry. More recently he was one of the founders of the Waffle Movement, an attempt to re-direct the energies of the New Democratic Party along economic-nationalist lines. Gonick is a Winnipeg-based politician-journalist (*Canadian Dimension*) and professor of economics at the University of Manitoba.

C

A thought-provoking departure from historical-analytical approaches is to examine a current economic situation with far-reaching implications. Canada's North affords the possibility of studying economics in microcosm. Past and present practices symbolize the confusion which has plagued national growth and development. Students can commence their investigations by making a number of comparisons:

> Northern Canada constitutes the last remaining treasure-trove of natural resources on the continent. Natural gas, oil, iron ore, lead, zinc, nickel, uranium, have undetermined potential The ownership and development of these non-renewable resources can be compared with past Canadian practice.

> One half of the total supply of fresh water in the world is in Canada. Much of that water is found in the drainage systems of the North. Will the preservation and use of this vital resource follow the pattern of the Columbia River Treaty and/or the Bennett dam of the British Columbia interior?

> Approximately 70 000 people live north of the 60th parallel in the Yukon and Northwest Territories. The rights of these people can be denied in the face of demands by the 22 000 000 people who live in the southern provinces. (A further comparison can be made with the rights of the total Canadian population and the pressures created by 225 000 000 Americans).

> Indian, Métis, and Inuit peoples comprise the majority of the

northern population. Their aspirations for control of their economic destiny can be contrasted with the track-record of past practice as found in treaties and the policies of the federal government and industry.

The North has no secondary industrial base. The exploitation of natural resources is the basis of a boom or bust economy. Plundering the North to satisfy the provinces parallels Canada's traditional role as a hewer of wood and drawer of water in the international community.

Northern Canadians live in the last remaining colony on the continent. Though a façade of representative government exists in Whitehorse and Yellowknife, decision-making of consequence is exclusively in the hands of Ottawa. Northern desires for autonomy can be compared with western feelings of alienation from Ottawa.

The Mackenzie Valley pipeline, like the James Bay Hydro Project, illustrates the critical problem of Canadian versus foreign control and domination.

D

Allusion has been made to two of the key elements in understanding Canadian economics, namely, regional diversity and disparity. National awareness initially and national concensus in the longer term are elusive ideals. Minimally, students can be given the chance to study:

The centralization of secondary industry in the Great Lakes-St. Lawrence seaway area and the resultant dependency of the rest of Canada.

The politics and economics of petroleum vis-á-vis western and eastern Canada.

The importance of a national transportation system and the equalization of freight rates (e.g., Crow's Nest Pass agreement of 1896 and its implications for the prairie farmer).

Provincial-federal jurisdictional disputes (e.g., offshore mineral rights in Atlantic Canada and British Columbia).

Government activity in the field of allocating industry on a regional basis (e.g., Air Canada servicing in Winnipeg; heavy-water production in Cape Breton).

E

Politics and economics share the same bed, with the latter often seducing the politician. William "Bible Bill" Aberhart, first Social

Credit premier of Alberta, was a disciple of the economic theories of Major Douglas. In turn, Aberhart's apostle E.C. Manning improved upon his mentor's ability to combine economics, politics, and religion in such a manner as to sustain the Social Credit Alberta government for three decades. For comparison purposes, students will be entertained, if not enlightened, by examining the economic ideas of W.A.C. Bennett and Réal Caouette, both Social Credit adherents but of a different stripe.

Remarkably enough, the same geographical area, the prairies, gave birth to the Cooperative Commonwealth Federation (C.C.F.), the first socialist party in Canada to achieve national recognition. The economic ideas expressed in this party's Regina Manifesto are useful as an indication of the direction Canada might have taken. The mélange of agrarian populism, religious fervour, economic dissent, and the availability of leaders gifted in histrionics were as characteristic of the socialist movement as they were of the Social Credit party. The transition from the C.C.F. to the N.D.P. provides further evidence of the problem encountered in trying to meet the economic needs of east (labour unions) and west (farmers, ranchers).

F

The economics of international relations will introduce students to a host of interrelated problems:

> Traditionally, it has proven difficult to establish a balance between the geographic pull exerted by the United States and the historic and subjective ties to the British Commonwealth.

> In more recent times the search for expanded markets has altered the traditional patterns of trade. Alvin Hamilton, agricultural minister in the federal cabinet of John Diefenbaker, helped to establish important wheat markets in China and the U.S.S.R. The revitalization of Japanese industry created a demand for coal mining in the Fernie, Natal, and Sparwood areas of British Columbia. Expanded C.P.R. rail services and the building of deepwater port facilities on the west coast were all links in the chain-reaction of events which followed.

> A study of the revolutionary government of Fidel Castro in Cuba will help to lay bare the crux of the foreign domination and control issue. Having severed relations with the United States, Cuba required manufactured products which Canada could supply. Frequently, before the business arrangements between the two countries were finalized, it was necessary for the Canadian government to apply pressure on the appropriate American parent firms. The approval of corporation executives, and even the American

government in certain instances, was required before the subsidiaries based in Canada could conclude the transactions.

Physics, economics, and morality are an unlikely triumvirate. The
sale of CANDU nuclear reactors to countries such as India and
Pakistan, Israel, and Arab states creates an issue of potentially
disastrous magnitude. The possible proliferation of the nuclear
club is dependent on the safeguards built into the sales agreements.

As a nation bounded by three oceans, Canada traditionally has de-
pended upon the sea for a portion of its economic growth. Atlantic and Pacific coast fisheries provide the livelihood of substantial
numbers of people. Technological advances have created a peril
of international consequence. The definition of national off-shore
limits remains unresolved. Japanese, Russian, and Scandinavian
trawlers are now common in fishing zones Canadians once considered theirs by right of geographical proximity. Law of the Sea
conferences and the ensuing deliberations can be the substance
of study on this question.

Shifting alliances and emerging power-blocs have an immense
effect on an exporting nation such as Canada. Study of the Oil
Producing and Exporting Countries (O.P.E.C.) and the Common
Market Countries, and attempts at establishing "contractual links"
will enable the student to understand more fully the interdepen-
dence of the international community.

For all of the apparent problems, Canada is one of the most fortunate countries in terms of its economic resources. The immediate question is:

> How can these resources be shared with the peoples of
> the Third World?

Answers to this pressing concern primarily will be found through
the education of future citizens.

G

The economics of education can be the lynch-pin of the learning
program. Virtually any classroom situation can be the setting for
examining:

> foreign control of the Canadian learning materials industry;
>
> foreign domination of educational bureaucracies (e.g., universi-
> ties, government departments);
>
> financing of education (schools, universities, research);
>
> constitutional implications (e.g., Section 93 of the B.N.A. Act);
>
> society's toleration and acceptance of conflicting economic
> theories (e.g., Marxism, socialism, capitalism).

Materials to facilitate study of these topics are listed below and in Chapter 6—Business Education, Chapter 22—Political Science, Chapter 25—Social Studies, and Chapter 26—Sociology.

♦ ♦ ♦ ♦

General References

Economic Thinking in a Canadian Context, Gordon F. Boreham and Richard Leftwich (Holt, 1971), 2 vols., $5.95 each. Student's study guide, $2.95.

Contemporary Economic Thinking, ed. Gordon F. Boreham (Holt, 1971), $4.95 pa. A book of readings illustrating the application of economic principles to Canadian problems and designed to accompany *Economic Thinking In A Canadian Context.*

Economics: A Search For Patterns, Alison Kemp Mitchell and Mary Austin Millard (Gage, 1971), $6.75. Also available notes and bibliography, 1972, $1.40.

A Nation Unaware: The Canadian Economic Culture, Herschel Hardin (J.J. Douglas, 1974), $6.95. An examination of two hundred years of economic history.

Economics: Contemporary Issues In Canada, Douglas Auld (Holt, 1972), $3.25 pa. Topics include: federalism, poverty, inflation, urban problems, unemployment.

Approaches to Canadian Economic History, ed. N.T. Easterbrook and M.H. Watkins (McClelland, 1967), $3.95 pa. A collection of essays.

Canada in a Wider Economic Community, H. Edward English, Bruce W. Wilkinson, and H.C. Eastman (U.T.P., 1973), $4.00 pa. Canada in an international perspective.

Contemporary Canada: Readings In Economics, ed. Timothy E. Reid (Holt, 1969), $6.00 pa. Topics include: poverty, automation, American investment in Canada, inflation, depression, credit, monopolies.

Inside Canada: Readings From the Financial Post, ed. Benjamin Vass (McGraw, 1970-72), 3 vols., $2.95 each pa. Issues of the 1970s are illustrated.

Cents & Non$ense: The Economics of Canadian Policy Issues,
Jack Carr, Frank Mathewson, and J.C. McManus (Holt, 1972),
$2.75 pa. Reference to foreign ownership, the C.B.C., prohibition
of cigarette advertising, the press, separatism, the N.H.L., bilingualism.

Exploiting Our Economic Potential, ed R. Shearer (Holt, 1968),
$4.95 pa. Topics encompass a broad range from educational policy
to industrial relations—primarily based on the experiences of
British Columbia.

Economics For Canadians, rev. ed., Helen and Kenneth Buckley
(Macmillan, 1968), $4.00. An introductory course.

Canadian Economic Issues, ed. I.D. Pal (Macmillan, 1971) $5.50
pa. A selection of readings.

Quebec

Initiation à la vie économique, Robert Thomassin et un groupe
de professeurs de l'Université Laval (C.P.P.), tome 1 $6.50, tome
2 $5.85, corrigé $4.50, cahier d'exercices $1.80 br. Une introduc-
tion générale aux grands themes de la vie économique dans les
contextes québecois et nord-américain.

Québec 1960-1980 La crise du développement, ed. Gabriel
Gagnon et Luc Martin (H.M.H.), $9.95. Indispensable à qui veut
suivre la trace de notre vie économique actuelle dans le contexte
des années passées et à venir.

Économie Québecoise, Robert Comeau and others (P.U.Q.),
$5.80.

Patronage et Pouvoir dans le Bas-Canada 1794-1812, Gilles Paquet
et Jean-Pierre Wallot (P.U.Q.), $5.00. Un essai d'économie his-
torique.

The Decolonization of Quebec: an analysis of left-wing nationalism,
Sheilagh Milner and Henry Milner (McClelland, 1973), $3.95 pa.

Socialist Interpretations

The Founding of Canada, 2nd ed, Stanley B. Ryerson (Progress,
1975), $3.95. Provides a Marxist approach to understanding the
early growth and development of Canada.

A History of Canadian Wealth, Gustavus Myers (James Lorimer,
1972), $3.95 pa. An analysis of business and political history be-
tween 1600 and 1900 with specific reference to the Hudson's
Bay Co. and the building of the C.P.R.

Let Us Prey, ed. Robert Chodos and Rae Murphy (James Lorimer, 1974), $4.95 pa. A collection of articles which initially appeared in the *Last Post* magazine; analyzes the practices and profits of such corporations as Bata Shoes, I.T.T., Brascan, Bell Canada; and individuals such as John Shaheen and his involvement in the economic life of the Maritime provinces.

Louder Voices: The Corporate Welfare Bums, David E. Lewis (James Lorimer, 1972), $1.95. The views of the former national leader of the N.D.P., David Lewis, on federal government economic policies, corporate taxation.

Anatomy of Big Business, Libbie Park and Frank Park (James Lorimer, 1973), $3.95 pa. A study of capitalism in Canada, first published in 1962.

Foreign Ownership

Foreign Ownership: Villain or Scapegoat, ed. Timothy E. Reid (Holt, 1971), $1.50 pa. An introductory text.

Corporate Canada: Fourteen probes into the workings of a branch-plant economy, ed. Robert Chodos and Nick Aufdermaur (James Lorimer, 1972), $2.50 pa.

The Americanization of Canada, Samuel Moffett (U.T.P., 1972), $10.00. An historical study of the forces leading to the assimilation of Canada into the American economic empire.

Getting It Back, ed. Abraham Rotstein and Gary Lax (Clarke, Irwin, 1974), $3.95 pa. A collection of papers by the Committee for an Independent Canada which illustrate the problem of returning control of the economy to Canadians.

Foreign Ownership: Canadian Critical Issues, Malcolm Levin and Christine Sylvester (General, 1972), $1.25 pa.

American Investment: Development or Domination, Victor J. Guenther (Dent, 1971), $2.25 pa.

Close the 49th Parallel, etc.: The Americanization of Canada, ed. Ian Lumsden (U.T.P., 1970), $3.75 pa. Essays by Mel Watkins, James Laxer, Bruce Kidd, Cy Gonick, Frank Piers.

Gordon to Watkins to You, ed. Dave Godfrey and Mel Watkins (New, 1970), $3.50 pa. Study of U.S.-Canadian relations.

Who Owns Canada? (cassette tape). 60 min, C.B.C. Learning Systems, $15.00. On foreign ownership and control of the economy.

Specific Issues

Canadian Economy in the Great Depression, A.E. Safarian (Mc-Clelland, 1971), $3.95 pa.

The Dirty Thirties: Canadians in the Great Depression, Michael Horn (Copp, 1971), $5.95 pa.

Inflation or Depression: The Continuing Crisis of the Canadian Economy, C.W. Gonick (James Lorimer, 1975), $6.95 pa.

Inequalities Within Canada, Angus M. Gunn (Oxford, 1974), $1.95. Regional and local disparities.

Canada and the Third World: What are the Choices, (Yorkminster). A paper presented at the Couchiching Conference.

The Surrender of the North: The Mackenzie Pipeline, Edgar J. Dosman (McClelland, 1975), $4.95 pa.

The Economic Background of Dominion Provincial Relations, W.A. MacIntosh (McClelland, 1964), $2.50 pa. A review of economic history from 1867 to 1930.

The Politics of Food, Don Mitchell (James Lorimer, 1975), $4.95 pa. Food and its politics in the overall context of the Canadian economy and policy.

Economic Thinking and Pollution Problems, ed. Douglas A.L. Auld (U.T.P., 1972), $2.75 pa.

Labour Economics in Canada, S. Ostry and M.A. Zaidi (Macmillan, 1972), $11.00.

Natural Resources: The Economics of Conservation, rev. ed., Anthony Scott (McClelland, 1973), $3.95 pa. An examination of international practices and policies.

Resource Use In Canada, Don C. Wilson and Angus M. Gunn (Oxford, 1974), $1.95.

Regional Disparities, ed. Hugh R. Innis (McGraw, 1972), $2.25 pa. From the Issues For the Seventies Series.

Economists

A New Theory of Value: The Canadian Economics of H.A. Innis, Robin Neill (U.T.P., 1972), $3.50 pa. An analysis of the thought of Harold Innis.

Storm Signals, Walter Gordon (McClelland, 1975), $3.95 pa.

Studying Industries

Canada's Science Policy and the Economy, N.H. Lithwick (Methuen, 1969), $5.95. A scholarly study of the relationship between scientific research and the economy.

Falconbridge: Portrait of a Canadian Mining Multi-National, John Deverell and the Latin American Working Group (James Lorimer, 1975), $4.95 pa.

Pioneers in Agriculture, Elizabeth Waterston (Clarke, Irwin, 1957), $3.70.

Titles from the Canada at Work series, McGraw:
  Canada's Railways; Automotive Industry; Oil Industry; Fisheries; Aviation Industry; Agriculture, boxed set of 6, $22.50, $4.25 each.

Oil and the Overlive Society (film). 14½ min, 16mm, col, Holt, $203.00. The place of oil in our society.

The Forest Economy (filmstrip). col, N.F.B., $5.00.

Periodical

Canadian Dimension, Canadian Periodical Publishers' Association. 8 issues annually, $6.00.

Chapter 11

ENGLISH

From the "Spud Islander" of the east to the "Stubble Jumper" of the west, and from the "Bluenoser" of the south to the "Northerner" of the Territories, English-speaking Canadians share an often emotional attachment to one item—defense of "their" language. "By the Lard Jasus, me old son, them b'ys in Upper Canada had better watch their step when it comes to tinkering with the way we talk" is one regional variation on a common theme. The English language is queen. Or so it appears at times.

Interestingly enough, there is seldom much discussion on what the term "English language" means. Historical antecedents can suggest a genealogical purity originating with the seeds of Chaucer with subsequent cultivation, fertilization, and pruning by Shakespeare and Milton. An equally vociferous defense is made of what is, in effect, Americanized English. Seldom do those people who feel most strongly about "our language" pay much heed to the Canadian English dialects.

For that matter, neither does anyone else. Schools follow as best they can the swing of the language pendulum: from England to the United States. The language of commerce is the language of the classroom. All that requires delineation is the nature of the economic empire to which Canada happens to belong. Once that is affirmed, the status of the study of English can be evaluated with less hypocrisy. Not only are conventional language learning materials essentially devoid of Canadian reference but, as noted in detail elsewhere, the preponderance of all materials are foreign in origin and are written, recorded, or otherwise prepared in a non-Canadian English dialect (including spelling, grammar, and pronunciation). This denial of Canadian contributions to the evolution of language is only compounded by the education-publishing approach to standardized language textbooks. As currently conceived, the teaching of "standard English" is regarded as being the great equalizer (i.e. a blenderized people speaking a puréed dialect). It is also, inevitably, the means of eradicating colourful idiom, unique perceptions as conveyed through the vernacular, and cultural pride and identity. Recommending that language study and learning materials in the English language be developed within a Canadian context may appear to be fanciful in the extreme. The options accessible in this respect suggest otherwise.

Two valuable resource books are available to assist the development of new approaches: *Speaking Canadian English* (M. Orkin, Toronto, General, 1970) and *The Dictionary of Canadianisms on Historical Principles* (Walter S. Avis and others, Toronto, Gage, 1967). The former provides contrasts and comparisons among American, British and Canadian variations in language. Uniquely Canadian spellings, pronunciations, words, and expressions are identified and explained. The latter book is the best one-volume collection of words and expressions of Canadian origin and/or adoption and modification. Reference materials such as these will make it possible to study Canadian English within any number of broad categories.

A

Geographical determination: Expressing location and direction is really quite simple. "Upper Canada" (Ontario), "out west" (the Prairie Provinces) and "the coast" (British Columbia) are readily translatable among Maritimers. Newfoundlanders might take one exception. In downtown St. John's, "going to the coast" likely implies Port aux Basques rather than Vancouver. "Down east" to a Calgarian means Ontario, specifically southern Ontario, and is not to be confused with the "east coast" which encompasses what's left after you leave Toronto. "Up north" is less precise. "Herring Chokers" from St. John may perceive Bathurst as "north". Similarly Sudbury is "up north" too—when you are in Hamilton. Possibly only in Edmonton does the term indicate what lies above the 60th parallel. Above that imaginary line, a refinement is made to distinguish "north" from the "high north, or Arctic", meaning above the Arctic Circle.

Within a region or province, similar if more localized colloquialisms are well understood, though less so by the "come from aways from up-along" (outsiders from the mainland, as defined in Newfoundland). In the Atlantic region "the Island" is Prince Edward

Island, Newfoundland and Cape Breton notwithstanding. Likewise, "the Valley" (Annapolis Valley) is as precise as is "the Okanagan" to western residents. On "the Island" Charlottetown could play host to visitors from "away up west" (possibly Summerside, "thirty-some" miles distant). In Victoria, visitors from Campbell River come from "up Island", while in Frobisher Bay "the top end of the Island" indicates Pond Inlet and environs in northern Baffin Island. "Going south" is a wintry preoccupation with many Canadians. Nova Scotians can dream of Florida, but an Inuvik resident might settle for Edmonton, which could prompt a smile in Manyberries, Alberta, where the location of their provincial capital brings to mind a different image.

Related to direction is the identification of local land formations. James M. Minifie in *Homesteader: Recollections of a Prairie Boyhood* (Toronto: Macmillan, 1972), recalls the confusion his father experienced over a particular Ottawa-inspired government form:

> "You can see this questionnaire was invented by those guys down east," Smaill said. "They think in terms of tamarack, swamps or beaver meadows."
>
> "Well," said my father, "there's plenty of hay in sloughs, but what are sloughs for the purposes of Form No. 11?"
>
> "Forget it," Smaill counselled again.
>
> "They'll think up some absurd word in the course of time. Sloughs will be potholes, and coulees will be ravines, so other bureaucrats can understand the language, whether you do or not." (Minifie, p. 142)

"Cheechakos" (Chinook dialect for tenderfoot or newcomers) trying to find their way around the prairies may marvel over the precision of these directions: ten miles south of the "Parkland" (rolling, wooded hills) go east to the "correction line" (a surveyor's definition) and watch for the "buffalo jump" (a cliff or bluff over which Indian hunters chased buffalo). Proceed south until you spot the "road allowance" (uncultivated land outside of the fenced quarter, half or full section of land). Stop at "the wash" (water eroded indentation in the rocks through which fragments of petrified bone or shell are often exposed or "washed"). (All of which likely expedites the journey with greater dispatch than, say, a trip on the "Newfie Bullet".)

Southerners who go "into" the North will be equally entranced by taking a boat "down the river" (going north on the Mackenzie which seemingly flows "up" on the map), assuming that they are careful to avoid "break-up" and "freeze-up". Having arrived in Fort

Good Hope, they might wish to go "into the bush", (quasi-forest) and eventually in Tuktoyaktuk to journey "out on the land" (above the tree line, on the barrens) to see a pingo. If this isn't satisfactory they can always go "out" (leave the North for the outside).

B

Occupations: An east coast fisherman using a long liner (in the N.W.T. a peterhead) can set his traps (lobster) "outside" (in deep water). A prairie "farmer" (grain grower, not to be confused with "rancher", who has rangeland) can bring a truckload of grain to the "Pool" (Wheat Pool) elevator where the "dockage" (amount of impurities, i.e. weeds) will be calculated. The farmer calls it "takeage". While the load is being "dumped" (emptied into a bin beneath the floor of the elevator), invariably a minute amount of the grain will find its way to the "boot" (bottom of the elevator shaft). Depending upon the time of year and the location, the farmer might have to leave hastily in order to "set his water" (in irrigated farm land, ditches or sprinkler systems require careful attention). In the north the major cashcrop lies in the harvest of natural resources. The "ratting" season refers to hunting for muskrats in the Mackenzie Delta, for example. This might require the assistance of a "bush pilot" flying a "Beaver", more likely a "Twin Otter". Prior to the convenience of single or double engine Canadian-made aircraft, there was much greater dependence on "cat trains" (Caterpillar tractors) for moving supplies and equipment.

C

Sins of the Flesh: The cares of the day can be such as to make one long for some "red eye" (beer and tomato juice), a "shandy", (beer and ginger ale), screech (rum and hot water) or if you are very "dry" (thirsty), a snort of "callibogus" (rum, molasses, and spruce beer). Fortunate Albertans may view the "Stampede" through the hazy glow of "sillibub". It is to be hoped that the end result will not be a "bust-up" (state of intoxication as expressed in the Maritimes).

James Gray in his *Red Lights on the Prairies* (Toronto: Macmillan, 1971), quotes from the *Calgary Herald* and *Edmonton Journal* to illustrate the bowdlerized prose used to denote prostitutes in the early years of those cities. The editorial writers of the *Herald* outstripped their Edmonton competitors in their use of "two languid ladies of the red glim variety," "four ladyettes," and "the elite sorority of sisters from across the Langevin Bridge." A climax of sorts was achieved in the choice of "demimondaines." The *Journal* settled for "disorderly women." The evasiveness of the prose did not seem to deter the males from the "ram pasture" (bunkhouses).

D

Word Games: Students could have a "time" (Maritime idiom for enjoyment, fun, party) trying to identify various objects as defined locally. A northern resident wearing a "parka", "parkie", "amouti" or "mother hubbard" may go to "the Bay" (store) to purchase a "kicker" (outboard motor) to be used when winter has passed and "white outs" (blizzard conditions) are no longer a danger. Around the "settlement" (community, village) occasionally can be seen a "sik-sik", which every prairie child would recognize as a "gopher" (Richardson's ground squirrel). Overhead, "green heads" (male mallards) may be migrating to prairie sloughs. In the shallows a voracious "jackfish" (northern pike or pickerel) might be lurking. The surrounding "buckbrush" (bushes) might conceal some "chickens" (prairie chickens), even a "white tail". But only a novice would give a second thought to a "fool hen" (spruce grouse), much less a "snearth". Back at the house it is time for "tea" and perhaps "squares" (brownies) or a "slice" (date or nut loaf).

E

Snippets of History: Going to the "I.G.A." (International Grenfell Association) in Labrador is as common as, well, going to the I.G.A. (supermarket chain) in Halifax. Tourists driving from the "Pass" (Crow's Nest Pass) to the "Hat" (Medicine Hat) will travel through a part of "Palliser's Triangle" (prairie grassland area which has five rather than three sides). Relations to be visited en route may have among their forebears "remittance men" (males who left England and settled in the west under something other than their own volition). Digging up the family tree should not cause any disturbance. In any event a "Ross Rifle" (World War I rifle with notoriously little reliability) can be kept handy.

F

Literature: Succeeding chapters suggest ways to use reading materials (primary through grade six) and literature (junior-senior high grades) within the framework of regional-ethnic diversity. Here it is useful to refer to four writers whose books exemplify the variety of dialects that enrich our expression. *Recollections of Labrador*

Life by Lambert De Bolieu (Toronto: Ryerson, 1969), originally
published in 1861, is a treasure-trove of colourful idiom including
"rattles" (waterfalls), "longers" (floor planks made from squared
trunks of trees), "rinding" (process of stripping bark from a tree for
roofing), an "household engine" (bucket of water kept at the ready
in case of a fire in the wooden chimney), and "water horses" (piles
of washed fish left to dry).

The "Namko" country is the setting for Paul St. Pierre's novels,
Boss of the Namko Drive and *Breaking Smith's Quarter Horse*
(Toronto: Ryerson, 1965, 1966). This mythical land, located in
the Cariboo country in the interior of British Columbia, is known
for hard-driving men chewing "snoose" (snuff) who head for the
"round-up" through the "buckbrush flats".

Will R. Bird is a prolific author of Maritime material. A browse
through *These Are The Maritimes* (Toronto: Ryerson, 1959), will
introduce the reader to "Charlie ox" (a cart); "baked beans dried
crunchy on a frypan"; a "grand" (fine) Cape Breton morning;" and
the self-effacing "don't think I'm dippy talking like this."

One of the most gifted writers of the descriptive wilderness adventure is southern Alberta author Andy Russell. *Grizzly Country,
Horns in the High Country, Trails of a Wilderness Wanderer* (Toronto:
Random House, 1967, 1971, 1973), amount, in many ways, to
guided tours through Russell's backyard—the foothills and the
Rockies from the Montana border to Alaska. Through "canyons"
and "coulees"; across "creeks" and over "bluffs" to the "high
country" itself, his vocabulary and choice of expressions make for
engaging comparisons with other writers.

"Hammer Down and Copper Fasten": This Newfoundland expression meaning the last word or the clinching argument can be
left to another writer with western roots, Wallace Stegner. His book
Wolf Willow (Toronto: Macmillan, 1962) strikes close to home on
the matter of studying and learning a language and its relevant dialects. School books, as he recalled, "didn't enlarge me, they dispersed me." The reasons were clear:

> You grow up speaking one dialect and reading and writing
> another. You grow out of touch with your dialect because
> learning and literature lead you another way unless you con-
> sciously resist (p. 26).

With what appears to be a shrug of resignation he concludes:

> For most of us the language of literature is to some extent un-
> real, because school has always been separate from life (p. 26).

Language study oriented to Canadian developments could help to diminish the separation of life from the classroom. It might even help in the search for the elusive, egg-laying "snearth." But for more on that consult the "Sweet Songstress of Saskatchewan," *Sarah Binks* (by Paul Hiebert, Toronto: McClelland, 1967). Prudent choices from the literature and reading bibliographies will provide the dialect character notably absent in the language arts materials listed here.

◆ ◆ ◆ ◆

Primary (K-3) Texts, Kits and Series

Language Patterns Program, ed. John R. Linn (Holt). Reading, language, complementary materials including the *Language Patterns Library,* in three levels of difficulty.

Primary Supplementary Materials

Children's World Core Kit (kit). (Holt), $195. Teacher's guide $9.85. A multi-media kit including recordings, an anthology of children's literature, filmstrips, books, cards encompassing topics such as transportation, home and community, special days, seasons, pets and animals.

Schoolhouse: A Word Attack Skills Kit (kit). Muriel Clark and Fleur Marsden; SRA, 1973, $84.50. Teacher's manual $1.75. Grades 1-4; 340 cards in ten units designed for independent work in phonetics and vocabulary.

Language Development Program (kit). SRA, $130.00. Teacher's manual, $8.40. K-6; 96 story cards plus dialogue papers for the writing of stories based on the pictorial material.

Language Involvement Program (kit). SRA, $51.00. Teacher's manual, $2.20. Grades 1-6; write-in storybooks on 18 themes; 20 copies of each theme included; stories are written on the basis of the sequenced illustrations.

Elementary (Grades 3-6) Texts, Kits and Series

Communication Program, Macmillan. 1971. Four textbooks with accompanying teacher idea books with an emphasis on the skills of listening, speaking, reading, and writing.

Gage Strategies for the Language Arts (teaching program). Elizabeth Thorn and others, Gage. Grades 4-6, includes reader, workbook, book on developing skills, and teacher's handbook for each grade. The readers are available in hard or soft cover:

People Like Me, 1972, $7.25. Five individual books, $9.75 pa.

Something to Remember, 1973, $7.25. Four individual items, $7.80 pa.

How Many Miles?, 1974, $7.25. Four individual items, $7.80 pa.

Language Stimulus Program, Nelson. Grades 3-8; includes core text book, set of support materials, and teacher's guidebook for each grade, plus one book of personal language checks.

Starting Points in Language (teaching program). Ed. William H. Moore, Ginn, 1973. Grades 4-8; includes four students' books (paper) and four teacher's handbooks.

Elementary Supplementary Materials

Schoolhouse: Comprehension Patterns (kit). Robert Ireland, SRA, $84.00. Teacher's manual $1.75. Grades 4-6; 195 exercises in 10 units covering sentence patterns, pronoun referents, function words and ambiguity.

The Writing Centre, 2nd rev. ed. (kit). Robert Madeley and Sylvia Gibb, Holt, 1974, $31.00. Grades 3-6; 46 ideas for writing prose and poetry in five general theme areas: adventure, animals, fantasy, mystery, and poetry. Two cards are provided for each of the 46 ideas.

Write On!, D. Golden and others. McGraw, 1973, $36.00. A creative writing kit and teacher's manual; 80 cartoon-style picture cards and 37 activity cards included.

Junior High Series and Texts

This Book is About Communication Series, 2nd ed., Gerry Bryars and George R. Hall, McGraw, 1976. Three textbooks for grades 7-9 encompassing aspects of communication: talk, textbooks, narrative, newspapers, radio, tape recorders, film, television, additional material on spelling, punctuation, and grammar.

Action English (teaching program). Gage, 1973. Grades 7-10; includes for each grade textbook, teacher's handbook and sets of recorded material on cassette tapes or reel-to-reel tapes.

The Probing of Experience. Ronald J. McMaster and W.C. McMaster (Longman, 1969), $2.75. Grade 7 composition skills.

The Craft of Writing, Ronald J. McMaster (Longman, 1962),

$2.30. Grade 8; aims, principles and techniques of good writing.

The Expression of Thought, Ronald J. McMaster and W.C. Mc-Master (Longman, 1963), $2.35. Grade 8; the nature of language.

Language Matters, Ronald T. Shephard and James Henderson (Nelson, 1974), two textbooks, *Language Is,* $5.50 and *Grammar Is,* $5.50.

Senior High School

Creative Composition, Ronald J. McMaster and W.C. McMaster (Longman, 1957), $3.25. Teacher's key, $1.25. Grades 10-11.

Guide to Modern English, Earl W. Buxton and others (Gage, 1959), $5.95. Teacher's key, $2.35.

Patterns of Thought: The Basic Language Skills Book, Cy Groves (Methuen, 1974), $2.95 pa. A handbook for senior high students who require assistance in verbal and written communication.

WEP: A Handbook for Writing, Editing and Polishing, Emma E. Plattor and Patrick D. Drysdale (Gage, 1975), $3.60. Teacher's edition, $3.60.

Mediascan, James Henderson (Nelson, 1976), $4.20 pa. Discussion, writing, and research activities for senior high students.

Junior-Senior High School Supplementary Materials

Now, the Newspaper, Ronald J. McMaster (Longman, 1972), $3.60. A textbook for grades 6-10 on understanding and analyzing newspapers and the field of journalism in general.

Mass Media and You, Austin Repath (Longman, 1966), $2.50. A source book for grades 9-12 on understanding the media and its influence on our society.

A Folio for Writers (kit). Bruce Vance and Michael Milne, Clarke, Irwin, 1969-70. Five booklets, *Advertising / Description / Exposition / Narration / Poetry,* $2.25 each. Includes over 25 visual models of actual advertising copy along with detailed suggestions and exercises in copywriting.

The Underground Press (cassette tape). 60 min, C.B.C. Learning Systems, $15.00. The press in Vancouver, Toronto, Montreal and Halifax.

The Press in the Maritimes (cassette tape). 30 min, C.B.C. Learning Systems, $8.00. Documents the control a few families have over the press.

English as a Second Language

English as a Second Language (teaching program). Collier-Macmillan. Includes student texts and workbooks, tapes, teacher guidebooks, lesson plan. First level available in fall 1976.

Dictionaries

Primary

Winston Primary Dictionary, rev. ed. (Holt, 1972), $2.00. Grades 1-3; 300 words, illustrated.

Dent's Primary Dictionaries, Joyce L. Morgan and Beverley Wilbur (Dent, 1970), level 1, $1.50, level 2, $2.50.

Elementary

Winston Canadian Dictionary for Schools (Holt, 1965), $3.50. Grades 3-6; 38 550 definitions.

Teaching Dictionary Skills (Holt, 1965), 95¢.

In Other Words: An Introductory Thesaurus, Murray Dobson and Patricia Hughes (Holt, 1969), $4.85. Grades 3-8; 2600 entries.

Words to Use, Patrick D. Drysdale (Gage, 1971), $4.85 pa. A primary thesaurus for grades 2-4; 6000 entries under 70 headings.

Words and Their Meanings, Donald Urquhart (Copp, 1962), $5.25.

The Beginning Dictionary, Walter S. Avis and others (Gage, 1963), $6.05. Grades 3-5; 24 000 entries; lesson on the use of a dictionary.

Nelson Canadian Elementary School Dictionary, F.R. Whitty (Nelson, 1975), $2.95 pa. Teacher's edition with 16-page handbook, $3.74. 13 000 entries.

Junior High

The Winston Dictionary of Canadian English: Intermediate Edition (Holt, 1969), $4.25. Grades 6-10; 65 000 vocabulary entries.

Compact Dictionary of Canadian English, ed. Thomas Paikeday (Holt, 1973), 50¢. Grades 7-9; 65 000 entries.

The Intermediate Dictionary, rev. ed., Walter S. Avis and others (Gage, 1972), $7.30. 64 000 entries.

Senior High

The Gage Canadian Dictionary, Walter S. Avis and others (Gage, 1973), $6.95 pa. 90 000 entries.

The Winston Canadian Dictionary for School, Home and Office (Holt, 1974), $3.25. 38 500 entries.

For Teachers

Speaking Canadian English, Mark M. Orkin (General, 1970), $7.95. An examination of the English language from the Canadian perspective of grammar, syntax, vocabulary, pronunciation, spelling and slang.

Dictionary of Canadianisms on Historical Principles, Walter S. Avis, D. Leachman and C.B. Crate (Gage, 1967), $25.00.

Canadian English: Origin and Structure, J. Chambers (Methuen, 1975), $5.95 pa. One item in a new linguistic series.

Looking at Language: Essays in Introductory Linguistics, M.H. Scargill and P.G. Penner (Gage, 1966), $4.30 pa.

Teaching Spelling: Canadian Word Lists and Instructional Techniques, Ves Thomas (Gage, 1974), $3.25 pa. Grades 1-6.

Teaching the Language Arts: Listening, Speaking, Reading and Writing, Elizabeth A. Thorn and Carl Braun (Gage, 1974), $6.95 pa. Grades 1-6.

Sounds Canadian: Languages and Cultures in Multi-Ethnic Society, ed. Paul Migus (Peter Martin, 1974), $12.00. A collection of papers on language, religion, education, multiculturalism.

Creative Communication: Teaching the Language Arts, Lillian M. Logan, Virgil G. Logan and Leona Paterson (McGraw, 1972), $8.50. Language arts methodologies.

Media for Discovery, Hans Moller (Maclean-Hunter, 1970), $4.00.

Teaching Children to Read and Write, Alfred F. Deverell (Holt, 1974), $6.95 pa. Of particular use to teachers of English as a second language.

Canadian English and Newspeak (cassette tape). 30 min, C.B.C. Learning Systems, $8.00. Mark Orkin, author of *Sounds Canadian* talks about the characteristics of Canadian language.

Chapter 12

ENVIRONMENT

Environmental education is relatively new. The *Report of the Provincial Committee on Aims and Objectives of Education in the Schools of Ontario: Living and Learning* contributed significantly to the growth of public awareness. The term itself has a Humpty Dumpty aura: environmental studies means "what I say it means, nothing more and nothing less". Some of the more common curriculum varieties are outdoor education, ecology, geography, conservation, nature studies, local studies, and local history.

Regardless of the terms used, the most coherent statements in support of the need for environmental education come from Alberta:

> In the face of rapid deterioration of earth's interlocked life support systems, we will need to explore quickly and accurately all the probabilities for survival—both to sustain life and give it meaning. Environmental education, therefore, must dominate our future horizon—if there is to be a future horizon.
>
> *Report of the Commission on Educational Planning,*
> Queen's Printer (Edmonton:1972 p. 192).

Both content and method of learning have been the concern of both Ontario and Alberta education authorities. The provincial reports warn against viewing environmental studies as an additional course to be tacked on the existing curricula:

> Environmental education obviously calls for an interdisciplinary approach. Just as ecology permeates our entire living pattern, so should it permeate our entire learning pattern. In fact, to separate environmental education from other education would be the ultimate in irony, treating its dynamic wholeness as though it were a specialized fragment—an optional course. . . . There is no option when it comes to environmental education. Hence, it should be

integrated with all, or nearly all, of the subjects taught in our schools. (*Report of the Commission on Educational Planning,* p. 192)

An indication of how the integration of conventionally separate, often isolated, subject areas might take place can be summarized in this fashion:

The sciences are natural elements in studies of the environment, but children must not be restricted, especially in the pre-adolescent years, to the confines of the sub-disciplines of science (e.g. biology, botany, chemistry, etc.). The geographical elements of social studies and much of applied mathematics may be properly included in such studies. The practical aspects of agriculture, of manual arts, of home and consumer economics, and much of what is called vocational training may also be identified with this area referred to as "Environmental Studies".

Living and Learning, (Toronto: Ontario Department of Education, 1968, p. 77)

The essence of environmental study is to make it possible for the individual to clarify concepts and attitudes about the interrelatedness of people, cultures, and ecological surroundings. The delicate yet sturdy spider's web illustrates visually the required transformation of learning. Placing the junior high student at the centre of the web, the subject areas become an interlaced, logical pattern of experiences. For example, study of prairie geography is enlivened when place names and land forms are combined with the wit and insight of W.O. Mitchell recounting the adventures of *Jake and the Kid* (Toronto: Macmillan, 1961) in Crocus, Saskatchewan. Similarly, study of Canada's primary industries (fish, forestry, furs) becomes more than an account of glum, dedicated souls decimating the wilderness when combined with the folk music of Edith Butler, John Allen Cameron, or Alan Mills.

Constructing networks for learning not only places information in a logical format, but, of equal importance, it infuses the otherwise detached assimilation of facts with feeling—a grasp of the beliefs people hold and have held about their relationship with their surroundings.

Pursuing this approach necessitates the selection of learning resources from many of these chapters. The materials as listed immediately following concentrate primarily on flora, fauna, and ecological concerns. These should be combined (as appropriate) with those listed in Chapters 4 (Art), 5 (Biology), 9 (Drama), 15 (Indian, Inuit, Métis), 17 (Literature), 19 (Music), 24 (Science), and 25 (Social Studies).

Through available items, grouped on a regional and/or provincial basis, it is possible to realize the interdisciplinary approach to learning. A suitable theme could be simply "People and their environments".

♦ ♦ ♦ ♦

General Reference

The Illustrated Natural History Library of Canada, Natural Science of Canada, 9 vols. $6.00 each. Distributed by McClelland and Stewart. The best basic reference library providing coverage of each geographical region.

The Fauna

The Birds of Canada, National Museum (Information Canada, 1966), $15.00.

Where to go Birdwatching in Canada, David Stirling and Jim Woodford (Hancock, 1975), $3.95 pa.

The Mammals of Canada, A.F. Banfield (U.T.P., 1974), $19.95.

Eyes on the Wilderness, Helmut Hirnschall (Hancock, 1975), $7.95. Illustrations and text describe a variety of animals in their wilderness setting.

Wolves and Wilderness, John B. Théberge (Dent, 1975), $4.95 pa.

Fresh Water Fishes in Canada (Information Canada, 1975), $12.75.

Checklist of Canadian Freshwater Fishes with Keys for Identification, W.B. Scott and E.J. Crossman (Royal Ontario Museum, 1969), $1.50. One hundred eighty-three species in 24 families.

Checklist of the Amphibians and Reptiles of Canada, Logier and Toner (Royal Ontario Museum, 1961), $3.50. Indicates the location of each species.

The Turtles of Canada, Barbara Froom (McClelland, 1976), $8.95.

Snakes of Canada, Barbara Froom (McClelland, 1972), $7.50.

Canadian Endangered Species, Darryl Stewart (Gage, 1974), $12.95. Illustrated in colour and black and white.

The World of Birds (filmstrip). col, sound, French or English, Cinemedia, set of 3, $47.50.

Cries of the Wild (l.p. recording). C.B.C. Publications Branch, $5.00. Recording of wildlife sounds.

The Flora

Native Trees of Canada, 7th ed., Dept. of Forestry and Fisheries and R.C. Hosie (Information Canada, 1970), $5.00 pa.

Forest Flora of Canada, Dept. of the Environment and G.C. Cunningham (Information Canada, 1969), $2.50 pa. Bilingual text.

Common Weeds of Canada / Les mauvaises herbes communes du Canada, Gerald A. Mulligan (McClelland, 1975), $4.95 pa.

Weeds of Canada, rev. ed., Dept. of Agriculture and Clarence Frankton (Information Canada, 1969), $3.00 pa. Two hundred species.

The Canadian Leaf Album, F.A. Urquhart (Gage, 1963), $3.95. Sixty-nine drawings of various leaves; 26 drawings of the most common deciduous trees.

Rocky Mountain Wildflowers, A.E. Porsild (National Museum, 1974), $5.00 pa. English or French.

Canada's Forests (multi-media kit). Harry Smith, $45.00.

Landscape (kit). O.I.S.E., complete kit on forest resource management, $120.00. Printed materials only, $20.00.

Geography – Geology

The Rivers of Canada, Hugh MacLennan, photos John de Visser (Macmillan, 1974), $30.00.

Rock and Mineral Collecting in Canada, vol 3 (Information Canada, 1972), $1.50 pa.

System of Soil Classification for Canada (Information Canada, 1974), $5.00 pa.

Prehistoric

Catalogue of Canadian Fossil Fishes, Brian G. Gardiner (Royal Ontario Museum, 1966), $3.50.

Environmental-Ecological Concerns

Pollution: An Ecological Approach, Robert G. Adamson (Book Society, 1971), $7.45.

This Good, Good Earth: Our Fight for Survival, Ralph O. Brinkhurst and Donald A. Chant (Macmillan, 1971), $3.50 pa.

The Plot to Save the World, Wade Rowland (Clarke, Irwin, 1973), $7.95. Canada's role at the Stockholm Environment Conference.

One Cosmic Instant: A Natural History of Human Arrogance, John Livingston (McClelland, 1973), $7.95.

A Citizen's Guide to Air Pollution, David Bates (McGill-Queen's, 1972), $2.95 pa.

Environment and Good Sense: An Introduction to Environmental Damage and Control in Canada, Maxwell J. Dunbar (McGill-Queen's, 1971), $2.50 pa.

Freshwater Pollution: Canadian Style, Peter A. Larkin (McGill-Queen's, 1974), $5.00.

People Pollution: Sociologic and Ecologic Viewpoints on the Prevalence of People, Milton R. Freeman (McGill-Queen's, 1974), $3.25 pa.

Pollution: The Effluence of Affluence, ed. F.J. Taylor, P.G. Kettle and R.Q. Putnam (Methuen, 1971), $4.35 pa. A collection of readings for senior high school students.

Endangered Animals (prints). col, Fitzhenry & Whiteside, $16.95. Set of 16 study prints with accompanying text for elementary students.

Historic

Canadian Naturalist, P.H. Gosse (Coles, 1971), $3.35 pa. First published in 1840.

Regional Environmental Materials

The North

The Green North, Richard Rohmer (Maclean-Hunter, 1970), $1.25 pa.

Freshwater Fishes of Northwestern Canada and Alaska (Information Canada, 1970), $8.50.

The Dangerous River, 2nd ed., Raymond Murray Patterson (Gray, 1966), $1.95 pa. The author's experiences in the Nahanni Valley, N.W.T.

Far Pastures, 2nd ed., Raymond Murray Patterson (Gray, 1973), $1.95 pa. Glimpses of the West and North.

Northern Survival (Information Canada, 1972), $2.50 pa.

The Idea of North (l.p. recording). C.B.C. Publications Branch, $5.00. Music which interprets the North.

British Columbia

The High West, Andy Russell (photos), Les Blacklock (Macmillan, 1974), $12.95. Text by Andy Russell, author of *Grizzly Country, Horns in the High Country* and *Trails of a Wilderness Wanderer.*

Taverner's Birds of Western Canada, P.A. Taverner (Coles, 1974), $11.00. First published in 1923.

British Columbia Game Fish, ed. Jack Grundle (Western Fish and Game, 1970), $8.95.

The Salmon People, Hugh W. McKervill (Gray, 1967), $5.80. The influence of the salmon fisheries on B.C. history.

The Whale People, R. Haig-Brown (Collins, 1962), $1.25 pa.

Rock and Mineral Collecting in British Columbia (Information Canada, 1975), $2.75 pa.

Milestones on Vancouver Island, 2nd ed., Ken Pattison (Milestone, 1974), $4.45 pa. A guide to the life and environment of the Island.

Titles from a series of films about British Columbia, Viking Films, 1972-73:

British Columbia: Mountains to the Sea, 27 min, col, $325.00.

Cariboo Country, 15 min, col, $195.00.

Kluane: Yukon Territory, 15 min, col, $185.00.

Last Frontier, 22 min, col, $285.00. Natural history of B.C.

A Place of Opportunity, 14½ min, col, $185.00 B.C. resource industries transportation, based on Vancouver.

Tied to the Sea, 15 min, col, $185.00. Salt water recreation and sports around Vancouver, Victoria, and the Gulf Islands.

Life of the Sockeye Salmon, 25 min, col, $125.00.

(There is a 14-day limit on preview copies of these films.)

The Prairies

Prairie Birds in Colour, Doug Gilroy (Western Producer, 1976), $17.95. One hundred fifty-four colour illustrations with descriptive text of 92 birds.

The Rockies, Andy Russell (Hurtig, 1975), $20.00. Lavishly illustrated.

Alberta: A Natural History, 2nd ed. (Hurtig, 1967), $8.95.

Birds of Alberta, Saskatchewan and Manitoba, David A. Hancock: illus. Jim Woodford (General, 1973), $5.95.

Mammals of Waterton Lakes National Park, Alberta (Information Canada, 1973), $1.25 pa.

Wild Flowers of the Prairies, J.B. Neufeld (Western Producer, 1968), $3.98. Photographs of 28 varieties with text.

Mammals from the St. Mary's River Formation, Sloan and Russell (Royal Ontario Museum, 1974), $2.00 pa.

The Paleontology of the Swan Hills Area of North Central Alberta, Russell (Royal Ontario Museum, 1967), $1.00 pa.

The Prairie Gardener, Bert Harp (Hurtig, 1970, $8.95.

Ontario and Quebec

A Naturalist's Guide to Ontario, ed. W.W. Judd and J. Murray Speirs (U.T.P., 1964), $2.96 pa.

Birds of Ontario and Quebec, David A. Hancock; Jim Woodford, illus. (General, 1973), $5.95.

Taverner's Birds of Eastern Canada, P.A. Taverner (Coles, 1974), $9.35.

Encyclopédie des oiseaux du Québec, W. Earl Godfrey (Homme), $6.00.

Freshwater Fishes of Eastern Canada 2nd ed., W.B. Scott (U.T.P., 1967), $3.50.

Les Mammifères du Québec, Elzéar J. Duchesnay (H.M.H.), $3.50.

Snakes of Ontario, E.B.S. Logier (U.T.P., 1958), $3.75 pa.

Wild Flowers of Eastern Canada, Katherine Mackenzie (Collins, 1973), $2.95 pa. Depicts 100 of the more common varieties with 90 full colour plates.

Rocks and Mineral for the Collector: Hull-Maniwaki, Quebec; Ottawa-Peterborough, Ontario (Information Canada, 1975), $2.75 pa.

Rocks and Minerals for the Collector: Ottawa to North Bay, Ontario; Hull to Waltham, Quebec (Information Canada, 1975), $2.75 pa.

Rocks and Minerals for the Collector: Ontario and Quebec: Cobalt-Belleterre-Timmins Region (Information Canada, 1974), $3.00 pa.

The Niagara Escarpment: From Tobermory to Niagara Falls, William H. Gillard and Thomas Tooke (U.T.P., 1974), $3.95 pa.

Al Purdy's Ontario (l.p. recording). C.B.C. Publications Branch, $5.00. Readings by the poet Al Purdy.

The Atlantic Region

Birds of the Atlantic Provinces, David A. Hancock, illus. Jim Woodford (General, 1973), $5.95.

The Birds of Nova Scotia, Robie W. Tufts, illus. Roger Tory Peterson (Nova Scotia Museum, 1973), $14.00.

Seabirds of Bonaventure Island, Newfoundland (Information Canada, 1973), 50¢ pa.

Waterfowl Studies (Information Canada, 1974), $3.00 pa.

Prince Edward Island Lobsterlore: Claws, Tales and Tomally,

George Leard and Merle Bigney (P.E.I. Heritage Foundation, 1975), $1.25 pa.

Textbook Series

Titles from the series Examining your Environment, Holt, $4.50 each. Grades 4-8; teacher's guide for each title; overview teacher's guide for the series; illustrated in colour; encourages independent exploration. Also available in packages of 6. Twelve titles:

Birds; Mini-Climates; Pollution; Running Water; Snow and Ice; Trees; Astronomy; Small Creatures; Ecology in Your Community; The Dandelion; Mapping Small Places; Your Senses.

Titles from the Ryerson Science in Action Series, McGraw. Grades 4-8; two core books and six companion books provide basic materials for involving the individual in a study of the environment.

Studies for Open Places, $2.85; *Studies for Woodlands,* $2.85; *Studying Birds,* $3.45; *Studying Soil,* $3.45; *Studying Insects,* $3.45; *Studying Streams,* $3.75; *Studying Plants,* $3.75; *Studying Mammals,* $3.95; *Teaching Outdoors: How, Why, When,* $4.75.

Titles from the series Collier-Macmillan Science Studies, Collier-Macmillan, $2.75 each. An interdisciplinary approach to relating people to their environment. Reading level—upper elementary—junior high; metric; teacher's guide for each unit.

Schoolyard and Beyond; The Living Community; Mechanics and Men; Astronomy without Telescopes.

Titles in preparation: *Water and Other Liquids; Measurement; Sound and Music; Electricity; Molecules.*

Titles from the Environment Series, Harvest. Senior high level.

Regional Planning in Canada, $8.50; *The Last Refuge,* $7.50; *Land: Private Property, Public Control,* $12.50; *The Last Seal Pup,* $2.00 pa.; *The Pollution Reader,* $3.50 pa.; *Water: Canadian Needs & Resources,* $3.50 pa.; *The Right to Housing,* $4.50 pa.; *Canadian Parks in Perspective,* $3.50 pa.; *Planning the Canadian Environment,* $4.50 pa.

Titres du série les millieux naturels du Québec, H.M.H. Quatre diaporama d'habitants du Québec; chacun des montages se presente en deux versions répondent à plusieurs types d'objectifs. Diapositives avec deux bandes sonores et guide méthodologique, chacun, $90.00.

Le littoral du bas St.-Laurent; Le Ruisseau; La toubière; La forêt de conifères.

Materials for Elementary Grades

A Book of Canadian Animals, Charles Paul May (Macmillan, 1962), $5.95.

A Second Book of Canadian Animals, Charles Paul May (Macmillan, 1962), $5.95.

A Book of Canadian Birds, Charles Paul May (Macmillan, 1967), $5.95.

A Book of Insects, Charles Paul May (Macmillan, 1972), $5.95.

A Book of Reptiles and Amphibians, Charles Paul May (Macmillan, 1968), $4.95.

Sharp Tooth: A Year of the Beaver, David Allenby Smith (Peter Martin, 1974), $6.95.

Wild Animals I have Known, Ernest Thompson Seton (Schocken, 1966), $2.00.

Biography of a Grizzly, Ernest Thompson Seton (Schocken, 1969), $2.69.

Into the Woods Beyond, Cy Hampson (Macmillan, 1971), $6.45.

Cry Wild, Ronald D. Lawrence (Nelson, 1970), $7.85. The story of a timber wolf.

The Harp Seal, David Terhune (Burns, 1973), $7.95.

Canadian Scout Handbook, Boy Scouts of Canada (Boy Scouts, 1973), $7.25.

Growing a Green Thumb, Lorraine Surcouf (Greey de Pencier, 1975), $3.95 pa. Individual and group gardening projects for young children.

Titles from a series of multi-media kits concerning British Columbia, Grolier:

   The Ocean's Edge, $21.00; *Timber,* $28.00; *Pulp and Paper.*

Junior High

Instant Weather Forecasting in Canada, Alan Watts (General, 1969), $3.95.

Watchers at the Pond, Franklin Russell (McClelland, 1961), $6.95. Life cycles of pond inhabitants.

Never Cry Wolf, Farley Mowat (McClelland, 1973), $8.95.

Wilderness Writers, James Polk (Clarke, Irwin, 1973), $3.50. Life stories of three writers who created realistic animal stories: Ernest Thompson Seton, Charles G.D. Roberts, Grey Owl.

Wilderness Man: The Strange Story of Grey Owl, Lovat Dickson (Macmillan, 1973), $9.95.

Titles by Grey Owl from Macmillan, $4.95 each:
Sajo and the Beaver People; A Book of Grey Owl; Tales of an Empty Cabin; Pilgrims of the Wild; The Men of the Last Frontier.

The Box of Noise (multi-media kit). Grolier, $16.00.

Senior High

Man's Physical Environment, Angus Gunn (E.B., 1973), $7.50.

Last of the Curlews, Fred Bodsworth (McClelland, 1963), $1.95 pa.

Holt Geo Resource Kit (kit). Holt, $265.00. Fifteen units with slides, guide book, and printed material on topics such as: Alpine Glacial Features, Coastal Features of Eastern Canada, Weathering and Landscape Change, Geology and Scenery of Ontario, Drumheller Badlands, Hot Springs and Geysers. Units can be purchased separately.

Periodicals

Nature Canada, Canadian Nature Federation. Four issues annually, $6.00.

Alternatives, Canadian Periodical Publishers' Association. Quarterly, $3.00. On pollution, resources, conservation and wilderness.

Outdoor Canada, Canadian Periodical Publishers' Association. Six issues annually, $3.50.

B.C. Outdoors, Canadian Periodical Publishers' Association. Six issues per year, $3.50.

Owl: The Outdoor and Wildlife Magazine for Children, Owl Magazine, 59 Front St. E., Toronto, M5E 1B3. Ten issues annually, $6.00.

For Teachers

Titles from a series developed by the Vancouver Environmental Education Project, (VEEP), B.C. Teachers' Federation. Guidebooks developed by teachers for use at various grade levels.

Primary

Kids and Kites, $2.00 pa.; *Forest Appreciation,* $2.00 pa.; *The Jolly Green Classroom,* $1.70; *Busing Around,* $1.70.

Intermediate

The Stump Book, $2.00; *There's Dirt in the Forest*, $1.15; *Creeks*, $1.65 pa.; *Cast Your Class to the Wind*, $1.70 pa.; *Science on a Kite String*, $2.00 pa.; *Super-8 Kids Film Book*, $2.00 pa.; *The Pond Book*, $2.00 pa.; *Herbal Happenings*, $2.00 pa.; *Classroom Camera*, $1.65 pa.; *Clay: You can Dig it*, $1.70 pa.; *Parachutes*, $1.55 pa.; *The Cabbage-White Butterfly Classroom Book*, $2.00 pa.; *Grounds for Erosion*, $1.55 pa.; *Measuring the Forest*, $2.00 pa.

Secondary

How to Get Your Hands in the Till, $1.70 pa.; *A Mouse by any Other Name*, $1.70 pa.

Chapter 13

FRENCH

To have the pupil feel that he is learning languages with nothing higher in view than a mastery of elementary grammar and the reading of a few simple texts, robs his work of a powerful incentive.

> *Modern Language Instruction In Canada* (Toronto: 1928, Vol. 1, p. XXXIII)

This observation concerning the status of language instruction made nearly half a century ago remains true of many classrooms today. Despite the recommendations of the Royal Commission on Bilingualism and Biculturalism, the status of French as one of the two official languages of Canada, and increased public awareness, there has been only slight improvement in the quality of French language instruction nationally. For many students attempting to learn French as a second language, the "higher view" is severely restricted. Exclusive of the education of teachers who understand and can teach in the various Canadian dialects, the major concern is the learning materials situation.

Relevant Canadian French language resources have had small impact on English-speaking classrooms. Most materials are from Paris with modifications to suit the needs of American pupils. If Canadian items are used, they are often a variation on the same theme; i.e. the sounds, words, structures, are European in derivation with frivolous substitutions made in order to "Canadianize" the edition.

Leaving aside the social implications of denying the existence of Acadian dialects, Manitoba and Alberta variations, and the dialects of Quebec itself, the majority of learning materials used in Canadian schools do not let the individual learn such things as the following:

Native speakers of Canadian French may use different phonemes from the international standard (e.g. Canadian French uses

118

phoneme /e/ in "mai" where the European version employs /E/).

In international French, stress normally falls on the last uttered syllable of a stress group; in Canadian French, the distribution of stress is somewhat different, owing to the presence of a rather strong secondary accent.

In closed short syllables, the international standard vowels /i/, /u/, /y/ may or may not be articulated by native speakers of Canadian French.

In Canadian French the four nasal vowels tend to show a different articulation from their European counterparts.

It is the usual practice in Canada to sound the "t" which comes at the end of a word and is preceded by a vowel (e.g. "tout" can be pronounced "tut" in Canada but "tu" in France).

Quebec and Acadian peoples can differ in the pronunciation of /t/ and /d/ followed by the close vowels /i/ and /y/. Québécois may pronounce these with a marked friction similar to the clusters /ts/ and /dz/ of the English words "bits" and "adze".

For more information *The Canadian Dictionary* (French/English), Jean-Paul Vinay, Pierre Daviault, Henry Alexander (Toronto: McClelland, 1962), is helpful.

Neglect of Canadian French phonology is only a part of the problem. Conventionally, mispronunciation can be overlooked because the speaker of French as a second language is at least making an effort to communicate. It is when words and phrases of European origin are employed in Chicoutimi, St. Boniface, or Ottawa that significant difficulties can be encountered. Erroneous information, double meanings, or lack of coherence can be the result of putting one's school French into practice. Consider, within the context of daily living, the following situations.

Government. Nominally, it should be expected that an understanding of the organization of the Canadian government in the French language is possible. With the increased attention paid to bilingualism in the civil service, career-minded students must have the chance to master the Canadian idiom. Knowing the Canadian derived terminology would be of assistance: la Chambre des communes, l'orateur, le chef de l'opposition, Receveur général du Canada. It might even save some embarrassment to know that a white collar worker is "un collet blanc" and not "un employé du bureau".

Environment. Canadian terminology is often not only more colorful but more precise than its European counterpart. In France, *le sapin* denotes both fir and spruce trees. In Canada *l'épinette* (spruce) and *le sapin* (fir) are employed. A wolverine is more than adequately described in the term *le glouton* or the more familiar *le carcajou,* rather than the European word *le blaireau du Labrador* (freely translated, the Labrador badger). The moose, an ungainly animal to be sure, is *l'orignal* (derived from *original,* meaning odd, queer, or eccentric). In France, the identification would be *l'élan.* The woodpecker is appropriately *le pic-bois* rather than the less adequate *le pevert. La poudrerie* indicates the potential severity of a Canadian snowstorm as opposed to *la tempête de neige.*

Around the Home. A typical rural Canadian farmhouse is likely to have a pantry, *la paneterie,* derived from *la panetière* meaning a bread bin, rather than *une dépense,* which approximates a storeroom. The veranda or porch is termed *la galérie,* while in France *le portique d'une maîson* would be valid. The upstairs in such a home would be *au deuxième étage* and not *au premier étage* as in Europe. An annual ritual in many homes is the spring-cleaning or *le grand ménage,* as opposed to the more cumbersome *le grand nettoyager du printemps* in France. And every house has the problem of garbage disposal, *le vidangeur* contrasted with *les ordures.*

Recreation. Whether the individual is watching a hockey puck, *le disque,* or a baseball batter, *un frappeur,* the munchies might be *les pinottes,* peanuts, rather than *les arachides.* All of which might be washed down with copious quantities of *un breuvage* rather than *une boisson.* After a quick visit to *la toilette* rather than the W.C., a pleasant interlude on a lagoon in *un canot,* a canoe, might be preferable to navigating in *une chaloupe,* a rowboat. (In France at nightfall, *à la brunante* rather than *à la tombée de nuit,* one might enjoy a visit to a nearby township, *le canton* as opposed to *la commune,* to dine on salad, *la laitue,* as contrasted with *la salade,* that's for sure—*certain,* not *pour sûr.* To be able to engage in these pastimes the individual should be successful. To succeed, *arracher,* is somewhat more descriptive than the European verb *réussir.* The Canadian word has overtones of extracting, wringing out, extorting, even screwing, appropriate to some business practices!

Laughter can be a deceptive cover for cold fury. Over one hundred years after Confederation, it is difficult to accept the fact that the language of more than one-third of the Canadian population is treated with virtual disdain in the nation's classrooms. It is doubtful if a more effective, efficient way to castrate the self-image, the dignity, of any people can be found then to deny them access to the study of their own Canadian language heritage. To suggest that non-French Canadian people should have a chance to become competent in the working languages of Acadiens, Manitobaines or Québécois is to state the obvious. The colour, the flavour, the substance of Canadian dialects can be learned along with the language variations found in Belgium, the provinces of France, or the Left Bank of the Seine. In French, as in English, students can build upon native developments to create better national and international understanding. The various textbook series can be combined with such relevant Canadian-dialect material as is available. Wherever possible, materials written in French pertinent to each subject area should be made available to students. A bilingual atlas, a biography of Norman Bethune, a drama by Gratien Gélinas, mathematics materials from l'Université de Sherbrooke, plus any number of other suggested items, must become accepted features of language learning, if study of Canadian French is to become something more than a perfunctory ritual in our schools. (N.B. Each chapter bibliography should be consulted for appropriate materials in the French language.)

♦ ♦ ♦ ♦

Textbook Series

Titles from the series Feuille d'érable, Nelson. K-10; teacher's handbooks, texts and workbooks for the students:

La maternelle / Au jardin fleuri, $2.10.

Première année

Remi et Aline première partie, $3.55 / Deuxième partie, $3.85. / *Contes bleus,* $4.25 / *Les enfants heureux,* $3.75, livre parallèle d'enrichissement, 3e trimestre.

2e—10e Annees

De belles histoires / Contes et poèmes / Le bon temps / Près de la fontaine / La vie canadienne / Aux quatre vents / Vers l'avenir / Nouvelles aventures, $3.95 each.

Titles from the series Le Français partout be Gordon Carruth and others, Holt. K-8; multi-media.

Kindergarten, years 1 and 2

Aux yeux des petits (kit). $112.50. Teacher's guide, $6.95. Activity pads, $2.45.

Year 7

Le Français partout, 1. Teacher's guide, $7.00. Wall charts, $29.95. Student l.p. recordings, $7.90. Student tests, $4.60. Key to tests, $2.00. Tape recorded material, 6 five inch reels, doubletrack, 3¾ i.p.s., $90.00.

Titles from the Macmillan French series, Macmillan. A six year program with an emphasis on conversation.

Commençons, Teacher's guide, $2.50. / *Jouons 1,* $1.90. Student text. / *Jouons 2,* $2.10.

Titles from the series Le plaisir d'apprendre et connaître, Gage. A two year program using illustrations to explain the language.

Le plaisir d'apprendre 1re année, $4.10 / *Le plaisir de connaître,* 2e année $4.80 / *Guide de maître,* $5.65.

Titles from the series Collection cathédrale, Gage. A three-year program with emphasis on *la méthode de lecture globale.*

Bientôt je lirai, $1.95. Préparation à la lecture. / *Viens voir,* Préparatoire 1, $1.85 / *Viens travailler, viens jouer,* Préparatoire 2, $1.85 / *Viens te promener,* Préparatoire 3, $1.95.

Titles from the series Grammaire français et livres de lecture les couleurs de la vie by Georges Galichet et Gaston Mondouaud, H.M.H. A five-year program for grades 3-7.

Je découvre la grammaire et l'orthographe par des méthodes actives, $3.25. 8-9 ans / Pochette plastique avec jetons de grammaire pour chaque élève, pour 3e, 4e, 5e, années, 60¢ / *Les couleurs de la vie,* $3.20. 8-9 ans / *Je découvre la grammaire de la langue parlée à l'orthographe par des méthodes actives,* $3.20. 9-10 ans / *Je découvre la grammaire et l'orthographe,* $3.20. Ouvrage européen pour ceux qui commencent l'étude des grammaires Galichet en 4e année. / *Les couleurs de la vie,* $3.40. 9-10 ans / *Je comprends la grammaire de la langue parlée à l'orthographe par des méthodes actives,* $3.35. 10-11 ans / *Les couleurs de la vie,* $3.50. 10-11 ans / *Grammaire des ensembles et orthographe de base,* $3.60. 11-12 ans / *Corrigé des exercices et conseils pédagogiques, Grammaire des ensembles,* $3.60.

Titles from the series Programme integré de langage à l'élémentaire. (PH.E), Nelson. A four-year program for ages 8-12.

Magie des saisons, $4.85. 8-9 ans / *Multimondes,* $4.85. 9-10 ans / *Mille lieux,* $4.85. 10-11 ans / *Media-sens,* $4.85. 11-12 ans / Teacher's guide for each level, $5.95.

Cours préliminaire, Holt. A multi-media pre-reading course;

grades 3-6; includes student's text, teacher's guide, wall charts, recordings, tapes, cutouts etc.

Titles from the series Collection communication, H.M.H. Textbooks and teacher's guide books; grades 4-7; emphasis on oral and written expression.

Arnold le hamster, $1.25. 9-10 ans / *Perouette*, $1.25. 10-11 ans / *Fil de fer*, $1.25. 11-12 ans / Teacher's guide for each level, $3.95.

Titles from the series Histoire de mon pays, Nelson. Social Studies materials for students in grades 5-10 who have developed reading competency.

La découverte, $3.50. 5e année / *La Nouvelle-France*, $3.50, 6e année / *Les deux Canadas*, $3.50. 7e année / *La Confédération*, $3.75. 8e année / *Notre héritage européen*, $3.75. 9e année / *Le Canada au XXe siècle*, $3.95. 10e année / *Notre héritage canadien 1*, $3.50. 7e and 8e années.

J'écoute, je parle, Gage. A four-year multi-media program for grades 7-10; includes teacher's guide, pupil's book, flash cards, posters, tapes etc. for each level.

Filmstrips, Multi-media Kits, Games

De chez nous (kit). O.I.S.E., $27.50. Based on the Quebec Winter Carnival; includes student newsmagazines, language games, listening tape and a teacher's guide; for high school students acquiring a second language.

Nelson Oral French Filmstrips, Nelson, $30.00. Five filmstrips with accompanying teacher's guides; titles include *Alouette, Au café, Les fêtes, Toronto/Montréal/Québec*.

Titles from a series of French language filmstrips with accompanying audio-tapes, O.I.S.E.:

Les papillons, $30.25. 5-7 ans / *La météo*. $20.35. 10-12 ans / *Bienvenue à Montréal*, $19.50. 14-15 ans / *Chansons et chansonniers*, $32.00. 16-17 ans / *Le temps des fêtes*, $27.50. 10-15 ans. Order from Prentice-Hall.

The Language of Modern Quebec (cassette tape). 30 min. C.B.C. Learning Systems, $8.00. A discussion of the difference between school French and the language of French Canadians.

Three kits from SRA can provide additional reading and writing material. The format in each instance is similar to SRA materials in English. Care should be taken to avoid duplication and needless expenditure.

Laboratoire de lecture, $142.00. Supplementary reading material for grades 4 to 7.

Dynamique d'apprentissage du langage, $130.00. Students can write their own stories based on the illustrations. Teacher's guide, $8.40.

Les jeunes auteurs, $51.00. Teacher's guide, $2.20. Illustrated booklets in which students can write their own stories.

Titles from a series of games, Jeux educatifs, H.M.H.:

Pas une faute avec le puzzle Colino, Trois séries, 7-9 ans, 10-14 ans, chacun, $8.75.

Jeux des familles de mots: *Coffret bleu,* $8.75. 1-5 ans / *Coffret rose,* $8.75. 6-10 ans.

Individual books

8-11 ans

L'aïcule qui venait de Dworitz, Ethel Vineberg (Tundra, 1969), $4.00. The illustrated story of a Jewish family that emigrated to Canada. In English, *Grandmother came from Dworitz.*

Jolly Jean-Pierre/Voyage extraordinaire de Jean-Pierre, Lyn Cook (Burns, 1973), $6.95. Bilingual, illustrated.

Titles from the series Collection Littérature de Jeunesse, Saannes. Illustrated French verse for young readers.

Comptines, $3.50 / *Ouram,* $2.50 / *La poulette grise,* $2.50.

Le petit sapin qui a poussé sur une étoile, Bussures (Saannes, 1974), $3.95.

12-14 ans

Aventure à Montréal, Omer Latour (Dent, 1968), $1.25. A story for junior high students.

Aventure en Gaspésie, Omer Latour and Claudette Robinson (Dent, 1969), $1.30. Junior high.

La photo mystérieuse, Maurice R. Smith and Anne Thompson (Dent, 1969), $1.25. Junior high.

It's Not Always a Game/Un été d'illusions, Russ Hazzard (All about us/Nous autres, 1974), $5.95. Written by students for students; bilingual.

Titles from the series Joie de lire collection, Holt, $1.50 each. Biographies and stories which require approximately two years of reading ability.

Banting / *Pauline Johnson: La fleur des bois* / *Le Père Albert Lacombe* / *Le Seigneur de Saguenay* / *Le mystère de l'Isle-au-Chêne* / *Le loup blanc.*

André et le loup-garou, Mary M. Green (Holt, 1971), $1.35. Suitable for students in third or fourth year of language study.

Cadieux, Mary M. Greene (Holt, 1971), $1.35. For students in third or fourth year of language study.

15-17 ans

Tales sur la pointe des pieds, Gilles Vigneault (Porcépic, 1972), $7.95. Collection of stories with English translation.

Conteurs du Canada et de la France, Carl R. Theodore and Rolland Legault (Gage, 1967), $4.55. Fifteen prose and three poetry selections.

Les belles histoires du Canada et de la France, Carl R. Theodore and Rolland Legault (Gage, 1964), $4.55. Ten prose and three poetry selections.

Fleurs de lis: Anthologie d'écrits du Canada-français, ed. Anthony Mollica, Donna Stefoff and Elizabeth Mollica (Copp, 1973), $3.95. For senior high grades; includes selections by Roger Lemelin, Gilles Vigneault, Yves Thériault, Anne Hébert, Roch Carrier, Alfred des Rochers and Robert Choquette.

Les ensembles, Monique Nemni and Geneviève Quillard (Prentice, 1975), $7.00. Text for senior high grades. Acadian literature from Les Éditions d'Acadie.

Ti-Jean, Melvin Gallant (Acadie, 1973), $3.00. Un recueil de huit contes qui prennent leur origine dans le folklore acadien; illustrations en noir et blanc.

Gabriel et Geneviève, Hector Charbonneau (Acadie, 1974), $4.00. Roman de la mer; ouvrage posthème et inédit du grand historien et écrivain des Îles de la Madeleine.

Charmante Miscou, Louis Haché (Acadie, 1974), $3.00. Recits poetiques de chasse et du peche dans l'Île de Miscou.

Mourir à Scoudouc, H. Chiasson (Acadie, 1974), $3.50. Recueil de poèmes profondement ancrés en terre acadienne.

Paysages en contrabande, Ronald Déprés (Acadie, 1974), $4.00. Choix de poèmes de 1956 à 1974.

Cri de terre, Raymond LeBlanc (Acadie, 1973), $2.00. Partage entre l'angoisse et la violence de vivre, le poète poursuit une recherche effrence de lui-meme et de l'homme acadien.

Saisons antérieures, Léonard Forest (Acadie, 1973), $3.50. Le poète chante sa patrie, cette femme qu'il désire réconquérir afin d'adoucir son sentiment d'exile; avec illustrations en couleur.

Acadie Rock, Guy Arsenault (Acadie, 1973), $2.00. Des poèmes destinés à exorciser le mal de vivre dans le monde moderne et en Acadie; avec illustrations en noir et blanc.

A Sampling of Books by Quebec Writers

Acadie et la mer, Rita Scalabrini (Leméac), $2.50.

Avant la violence, ou la révolution de mai comme préliminaire? Michel Belair and others (Leméac), $1.00.

Bataille du livre au Québec, Pierre de Bellefeuille et Alain Pontaut (Leméac), $2.50.

C'est toujours la même histoire, Claude Jasmin (Leméac), $1.95.

Chocola Cho, Rita Scalabrini (Leméac), $3.50.

Gilles Vignault, Aline Robitaille (Leméac-Hexagone, 1971), $3.75.

Materials for Teachers

Speaking Canadian French, Mark M. Orkin (General, 1970), $5.95. An informed study of the French language as spoken in Quebec.

Practical Handbook of Canadian French/Manuel pratique du français canadien, Sinclair Robinson and Donald Smith (Macmillan, 1973), $3.50. Lists common expressions used in Quebec and gives their Parisian and English equivalents.

Les indices d'utilité du vocabulaire fondamental français, Jean-Guy Savard et Jack Richards (P.U.L.) $4.00 br. La selection du vocabulaire utile à apprentissage d'une langue seconde.

Canadianismes de bon aloi, 2e ed. Maurice Beaulieu et Gaston Dulong (Ed. Officiel, 1975), 75¢ br.

Petit dictionnaire du joual au français, Augustin Turenne (Homme), $2.00 br. Indispensable source book.

Les anglicismes au Québec, Gilles Colpron (Beauchemin, 1970), $7.95. A comprehensive study of the influence of English on the language of French Canada, including vocabulary and structure.

Periodicals

C'est-à-dire: Le compte de linguistique Radio-Canada, Société Radio-Canada, Case Postale 6000, Montreal P.Q. H3C 3A8. Newsletter of Radio-Canada.

Nous journal, All About Us/Nous autres. Quarterly, $1.50. Newsletter for students, bilingual.

Useful Sources of Bilingual and/or French language materials

Information Canada (Now Publishing Centre, Supply and Services Canada).

Les Editions Leméac (LEMAC)

Les Editions HRW

Harvest House

Les Editions d'Acadie

Les Editions Hurtubise-H.M.H.

Les Editions de l'Homme

Les Editions Pédagogia

Les Livres Toundra

Chapter 14

HOME ECONOMICS

Home Economics may well be the subject with the greatest potential for influencing practical aspects of adult life. The fact that this potential is largely unrealized is due only in part to the slender array of available Canadian learning materials. Responsibility rests also with both educators and public expectations. The popular image of Home Economics is often limited to gaining skills with pots and pans or needles and pins. Social customs compound the problem. Old ways die slowly when it comes to recognizing, within and without the school, that the hand rocking the cradle, the fingers threading the bobbin, the knuckles kneading the dough, are not by definition female. Home Economics could be the centre for developing skills of living for every student, regardless of sex, from the late elementary years through high school. Five ingredients are essential in the curriculum if this area of learning is to receive the attention it deserves.

A

Emphasis should be placed on changing life styles and their implications for the developing attitudes and values of the individual. Examination of the proportionate female/male enrollment in Home Economics classes could serve to open for discussion the question of sexist stereotyping. The convenience of time-tabling "home management" in tandem with "wood working" could be weighed along with community opinion regarding expectations for daughters and sons. The best intentions of the school to make equal opportunity a reality may run counter to deep-seated parental convictions. Similarly, study of viewpoints regarding single parent families, monogamous relationships, and zero population growth all call into question long-established values. (N.B. For suitable learning materials refer

to Chapter 8—Counselling.) Day care centres, government involvement in child welfare, remuneration for housewives, reversal of
traditional roles (i.e. father at home/wife pursuing a career) likewise
raise questions that may threaten cherished beliefs.

Providing opportunities for young people to discuss these issues
and arrive at their own conclusions is an urgent necessity. Discus-
sions and decisions can take place within a broad general perspective
as well as within a socio-economic context. Caution must be exercised to ensure that generalizations of middle class origin are not
applied willy-nilly to all individuals and groups. More emphatically,
Home Economics should not convey a *Chatelaine* magazine mentality.
Model homes, like model lives, are a figment of the glossy periodical's imagination rather than a practical possibility for the vast
majority of young learners.

B

Skills required to raise children are such an apparent social need
that it is astonishing that they are left mainly to chance. Any understanding an adolescent may develop probably stems more from
fortuitous circumstances in the home than from anything provided
by the formal school program. Information on nutrition, health,
psychology, and the economics of family living is basic. Study of
comparative child-rearing practices among various societies and cultures would be an enriching experience. The notion conveyed by
many materials that there is one "right" way (i.e. the middle class
way) to raise a family, would be destroyed. Equally important,
students could learn from others. An excursion into the anthropology of Indian and Inuit peoples might create a heightened sensitivity toward those much-abused terms, love, affection, and discipline. Mother/father responsibilities can be studied in the same
manner, with comparisons drawn between rural/urban or rich/poor
families, as cases in point. Becoming aware of socio-economic conditions and how these affect families is only one beneficial by-
product of this approach. The development of a social conscience
should be the overall aim.

C

Technology and the consumer society combine to exact their toll
of the home manager's energies. It is an understatement to suggest
that operating a home requires the versatility of a handyperson and
the mind of a mini-calculator. The electric domicile of the seventies

is just one example of how society has been transformed in little more than a generation. Labour-saving devices have not only influenced living patterns (e.g., leisure pursuits), but, of equal concern, have created a dependency bordering on a false sense of security. Nothing can go wrong. Until, that is, an electrical brown-out cripples a metropolis, or energy sources, heretofore taken for granted, vanish. People must be prepared to cope with these eventualities. Alternatives, particularly in the area of self-reliant skills, must be explored. On a more elementary level, developing abilities in maintenance, repair, adaptation, and recycling constitute survival skills for apartment dwellers and rural citizens alike. Related to these considerations are the implications of the inflated dollar and the subtle-sell of the merchants of easy-credit. Living in debt has become the accepted way of life. Money management courses are essential. (Refer to Chapter 6—Business for suggested materials).

D

Food sciences, or just plain cooking, is as old as the term Domestic Science itself. Sadly, years of practice have not made perfect this aspect of the curriculum. In many instances there appears to be a remorseless pursuit of the ideal bland diet. Juggling calories and portions with the finesse of a chemist, the end products often approximate a laboratory experiment in which the principal elements are alfalfa and gelatin. The unpalatable results are inexcusable, as this is the one aspect of the Home Economics program where distinctive Canadian learning materials are available. Cookbooks of ethnic, cultural and/or regional interest should be quickly substituted for the conventional recipes that can make the individual yearn for the famine and not the feast.

E

The garment and place mat industry need not be threatened by what takes place in many sewing labs. Like the dedicated search for the flawlessly boiled dinner in the kitchen is the devotion to the production of the symetrically precise cushion manufactured from two face cloths and a supply of used panty hose in the fashion and design program. Labelling Home Economics as a frill is not without justification in view of classrooms full of young women simultaneously engaged in the production of dainty aprons, followed by a "girl scout blouse" and culminating with the pièce de resistance— a jumper (from the pages of *Seventeen,* or some other journal of sugar n'spice wholesomeness). In the upside-down real world, where dressing-down equals high fashion, it is not hard to recognize the "denim curtain" which separates the "far-out", yet "in" qualities of youthful fashions from the efforts of typical sewing classes. In fairness to the schools, sources of ideas or learning materials that would provide a Canadian orientation are few in number. (N.B. Refer to Chapter 4—Art for some suggestions.) Items portraying the contributions of Canadian design artists and ethnic or regional developments (from weaving in Pangnirtung to the Winnipeg-Edmonton garment industries) should be available if assimilation into the American "admass" society is to be halted. The resources currently available hardly activate the taste buds, let alone satisfy the appetite.

◆ ◆ ◆ ◆

Cookbooks

The Canadiana Cookbook, Jehane Bénoit (Pagonan, 1970), $7.25.

The Laura Secord Canadian Cook Book, Canadian Home Economics Association, ed. Sally Henry (McClelland, 1966), $4.85.

Classic Canadian Cooking, Elizabeth Baird (James Lorimer, 1974), $8.95. Four hundred and fifty recipes including fiddleheads, maple syrup, smelts, salmon, whitefish, and blueberries.

Canadian Country Preserves and Wines, Blanche P. Garrett (James Lorimer, 1974), $8.95. Recipes using garden produce and wild plants.

Recipes For Healthier Families, Redman (Gage, 1976), $4.95 pa.

Cookbooks of Historical or Unique Interest

Canadian Home Cookbook (Coles', 1970), $3.95.

Traditional Ukrainian Cookery, 5th ed., Savella Stechishin (Trident, 1971), $9.00. Over 650 recipes.

Yukon Cookbook, Leona Kananen (J.J. Douglas, 1975), $3.50 pa.

A French Canadian Cookbook, Donald E. Asselin (Hurtig, 1968), $4.25. Over 300 recipes, illustrated.

Out of Old Nova Scotia Kitchens, Marie Nightingale (Petheric, 1970), $4.25 pa.

The Mennonite Treasury of Recipes (Derksen), $4.50.

The Ann Wilson Cookbook, Ann Wilson (Mitchell, 1967), $7.50. Sixteen hundred recipes originally published in *Western Homes and Living.*

Northern Cook Book, Eleanora Ellis (Information Canada, 1968), $3.50 pa. Recipes from the N.W.T.

Managing the Home

House and Home, Marvin Tameanko (General, 1968), $3.60.

Home Management and Nutrition, Helen Wattie (General, 1967), $3.80.

Food à la Canadienne, Dept. of Agriculture (Information Canada, 1968), $1.50 pa. Bilingual text.

The Right Combination: A Guide to Food and Nutrition, Elizabeth Chant Robertson (Gage, 1975), $7.95.

Poultry: How To Buy: How To Cook, Dept. of Agriculture (Information Canada, 1964), $1.00 pa.

Meat: How To Buy: How To Cook, Dept. of Agriculture (Information Canada, 1968), $1.00 pa.

Freezing Foods, (Information Canada, 1973), 35¢ pa.

Healthful Eating, (Information Canada, 1973), 50¢ pa.

Growing Herbs for the Kitchen, Betty E.M. Jacobs (Gray, 1972), $5.95. Information on herb culture plus cooking guide.

Fashions

Fashions, Barbara Hatcher (General, 1967), $3.75.

Crafts

A Heritage of Canadian Handicrafts, ed. H.G. Green (McClelland, 1967), $8.95.

Families

Families, A. Jean Erwin (General, 1967), $3.75.

Historical Interpretations of Domestic Life

God Bless Our Home: Domestic Life in 19th Century Canada, Una Abrahamson (Burns, 1966), $9.50. Recipes, home remedies, child raising, games, songs, pastimes of the 1800s.

At Home In Upper Canada, Jeanne Minhinnick (Clarke, Irwin, 1970), $22.50. Life styles of early pioneers.

The Food Services Industry

Where to Eat in Canada, Anne Hardy (Oberon), $3.50. An annual guide to the best places to eat.

The Gourmet's Canada, Sandra Gotlieb (New, 1972), $8.95. A guide to eating establishments.

Textbook Series

Home Economics I and *Home Economics II,* Yvonne M. Brand (Dent, 1968, 1970), $2.55 and $2.65.

Films

Films on cooking, sewing and nursing are available from Moreland-Latchford: 16mm, col, English or French, from $140.00 to $205.00 or rental, 3 days $16.95.

Periodicals

Chatelaine, MacLean-Hunter. 12 issues annually, $6.00.

For Teachers

Play for Preschoolers, (Information Canada, 1971), 50¢ pa.

Chapter 15

INDIAN – INUIT – MÉTIS

Four quotations can be used as examples of the kind of bias in learning materials that can influence students against native people.

The clapboards on the national shrine to novelist Lucy Maud Montgomery at Cavendish, P.E.I. may rattle ever so slightly at the mention of her particular assessment of Indians and Métis.

> There is no worse enemy in all the world than a half-breed. Your true Indian is bad enough, but his diluted descendant is ten times worse.
>
> L.M. Montgomery, *Further Chronicles of Avonlea* (Toronto: Ryerson, 1920, p. 288)

This should not be interpreted as an attempt at a hatchet-job on the virginal image of *Anne of Green Gables.* But Montgomery's choice of expression does illustrate that children's literature can be the vehicle for indoctrinating and/or reinforcing bigotry in the minds of even the youngest readers.

If Montgomery ranks with the most esteemed children's novelists, Arthur Lower occupies a position of similar stature among historians. His book, *Canada: An Outline History* is one of the most popular items of its kind. An examination of the index will reveal an omission common to many survey-type textbooks. The Inuit are ignored. As for Indian peoples in general, and his interpretation of events surrounding the life of Louis Riel specifically, Lower's views are not unique:

> A Mounted Police force was ambushed and attacks on outlying white settlements took place, but as most of these raids were committed by roving bands of savage Indians, the English half-breeds and many Métis were reluctant to take part in what looked more and more like an Indian uprising;
>
> J.A. Lower, *Canada: An Outline History* (Toronto: Ryerson, 1966, p. 135)

The facility with which words such as "ambushed", "raids", "savage", "half-breeds" and "uprising" are worked into a simple forty-nine word sentence is an historigraphical skill not to be dismissed lightly.

The marriage of historical distortion with the well-turned but evasive government phrase, compounds the problem of finding accurate reference materials. In a publication issued under the authority of the Minister of Industry, Trade and Commerce, the sub-section devoted to the Inuit concludes with these interesting statements:

> The future of the Canadian Inuit is one which has caused some concern. In the development of the Canadian North it is of highest importance to the government.
>
> *Canada 1974: The Handbook of Present Conditions and Recent Progress* (Ottawa: Information Canada, 1974, p. 45)

What does the phrase "some concern" imply? Would the facts of Inuit existence such as a high infant mortality rate, low life expectancy, and the absence of a wage-earning economy be implicit in this comment? Similarly, one should decipher with trepidation those innocuous words, "highest importance to the government." Can these words be literally translated as meaning a burgeoning, benevolent bureaucracy will forever look after its people? Or, is there, too, the suggestion that hereditary territorial rights will be defended in the face of the ceaseless exploitation of northern resources? A valiant effort is needed on the part of teachers and students alike if government information services are to be prevented from lulling one and all into an uneasy sleep.

An item in the McGraw-Hill, Ryerson *Issues for the Seventies* series entitled *Canada's Indians* provides an example of perhaps the most serious problem in native studies. The word "culture" is commonly grossly misunderstood. An excerpt quoted from a federal government publication, *Discussion Handbook for the Indian People,* makes the point.

> The Indian people have made a great contribution to Canadian culture. They should have the opportunity to preserve Indian arts, crafts, handiwork and legends.
>
> N. Sheffe, ed., *Canada's Indians* (Toronto: McGraw, 1970, p. 19)

Culture is more than material products like beadwork, and more than stories and mythology. Learning about Indian/Inuit handicrafts will not provide a student with anything like a complete

understanding of the people's attitudes towards their environment,
their kinship relationships, or their concept of the supernatural.
When culture is defined as a finite collection of objects, a particularly
erroneous attitude can develop. Learning the Métis culture supposedly
can be handled with the same dispatch as mastering the birthdates of
the several prime ministers. Once certain details have been memorized,
Métis peoples have been "covered" (synonomous with "finished")
never to be heard from again. Ignoring the dynamic, evolutionary
character of any culture is a dangerous practice.

Throughout these pages stress has been placed on integrating the
study of cultural attributes with every aspect of the curriculum.
Nowhere is this emphasis more important than with the Indians,
Inuit and Métis. The reason is clear. Following the established
pattern of historians, schools have tended to treat native peoples
as but a short, introductory chapter in an European-dominated
story. With the growing supply of learning materials, many of which
have been authored, illustrated, and recorded by native peoples,
there is now the possibility of both extending the coverage throughout several grade levels and incorporating native studies in most
subject areas: art, history, literature, music, science, and technology
among them. In the lists that follow, categories have been established
to ease the selection of appropriate items for a variety of curriculum
possibilities.

◆ ◆ ◆ ◆

Language

A Bibliography of the Athapaskan Languages, Richard T. Parr
(National Museum, 1974), $3.50.

Meet Cree: A Practical Guide to the Cree Language, Christopher
H. Wolfart and Janet F. Carroll (Univ. of Alberta, 1973), $4.00
pa. A concise discussion of the Cree language based on linguistic
research.

Dictionnaire Montagnais-français, Antoine Silvy (P.U.Q.), $5.00.

A Thousand Words of Mohawk, Gunther Michelson (National
Museum, 1973), $2.00. Brief introduction to Mohawk grammar
followed by a root list from Mohawk to English and English to
Mohawk.

Write On: A Sourcebook for Teachers of Indian Languages and Writing Systems for Indian Students, Rathjen (Coyoti Prints). $5.00 pa. Emphasis is on the Chilcotin linguistic group.

Moose Factory Cree, Daisy Turner (Highway Book Shop, 1974), $2.00 pa. An illustrated introduction to Cree syllabics.

Some Aspects of the Grammar of the Eskimo Dialects of Cumberland Peninsula and North Baffin Island, Kenn Harper (National Museum, 1974), $1.25 pa.

Inuktituorutit: Grammaire purement Eskimaude, Lucien Schneider (Ed. Officiel), $2.00 br. Premier cycle en 40 leçons.

Dictionnaire des infixes de l'eskimau de l'Ungava, Lucien Schneider (Ed. Officiel), $2.00 br.

Esquimaux, peuple du Québec, (Ed. Officiel), $1.00 br. Catalogue de l'exposition d'art et d'objets d'usage courant des Esquimaux du Nouveau-Québec.

Eskimos and Indians and the English Language, (cassette tape). 30 min, C.B.C. Learning Systems, $8.00. The pros and cons of teaching English to Indian and Inuit children are discussed.

Sociology

Reservations are for Indians, Heather Robertson (James Lorimer, 1970), $3.95 pa. A thought-provoking, often disturbing account of life as it is for many Indian peoples.

Notice: This is an Indian Reserve, ed. Sheila and Kent Gooderham (Griffin, 1972), $4.50 pa. Black and white photographs plus a minimum of text portray aspects of reserve life.

Indians in Transition, Gerald Walsh (McClelland, 1971), $2.70 pa. The changes in lifestyles of native peoples.

I Once Knew an Indian Woman, Ebbitt Cutler (Tundra, 1974), $3.95. Winner of the first prize in the 1967 Centennial Literary Awards, story of an Indian woman who lived according to her own code of values in the midst of French and English society in the 1930s.

Indians: The Urban Dilemma, Edgar J. Dosman (McClelland, 1972), $3.95 pa.

Indians without Tipis, Verna J. Kirkness and D. Bruce Sealey (Book Society, 1974), $6.95. A compendium of views on Indian peoples.

Totem, Tipi and Tumpline, Olive M. Fisher and Clara L. Tyner (Dent, 1955), $4.95 pa. Life, work, and mythology are portrayed in story and drama.

The Only Good Indian, ed. Waubegeshig (New, 1970), $1.75 pa. A collection of essays by native writers.

Indian Summer, (Information Canada, 1972), 75¢ pa. Vivid illustrations combine with a minimum of text to portray aspects of Indian life; French ed., *En été chez les indiens.*

Success and Failure: Indians in Urban Society, W.T. Stanbury (U.B.C. Press, 1975), $17.95. A statistical study of status Indian peoples living off the reserves in B.C.

Visitors who Never Left: The Origin of the People of Damelahamid, ed. and tr. Kenneth Harris (U.B.C. Press, 1975), $4.95. Chief K.B. Harris provides an account of the Gitshian (Gitskan) Indian people of British Columbia.

Sea and Cedar: How the North West Coast Indians Lived, Lois McConkey (J.J. Douglas, 1974), $5.95. An illustrated historical account for elementary classes.

Potlatch, George Clutesi (Gray, 1973), $2.95 pa. An insight into the rites and drama of the last great potlatch of the B.C. Indian peoples.

The Gitskan Potlatch, John W. Adams (Holt, 1973), $3.25.

Salish Indian Mental Health and Cultural Change, Wolfgang G. Jilek (Holt, 1974), $3.50.

Opasquiak: The Pas Indian Reserve, Leonard Stanley Wilson (Holt, 1973), $1.50.

The Northern Ojibway and the Fur Trade, Charles A. Bishop (Holt, 1974), $4.95.

Les Iroquois, Bernard Assiniwi (Leméac), $2.25 br. La structure sociale des Iroquois; la culture materielle, les jeux, les costumes et une brève description de l'Iroquois contemporain.

Makwa: Le petit Algonquin, Bernard Assiniwi (Leméac), $2.25 br. La vie d'un petit Algonquin qui vit selon les anciennes coutumes des Algonquins de l'est du Canada.

Ethnics and Indians: Social Relations in a Northwestern Ontario Town, David H. Stymeist (Peter Martin, 1975), $3.95 pa.

The People's Land, Hugh Brody (Penguin, 1975), $2.95 pa. A valuable examination of Inuit-white relationships and concerns in the eastern Arctic.

An Arctic Settlement: Pangnirtung, Kenneth Dudley (Ginn, 1971), package of 5, $5.00.

Then and Now in Frobisher Bay, T.W. Martin (Gage, 1969), 96¢ each; package of 10 with teacher's guide, $9.00; multi-media kit, $42.00.

In the Manner of a Man (cassette tape). 30 min, C.B.C. Learning Systems, set of 3, $8.00 each. People of the Mackenzie delta discuss the impact of change on their lives.

Canada's Indians (cassette tape). 60 min, C.B.C. Learning Systems, $15.00. Discussion on the place of the Indian in society, including interviews with noted Indian spokesmen Harold Cardinal and Wilfred Pelletier.

Transition (cassette tape). 60 min, C.B.C. Learning Systems, $15.00. Describes the cultural shift made by Inuit children when they attend schools of the white people.

The Way of the People (cassette tape). 60 min, C.B.C. Learning Systems, $15.00. Music, poetry and conversation which express aspects of Indian culture as experienced by a young white woman who lived for a year in northern Manitoba.

On my Way to School (cassette tape). 60 min, C.B.C. Learning Systems, $15.00. Describes racial discrimination involving a 17-year-old Indian girl.

A Conversation with Duke Redbird (cassette tape). 60 min, C.B.C. Learning Systems, $15.00. The Indian poet, Duke Redbird discusses problems confronting his people.

Childhood on an Indian Reservation (cassette tape). 30 min, C.B.C. Learning Systems, $8.00. Interviews with Indian peoples in which they discuss their early childhood experiences.

Moccasin Flats (film). 28 min, 16mm, col, International Tele-Film Enterprises, $360.00 or rental $30.00 per day. Portrays life in a Cree village.

Anthropology

The series Royal Ontario Museum Booklets on the Indians and Eskimos of Canada, Royal Ontario Museum, 50¢ each for 6 booklets.

Cultural Ecology: Readings on the Canadian Indians and Eskimos, ed. Bruce Cox (McClelland, 1973), $4.95.

Eskimo of the Canadian Arctic, Victor Valentine and Frank G. Vallée (McClelland, 1969), $2.50 pa.

The Indians of Canada, Diamond Jenness (Information Canada, 1972), $9.75. The most comprehensive book available.

Indian Tribes of Canada, Eileen Jenness (McGraw, 1966), $2.25 pa. A concise reference book.

People of Light and Dark, Maja Van Steensal (Information Canada, 1966), $3.00 pa. A collection of informative papers on Northern peoples.

Makkovik: Eskimos and Settlers in a Labrador Community,
Samuel Ben-Dor (Social and Economic Research, Memorial University, 1966), $2.50 pa. Reprint of a university conducted community study.

Kabloona and Eskimo, Frank G. Vallée (Canadian Research
Centre for Anthropology, University of Ottawa, 1967), $5.95 pa.

Arctic Townsmen, John and Irma Honigman (Canadian Research
Centre for Anthropology, University of Ottawa, 1970), $6.95 pa.

They Shared to Survive: The Native Peoples of Canada, Selwyn
Dewdney (Macmillan, 1975), $6.95 pa.

Never in Anger, Briggs (Book Centre, 1970), $3.50 pa. Definitive
study of life among the Inuit of the central Arctic.

*Hunters in the Barrens: The Naskapi on the edge of the White
Man's World,* George Hendriksen (Social and Economic Research,
Memorial University, 1973), $4.00 pa. A scholarly study of contrast and conflict among Naskapi peoples of Labrador.

Our People: Indians of the Plains, Lee Updike (Western Producer,
1973), $1.00 pa. Hand-lettered text with half-page illustrations
that create an image of life on the plains.

Indians of the Plains, A. Joan Hall and others (Fitzhenry and
Whiteside, 1972), $1.92 pa. Teacher's guide, 80¢. Filmstrip,
$5.95.

Eskimo: Journey through Time, Alan C. Bennett and others
(Fitzhenry and Whiteside, 1972), $1.92 pa. Teacher's guide, 82¢.
Filmstrip I, $5.95. Filmstrip II, $5.95.

Métis of the Mackenzie District, R. Slobodin (Canadian Research
Centre for Anthropology, University of Ottawa, 1966), $4.95 pa.

The Dogrib Handgame, June Helm and Nancy Lurie (National
Museum, 1966), $2.50 pa.

Food

Traditional Indian Recipes, Juliette Iserhof and others (Highway
Book Shop, 1971), $1.50 pa. A collection of food and medicinal
recipes of Cree people, written in Cree and English.

Art
Four pocket guides from J.J. Douglas, $1.50 each pa.

*The Totem Poles in Stanley Park / Kwakiutl House and the
Totem Poles / Haida Totems in Wood and Argillite / The Totem
Poles of B.C.*

Titles from the series People of Native Ancestry, Fitzhenry and

Whiteside. Artistic expression of selected Indian peoples together with glimpses of their lives today; elementary level; $2.95 each pa.

Bark, Corn and Leather: Iroquois Crafts / Charcoal, Wood and Road: Ojibway Crafts / Clay, Beads and Dye: Cree Crafts / Fort Albany Reserve, Northern Ontario / St. Regis Reserve, St. Lawrence River Valley.

Tailfeathers: Indian Artist, Hugh A. Dempsey (Glenbow, 1970), $2.00 pa. Biography of Indian Artist Gerald Tailfeathers.

People from Our Side: An Inuit Record of Seekooseelak, The Land of the People of Cape Dorset, Peter Pitseolak with Dorothy Eber (Hurtig, 1975), $8.95 pa. Inuit artist Peter Pitseolak has recorded in photographs and text a history of his people.

Totem Poles (film strip). Scholar's Choice, $8.95.

Please refer to Chapter 4, Art, for further listings.

Historical Reference

The Canadian Indian, E. Palmer Patterson (Collier-Macmillan, 1971), $6.95. Historical survey.

The Eskimos of Canada, Anne H. Power (Collier-Macmillan, 1971), $1.40 pa.

The Changing People, Palmer Patterson (Collier-Macmillan, 1971), $1.40 pa. Indian peoples.

A History of the Original Peoples of Northern Canada, Keith J. Crowe (McGill-Queen's, 1974), $4.00 pa. The definitive work on Indian, Inuit and Métis people of the North.

As Long as This Land Shall Last, René Fumoleau (McClelland, 1975), $5.95 pa. A thorough examination of two important treaties (number 8 and 11) signed with Northern Indian peoples.

Titles from a series about native people from Ginn, set of 5, $5.50:

Nomads of the Shield / The Ojibway Indians / Seafaring Warriors of the West / The Nootka Indians / Hunters of the Plains / Assiniboine Indians / Treaties and Promises.

White Sioux, Iris Allen (Gray, 1969), $5.95. A history of the era of Chief Sitting Bull and Major Walsh of the Royal North West Mounted Police.

Across the Medicine Line, C. Frank Turner (McClelland, 1973), $8.95. Recounts the events involving Chief Sitting Bull and Major Walsh.

Voices of the Plains Cree, Edward Ahenakew (McClelland, 1973),

$7.95. Life of the Plains Cree people recorded by an Indian author.

Indians of the Prairies, Maria Campbell (J.J. Douglas, 1975), $5.95. Indian artist Shannon Twofeathers has illustrated this account of early prairie Indian life by a Métis woman; elementary level.

The Helping Hand, ed. Francis C. Hardwick (Tantalus, 1972), $2.50 pa. Documents and graphics on the debt of explorers Mackenzie and Fraser to the Indian people.

When Strangers Meet, Francis C. Hardwick (Tantalus, 1973), $2.50 pa. Documents and graphics relating to the initial contact between Indian and European peoples in B.C.

Indian Names for Alberta Communities, Hugh A. Dempsey (Glenbow, 1969), 75¢ pa.

Nestum Asa, Kent Gooderham (Griffin, 1970), $1.50 pa. Kit, $5.00.

The Canadian Indian Nations (cassette tape). 30 min, C.B.C. Learning Systems, $8.00. Discussion of the past and present.

Indians of Canada (kit). Griffin, $3.70.

Day of the Treaties (kit). Griffin, $6.95.

Political — Legal

Native Rights in Canada, 2nd ed., eds. Peter A. Cumming and Neil H. Mickenburg (General, 1972), $7.95 pa. A source book on the rights and claims of Indian, Inuit and Métis peoples.

Canada's Indians, Norman Sheffe (McGraw, 1970), $2.10 pa. Part of the Issues for the Seventies series.

Canadian Indians and the Law: Selected Documents, 1663-1972, Derek G. Smith (McClelland, 1975), $4.95 pa.

The White Man's Laws, Christine Daniels and Ron Christiansen (Hurtig, 1975), $3.95 pa. An interpretation of the white man's legal system and its applications to the lives of Indian and Métis citizens.

This Land Is Not for Sale: Canada's Original People and Their Land, a Saga of Neglect, Exploitation and Conflict, McCullum and McCullum (Anglican Book Centre, 1976), $3.95 pa. The effects of massive industrial developments on the lives of native peoples in the Yukon, N.W.T., northern Manitoba, B.C., and James Bay.

Strangers Devour the Land: The Cree Hunters of the James Bay Area versus Premier Bourassa and the James Bay Development Corporation, Boyce Richardson (Macmillan, 1976), $13.95.

Ruffled Feathers: Indians in Canadian Society, William I.C. Wuttunee (Bell, 1971), $2.50. A Calgary lawyer and Indian spokesman take a critical view of the native rights movement in Canada.

The Unjust Society, Harold Cardinal (Hurtig, 1969), $2.75 pa. An articulate portrayal of the desires of Indian peoples by Alberta Indian leader, Harold Cardinal.

Prison of Grass: Canada from the Native Point of View, Howard Adams (New, 1975), $10.95. A volume in the Trent University Native series.

The Fourth World, George Manuel (Collier-Macmillan, 1974), $7.95. President of the National Indian Brotherhood, George Manuel explores the status of native peoples in Canada within the perspective of the 'fourth world'.

Indians and Métis (cassette tape). 60 min, C.B.C. Learning Systems, $15.00. Discussions on establishing a new relationship with the federal government by native peoples.

Biographical

Strange Empire: Louis Riel and the Métis People, Joseph Howard (James Lorimer, 1974), $5.95 pa.

Louis Riel: The Rebel and the Hero, Hartwell Bowsfield (O.U.P., 1971), $3.50.

La révolte des Métis Louis Riel, héros ou rebelle, G.C. de Salagnac (H.M.H.), $4.50.

The Man who had to Hang, E.B. Osler (Longman, 1966), $5.00.

Louis Riel, Stanley Pearl and others (Maclean-Hunter), package of 6, $4.80.

The Life of Louis Riel, Peter Charlebois (N.C. Press, 1975), $7.95 pa.

Gabriel Dumont, George Woodcock (Hurtig, 1975), $8.95. A superb biography of the leader of the Saskatchewan Métis peoples in the 1870s.

Crowfoot: Chief of the Blackfeet, Hugh A. Dempsey (Hurtig, 1972), $8.95.

Poundmaker, Norma Sluman (McGraw, 1967), $5.95.

Jerry Potts, Plainsman, Hugh A. Dempsey (Glenbow, 1966), 75¢ pa. Biography of a noted Métis guide in the early years of Alberta history.

Sitting Bull: The Years in Canada, J.W. Grant MacEwan (Hurtig, 1973), $8.95.

Tatanga Mani: Walking Buffalo of the Stonies, J.W. Grant Mac-
Ewan (Hurtig, 1969), $3.95 pa.

Pauline Johnson: Her Life and Work, Marcus Van Steen (Musson,
1965), $6.45.

Autobiographies and Biographies by Native Writers

First Among the Hurons, Max Gros-Louis (Harvest, 1974), $3.50
pa. Max Gros-Louis, chief of the Huron people at Loretteville,
P.Q.

An Indian Remembers, Tom Boulanger (Peguis, 1971), $2.00 pa.
Biography of a man who spent his life as a hunter, trapper, and
fisherman in northern Manitoba.

Chief Peguis and his Descendants, Albert Edward Thompson
(Peguis, 1973), $2.00 pa. Biography of a Saulteaux chief of the
Netley Creek area of Manitoba written by his great-great grandson.

Recollections of an Assiniboine Chief, Dan Kennedy (McClelland,
1972), $7.95. Autobiography of Chief Dan Kennedy.

My Heart Soars, Dan George (Hancock, 1974), $9.95. Poetry and
recollections of Chief Dan George.

Chiefly Indian, Henry Pennier (Greydonald, 1972), $2.95. A
Métis logger from B.C. recounts his life experiences.

Trapping is my Life, John Tetso (Peter Martin, 1970), $4.95.
Autobiography of a former resident of the Fort Simpson area of
the N.W.T.

Half-Breed, Maria Campbell (McClelland, 1973), $5.95. Auto-
biography of a Métis woman.

I, Nuligak, ed Maurice Metayer (Simon and Schuster, 1971),
$1.25 pa. Autobiography of a former resident of the Arctic coast.

Geniesh: An Indian Girlhood, Jane Willis (New, 1973), $8.50.
Autobiography of a Cree resident of the James Bay area.

Guests Never Leave Hungry: The Autobiography of James Sewid,
a Kwakiutl Indian, ed. James Spradley (McGill-Queen's, 1972),
$3.95 pa.

No Foreign Land: The Biography of a North American Indian,
Wilfred Pelletier and Ted Poole (McClelland, 1973), $3.95 pa.

Buffalo Days and Nights, Peter Erasmus (McClelland, 1975),
$12.50. Biography of a Métis guide whose experiences spanned
the latter portion of the 19th and early years of the 20th centuries
in western Canada.

To Louis from Your Sister Who Loves You—Sara Riel, ed. Mary

Jordan (Griffin, 1974), $8.95. Letters written to Louis Riel by his sister.

Stories, Poetry and Legends by Native Writers

Son of Raven, Son of Deer, George Clutesi (Gray, 1967), $4.75. Stories of the Tse-Shaht Indian people of B.C.

Tales from the Long House, B.C. Indian Arts Society (Gray), $4.95. Stories written by Indian children of Vancouver Island and Kingcome Inlet, B.C.

Wild Drums, Alex Grisdale (Peguis, 1972), $2.50 pa. Fourteen legends of Plains Indian peoples; illustrations by Chipewyan artist Jim Ellis.

Legends of Vancouver, E. Pauline Johnson (McClelland, 1961) $5.95. A classic first published in 1911.

Harpoon of the Hunter, Markoosie (McGill-Queen's, 1974), $4.95. Novel by a resident of Resolute Bay, N.W.T.

Here are the News, Edith Josie (Clarke, Irwin, 1966), $5.00. Newspaper correspondent Edith Josie of Old Crow, Yukon, gives her views of events as these affect people in her community.

Eskimo Stories, Arima, Nungak (Information Canada, 1970), $3.00.

I am an Indian, ed. Kent Gooderham (Dent, 1969), $2.50 pa. An anthology of Indian writing.

Tales from the Igloo, ed. Maurice Metayer (Hurtig, 1972), $4.95. Twenty-two legends of the Copper Eskimo people with illustrations by Inuit artist Agnes Nanogak.

Red Earth: Tales of the Micmacs, Robertson (Nova Scotia Museum), $2.00 pa.

Tales of the Mohawks, Alma Greene (Dent, 1975), $6.95. Twentieth century stories from the Six Nations Reserve, illustrations by Indian artist G. Miller.

There is my People Sleeping, 2nd ed., Sarain Stump (Gray, 1974), $2.95 pa. Poetry and drawings by an Alberta Indian artist.

Tales from the Cree, George W. Bauer (Highway Book Shop, 1973), $2.00 pa. Legends from the Fort George area in Ontario, translated from Cree.

Why the Beaver has a Broad Tail, Mary Lou Fox (Highway Book Shop, 1974), $1.00 pa. Legend from Manitoulin Island, Ont. Written in Ojibwe and English.

Shadows, Tagoona (Oberon, 1975), $17.50. Stories and illustrations by Inuit writer and artist Armand Tagoona of Baker Lake, N.W.T.

Anthologies of Stories and Legends

Indian Legends of Canada, Ella E. Clark (McClelland, 1960), $5.65.

Indian Legends of Canada, Claude Melançon (Gage, 1974), $6.05 pa.

Thirty Indian Legends of Canada, Margaret Beminster (J.J. Douglas, 1973), $7.95.

The Corn Goddess and other Tales, National Museum and Diamond Jenness (Information Canda, 1966), $2.62 pa.

Glooscap and His Magic; Legends of the Wabanaki, Kay Hill (McClelland, 1963), $5.50.

More Glooscap Stories: Legends of the Wabanaki Indians, Kay Hill (McClelland, 1970), $5.30.

The Day Tuk became a Hunter and Other Eskimo Stories, Ronald Melzack (McClelland, 1967), $5.30.

Raven, Creator of the World, Ronald Melzack (McClelland, 1970), $5.30.

Elik, Herbert T. Schwarz (McClelland, 1970), $5.95. Stories from the Mackenzie Delta area.

Windigo and Other Tales of the Ojibway, Herbert T. Schwarz (McClelland, 1969), $5.95. Illustrated by Indian artist Norval Morriseau.

What They Used to Tell about: Indian Legends from Labrador, ed. Peter Desbarats (McClelland, 1969), $7.95.

The Girl who Married the Bear: A Masterpiece of Indian Oral Tradition, Catharine McClennan (National Museum, 1970), $2.75. A Yukon legend written in 7 versions.

Poetry

Beyond the High Hills, ed. Knud V. Rasmussen (Nelson, Foster, 1961), $4.75. Poetry of Baffin Island.

Songs of the Dream People, James Houston (Longman, 1972), $5.95.

Flint and Feather, E. Pauline Johnson (General, 1972), $4.95.

Beothuk Poems, Sid Stephen (Oberon, 1976), $2.50 pa. Poems about the fate of the original inhabitants of Newfoundland; illustrations by Shawnadithit, the last surviving Beothuk Indian.

Drama Please refer to Chapter 9 — Drama.

Music

Drum Dance: Legends, Ceremonies, Dances and Songs of the Eskimo, C. Hoffman (Gage, 1974), $4.95 pa.

Sepass Tales, Eloise Street (Mitchell, 1974), $4.95. The songs of the Chilliwack Indian peoples as recorded by the author, with illustrations by Indian artist-writer, George Clutesi.

Charlie Panigoniak (records). 45 r.p.m., C.B.C. Northern Service, $2.00 for two records. Original songs composed and sung in the Inuit language by this resident of Eskimo Point, N.W.T.

Indian Stories for Beginning Readers

Titles from the series about Nanabush, Ginn, set of 10, $6.25. Illustrations by Indian artist Daphne Beavon "Odjig".

Nanabush and the Dancing Duck / Nanabush and the Rabbit / Nanabush Loses his Eyeballs / Nanabush and Mandomin / Nanabush and the Chipmunk / Nanabush Punishes the Raccoon / Nanabush and the Spirit of Thunder / Nanabush and the Wild Rosebushes / Nanabush and the Spirit of Winter / Nanabush and the Wild Geese.

Normie's Goose Hunt and *Normie's Moose Hunt,* V. Crowell (Copp, 1968), $1.05 each, pa. Text and illustrations for primary reader.

Titles by James Houston for young readers about Inuit and Indians, Longman:

Eagle Mask, 1966, $3.95 / *Ghost Paddle,* 1972, $4.85 / *Tikta'liktak,* 1965, $3.90 / *Kiviok's Magic Journey,* 1973, $5.95 / *Akavak,* 1968, $3.95 / *The White Archer,* 1967, $4.30 / *Wolf Run,* 1971, $4.25.

Watch for The People of Native Ancestry series (PONA), a multi-media programme of nine books, four audio-filmstrips and a set of study cards for primary students. Write: Canadian Association in Support of Native Peoples for purchasing information.

Stories and Novels for Older Readers

Once More Upon a Totem, Christie Harris (McClelland, 1973), $5.65.

Riverrun, Peter Such (Clarke, Irwin, 1973), $5.95. Story of the last survivors of the Beothuk Indian peoples of Newfoundland.

The Downfall of Temlaham, 2nd ed. Marius Barbeau (Hurtig, 1973), $9.95. A classic of western Canadian folklore.

I Heard the Owl Call My Name, Margaret Craven (Clarke, Irwin,

1967), $1.00 pa. An outstanding novel of the involvement of a young priest in the lives of a group of B.C. Indian peoples.

Ashini, Yves Thériault (Harvest, 1972), $2.50. A fictionalized autobiography of a Montagnais Indian hunter.

Agouhanna, Claude Aubrey (General, 1973), 95¢ pa. A novel based on the experiences of a young Iroquois Indian.

Ayorama, Raymond de Coccola and Paul King, (General, 1973), $1.95 pa. A novel set in the Arctic.

White Dawn, James Houston (Longman, 1971), $8.95. An Inuit saga, now a feature motion picture.

L'aube blanche, James Houston (H.M.H.), $6.95.

Two legends for young readers illustrated by Elizabeth Cleaver and written by William Toye, Oxford:

> *The Mountain Goats of Temlaham,* 1969, $3.95.
>
> *How Summer Came to Canada,* 1969, $3.95.

Pictorial

People of the Seal (prints). Gunn, 16½" x 21¼", col, E.B., set of 10, $19.90. Portrays the traditional ways of life among the Netsilik Inuit peoples of Pelly Bay, N.W.T.

The Crowfoot Poster (poster). 18" x 24", b&w, photograph of Chief Crowfoot, Hurtig, $1.95.

Series of posters, col, Musson, $3.00 each:

> *Naskapi Wall Chart / Musical Instruments of Indian Peoples / Cree Wall Chart / Assiniboine Wall Chart / Toys and Games.*

Seasons of the Eskimo, Fred Bruemmer (McClelland, 1971), $19.95. The vanishing lifestyles of Inuit peoples captured in photography and text.

Reprints

Titles from the Coles Canadiana Collection:

> *Treaties of Canada with the Indians,* Alexander Morris (Coles, 1971), $4.95. First published 1880.
>
> *The Central Eskimo,* Franz Boas (Coles, 1974), $3.35. First published 1888.

Multi-Media Kits

Manowan (kit), Harry Smith, $75.00. Includes history booklet, 16 b&w photographs, 4 toys, maps. Specify language, English,

Cree, or French. Also includes five sound filmstrips:

> *History of Manowan* Part 1 / *History of Manowan* Part 2 /
> *Canoe* / *Moose Call* / *Snow Shoes*;
> two slide sets: *Jeremie Quitish at Home* / *Children at play*;
> and two wall charts: *Children's Winter in Manowan (Making Skis)* / *Toys from Manowan.*

Tawow (kit). Book Society, $150.00. Includes study and photo cards, cassette tapes, filmstrip, resource book, quiz, teacher's handbook.

Tales from the Treetops (filmstrip). col, sound, English or French, Cinemedia, set of 4, $59.00. Indian legends with narration by Chief Dan George.

Legends of the Micmac (filmstrip). col, sound, Cinemedia, set of 4, $59.00. Legends as performed by puppets with an explanation of the puppetry provided by the Mermaid Theatre, Nova Scotia.

The Arctic Through Eskimo Eyes (filmstrip). col, sound, Cinemedia, set of 4, $59.00. Features music, drawings, and writings of Cape Dorset Eskimo peoples.

The Indian Studies File (kit). O.I.S.E., $300.00. Over 200 items based on the culture of the Blackfoot peoples of southern Alberta; includes copies of treaties, autobiographies, recorded ballads, artifact photo albums, slide sets, films, filmstrips, maps.

Newspapers and Periodicals

Canadian Association in Support of Native Peoples Bulletin, $10.00 annual membership fee.

Inuttitut, Information Canada. English, Inuit, and French languages are used in this government periodical about Inuit peoples.

The Indian News, Information Canada. Government newsletter.

Native Press, N.W.T. Indian Brotherhood, $8.00. Best item available for keeping informed about developments affecting Northern native peoples.

The Kainai News, Box 808, Cardston, Alberta, $8.00. One of the best Indian newspapers available.

Indian Record, 1301 Wellington Crescent, Winnipeg R3N 0A9. Newsletter of the Oblate Fathers.

Eskimo, Eskimo Museum, Churchill, Manitoba. Journal about Inuit life.

Native People, 11427 Jasper Avenue, Edmonton Alberta. Newspaper.

Micmac News, Box 961, Sydney, Nova Scotia, $3.00. Monthly newspaper.

Saskatchewan Indian, 1114 Central Avenue, Prince Albert, Sask., $5.00. Periodical.

Nesika, 2140 West 12th Avenue, Vancouver, B.C., $5.00. Newspaper.

For Teachers

Indian Control of Indian Education, (National Indian Brotherhood, 1973), $2.00 pa. The definitive policy statement.

The Shocking Truth about Indians in Textbooks: Textbook Evaluation (Manitoba Indian Brotherhood).

Defeathering the Indian: A Handbook on Native Studies, Emma LaRoque (Book Society, 1975), $2.95 pa.

About Indians: A Listing of Books, (Information Canada). Over 600 books about North American Indian peoples have been annotated by Indian university students.

A Canadian Indian Bibliography: 1960-1970, Tom Abler (U.T.P., 1974), $35.00.

Native Writers and Artists of Canada, Paul Robinson (Atlantic Institute of Education), $1.00 pa. Fifty-three Indian, Inuit, and Métis authors and artists are the subject of attention.

Indians of British Columbia School Package: Book List and Teacher's Guide, Boston (Educational Research Institute of British Columbia. An annotated bibliography on British Columbia and Canadian native peoples

Useful Addresses

Canadian Association in Support of Native Peoples,
Library and Information Centre,
277 Victoria Street, Toronto, M5V 1W2

Inuit Tapirisat of Canada,
222 Somerset St. W.,
Ottawa, K2P 2G3 (National Inuit Brotherhood)

National Indian Brotherhood,
Suite 1610, Varette Bldg.,
130 Albert Street,
Ottawa, K1P 5G4

Department of Indian and Northern Affairs,
Centennial Towers,
400 Laurier Ave. W.,
Ottawa.

National Museums of Canada, Information and Education Division,
Victoria Memorial Building
McLeod and Metcalfe Street
Ottawa (Write for information re sample artifacts, films, etc.)

Peoples Library
Manitoba Indian Brotherhood
600-191 Lombard Ave.
Winnipeg, Man., R3B 0X1

Woodland Indian Cultural Centre,
P.O. Box 1506,
Brantford, Ont.

Programme Development Division,
Department of Education,
Government of the N.W.T.
Yellowknife, N.W.T. X0E 1H0

Information Services Co-ordinator,
Native Council of Canada,
77 Metcalfe St.,
Ottawa, Ont. (List of books on the Métis people).

Aboriginal Institute of Canada,
4 Newgate St., Ottawa,
(List of newspapers and periodicals).

Native Peoples Resource Centre,
1467 Richmond St.,
Westminister College,
London, Ont. (Catalogue of video-tapes for rental or
purchase is available).

Library,
Saskatchewan Indian Cultural College,
1402 Quebec Ave.,
Saskatoon, Sask. (Catalogue of materials is available).

Iroqrafts,
R.R. #2,
Oshweken, Ont.
(Source of Iroquois music)

Indian and Northern Curriculum Resources Centre,
College of Education,
University of Saskatchewan,
Saskatoon, Sask.

Chapter 16

LAW

At 4 a.m. on October 6, 1970, the Federal Cabinet approved emergency powers to preserve public order in Canada, using as its authority the long-standing War Measures Act. The relative ease with which this legislation was invoked despite its curtailment of civil liberties, and the limited public response following its implementation, are significant comments on the legal awareness and understanding of many Canadians.

At the time, majority popular opinion was complacent, bordering on acquiescence. An attitude of unspoken faith in strong, even stern leadership seemed to prevail throughout Canadian society. With dispatch, individual freedom and civil rights were suppressed by the government. It would be a mistake to assume that this majority support was based on understanding of the law in all its consequences. It is probable that indifference stems in large part from ignorance of the law. Unlike the more populist government system found in the United States, the Canadian federal state is essentially detached from direct public involvement. Mining legislation in British Columbia, government automobile insurance in Manitoba, language legislation in Quebec, have greater immediate impact within the provinces than does federal intervention in the basic area of civil liberties.

If awareness and understanding are to be deepened, a fuller comprehension of the entire legal process must be developed, beginning with a reform in existing law curricula in the schools.

A brief review of the history of the War Measures Act, combined with a synopsis of six legal case studies, indicates the type of information students need. Providing access to legislative-judicial understanding is one means of bringing the law out of the courtroom and into the classroom.

The War Measures Act

The War Measures Act was passed originally during a special session of Parliament held at the outbreak of World War I. It was enacted under Section 91 of the British North America Act, which grants to the Parliament of Canada the right to make "Laws for the Peace, Order and Good Government of Canada" in all matters not exclusively assigned to the provinces under other sections (notably 92). In the words of historian Arthur Lower, the statute was short and to the point.

> It simply handed over to the Government (that is, the Cabinet) all the powers of Parliament. Parliament in passing it, superseded itself, and so far as the words of the Act go, committed suicide.
>
> Arthur Lower, *Colony to Nation* (Toronto: Longman, 1946, p. 469)

R. MacGregor Dawson in his definitive political science study, *The Government of Canada,* (Toronto: U.T.P., 1947) was equally concise.

> The War Measures Act gave authority to the Governor-in-Council (i.e. the Cabinet) to make such orders and regulations as it "may deem necessary or advisable for the security, defence, peace, order and welfare of Canada so long as the war emergency should continue—a grant of powers so sweeping that it conveyed to the Governor-in-Council most of the enormous war-time emergency powers made available to the Dominion Parliament under the "peace, order, and good government" clause of the British North America Act. (p. 315)

The unilateral authority that this Act vests in the Federal Cabinet raises a question. What type of circumstances must be presumed to exist before the Act can be invoked?

> The clear justification for so comprehensive a delegation (of power) was of course the national safety. (Dawson, p. 316)

> The federal statutes known as the War Measures Act . . . have been used to authorize the federal Cabinet to take the necessary speedy action in time of real or apprehended war, invasion, insurrection, or national emergency. . . . (Dawson, pp. 109-110)

In retrospect, the justification given during the "October Crisis" of 1970 was a state of "apprehended insurrection." During a televised interview a few days following the assassination of Quebec's House Leader and Labour Minister, Pierre Laporte, Prime Minister Trudeau described the situation in these terms:

Society must take every means at its disposal to defend itself against the emergence of a parallel power (i.e. the F.L.Q.) in this country. . . . I think it's only weak-kneed, bleeding hearts who are afraid to take these measures. (*Time* [*Canada*] October 26, 1970)

In the language of laypeople, the measures referred to included: the right of police to conduct searches and make arrests without warrants; the outlawing of the F.L.Q. and any other organizations advocating the use of force or criminal acts to change the government; the right to hold suspects for up to twenty-one days without laying charges (the date of trial needed only to be set within ninety days); reversal of the principle that a person is presumed innocent until proven guilty; placing the burden of proof on the individual to substantiate that he/she was not an F.L.Q. member (anyone who ever attended a meeting, spoke publicly in support of the Front, or acted as its representative, was considered to be a member). Clearly, the individual would trifle with this legislation at his peril.

It is reassuring to know that since 1914 creditable authorities have questioned the War Measures Act in no uncertain terms. Among the "weak-kneed, bleeding hearts", is F.R. Scott, an expert in constitutional law and former Dean of the Law Faculty at McGill University, who referred to the use of this Act during World War II as "adaptation with a vengeance".

> Let it no longer be said that totalitarian regimes can act more expeditiously and efficiently than democracies. And though there are dangers in this situation, let it not be said either that this is no different from totalitarianism.
>
> Scott, "Constitutional Adaptations to Changing Functions of Government", *Canadian Journal of Economics and Political Science,* Aug., 1945.

The views of Lower were similarly sweeping and critical. He described the enactment of the War Measures Act in 1914 as the most complete surrender of parliamentary powers made in any English-speaking country since the time of Henry VIII.

> It speaks volumes for the immaturity of Canadian society and the weakness of Canadian traditions of freedom, that these Regulations (i.e. War Measures Act) went virtually without protest.
>
> Lower, op. cit., pp. 469, 470.

The absence of opposition which Lower noted at the outset of World War I had its parallel in 1970. A Gallup poll, as recorded in the December 14, 1970 issue of the Montreal newspaper, *Le Devoir,* indicated that 87 per cent of Canadians supported the War Measures Act. The support was almost equally divided between English and

French-speaking citizens. Within the House of Commons, where the vote on the use of emergency powers took place after the fact (October 19), the legislation introduced by the Liberal government was overwhelmingly supported by a vote of 190 to 16.

Among those who did voice a protest, three political leaders can be mentioned. Gérard Pelletier, a member of the Liberal Cabinet, admitted to a degree of uncertainty.

> It is not easy to account for the fact that the Government to which one belongs has considerably augmented the powers of the police. One knows that such an operation is not without its risks. One fears abuses and one's only desire is to be in a position to rescind all exceptional measures.
>
> Pelletier, *The October Crisis* (Toronto: McClelland, 1971, p. 17)

In the House of Commons on October 17, 1970, T.C. Douglas, national leader of the New Democratic Party, questioned the validity of equating civil disturbance with "apprehended insurrection." He pointed out that the War Measures Act had not previously been used in peacetime even though severe unrest and riots had taken place (e.g. Winnipeg General Strike). He referred to the government's intent regarding the events of October, 1970, as being:

> . . . overkill on a gargantuan scale. The Government, I submit, is using a sledge-hammer to crack a peanut (House of Commons Debate, October 17, 1970).

René Lévesque, whose political organization, Parti Québecois, came dangerously close in the minds of substantial numbers of people to being tarred with the same brush as the F.L.Q., termed the imposition of the War Measures Act as "the most incredible piece of craziness I've seen (*Time* [*Canada*], March 8, 1971, p. 10).

Neither the government nor society generally were prepared to accept the reservations, the logical rebuttals, or the spontaneous remarks of the critics.

Six Sample Case Studies

A

The Padlock Law of 1937. Maurice Duplessis, Prime Minister of Quebec, justified this legislation as a means of protecting the province from communism. Some of its provisions were similar to those of the War Measures Act. The provincial Attorney General could, without court action, close for one year premises suspected of being used to propagate communism (no definition of the term was provided); homes could be searched without a warrant and padlocked; people could be effectively excluded from their place of residence. No redress for individuals was available unless they proved themselves to be innocent.

B

The Manitoba Schools Question of the 1890s remains an unresolved political issue to the present time. The Manitoba Act of 1870 decreed that no law on education should prejudicially affect any existing right or privilege enjoyed by the denominational schools at the time of union with Canada. Subsequent attempts at restructuring the financing of Manitoba schools have aroused repeated controversy between Roman Catholic separate school supporters and the public school system.

C

Bill 22, the language legislation introduced by the Quebec government of Premier Robert Bourassa in 1974, is a similar example of a law inflaming the passions, if not the intellect. Designed to support and extend the use of the French language, it has been heartily condemned on one side for infringing on the rights of the English-speaking minority, on another for not going far enough, and from a third viewpoint by people whose native language is neither English nor French (e.g. Italians who wanted their children to learn English).

The possibility of federal disallowance of Bill 22 on the grounds of unconstitutionality could put an impossible strain on confederation.

D

Decisions affecting the liberties of the individual do not stem from direct government legislation alone. Joseph Drybones is a little-known Dogrib Indian resident of the Northwest Territories. His lengthy involvement with the courts led to a Supreme Court of Canada decision with extensive implications. The Court ruled that unless the Parliament of Canada deems otherwise, the 1960 Canadian Bill of Rights prevails over any other parliamentary statutes that would take away the rights guaranteed under the Bill. In the Drybones' case, the charge of intoxication under the Indian Act subjected him to stiffer penalties than had he been a white person convicted of the same offence. It was the Court's opinion that the right of Mr. Drybones to equality before the law was protected by

the Bill of Rights. Other judicial decisions have since been made on
the grounds that any law which discriminates between individuals
or groups so that one is treated more harshly than others is a contra-
vention of the Bill of Rights.

E

Three issues central to the equal status of women in society have
legal implications as emotional as they are profound. In 1973, the
Supreme Court of Canada ruled that a wife has no legal right to a
share in the land that she has helped to work. By common law the
land belongs to the husband (Murdoch vs. the Queen). In the spring
of 1975, the Alberta Supreme Court made a similar decision: Mrs.
Fieldler, whose husband had won an uncontested divorce, did not
have "an equal interest" in the 1120 acres purchased during their
twenty-two year marriage. An appeal by Mrs. Fieldler to the Supreme Court of Canada is pending (at time of writing).

The crime of rape calls into question the stereotypes of aggressive
male and passive female and the myth that women subconsciously
want to be taken by force and are perpetually available. It raises
the issue of male chauvinism in the police detachment, the legal
profession, the courtroom, and the legislative process itself. Throughout the interrogation of the victim, the defence proceedings, the
prosecution by the Crown, and the enactment of laws protecting
society from rapists, the decisions have traditionally been in the
hands of males. Women in groups (e.g. Voice of Women) and as individuals are calling into question a system of justice which can
harm rather than help the victim.

Similarly with abortion. The right of a woman to have control
over her own body and to seek an abortion on demand has been
highlighted in the trial of Dr. Henry Morgentaler. At specific issue
is the question of equal rights (as guaranteed in the Bill of Rights)
to an abortion as spelled out in Section 251 of the Criminal Code.

F

"Get it in writing" is an admonition almost as deeply ingrained as
belief in the integrity of the judicial system. The importance of
reading the fine print in everything from a bank loan to a major
purchase is evident in the light of Indian experiences with treaties.
What was so artfully written in the treaties (as in contracts) is subject
to interpretation. Deciphering legal terminology is a survival skill
of more than passing interest.

Case studies such as the foregoing indicate how knowledge of the law and the legal system touches everyone's life. An acquaintance with the personal characteristics and career experiences of jurists, parliamentarians, and lawyers will enrich students' understanding of the legal process.

Two suggestions for reading are the memoirs of Judge Jack Sissons (*Judge of the Far North*, Toronto: McClelland, 1968), and of the Rt. Hon. John Diefenbaker. Judge Sissons' memoirs are of particular significance given the increased public awareness of the development of northern Canada and the aspirations of the native peoples who reside there. The legal career of John Diefenbaker, reaching from the era of the Klu Klux Klan in Saskatchewan through to the passage of the Bill of Rights during his term as Prime Minister, is a story even his detractors can scarcely tarnish. In introducing the Bill of Rights to the House of Commons on July 1, 1960, his remarks more accurately suggest where Canada might go than where it has been.

> I am a Canadian, a free Canadian, free to speak without fear, free to worship God in my own way, free to stand for what I think right, free to oppose what I believe wrong, free to choose those who shall govern my country. The heritage of freedom I pledge to uphold for myself and all mankind.
> (House of Commons Debate, July 1, 1960)

This eloquent statement emphasizes the discrepancy between what is and what might be. While study of the law in classrooms will not create a society of legal beagles, it will help to develop an informed population. Upon that, the defense of personal freedom rests.

◆　◆　◆　◆

General References

The Government of Canada, 5th ed., R.M. Dawson (U.T.P., 1970), $15.00.

Fundamentals of Canadian Law, 2nd ed. F.A.R. Chapman (McGraw, 1974), $6.95.

Introduction to Canadian Law, Gibson, King, Milliken and others (Wiley, 1975), $8.70. A text for high school.

Your Canadian Law, A.B. Wilkenson (Hodder, Stoughton, 1975), $2.95 pa.

Civil Rights in Canada, P. Michael Bolton (Int'l. Self-Counsel, 1975), $1.95 pa.

Crime in Canada, Keith Hubbard and others (Maclean-Hunter, 1972), $1.00 pa.

Protest, Violence and Social Change, J.L. Hanley and others (Prentice, 1972), $4.95 pa. Part of the Canada: Issues and Options series.

Connaissez-vous la loi? 2nd ed. Robert Millet (Homme, 1962), $2.00.

Le dictionnaire de la loi, Robert Millet (Homme, 1965), $2.50.

La loi et vos droits, Paul-Émile Marchand (Homme, 1971), $4.00.

Biography

One Canada: The Crusading Years, 1895-1956, John Diefenbaker (Macmillan, 1975), $15.00.

Renegade in Power: The Diefenbaker Years, Peter C. Newman McClelland, 1963), $4.95 pa.

Judge of the Far North: The Memoirs of Jack Sissons, Jack Sissons (McClelland, 1968), $8.95.

Rankin's Law: Recollections of a Radical, Harry Rankin (November House, 1975), $7.95 pa. Autobiographical account of thirty years of British Columbia courtroom appearances.

October Crisis 1970

The October Crisis, Gérard Pelletier (McClelland, 1971), $6.95.

The Drybones Precedent

Those Things We Treasure, John G. Diefenbaker (Macmillan, 1972), $1.50 pa.

Quebec

Le bill soixante et la société québécoise, L. Dion (H.M.H.), $3.95.

Canadiens, Canadians and Québécois, R.W. Bowles and others (Prentice, 1974), $4.95 pa. Part of the Canada: Issues and Options series.

La justice au délà du 50ième parallèle, Jerôme Choquette (Ed. Officiel, 1973), $3.00 br.

Abortion

Morgentaler: The Physician Who Couldn't Turn Away, Eleanor W. Pelrine (Gage, 1975), $9.95.

Prison

Don't Steal This Book, ed. Ronald Marken (Green Tree, 1974), $7.95. Poetry written by inmates of the Saskatchewan Penitentiary at Prince Albert, Saskatchewan provides insight into prison life.

Shaking It Rough, Andreas Schroeder (Doubleday, 1976), $9.95.

Family

A Guide to Family Law, Penelope John and Charles Campbell (Anansi, 1975), $4.95 pa. Marriage, adoption, divorce, welfare, family courts, legal aid.

Immigration

How to Immigrate into Canada, Gary L. Segal (Int'l. Self-Counsel, 1974), $2.95 pa.

Taxation

Layman's Guide to Income Tax in Canada, David Ingram (Int'l. Self-Counsel, 1975), $2.95 pa.

Consumers

Canadian Consumer Law, 2nd ed., Alan Parker (Int'l. Self-Counsel, 1974), $2.95 pa.

Civil Rights

Civil Rights in Canada, P. Michael Bolton (Int'l. Self-Counsel, 1975), $2.50 pa.

Law, Law, Law, Paul Copeland, Clayton Ruby, and others (Anansi, 1975), $2.95 pa. A citizen's handbook.

For Teachers

The Legal Status of the Canadian Public School Pupil, P.F. Bargen (Macmillan, 1961), $4.00.

The Legal Status of the Canadian School Board, Frederick Enns, (Macmillan, 1963), $4.95.

The Legal Status of the Canadian Teacher, Sherburne G. McCurdy (Macmillan, 1968), $5.00.

Chapter 17

LITERATURE

Margaret Atwood's influential book *Survival: A Thematic Guide To Canadian Literature* (Toronto: Anansi, 1972), is symbolic of a renaissance in the use of Canadian material in literature courses. A growing abundance of materials, innovative developments within schools, and closer association between the literary and education communities combine to create a favourable classroom situation. Or do they?

The results of two studies on the status of Canadian literature in high schools provide an insight into the stark realities. *Course Countdown*, (Toronto: CANLIT, 1974) the report of a national survey of high school English curricula published by a research cooperative based at Glendon College, York University, indicated the dimensions of the problem. Exclusive of schools in Ontario and English-speaking Quebec, over 85 per cent of the schools surveyed did not offer even one semester of Canadian literature to their students. If available in the curriculum at all, Canadian literature was most likely to be afforded "some emphasis". Four-fifths of the questionnaire respondents indicated that Canadian literature was a part of the curriculum, but not a subject meriting attention in its own right.

A 1973 report, *Barometer Rising,* published by the Canadian Council of Teachers of English, and focusing primarily on the schools of the Atlantic region, suggests that even when Canadian literature is a portion of other courses it is likely to receive little stress. Three-quarters of the teachers surveyed interpreted "some emphasis" as being zero to 15 per cent Canadian content. Two out of five teachers reported using none, or a minimal amount of Canadian material.

Other less apparent but equally disturbing considerations arise from these studies. Where Canadian literature is offered as a course of study, the student audience is likely to be severely restricted. Academic high school students probably have the best opportunity.

161

For the majority of young people, any exposure they receive will be in general survey courses where Canadian literature is lumped together with everything else (Duncan Campbell Scott and Bliss Carman sit cheek by jowl with Longfellow, Shelley, and Keats). More significantly, teachers who wish to provide comprehensive instruction frequently are restricted by a lack of materials. In 1972-73, according to *Course Countdown*, the province of Alberta had the highest percentage of Canadian titles in its literature curriculum, an unimpressive 16 per cent. Even when Canadian writers are included in recommended lists, the concentration is on a select few, usually writers from the Toronto/Montreal literary communities. Literature is not much used as a means of developing cultural and/or regional awareness and understanding.

Two reasons can be advanced. The work of talented but unrecognized writers is more likely to be published by small, independent firms rather than by the more influential national or multinational corporations. Publishers such as Borealis, Fiddlehead, and Tecumseh have some excellent titles which would be valuable additions to any classroom. Yet their use remains limited. The extensive advertising, sales, and distribution networks of the larger publishers are more likely to catch the eye of curriculum authorities as well as teachers. The situation can be expected to improve. Through affiliations such as Belford Book Distributing, Canadian Basic books, and Canadabooks: Books for Canadian Education, wider circulation of such information among educators is to be anticipated.

The other reason is more difficult to explain and justify. Novelist Mordecai Richler expressed it well in his article "Letters From Ottawa" (*Harper's,* June, 1975, pp. 28-32). With reference to the "nationalists," who have the temerity to advance the importance of "Canadian letters", Richler made the following comment:

> . . . the nationalists have made it clear that they are determined to win through legislation, for the second-rate but homegrown writer, what talent alone has hitherto denied him: an audience, applause.

Richler's attitude suggests an intellectual snobbery totally at odds with reality. Support for Canadian literary endeavours is not in itself synonomous with "applause" for the "second rate". In a country where continental cultural homogeneity is the rule, it can be difficult, if not impossible, for talented new writers to receive recognition. Particularly is this true with respect to school literature curricula. If a handful of select, competent writers, including Richler, are fortunate enough to have their books promoted by multi-national and major Canadian publishers and distributors, then students can receive exposure to a part of their literary heritage. For other equally capable writers, struggling to survive in the face of foreign saturation of the marketplace, such recognition may be remote. Does this mean that the search for quality writers should be held in abeyance until such time as the Book-of-the-Month Club places its stamp of approval on the Canadian author? From a pragmatic dollars and cents point of view, it would be logical if an increased percentage of the hundreds of millions of dollars spent annually on learning materials in Canada were diverted to support competent but unknown writers. Through purchase of their books, not only would the writers have a livelihood, but as importantly, Canadian-owned publishers would have more money for the further encouragement of Canadian writers.

A bibliography, even as limited as the one provided here, speaks volumes for the potential of Canadian literature in the schools. Whether periodicals, cassette tapes, general reference works, or paperback novels, poetry, and literary criticism, a comprehensive range of materials can be incorporated throughout the junior and senior high school years. (Materials for younger students are included in Chapter 23—Reading).

♦ ♦ ♦ ♦

Anthologies—the Basic Reference Shelf

Oxford Anthology of Canadian Literature, ed. Robert Weaver and William Toye (Oxford, 1973), $5.50 pa.

The Oxford Companion to Canadian History and Literature, Norah Story (Oxford, 1967), $18.50.

Supplement to the Oxford Companion to Canadian History and Literature, gen. ed. William Toye (Oxford, 1973), $9.50.

Canadian Short Stories, ed. Robert Weaver (Oxford, 1966), $2.95 pa.

Canadian Short Stories: Second Series, ed. Robert Weaver (Oxford, 1968), $2.95 pa.

Kaleidescope: Canadian Stories, ed. John Metcalf (Van Nostrand, 1972), $2.00 pa. Twelve Canadian writers including Stein, Garner, Laurence, Hood, Callaghan, Munro, and Ross.

Singing Under Ice, Grace Mersereau (Macmillan, 1974), $3.95 pa. Twenty-seven selections including short stories and non-fiction.

Colony and Confederation: Early Canadian Poets and their Background, ed. George Woodcock (U.B.C. Press, 1974), $6.50 pa.

The Book of Canadian Poetry: A Critical and Historical Anthology, 3rd ed. A.J.M. Smith (Gage, 1957), $11.30.

How Do I Love Thee, ed. John Robert Colombo (Hurtig, 1970), $2.95 pa. Selections from 60 poets.

Fifteen Canadian Poets, ed. Gary Geddes (Oxford, 1971), $3.95 pa.

The Oxford Book of Canadian Verse, ed. A.J.M. Smith (Oxford, 1965), $3.20 pa.

Four Parts Sand, Earle Birney, Bill Bissett, Judith Copithorne, and Andrew Suknarski (Oberon, 1972), $6.95. Poetry of four writers.

Marked by the Wild, ed. Bruce Littlejohn and Jon Pearce (McClelland, 1973), $3.95 pa. Anthology of prose and poetry; includes selections by Birney, Roberts, Pratt, Creighton, Layton, Mowat and Berton.

Canadian Anthology, 3rd ed., ed. Carl F. Klinck and R.E. Watters (Gage, 1974), $12.95. Prose and poetry plus biographical and bibliographical information.

Short stories from Coach House:
   The Story so Far 1, 1971. $3.00 pa.
   The Story so Far 2, 1973. $3.00 pa.
   The Story so Far 3, 1974. $4.95 pa.
   Writers are Atwood, Nichol, Cohen, Kent, Carlson, Nowlan, McFadden, Smith, Harrison, Hewko, Laurence, Heath.

Titles from the Canadian Short Story Library, University of Ottawa Press:
   Selected Stories of Raymond Knister, $3.75.
   Selected Stories of E.W. Thomson, $3.75.
   Selected Stories of Duncan Campbell Scott, $3.75.
   Waken Lords and Ladies Gay: Selected Stories of Desmond Pacey, $4.80.
   Stories and Tales of Isabella Valency Crawford, $4.80.

Literature in an Historical Perspective

Literary History of Canada: Canadian Literature in English, 2nd ed., ed. Carl F. Klinck (U.T.P., 1976), 3 vol., $8.95 each pa. A basic reference source.

The Evolution of Canadian Literature in English: Beginnings to

1867, vol. 1, ed. Mary Jane Edwards (Holt, 1973), $6.25 pa.
Eighteen writers from the 1700s to 1867, including Susanna Moodie,
Joseph Howe, and Charles Sangster.
Vol. 2, 1867-1914, ed. George L. Parker and Mary Jane Edwards
(Holt, 1973), $6.25 pa. Includes Bliss Carman, L.M. Montgomery,
and Stephen Leacock.
Vol. 3, 1914-1945, ed. George L. Parker (Holt, 1973), $6.25 pa.
Literature of the Great Depression including writing by Mazo de
la Roche, E.J. Pratt, Morley Callaghan, and W.E. Ross.
Vol. 4, 1945-1970, ed. William Paul Denham (Holt, 1973), $6.25
pa. Twenty-three authors of the post-World War II era, including
Earle Birney, Irving Layton, Alice Munro, Margaret Atwood, and
Leonard Cohen.

The Sixties: Canadian Writing and Writers of the Decade, ed.
George Woodcock (U.B.C. Press, 1969), $3.50 pa. Essays in criti-
cism and literary history by nineteen writers including Mordecai
Richler, Al Purdy, and Margaret Laurence.

*From There to Here: A Guide to English Canadian Literature since
1960,* Frank Davey (Porcepic, 1974), $4.95 pa. Volume 2 of *Our
Nature, Our Voices* series, includes short chapters on Milton Acorn,
Margaret Atwood, Alice Munro, Alden Nowlan and many others.

The Colonial Century, ed. A.J.M. Smith (Gage, 1973), $4.85 pa.

The Canadian Century, ed. A.J.M. Smith (Gage, 1974), $8.50 pa.

Panorama littéraire du Canada français, Paul Gay (H.M.H., 1974)
vol. 1 *Notre roman;* vol. 2 *Notre poesie;* vol. 3 *Notre theatre;*
each $3.75.

Look Through a Diamond, ed. Joan Forman (Holt, 1971), $4.75.
An anthology of 230 poems from the nineteenth and twentieth
centuries, presented in pairs for comparison.

Atlantic Canada

Collections and Anthologies

Stories from Atlantic Canada, Kent Thompson (Macmillan, 1973),
$2.50 pa.

Sunrise North, Elizabeth Brewster (Clarke, Irwin, 1972), $3.95.
A collection of poems on life in the Maritimes and on the Prairies.

New Atlantic Writing, ed. P. Grant and F. Martin (Square Deal,
1975), $3.50 pa.
Ninety Seasons: Modern Poems from the Maritimes, ed. Robert
Cockburn and Robert Gibbs (McClelland, 1974), $6.95.

Doryloads: Newfoundland Writings and Art, ed. K. Major
(Breakwater, 1974), $3.75 pa.

Novels

> *The Mountain and the Valley,* Ernest Buckler (McClelland, 1961), $1.95 pa.

> *At the Tide's Turn,* Thomas Raddall (McClelland, 1959), $1.95 pa.

> *Anne of Green Gables,* L.M. Montgomery (McGraw, 1942), $4.85 pa.

> *The God Tree,* James Demers (Musson, 1974), $6.95. Experiences of a young boy growing up in the Madawaska area of northern New Brunswick.

> *Tomorrow will be Sunday,* Harold Horwood (General, 1975), $1.95 pa.

Poetry

> *My Newfoundland: Stories, Poems, Songs,* A.R. Scammell (Harvest, 1971), $2.50.

> *The Island Means Minago,* Milton Acorn (N.C. Press, 1975), $3.95 pa. Poetry based on the history of Prince Edward Island from 1758 to 1896.

Historical

> *Halifax: Warden of the North,* Thomas Raddall (McClelland, 1971), $5.95.

Autobiographical

> *The Alpine Path: The Story of my Career,* L.M. Montgomery (Fitzhenry and Whiteside, 1974), $6.50.

> *Helen Creighton: A Life in Folklore,* Helen Creighton (McGraw, 1975), $8.95.

Quebec

Collection and Anthologies

> *Littérature canadienne,* R. Turcotte (P.U.Q.), $2.50.

> *L'age de la littérature canadienne,* Clément Moisan (H.M.H.), $3.95.

> *Québec: hier et aujourd'hui vu par ses écrivains: Jean Ethier-Blais, Louis Daigneau, Laurier LaPierre,* Raymond Turcotte (H.M.H.), $5.95.

> *Porte ouverte,* ed. M.G. Hesse and L.T. Cormier (Book Society, 1974), $4.95. An anthology of prose.

> *Poésie du Québec,* Alain Bosquet (H.M.H.), $3.75. Comprehensive anthology of contemporary poetry.

Le temps des poètes, Gilles Marcotte (H.M.H., 1969), $4.75. Study of French Canadian poets of the 1953-1969 period.

Ellipse, La faculté des arts, Université de Sherbrooke, (H.M.H.), $1.50 each for 15 volumes of poetry.

Voix et images du pays, Rénald Berubé (P.U.Q.). A nine volume series of literature.

Novels

Le voyage, Gilles Marcotte (H.M.H.), $3.95.

La route d'altamont, Gabrielle Roy (H.M.H., 1967), $3.75.

Max au rallye, Monique Corriveau (Book Society), $2.50 pa.

La chanette, Jacques Ferron (H.M.H., 1968), $3.95.

La fin des loups-garous, Madeleine Ferron (H.M.H., 1967), $2.95.

Nouvelles singulières, Jean Hamelin (H.M.H.), $2.95.

English Translations

The French Writers of Canada series, Harvest, includes representative works of fiction by French Canadian authors. Titles are available from the publisher.

The Poetry of French Canada in Translation, John Glassco (Oxford, 1970), $4.50 pa.

One Hundred Poems of Modern Quebec, ed. and tr. Fred Cogswell (Fiddlehead), $2.00 pa.

Kamouraska, Anne Hébert (General, 1974), $1.95 pa.

Tales from the Uncertain Country, Jacques Ferron (Anansi, 1972), $6.50. A collection of short stories.

Maria Chapdelaine, Louis Hémon (Macmillan, 1972), $1.95 pa.

Boss of the River, Félix-Antoine Savard (Harvest, 1975), $2.50 pa. A novel that describes the bitterness of a veteran of the log drive over the exploitation of Quebec resources by foreign capital.

English Writing about Quebec

Saturday Night at the Bagel Factory, Don Bell (McClelland, 1972), $6.95. Eighteen stories based on life in Montreal.

Four Montreal Poets, David Solway (Fiddlehead, 1973), $2.50 pa.

The Revolution Script, Brian Moore (Simon & Schuster, 1972), $1.25 pa. A story of the FLQ crisis.

The Apprenticeship of Duddy Kravitz, Mordecai Richler (McClelland, 1969), $1.50 pa. Insight into Jewish life in Montreal.

Going Down Slow, John Metcalf (McClelland, 1972), $6.95. Experiences of a young Montreal school teacher.

Ontario

Collections and Anthologies

Stories from Ontario, ed. Germaine Warkentin (Macmillan, 1974), $2.95 pa.

Novel

Cabbagetown, Hugh Garner (Simon & Schuster, 1971) 95¢ pa. Life in a Toronto slum during the Depression.

Poetry

Poets of the Capital, ed. Frank M. Tierney and Stephen Gill (Borealis, 1974), $5.95. An anthology of the works of 50 poets living in the Ottawa area.

Lure of Lanark, David Andrew (Borealis, 1974), $4.50. Poetry of Lanark County, Ontario.

Glengarry Forever, Douglas Fales (Borealis, 1973), $3.95. Poetry of Glengarry County, Ontario in earlier times.

Short Stories

Selected Stories of E.W. Thomson, ed. Lorraine McMullen (Univ. of Ottawa Press, 1973), $3.75. Humorous expressions of life in Glengarry county and the Ottawa valley region.

Homebrew and Patches, Harry Boyle (General, 1972), $1.25 pa. Humorous, often touching episodes of rural life in the 1930s.

Western Canada

Collections and Anthologies

Writers of the Prairies, Donald Stephens (U.B.C. Press, 1973), $5.50. A selection of essays by and about eleven prairie novelists from Ralph Connor and Robert Stead to Margaret Laurence and Robert Kroetsch.

Stories from Western Canada, ed. Rudy Wiebe (Macmillan, 1972), $2.95 pa.

Skookum Wawa: Writings of the Canadian Northwest, ed. Gary Geddes (Oxford, 1975), $6.50 pa. An anthology of over eighty selections from writers of the Pacific Northwest.

The Truth and Other Stories, Terrence Heath (Anansi, 1972), $2.50 pa. Glimpses of prairie life.

The Best of Edna Jacques, 3rd ed., Edna Jacques (Western Producer, 1974), $4.95. An anthology of 75 poems of pioneer life in western Canada.

The Longest Day of the Year, Helen Marquis (General, 1974), $1.25 pa. A prairie blizzard maroons three young children on Christmas eve; setting is Holbein, Saskatchewan.

Breakaway, Cecelia Frey (Macmillan, 1974), $7.95. A sensitive novel about a young girl growing up in Alberta.

Lonesome Hero, Fred Stenson (Macmillan, 1974), $7.95. A humorous novel based on the life of a young man reared in southern Alberta.

Boss of the Namko Drive, Paul St. Pierre (McGraw 1965), $1.95 pa. Story of a cattle drive in the British Columbia interior.

The novels of W.O. Mitchell from Macmillan:
   Jake and the Kid, (1961), 1974. $2.95 pa.
   The Kite, (1962), 1974. $3.50 pa.
   Who has seen the Wind? (1947), 1961. $1.95 pa.
   The Vanishing Point, 1973. $4.50 pa.

Wolf Willow, Wallace Stegner (Macmillan, 1967), $3.15 pa. A novel set in the Cypress Hills of southern Alberta and Saskatchewan.

Over Prairie Trails, F.P. Grove (McClelland, 1970), $1.95 pa.

Jim Tweed, John Lloyd Parr (Queenston, 1975), $6.95 pa. A humorous nostalgic novel of growing up in Manitoba during World War II.

Hungry Hills, George Ryga (Talonbooks, 1974), $4.95 pa. A novel set in the Alberta foothills.

Poetry

The Poet's Record, ed. Elva Motherall and K. Wilson (Peguis, 1975), $3.25. Poetry by Manitoba writers.

Salamandre, Paul Savoie (Editions du Blé, 1974), $7.00. Poetry with illustrations by a Franco-Manitoban.

Titles from the series Manitoba Poets and their Works, Peguis:
   Responses, Mary Elizabeth Bayer (Peguis, 1972), $3.75 pa.
   Red River of the North, Thomas Saunders (Peguis, 1969), $3.95 pa.

Titles from the Peguis Poetry series, Peguis. (These books resulted from the efforts in 1972 of the Manitoba Arts Council to promote the poetry of the province.)
   Rib by Rib, K. Karsten Kossman (Peguis, 1973), $2.50.
   Story for a Rainy Day, S. Allen Mann (Peguis, 1973), $2.50.
   Three Parallels of Grass, Jeannette Quajar (Peguis, 1973), $2.50.

Alberta Days, W. Glenn Clever (Borealis, 1974), $4.50. Two illustrated narrative poems about Alberta life.

The Vancouver Poems, Daphne Marlett (Coach House, 1972), $3.00. A free-form collection of poems based on Vancouver life.

The North

Stories from Pacific and Arctic Canada, Ed. Rudy Wiebe and Andreas Schroeder (Macmillan, 1974), $2.50 pa.

Descriptive Narrative

People of the Deer, rev. ed., Farley Mowat (McClelland, 1975), $5.95.

Never Cry Wolf, rev. ed. Farley Mowat (McClelland, 1973), $1.75 text.

Land of the Long Day, Douglas Wilkinson (Clarke, Irwin, 1966), $2.50.

Novel

The Sparrow's Fall, Fred Bodsworth (New American Library, 1966), $1.25 pa. The struggle for life in the Canadian Shield-Hudson Bay Lowlands area; winner of the Governor General's Award for Fiction.

Poetry

Poetry of Robert Service, McGraw:
  Best of Robert Service, 1907, $3.50 pa.
  Songs of a Sourdough, 1907, $1.50.
  Songs of the High North, 1964, $1.50.

Historical

The Last Voyage of the Unicorn, Delbert A. Young (Clarke, Irwin, 1969), $5.50. A true story of the search for the Northwest Passage in 1619.

N.B.— Please refer to Chapter 15—Indians—Inuit—Métis—for books authored by Northern native peoples—John Tetso, Markoosie, Pitseolak.

Listening to Literature

My Country 'Tis of Thee (cassette tape). 60 min, C.B.C. Learning Systems, $15.00. A group of writers express their thoughts and feelings about Canada.

Canadian Poets I (l.p., 2 records). C.B.C. Publications Branch, $7.50. Poets reading their works; includes Webb, Birney, Newlove, Purdy, Layton, Cohen, Bowering and MacEwen.

Canadian Poets II (l.p. record). C.B.C. Publications Branch, $5.00.

Margaret Atwood reads a cycle of her poems invoking the life and thoughts of an immigrant in the 1800s.

Canadian Poets on Tape (cassette tape or reel-to-reel). Van Nostrand, $9.95 each. Complete set, cassette, $44.95, reel-to-reel, $89.95. *Purdy and Mandel; Birney and Layton; Reaney and Waddington; Livesay and MacEwan; Scott and Souster.*

Open Secret (l.p. record). C.B.C. Publications Branch, $5.00. Gwendolyn MacEwen reads selections from her books *A Breakfast for Barbarians, The Shadow Maker* and *The Armies of the Moon.*

Canadian Writers on Tape (cassette tape or reel-to-reel). Van Nostrand, $9.95 each. Complete set, cassette, $27.50; reel-to-reel, $54.95. *Laurence and MacLennan; Ross and Richler; Garner and Callaghan.*

The Green Beyond (l.p. record). C.B.C. Publications Branch, $5.00. Louis Dudek reads his poetry.

John Drainie reads Stephen Leacock (l.p. record). London Records, $5.98.

The Spell of the Yukon (l.p. record). Ringside Records, $3.95. J. Frank Willis reads the poetry of Robert Service.

Literary Study and Criticism

Eleven Canadian Novelists: Interviewed and Photographed, Graeme Gibson (Anansi, 1973), $2.75 pa.

Northrop Frye, Ross Bates (McClelland, 1971), $1.25 pa. Life and works of the eminent literary critic.

The Novels of Hugh MacLennan, Robert Cockburn (Harvest, 1970), $2.95 pa.

Survival: A Thematic Guide to Canadian Literature, Margaret Atwood (Anansi, 1972), $3.25 pa.

Titles from the series Studies in Canadian Literature, McGill-Queen's, $2.15 each. Each deals with one writer—biographical details, critical analysis, and detailed bibliography. *Charles G.D. Roberts; Brian Moore; Frederick Philip Grove; Morley Callaghan; Hugh MacLennan; Al Purdy; Margaret Avison; A.M. Klein; Earle Birney; E.J. Pratt.*

The Wheel of Things: A Biography of Lucy Maud Montgomery, Mollie Gillen (Fitzhenry and Whiteside, 1975), $9.95. The life of the creator of *Anne of Green Gables.*

Emily, Florence McNeil (Clarke, Irwin, 1975), $5.95. Poetry about the life and times of Emily Carr.

Selected Stories of Duncan Campbell Scott, ed. W. Glenn Clever (University of Ottawa, 1972), $3.75. Introduction and stories.

Selected Stories of Raymond Knister, ed. Michael Gnarowski (University of Ottawa, 1972), $3.75. Selection of 6 stories accompanied by a critique.

The Creative Writer, Earle Birney (C.B.C. Publications Branch, 1966), $1.75 pa. Birney explains techniques of creativity in prose and poetry.

Titles from the series Aspects of English, Holt, gen ed. Roy Bentley:

The Cow Jumped Over the Moon, Earle Birney (Holt, 1972), $2.95. Birney introduces poetry through a blend of theory and autobiography.

New Directions in Canadian Poetry, ed. J.R. Colombo (Holt, 1971), $2.50. The poetry of 8 writers.

Rhymes and Reasons, ed. J.R. Colombo (Holt, 1971), $2.50. The works of 9 poets with prose description of each poem.

Contemporary Satire, David J. Dooley (Holt, 1971), $2.50. The nature and techniques of satire, illustrated.

The Canadian Short Story, ed. Tony Kilgallin (Holt, 1971), $2.50. Stories by Hugh Hood, David Helwig, John Metcalf, Mordecai Richler, and Malcolm Lowry.

Eight More Canadian Poets, ed. Eli Mandel (Holt, 1972), $2.50. This volume complements the poetry found in *New Directions in Canadian Poetry* and *Rhymes and Reasons.*

Five Modern Canadian Poets, ed. Eli Mandel (Holt, 1970), $2.50. Sampling of the works of Earle Birney, Irving Layton, Al Purdy, Margaret Atwood, and Leonard Cohen.

Four Canadian Playwrights, ed. Mavor Moore (Holt, 1973), $2.95. An analysis of the works of Robertson Davies, Gratien Gélinas, James Reaney, and George Ryga.

One Man's Media and How to Write for Them, Eric Nichol (Holt, 1973), $3.25. A light-hearted, comprehensive look at writing for the media.

Engagements, Irving Layton (McClelland, 1972), $8.95. Short fiction, articles, letters and reviews.

Titles from the series Themes in Canadian Literature, Macmillan. Discussion questions and topics for further study, high school level, $3.25 each pa.

Canadian Humour and Satire; The Frontier Experience; The Immigrant Experience; Isolation in Canadian Literature; The Maritime Experience; Native Peoples in Canadian Literature; The Prairie Experience; The Role of Women in Canadian Literature; The Search for Identity.

Poetry of Relevance, Homer Hogan (Methuen, 1970), 2 vols. $3.50 each pa. Canadian and non-Canadian material for senior high school students.

Prose of Relevance, Kenneth J. Weber (Methuen, 1971), 2 vols. $3.50 each pa. Canadian and non-Canadian material for senior high school students.

Truth and Fantasy, ed. Kenneth J. Weber and Homer Hogan (Methuen, 1972), $3.50 pa. Teacher's guide, $3.50. A senior high anthology of Canadian and non-Canadian poetry.

Listen: Songs and Poems of Canada, ed. Homer Hogan (Methuen, 1972), $3.40 pa. Teacher's guide, free upon request. Senior high.

Survey: A Short History of Canadian Literature, Elizabeth Waterson (Methuen, 1973), $3.95 pa. High school.

Strawberries and Other Secrets, ed. James MacNeil and Glen Sorestad (Nelson, 1969), $3.25 pa. Teacher's edition, $1.95. Anthology of short stories.

Humour

The Treasury of Great Canadian Humour, Alan Walker (McGraw, 1974), $12.50.

A Treasury of Canadian Humour, Robert Thomas Allen (McClelland, 1961), $4.95 pa.

Canadians: An Anthology of Nostalgia, Humorous and Satirical Writing for Secondary Schools, G. Huffman (McClelland, 1970), $2.75 pa.

O Can, W. Glenn Clever (Borealis, 1972), $3.95. Book of satirical verse.

The Old Judge, or Life in a Colony, Haliburton (Clarke, Irwin, 1968), $2.50 pa.

The Sam Slick Anthology, Haliburton (Clarke, Irwin, 1969), $2.75 pa.

The Flying Bull and Other Tall Tales, Watson Kirkconnell (Clarke, Irwin, 1949), $1.25. Tall tales by some snow-bound travellers.

With a Pinch of Sin, Harry Boyle (General, 1973), $1.50 pa.

Sunshine Sketches of a Little Town, Stephen Leacock (McClelland, 1960), $1.50 pa.

Still a Nichol, Eric Nichol (McGraw, 1972), $7.95. A varied collection of the B.C. writer's works from 1943 to 1971.

The Battle of Mole Run, Howard T. Mitchell (Mitchell, 1966), $1.25 pa. Anthology of humorous articles from such publications as *Western Homes and Living* and *Ontario Homes and Living.*

The Best of Bob Edwards, ed. Hugh A. Dempsey (Hurtig, 1975), $8.95. Satire, editorial comment, reflections, and observations by Bob Edwards, editor of the *Calgary Eye-Opener* from 1902-1922.

The Boat who Wouldn't Float, Farley Mowat (McClelland, 1969), $2.95 pa.

And Now . . . Here's Max, Max Ferguson (McGraw, 1967), $1.50 pa.

Good Buy Canada, Murray Soupcoff and others, (James Lorimer, 1975), $5.95 pa. Satire drawn from the C.B.C. Radio series, "Inside from the Outside".

Seven Award-Winning Titles

Bird at the Window, Jan Truss (Macmillan, 1974), $7.95. A first novel by an Alberta writer, winner of 1971 Search-for-a-new-Alberta-novelist Contest.

The Collected Works of Billy the Kid, Michael Ondaatje (Anansi, 1971), $2.95 pa. Governor General's Award for Poetry.

Civil Elegies and Other Poems, Dennis Lee (Anansi, 1972), $2.75 pa. Governor General's Award for Poetry, 1972.

Bread, Wine and Salt, Alden Nowlan (Clarke, Irwin, 1973), $2.50. Governor General's Award for Poetry.

Cross Country, Hugh MacLennan (Hurtig, 1971), $5.95. Reprint of the Governor General's Award-winning collection of essays.

The Temptations of Big Bear, Rudy Wiebe (McClelland, 1973), $4.95 pa. Governor General's Award for Fiction, 1974.

Sarah Binks, Paul Hiebert (McClelland, 1971), $1.75 pa. Stephen Leacock Medal for Humour, 1964. The immortalization of a non-existent nobody, Sarah Binks, the "sweet songstress of Saskatchewan".

Literature and Other Curriculum Subjects

Counselling: Growing Up

Just Gin, Wallis Kendal (Macmillan, 1973), $5.95. A novel of the pre-teen and early teenage years of a young girl.

Science: Science Fiction

North by 2000: A Collection of Canadian Science Fiction, Henry Allen Hargreaves (Peter Martin, 1975), $3.95 pa.

Business

> *The Devil's Lighter,* John Ballem, (General, 1974), $1.75 pa. The oil industry is the background to this novel.

Social Studies: Biography

> *And the Dying Sky like Blood,* Peter Stevens (Borealis, 1974), $5.50. A tribute to Dr. Norman Bethune.

Social Studies: English/French Identities

> *Two Solitudes,* Hugh MacLennan, (Macmillan, 1951), $1.25 pa.

Social Studies: Black/White Relationships

> *When He was Free and Young and He Used to Wear Silks,* Austin Clarke (Anansi, 1971), $2.95 pa. A collection of short stories about black people in Canada.

Social Studies: Military

> *War: Perspectives on Violence,* Gerald Karpinka and others (Gage, 1971), $1.55 pa. Teacher's guide, $1.90. Poems, short stories, and extracts from novels on three themes: patriotism, sensitivity, and attitudes.

> *Turvey,* Earle Birney (McClelland, 1963), $1.75 pa. Novel of World War I.

> *Barometer Rising,* Hugh MacLennan (Macmillan, 1969), $2.25. The Halifax explosion of 1917.

Social Studies: The Twenties

> *That Summer in Paris,* Morley Callaghan (Macmillan, 1973), $3.95 pa. Life in the Parisian artistic community with glimpses of Ernest Hemingway and F. Scott Fitzgerald.

Social Studies: The Thirties

> *The Watch that Ends the Night,* Hugh MacLennan (New American Library, 1961), $1.25 pa.

Language Arts: The Multi-Language Society

> *Volvox: Poetry from the Unofficial Languages of Canada in English Translation,* ed. J. Michael Yates and Charles Lillard (Sono, 1971), $7.95.

Reading

> *Read Canadian: A Book About Canadian Books,* ed. Robert Fulford and others (James Lorimer, 1972), $1.95 pa. Essays about writing and writers; useful bibliographies.

Sociology: Culture, Youth, Prejudice

> *Shovelling Trouble,* Mordecai Richler (McClelland, 1972), $6.95. Essays on culture, hippies, and anti-semitism.

Sociology: Change

> *The Immoral Moralists,* Patricia Morley (Clarke, Irwin, 1973), $2.75 pa. A reflection of significant changes in society as shown in the writings of Hugh MacLennan and Leonard Cohen.

Sociology: Social Maturity

> *Various Persons Named Kevin O'Brien,* Alden Nowlan (Clarke, Irwin, 1973), $6.95. A story of coming of age.

Sociology: Nostalgia

> *Jalna,* Mazo de la Roche (Collins), $1.25 pa. Romantic view of life at the turn of the twentieth century.

Sociology: Cultural Identity

> *Surfacing,* Margaret Atwood (General, 1973), $1.75 pa.

Sociology: Sexual Identity

> *A Jest of God,* Margaret Laurence (McClelland, 1974), 60¢ pa. Also published as *Rachel, Rachel.*

> *I am Mary Dunne,* Brian Moore (McClelland, 1968), $1.75 pa.

Pick a Poet, Novelist, or . . .

> Margaret Atwood, *Journals of Susanna Moodie* (Oxford, 1970), $1.95 pa.

> G. Balderstone, *Where the Words are Unspoken* (Fiddlehead, 1972), 50¢.

> Marie-Claire Blais, *Mad Shadows* (McClelland, 1971), $1.75 pa.

> Fred Bodsworth, *Last of the Curlews* (McClelland, 1963), $1.50 pa.

> L.A. Booth, *For the Record* (Fiddlehead, 1965), $2.50 pa.

> Morley Callaghan, *Morley Callaghan's Stories* (Macmillan, 1967), $1.25 pa.

> Fred Cogswell, *The House without a Door* (Fiddlehead, 1973), $1.00 pa.

> Leonard Cohen, *Spice Box of Earth* (McClelland, 1961), $2.95 pa.

> Matt Cohen, *Columbus and the Fat Lady* (Anansi, 1972), $8.95.

> Robertson Davies, *Tempest-Tost* (Clarke, Irwin, 1951), $1.95 pa.

> John Glassco, *Selected Poems* (Oxford, 1971), $2.95 pa.

> George Johnston, *Happy Enough: Poems 1935-1971* (Oxford, 1972), $2.95 pa.

> Henry Kreisel, *The Betrayal* (McClelland, 1971), $2.95 pa.

> Irving Layton, *Collected Poems* (McClelland, 1971), $3.95 pa.

Wyndham Lewis, *Self Condemned* (McClelland, 1974), $2.95 pa.

Jay Macpherson, *The Boatman and other Poems* (Oxford, 1968). $3.25 pa.

Alden Nowlan, *Miracle at Indian River,* (Clarke, Irwin, $3.95.

Gabrielle Roy, *Where Nests the Water Hen* (McClelland, 1961), $1.95 pa.

F.R. Scott, *Selected Poems* (Oxford, 1971), $3.25 pa.

A.J.M. Smith, *Poems: New and Collected* (Oxford, 1967), $2.50 pa.

Wayne Stedingh, *From A Bell Tower* (Sono, 1970), $2.50.

F.M. Tierney, *Come Climb a Mountain* (University of Ottawa, 1970), $3.95.

Miriam Waddington, *Driving Home* (Oxford, 1972), $2.95 pa.

Rudy Wiebe, *Blue Mountains of China* (McClelland, 1975), $2.95 pa.

Delbert A. Young, *According to Hakluyt* (Clarke, Irwin, 1973), $6.95.

Specific Materials for the Classroom

The Novel Lab Series (kit). General, $69.95. Junior and senior high; each kit contains study cards, student study booklet and teacher's guide. Designed to stimulate critical analysis.

Solo Flight (kit). Grolier, $48.50. Junior, senior high; a multi-media kit of booklets, tapes, posters, manuscripts, overhead transparencies dealing with the works of over 50 poets.

Touchstones 2: A Teaching Anthology of Poetry, ed. M.G. Benton and others (Musson, 1972), $2.25. Study of basic poetic ideas.

The Leaf Not the Tree: Teaching Poetry through Film and Tape (kit). Gage. Junior, senior high; a variety of materials—books, tapes, photographs, slides, film.

Mirrors: Recent Canadian Verse, ed. Jon Pierce (Gage, 1975), $2.95 pa. Teacher's guide, $1.25. An anthology of over 150 poems divided into 9 themes: growing up, nature and environment, urban life, alienation, satire, portraits of people loving, poetry, old age, death.

Titles from the Action series, Macmillan, $3.95 each. Teacher's Guide for each, $2.50.

    Challenge, Grade 7; *Viewpoint,* Grade 8; *Dialogue,* Grade 9.

Signatures, Nelson, Books 1, 2, 3, $1.80 each. Teacher's handbook,

$2.80. Poetry anthologies including poems by Souster, Pickthall, Gotleib, Birney, and Lampman.

Books for Teachers

A Curriculum in Film, John S. Katz and others (O.I.S.E., 1972), $4.50. The integration of the study of film with the study of literature.

An Introduction to Teaching Canadian Literature, Hale (Atlantic Institute of Education), $3.00 pa.

Montréal dans le roman canadien, Antoine Sirois (Didier), $7.50. Comparative studies of French-English novelists in Montreal.

Making Poetry: Approaches to Teaching from Classrooms around the World, Brian S. Powell (Collier-Macmillan, 1973), $3.00 pa. A manual on teaching creative writing through poetry.

Periodicals

The Far Point, University of Manitoba Press. 2 issues annually for 2 years, $3.50.

Canadian Literature, University of British Columbia. Quarterly, $5.50. Literary criticism.

Exile, Canadian Periodical Publishers' Association. Quarterly, $7.00. Original imaginative fiction.

Quarry, Canadian Periodical Publishers' Association. Quarterly, $4.00. Poetry, short fiction, and book reviews.

The Canadian Fiction Magazine, Canadian Periodical Publishers' Association. Quarterly, $7.00. Fiction, reviews, graphics, interviews.

The Tamarack Review, Canadian Periodical Publishers' Association. Quarterly, $7.50. Fiction, poetry, general articles, and reviews.

Copperfield, Canadian Periodical Publishers' Association. 2 issues annually for 2 years, $4.00. Poetry, fiction, art, reviews.

Northern Light, Canadian Periodical Publishers' Association. 2 issues annually for 2 years, $5.00. Poetry.

The Fiddlehead, Canadian Periodical Publishers' Association. Quarterly, $6.00. Review and criticism.

Open Letter, Canadian Periodical Publishers' Association. Quarterly, $7.25. Reviews and criticism.

Journal of Canadian Fiction, Canadian Periodical Publishers' Association. Quarterly, $9.00. Fiction, criticism, reviews; an annual annotated bibliography of Canadian literature.

Canadian Review, Canadian Periodical Publishers' Association. 10 Issues, $6.50. Poetry, art, fiction, reviews.

Waves, Canadian Periodical Publishers' Association. 3 issues annually, $3.00. Fiction, poetry, graphics, translations.

Ellipse, Canadian Periodical Publishers' Association. Quarterly. $5.00. Presents parallel French-English, English-French literary translations and critical articles.

Saturday Night, New Leaf Publications. 10 issues annually, $8.00. Fiction, reviews, contemporary comment.

Chapter 18

MATHEMATICS

General Directions for Students

Body:
The pupil should face the desk with both shoulders at the same height, with body straight and slightly inclined forward, but not bent over to bring the eyes too near the work. The body should be far enough from the desk to admit a free movement of the arm in any direction.

Right Hand:
The right hand should be perpendicular, or nearly so, to the line being drawn.

Left Arm:
The left arm should rest on the desk, so that the hand may be used to refer to the printed copies, or to adjust and keep the paper at rest, on which the drawings are being made.

Pencil:
An "H.B." pencil, cut to a medium point is the best. It should be held with an easy grasp between the first and second fingers and the thumb, very slightly bent. The third and fourth fingers would be turned in towards the palm of the hand a trifle more than the others. A pencil of less than four inches long should be used with a holder. The point of the pencil should not be moistened by the pupil.

Book:
The book should be placed with its edges parallel with those of the desk, and far enough from its lower edge to allow the forearm to rest upon it. The book may be moved slightly, to the left or right, upwards

180

or downwards, to bring the work more nearly in front of the pupil, or to accomodate it to the hand. Do not change position of book or paper to draw lines in different directions, but change the position of hand, arm, and pencil if necessary.

"Are there any questions? If not, you may commence the examination."

Values	Time — One and a Half Hours
15	1. Draw a circle through three points, not in a straight line.
15	2. In an angle of 45 degrees, inscribe a circle of one inch radius, which shall touch the sides of the angle.
15	3. On a line, 2 inches in length, construct, by a special method, a regular octagon.
15	4. Upon a diagonal, 4 inches in length, construct a square, and trisect one of the angles formed by the diagonal.
20	5. In an equilateral triangle, of which the base is 3 inches, inscribe three equal circles, each touching two sides and two circles.
20	6. Show general method of inscribing, in a circle, a regular polygon, of any number of sides.

"Time's up, hand in your papers!"

The foregoing is representative of the approach to the study of geometry in the late nineteenth century in Ontario (McFaul, *The Public School Drawing Manual: For Teachers and Students,* Toronto: Canada Publishing, 1892). From the inception of school systems, mathematics (including arithmetic, algebra, and geometry) has enjoyed a prominent place in the curriculum—a charter member of the "triple threat"—reading, writing, and arithmetic—which influences primary and elementary education particularly, and which is queen of the sciences in the higher grades.

A glance at the general characteristics of the curriculum over the past century will illustrate the influential position occupied by this subject.

In the 1840s in Upper Canada the common subjects were spelling, reading, writing, *arithmetic,* grammar, geography and some British history.

> Janzen, *Curriculum Change in a Canadian Context,* (Toronto: Gage, 1970, p. 30)

In the early 1900s in most elementary schools, the simple fare was reading, writing, *arithmetic,* supplemented with grammar and geography in the higher grades. (Ibid, p. 36)

By mid twentieth century the number one objective related to academic development, as expressed in the "Report on the Canadian Conference of Education" (Ottawa, 1958), was:

> To teach the pupils the skills of reading, writing, spelling, oral expression, written language, *mathematics,* and the simple graphic arts.

The priority status of mathematics in the learning program raises the question of the quality of the curriculum.

In his thorough study of the history of education in Alberta, J.W. Chalmers synopsizes the changing philosophy and methodology of this subject. Four approaches can be noted. In the nineteenth and early twentieth century, mathematics was perceived as one of the important mental disciplines. Through intensive study, a general mental improvement affecting other aspects of learning was to be expected. The investigations of the Russian psychologist Pavlov into the effects of conditioning on dogs, in turn, influenced the research of Watson and Thorndike in the United States. The latter established the theory that the myriad arithmetical facts that the individual needed to learn could be most effectively undertaken through stimulus-response bonds. Repetition (i.e. drill) was required to reinforce these S-R bonds. By the 1930s the influence of American philosopher John Dewey was felt. The "enterprise" method of learning entered the classrooms. Mathematics now became one part of the integrated curriculum, correlated with the social sciences, languages, and the fine arts. No longer was this subject to be treated in isolation. The "queen" was dethroned in the ensuing upheaval in the curriculum. The revolution did not proceed smoothly.

> To claim it (i.e. the Enterprise method) has been an unqualified success would be unjustified. Critics have attacked its basic philosophy—with its rejections of the sanctions of authority per se, whatever its source, and its concept of truth as that which works, changing rather than immutable, relative rather than absolute—as

un-Christian, even anti-religious, possibly communist.

> Chalmers, *Schools of the Foothills Province,*
> (Toronto: U.T.P., 1967, p. 91)

Interestingly enough it was the U.S.S.R. that inspired the next change in mathematics teaching. The first Sputnik shot the curriculum into a different orbit. American educational authorities bore the brunt of the criticism for having allowed their society to become a runner-up in the science-technology sweepstakes. What "Ivan" presumably knew, and what "Johnny" did not, centred largely on mathematical understanding. New methods and programs were needed. A spate of "new maths" followed, Greater Cleveland, Ball State, and Texas Curriculum Studies among them. Hard on the heels of the research came the flood of materials: Experiences in . . .", "Exploring modern . . .", "Seeing Through . . .", the profusion of which could often be conveyed more readily by acronyms. ("Are you using S.T.A.?" "No, I'm using S.M.S.G." "What's that?" "I'm not sure, but it was developed in California, I think.")

Meanwhile, back in Canada educational progress followed its traditional pattern. What was sauce for the American gander was adequate for the Canadian goose. The rush was soon on to purchase the latest, if not the best, in American mathematics materials. One province no sooner opted for the Addison-Wesley program, when its neighbour would take the plunge in whatever Scott-Foresman (a competing American publisher) had to offer. The fact that literally no Canadian teachers were prepared to teach these programs was a secondary consideration. Some questioned the need for Canadians to make changes based on American preoccupation with the race to the moon. But in general Canadian faculties of education mounted an attack on the problems of an inadequately prepared teaching force for the mathematics classroom. American professors or American-educated Canadians, together with foreign textbooks and other materials, were rushed into the breach. Canada, if not quite up there with (or in) the stars, was not to be ignored either. Johnny Canuck might be outhustled by a "Vyacheslav" and a "Yuri" on the hockey rink, but not in the theory of sets.

The reverberations of this approach to changing the quality of Canadian mathematics are still being felt. Nearly two decades after Sputnik, the reaction has commenced—adequately summed-up in the phrase, "Now what?" There is much concern for the mathematical understanding of the initial "space-age" generation of students.

Universities, businesses, technology institutes, and parents have questioned the effectiveness of the new math.

Perhaps it is timely to suggest that in this field of learning, too, Canadians should search for the answers within the needs and resources of their own society. Rather than relying exclusively on the most recent Canadianized version of American materials, should thought not be given to developing programs designed for our society? The research of Jean Piaget (Switzerland); the developments of the Nuffield Foundation (Great Britain); the work of Van Engen and Stern (U.S.A.), can be drawn upon and incorporated as appropriate. But the work of Zolten Dienes at the Université de Sherbrooke, Doyal Nelson at the University of Alberta, Werner Liedtke at the University of Victoria, and James MacLean, former president of the Ontario Association of Teachers of Mathematics can also receive greater attention than formerly. In a similar fashion, materials such as *Project Mathematics* (Holt) which are available in French as well as English editions, should find a receptive clientele in a bilingual nation. Interpreting this as a plea for "Canadian Calculus" is to miss the mark by a wide margin. Meeting unique social, scientific, technological, and economic needs is the function of the mathematics curriculum.

◆ ◆ ◆ ◆

Primary-Elementary

Mathways (teaching program). W.W. Bates and others, Copp, 1974. Grades 1-6; metric.

Mathex (teaching program). L.D. Nelson and W.W. Sawyer, E.B., 1970. School set, $150.00. Primary set, $150.00. Junior set, $150.00. Grades 1-6; may be purchased in individual units or sample sets; materials for students and teachers included.

Titles from the Dent Metric series, Dent. Puzzles, pictures, activities, games; primary-elementary grades.
  Primary Book 1—We Measure Length, Mary E. Thomas and and others (Dent, 1974), $1.35.
  Junior Book 1—More About Length, Mary E. Thomas and others (Dent, 1975), $1.50.

Project Mathematics (teaching program). H. Andrew Elliott and others, Holt, 1973. K-6 An activity-centred math program which incorporates some of the methodology and philosophy of the Nuffield Math Project; includes teacher handbooks, student textbooks, workbooks, metric edition available.

Mathématiques contemporaines (teaching program). Alfred P. Hanwell, Holt, 1965. Grades 1-6; French; includes teacher handbooks, student textbooks and workbooks.

Mathematics (teaching program). Book Society. Student books, 1-5, $1.75 each. Teacher guides, 1-5, $1.00 each. Grades 3-7; set of all-metric exercises on linear, area, volume, liquid measurement, temperature, mass.

L'univers des nombres (teaching program). Alexandre Deschamps et Léopold Lacroix, Holt, 1966. Grades 1-6; French; includes teacher handbooks, student textbooks and workbooks.

Mathématique vivante (teaching program). Z.P. Dienes and A. Tellier, H.M.H.
Primary; *Zoo éléphant* 1&2; *Zoo chien* 1&2; *Zoo ours* 1&2; *Zoo chat* 1&2, $1.50 each. OR *Zoo*; collection des huit livres, $11.00. Livre du maître, $3.60.
Pour la classe, trousse de fiches, 1, 2, 3, $48.00; pour l'élève, fiches individuelles, $1.80; pour le professeur, commentaires généraux, $1.80; guide de l'unite 1, 2, 3, $4.85 each.

Kits and Materials for Primary-Elementary Grades

Materials developed by Z.P. Dienes, Scholar's Choice:

Dienes Logic Starter Set, $12.60. One tabletop set of logiblocs, one set of 72 logic symbol cards, one set of logic symbol dice, one handbook; *Dienes Logiblocs,* 48 pieces, $17.82; *Dienes Logiblocs Handbook,* 38¢; *Logic Dice,* $1.14; *Logic Cards,* $2.08; *Teacher's Handbook,* $1.66; *Dienes Flipover Logic Tracks,* $7.60; *Logic and Set Work Cards,* Set A & B, $7.60 each; *Dienes Relation Plates Handbook,* $1.66; *Dienes Multi-base Set,* $106.35.

Primary Mathematics Involvement Program, (kit). SRA, $189.00. Two hundred and forty activity cards in 5 levels, K-4, organized around topics of number, geometry, and measurement.

Mathematics Involvement Program (kit). SRA, $205.00. Two hundred and fifty activity cards in 7 levels, K-6, organized by topics of number, geometry, and measurement.

Mathex Models (kit). E.B., $8.50. Fourteen plastic models of geometric solids.

Think Metric Kit (kit). Scholar's Choice, $5.95. Includes 8 posters, metric conversion slide, graph paper and teacher's handbook.

Models for Mathematics (kit). Holt, $24.95. A set of 26 wooden geometric solids and 100 plane figures in plastic; green, yellow, orange, red.

Supplementary Items for Primary-Elementary

The Metric Book of Amusing Things to Do, E. Hallamore and L. Bucholtz (Greey de Pencier, 1974), $2.50 pa. Games, puzzles, projects to involve the young child in using metric measure.

Easy to Use Metric Conversion Tables, Scholar's Choice, $1.75. The Desi Decimal series, George Calogeridis, Lee Hutton and Guy Richard, Holt, 1973. $5.85 each. Books with an uncomplicated approach to the principles of conversion and the terminology of metric measurement.

Fun with Figures, General, $2.00. Puzzles and *More Fun with Figures,* General, $1.75. Brainteasers.

One to Fifty Book, ed. Anne Wyse (U.T.P., 1973), $2.75. A counting book based on children's illustrations.

The Great Canadian How to Go Metric and Like it Book, Del Grande (Gage, 1975), $2.95 pa.

Junior High

Math Is, Frank Ebos and Robert Robertson (Nelson, 1974), Book 1 & 2, $6.95 each. Grades 7 & 8. Teacher's guides, $8.75 each. Answer keys, $1.85 each.

Gage Mathematics (Gage, 1974), Grades 7-9, metric. Books 1&2, $6.50 each. Book 3, $7.50. Answer Keys $2.20 each. Teacher's Manual, $2.20 each.

Kits for Junior High

Mathset Measurement (kit). Gage, 1970, $16.50. Two hundred and sixty-eight cards plus teacher's handbook.

Mathset Geometry (kit). Gage, 1969, $16.50. Two hundred and forty cards plus teacher's handbook.

Materials for Teachers

Mathematical Experiences in Early Childhood, H.D. Nelson and W.W. Liedtke (E.B., 1972), $3.75.

Geometry: Kindergarten to Grade Thirteen, (O.I.S.E., 1967), $3.95.

Modern Mathematics, A.B. Evenson (Gage, 1966), $6.60. Provides background to changes taking place in junior-senior high mathematics.

Quelques aspects du renouveau de l'enseignement des mathématiques à l'élémentaire, Hélène Kayler (P.Ú.Q.), $2.50.

Elements of Modern Mathematics: Algebra, A.J. Coleman and others (Gage, 1973), $6.90.

Geoboards and Motion Geometry for Teachers, Del Grande (Gage, 1975) $5.50 pa.

Geometry in the Classroom: New Concepts and Methods, H.A. Elliott, James R. MacLean, and J.M. Jordan (Holt, 1968), $5.50 pa.

Materials for Teachers in French

Titles by Z.P. Dienes from H.M.H.:

Nombres naturels, entiers, rationels, $4.50; *Rélations et fonctions,* $4.50; *Les ensembles et leur logique,* $5.95; *Logique et jeux logiques,* $2.25; *Ensembles, nombres et puissances,* $2.25; *Explorations de l'espace et pratique de la mesure,* $2.25; *Mathématiques pour tous,* $4.90; *Les six étapes du processus d'apprentissage en mathématique,* $3.30; *La Mathématique moderne dans l'enseignement primaire,* $2.65; *Comprendre la mathématique,* $4.95; *Pensée et structure,* $4.30; *Tapologie, géometrie projective et affine,* $3.75; *Géometrie euclidienne,* tome 2, $3.75; *Groupes et coordonnes,* tome 3, $3.75.

Periodicals

Math Letter, O.I.S.E. Four issues annually, $1.00. Grades 7-10.

Plaisir des mathématiques, O.I.S.E. Four issues annually, $1.00. Grades 7-10.

Fun with Mathematics, O.I.S.E. Seven issues annually, $1.00. Sold in sets of 12. Grades 4-6.

Chapter 19

MUSIC

A visit to a record and tape store and a reading of music curricula have much in common. In both instances Canadian music lies somewhere between country and ethnic in its importance—an item to be found in the extensive collection of Clyde Gilmour, ("Gilmour's Albums," C.B.C. Radio) perhaps, but not of much consequence. Were it not for the stand taken by the Canadian Radio and Television Commission (C.R.T.C.) to ensure that Canadian content be made available through the media, it is probable that there would be little interest in this aspect of cultural life. Yet this nation has produced composers Claude Champagne and Louis Applebaum, operatic soprano Lois Marshall, violinist Betty Jean Hagen, pianist Glenn Gould, contralto Maureen Forrester, orchestral conductor Alexander Brott and ballerina Veronica Tennant, to select but a few from the field of classical music. Nor has the folk music field been wanting in distinctive composers and performers—Ian and Sylvia Tyson, Oscar Brand, Bob Ruzicka, and Gordon Lightfoot. Sir Ernest MacMillan, himself a distinguished composer and conductor, put his finger on what must be the fundamental Canadian proverb, "a prophet is not without honour except in his own country." Nearly twenty years ago he wrote:

> The pity of it is that Canadians are still slow to recognize excellence in their own young musicians until other countries put upon them the stamp of approval.
> MacMillan, *Encyclopedia Canadiana,* (Toronto: Grolier, vol. 7, p. 225, 1958)

Nowhere is this observation more valid than in the music programs offered in most Canadian schools. The preoccupation has been with performance, commencing with the rhythm band of the primary years and terminating with choral, band, or orchestral productions at the high school level. In themselves, these developments are justifiable so long as music is perceived as an isolated subject for the select and talented few.

The concern for the education of musicians is fortified by the search for the appropriate teaching method. Largely dependent upon the course in music methodology offered at the university level, the specialist teacher will be equipped with the Japanese developments of Suzuki, the American initiatives of Mary Helen Richards, the German contributions of Orff, or the Hungarian Kodaly method. A Canadian-developed program, like an adequate curriculum in other than large urban schools, is rare. Rarer still is a methodology, regardless of its source, adapted to Canadian circumstances.

A multi-language society poses its own particular educational problems. The work of Orff and Suzuki lends itself to employing music as a means of teaching languages. Writing in *Schulwerke, Music For Children*, Orff emphasized the underlying basic patterns from which music can grow. The intellectual centre of his work is language. Through speech leading to the use of percussion instruments, the student can become involved in music. The emphasis is on "doing", "taking part" and "experiencing".

The Suzuki teaching method can be defined as a method of education in the native language applied without any essential modification to music education. Fundamental points to consider in this mother tongue approach include:

— having mothers taught the music so that they can teach their children;

— emphasis on repetition;

— the importance of the individual listening to recordings before attempting to play an instrument;

— using means other than language to communicate with students;

— selecting music which conveys emotional involvement.

It is useful to note that Dr. Suzuki has adapted this method of teaching to all stringed instruments, as well as mathematics, art, writing, and the teaching of English to Japanese children.

In as variable a society as Canada's, it would be practical to draw upon these and similar developments with adaptations to meet special needs. This approach would be beneficial in many ways. not the least of which would be the exposure of every individual to music. Opportunities for specialization can complement this approach. It is obvious that not every child has the desire or the aptitude to become a performer, and yet every student will be tuned-in to the latest in f.m., stereo, or quadraphonic sound at some point in life. Music for entertainment and relaxation is not a phenomenon confined to the adolescent years alone. As a lifelong experience in developing discriminating taste, the potential of music has few equals.

Five suggestions to consider:

1. Folk Music: the history and evolution of Canadian folk songs. Utilizing an extensive collection such as the R.C.A. Victor Centennial edition of long play recordings, *Canadian Folk Songs* (No. CS 100) as a basic resource, the following topics could be studied through listening:

   — Riddles and Traditional: "I'll Give My Love An Apple" and "Où Vas-tu, Mon P'tit Garçon"

   — Legendary and Historical: "Come All Ye Bold Canadians", "Chanson de Louis Riel", "O Canada"

   — Romantic Adventure and Tragedies: "Henry, My Son" and "A Maid, I Am In Love"

   — Love Ballads and Laments: "À La Claire Fontaine" and "The Bold Fisherman"

   — Love's Labour Lost: "Red River Valley" and "Hemmer Jane"

   — Courtship and Marriage: "Cod Liver Oil" and "Je sais bien quelque chose"

   — Songs and Ballads of the Lumber Camps: "The Lumberman's Alphabet" and "Ye Maidens of Ontario"

   — Work Songs: "The Klondike Gold Rush", "Four Strong Winds", and "Bud the Spud"

   — Social Comment: "Vive La Canadienne", "Feller From Fortune", and "Saskatchewan"

2. Music and the Environment: The Service Department of the Canadian Nature Federation, 46 Elgin Street, Ottawa, has available a variety of recordings of the sounds of nature. Many of these items lend themselves to developing an appreciation of music in the environment. More importantly, they can be used with good effect with young learners in helping them to discriminate among sounds (i.e. pitch, tone, intensity). Trying to identify the sounds of insects, birds, and animals is an enjoyable pastime in itself. At a more advanced level of study, students can compare the actual sounds with the interpretations provided by composers and artists (e.g. "The Flight of the Bumble Bee" by Rimsky-Korsakov; "Morning" by Edward Greig). Some sample titles to consider:

A Day In Algonquin Park
Prairie Spring
Cries of the Wild
The Language and Music of the Wolves
Land of the Loon
Voices of the North Woods
The Songs of Insects
Bird Songs In Literature
Songs of the Humpback Whale

(N.B. Write to the Canadian Nature Federation for a current price list.)

3. Music and Local History: No study of a region of Canada is complete without reference to the authentic music of that area. The National Museums of Canada have anthologies available which provide excellent source material (e.g. *Folksongs from Southern New Brunswick* by Helen Creighton (1971, $7.95) and *Songs of the Newfoundland Outports* by Kenneth Peacock (1966, $15.00 for three volumes). Musical transcriptions are included throughout.) Also available in book format is *Maritime Folk Songs* by Helen Creighton (McGraw: 1962, $4.95). Recorded material is in increasing supply. Study of Northern Canada will be enhanced by including *Straight North* (Damon Label, No. 1004). The material was composed by Edmonton folk-artist Bob Ruzicka; Ted Wesley sings the ten selections. A two-volume collection by Monique Leyrac (Columbia label, No. G.F.S. 90009) provides twenty selections, representative, in part, of French Canadian music. *Trade Winds: The Saga of Newfoundland In Song* by Omar Blondahl (Rodeo label No. RLP-5) includes "We'll Rant and We'll Roar" and "I'se the B'y". A useful one-record edition of thirteen representative songs is *Folk Music of Canada* (Bowmar label No. B-100). For each area from east to west (but not north), one representative selection is performed. A companion album is *Canadian Folk Dances* (Bowmar label No. B216). Seven selections, with instructions for performing each dance, are included. Providing a finale to the study of music as related to cultural heritage is the *Canadian Centennial Celebration* (London Label No. 99432). Stirring martial music is combined with the Peace Tower Bells in Ottawa and quotations from Sir John A. Macdonald and former Governor General Georges P. Vanier.

4. Without the C.B.C. Publications Department, access to a comprehensive classical music collection would be very difficult.

Their catalogue should be regarded as an essential reference. In the bibliography following, only a representative selection is mentioned in order to demonstrate the many alternatives for teaching appreciatio.¡ of classical music (e.g. regional developments, orchestral, ensemble, choral, soloist, string, wind instrumental . . .).

5. Junior-Senior high school students will benefit from having easy access to current issues of the various music periodicals. The coverage is comprehensive: opera, ballet, jazz, folk music, rock. Reviews of recorded material, coupled with evaluations of developments in the electronic music industry, provide interesting, informative reading. The potential for relating student interest to other aspects of the curriculum is apparent. From the technology of building a stereo-sound system to the social comment in the songs of Murray McLaughlin, music can play a significant part in any student's educational life. The communications revolution wrought by the transistor and the cassette should alter the isolated approach to the study of music characteristic of many classrooms.

♦ ♦ ♦ ♦

General Reference

The Sounds of Music, Don Cowan (Macmillan, 1970), $4.25. Ideas for developing music appreciation among junior high students.

Famous Musicians, Louise G. McCready (Clarke, Irwin, 1957), $2.75 pa. Careers of Sir Ernest MacMillan, Dr. Edward Johnson, Dr. W. Pelletier, and Dr. Healey Willan.

Soundprints, Peter Such (Clarke, Irwin, 1973), $3.50. The careers of six Canadian composers.

Tenor of his Time: Edward Johnson of the Met, Ruby Mercer (Clarke, Irwin, 1975), $9.50. Biography of the internationally acclaimed opera singer.

Wanna fight, Kid?, Chester Duncan (Queenston, 1975), $2.50 pa. Autobiography of Winnipeg-born conductor, Chester Duncan.

Canadian Composer series, U.T.P., $15.00 each. Biography of Harry Sommers currently available, other titles projected.

Traditional Canadian Dances, Everett (Canadian F.D.S. Audio

Visual), $1.65 pa. Booklet of dances with performance instructions.

A History of Music in Canada, 1534-1914, Helmut Kallmann (U.T.P., 1960), $3.00 pa.

Roll Back the Years: A History of Canadian Recorded Sound and its Legacy: Genesis to 1930, National Library (Information Canada, 1975), $12.75.

Colas et Collinette, ou Le Bailli dupé, Joseph Quesnel (Ré-Édition Québecois), $3.30 br. Premier opéra québecoise, écrit en 1790.

The Bands Canadians Danced to, Helen McNamara and Jack Lomas (Griffin, 1973), $10.95. An illustrated account of the Canadian dance band scene, 1920-1960.

Axes, Chops and Hot Licks, Ritchie Yorke (Hurtig, 1971), $2.95 pa. A survey of the rock music scene in Canada.

Series

Music for Young Canada, Kenneth Bray and others (Gage, 1967-69). Six student song books for grades 3-8.

Songtime, Vera Russell and others (Holt, 1963-70). Folksong collections from around the world for grades 2-8; includes teacher handbooks, student textbooks and l.p. recordings.

Basic Goals in Music, Lloyd H. Slind and others (McGraw, 1966). K-8; an integrated program of textbooks, charts, and teacher's handbooks.

Folk Song Books

Canada's Story in Song, Edith Fowke and Alan Mills (Gage, 1965), $6.95. Seventy-three songs with piano and guitar accompaniments.

Singin' About Us, Ed. R. Davis (Lorimer, 1976), $5.95. Sixty-seven songs from seventeen of the best singers and composers in Canada today.

Songs of the Great Dominion, W.D. Lighthall (Coles, 1971), $4.95 pa.

Canadian Folk Songs for the Young, Barbara Cass-Beggs (J.J. Douglas, 1975), $5.95. Thirty-two songs from across Canada including those of Indian and Inuit peoples.

Canadian Vibrations, Edith Fowke (Macmillan, 1972), $3.95 pa.

Seventy popular songs with melody line, words, and chords for guitar and autoharp.

Folk Songs of Canada, Edith Fowke and Richard Johnston (Waterloo Music, 1954), $7.50. Choral ed. $2.50. Seventy folk songs from across Canada.

More Folk Songs of Canada, Edith Fowke and Richard Johnston (Waterloo Music, 1967), $7.50. Seventy-seven additional songs.

Songs to a Seagull, R. Evans (McGraw, 1969), $4.95. A collection of folksongs from artists such as Ian Tyson, Joni Mitchell, Oscar Brand, combined with the verse of poets such as Leonard Cohen, Joan Finnigan and Al Purdy.

Chansons de Québec, Edith Fowke and Richard Johnston (Waterloo Music, 1973), $2.00. Forty French Canadian songs; also available in English.

Gaelic Songs in Nova Scotia, Helen Creighton and Calum MacLeod (National Museum, 1964), $8.00 pa.

Men of the Deeps, John C. O'Donnell (Clarke, Irwin, 1975), $1.95 pa. Songs of the Cape Breton Coal Miners' Chorus; also available in l.p. recording from the Waterloo Music Company.

Songs and Ballads from Nova Scotia, Helen Creighton (General, 1966), $3.50 pa.

Folk Ballads and Songs of the Lower Labrador Coast, MacEdward Leach (National Museum, 1965), $9.00 pa.

Songs of Miramichi, Louise Manny (Brunswick, 1968), $6.95 pa. Songs of the Miramichi River area of northern New Brunswick.

Born a Woman: The Rita MacNeil Songbook, Rita MacNeil (Canadian Women's Educational Press, 1975), $4.75. Lyrics and melodies by a Cape Breton artist.

Sally go Round the Sun, Edith Fowke (McClelland, 1969), $7.95. With l.p. recording, $9.95. Recording only, $4.95. A beautifully illustrated collection of songs for young children.

If Snowflakes Fell in Flavours . . . and Other Super Songs for Nursery School, Kindergarten and Up, Offenheim, Clark and Cruikshank (Berandol Music, 1974), $2.50 pa. Twenty great songs for today's children; also available on l.p. recording.

All the Bees and All the Keys, James Reaney and John Beckwith (Porcepic, 1975), $3.95 pa. Primary.

Recorded Folk Songs

Folk Songs of Canada (l.p. recording). Joyce Sullivan and Charles Jordan., Canadian F.D.S. Audio-Visual, $5.79.

Maple Sugar: Songs of Early Canada (record). Methuen, 2 record album, $12.00. Twenty-two songs performed by 35 musicians and singers; notes, bibliographies, and a folk map of Canada are included.

Multi-media Kit

Creative Rhythmic Approach (kit). SRA, $295.00. For any grade level, includes six 60-min cassette tapes, 92 overhead transparencies, and teacher's handbook.

Classical Music for Listening

A variety of reasonably priced stereo l.p. recordings are available from C.B.C. Publications, $4.00 each. Titles include:

Atlantic Symphony Orchestra, #SM-132.

The Halifax Trio, #RC1-229. The music of Alexis Constant, a pioneer in Canadian music.

Atlantic Brass Ensemble, #SM-195.

The Orford String Quartet, #SM-153. The quartet was formed by the Jeunesses Musicales Summer Camp at Mount Orford, P.Q. in 1965.

The Tudor Singers of Montreal, #SM-86. Performance of unaccompanied music of the Tudor, baroque, and contemporary periods.

McGill Chamber Orchestra, #RC1-216. The music of French-Canadian composer, Claude Champagne.

Société du Musique Contemporaire du Québec, #RC1-358.

The Monks of St. Bénoit-du-Lac, #RC1-383. Gregorian chants performed by the Benedictine monks.

The Toronto Symphony Orchestra, #SM-150. A recording of a live session at Massey Hall, Toronto, in 1972.

C.B.C. Toronto Chorus and Symphony Orchestra, #RC1-214. Combines the oratory of Barry Morse with the soprano voice of Mary Morrison.

C.B.C. Winnipeg Orchestra, #SM-119. Includes selections composed by Violet Archer, University of Alberta; E. Rathburn, a native of New Brunswick; and one selection based on an original Copper Inuit tune.

The Baroque Strings of Vancouver, #SM-136.

The Lyric Arts Trio of Canada, #SM-96.

C.B.C. Orchestra, #RC1-291. Includes a musical description of Montreal's historical, cultural, and civic landmarks and the 'Miramichi Ballad', based on New Brunswick folk songs.

National Arts Centre Orchestra, #SM-197. Selections from Brahms.

The Festival Singers of Canada and the Community Brass, #SM-203.

Music of Today by Contemporary Composers, #RC-298-299-300-301. Four records, $12.00.

Carrefour, #RC1-373. Electro-acoustic music by seven Canadian composers.

Cassenti Players, #SM-97. An instrumental ensemble organized by bassoonist George Zukerman.

Donald Bell, #SM-111. Bass baritone, native of South Burnaby, B.C.

Claude Corbeil, #RC-296. Bass, native of Rimouski, P.Q.

Robert Silverman, #SM-90. Montreal-born pianist.

Elizabeth Benson Guy, #SM-92. Soprano, native of Bridgewater, N.S.; accompanied on the harpsichord by Greta Kraus.

Hugh McLean, #SM-129. Organist, pianist, harpsichordist; native of Winnipeg.

Books for Teachers

Music for Fun, Music for Learning, Lois Birkenshaw (Holt, 1974), $6.95. A book of games, songs, activities.

The New Approach to Music, H. Perrin and others (Holt, 1972), Junior ed., $5.95. Primary ed. $5.95. Two books developed by the Ontario Institute for Studies in Education which stress a personal, creative approach to listening, singing, reading, and writing of music.

Teaching Music in Canadian Schools, Vera Russell (Holt, 1967), $2.50. A textbook on the aims, essentials, and problems of the music program, K-8.

To Listen, To Like, To Learn, Barbara Cass-Beggs (Peter Martin, 1974), $6.95 pa. Rhythm, melody, and form with teaching suggestions; songs, books, recordings; 80 pages of music combining an emphasis on Canadian folk music with the Kodaly and Orff methods.

Lucile Panabaker's Song Book, Lucile Panabaker (Peter Martin, 1968), $4.50. Pre-school and kindergarten.

More Songs From Lucile Panabaker, Lucile Panabaker (Peter Martin, 1975), $6.50 pa.

Classroom Ukulele Method, J. Chalmers Doane (Waterloo Music, 1971), $2.75.

Cheerleading and Songleading, Ron Humphrey (Hurtig, 1970), $6.50. Handbook of ideas, materials.

Periodicals

Beetle, Canadian Periodical Publishers' Association. 12 issues annually, $7.50. Emphasis on contemporary music.

Sound, Canadian Periodical Publishers' Association. 10 issues annually, $4.00. Music reviews by Clyde Gilmour, B.B. King, Oscar Peterson; information on purchasing audio equipment.

Opera Canada, Canadian Periodical Publishers' Association. Quarterly, $6.00.

Dance in Canada, Canadian Periodical Publishers' Association. Quarterly, $6.50. Emphasis on ballet.

Coda, Canadian Periodical Publishers' Association. 10 issues annually, $7.00. Jazz magazine.

Chapter 20

PHYSICAL EDUCATION

Summer and Winter Games, Commonwealth and Pan American
Games, international tournaments and competitions of all descriptions, and the Olympics themselves have become virtually routine
events in the nation's life, but serious physical education in the
schools is rare. There are obviously exceptions where enlightened
leadership, specialized staff, and adequate budgets exist; but if the
concern is for "sound minds in sound bodies" on a national scale,
then Canadian students generally are poorly served in this area.

Many factors are associated with the low importance accorded
"Phys. Ed.", or "P.T.". Historically, an economy based on agriculture and primary resource industry had neither need nor inclina-
tion for such a school subject. Rolling back the forests, furrowing
the soil harvesting the resources, treading the path up hill and down
dale to the little red school house made formal exercise redundant.
Physical exercise was equated with education in physical development—a confusion in terminology which has persisted to the present
day.

With few exceptions, the history of physical education as a
formal school subject is of brief duration, particularly in the
junior-senior high grades. In 1852 Egerton Ryerson wrote a series
of articles which included tables for gymnastic exercises and described movements for the horizontal bar and the wooden horse. In
1919 the Province of Alberta made physical education a compulsory
subject in the junior high curriculum. In both cases, school authorities moved to implement these ideas with the speed of a slow march
rather than a hundred metre sprint. In Saskatchewan it was not
until the 1944-45 school year that physical education was considered
to be a "core" (i.e. compulsory) subject in high school. Even then,
students received no credit value for the course. In 1950 a revised
high school program introduced in British Columbia required three

years of study in health and personal development, one facet of which was to be physical education.

Only in recent times has the remarkable shift in patterns of living prompted much interest in this subject. Revolutions in technology, growth in service industries, changes in work habits, and migrations of people from rural areas to cities have combined to arouse an uneasy concern for physical health. Schools are faced with several hurdles if they are to meet the demands and needs fostered by these changes.

One such obstacle to be overcome falls into the category of folklore—widely held, if mistaken, beliefs about the position of athletes and athletics in the nation's life. As a country, Canada lacks the "battles are won on the playing fields of Eton" tradition. (The one sporting exception occurred on a summer day in June, 1763. A couple of teams of Indian lacrosse players got together for a friendly match on the "playing field" near Michilimackinac. A craftily executed passing play sent a pin-point shot through the open door of the fort. What followed makes contemporary mayhem on ice look tame by comparison.) Nevertheless, there is a thread of earthy ruggedness running through the folk culture. From Gordie Howe stuffing copies of Eaton's catalogues into his socks for shinpads and chasing frozen "prairie apples" (horse manure) over icy sloughs in sub-zero temperatures, to the superstar status of Bobby Clarke, these "legends in their own time" become the yardsticks for measuring athletic endeavour. The result is not only public concentration on the "star", but also perpetuation of the notion that "anyone can make it if you only try". The saga "from stockroom clerk to corporation president" has its parallel in sports. Hockey authority Howie Meeker is worth noting in this regard.

> It seems our interest in a player or team is aroused only when we face the prospect of having a "winner". Now there is nothing wrong with an adult using his hockey talent as a commodity, to be bought, sold or bartered. But when kids barely into their teens are pressured into this commodity market, there's something wrong somewhere.
>
> Once a few teenagers become nationally known through amateur hockey, the parents of the other 99 percent figure their youngster isn't measuring up. So the minor league pressure cooker is heated up a few more degrees—win, win, win. Who's got the time for basic training? If a youngster concentrates on fundamentals while he is 13, how the hell can he be a junior star at 15?
>
> But that still doesn't explain why hockey is the one major sport where basic training is most neglected. The myth that stardom

lies ahead for every raggedy-assed kid with mail order catalogue
shin pads who learns to skate on a frozen pond should be demolished.

Meeker, H., *Howie Meeker's Hockey Basics*
(Toronto: Prentice, 1973, pp. 137-138)

An interesting addition to Meeker's observation was the problem
confronting the World Hockey Federation in 1963. Three prizes
were to be awarded to the best players of the tournament among
the prize-winning teams, except for the championship team. The
president of the Federation and the coach of the winning team (the
U.S.S.R.) explained that on this team there were no stars, and therefore the awards could not be given. The team of the U.S.S.R. emphasized collective rather than individual superiority. (Tarasov, *Russian
Hockey Secrets*. Toronto: Simon & Schuster, 1972, p. 28). Unfortunately, schools too have extolled the merits of the few to the dis-
advantage of the many, whether on the basketball court, the football
field, or the ice arena. Fielding the best available competitive team
becomes more important than participation by the majority. Curriculum experts and coaches alike could benefit from studying the
traditional beliefs of Indian and Inuit peoples. Involvement and
amusement were basic. It was preferable to remain submerged within
the group until such time as one's specific skills or assistance were
called for. There was no need to seek overtly to lead or attempt to
dominate. The group was more important than any individual.

If historical antecedents and current attitudes discourage educational change, then practical teacher considerations lengthen the
odds perceptibly. At the primary levels, unless a specialized teacher
is available, teaching physical education can be in the same league
as teaching fine arts. It is a filler of time and especially useful when
children are restless. A game of "I'm a little teapot short and stout.
Here is my handle, here is my spout", followed by a rousing spell
of dodge-ball on the playground, will quickly revitalize the lethargic
learner. A sporadic skirmish on the volleyball court, followed by a
cold shower, will douse carnal thoughts and uncontrolled desires in
the adolescent years. Physical education is seldom related to language
(e.g. body movement), artistic expression (gymnastics, ballet), or
muscle development (isometrics). Nor is much emphasis placed on
developing recreational pursuits which would stand students in good
stead in adult life. Team sports with little or no carry-over value
are frequently the priority concern. Even where competent teachers
are available, their initiatives can be frustrated by administrative
rigidity. Getting one's class to the gym can be construed as more of
a treat or a reward for academic performance than as an integral

aspect of learning and development. One or two fragmentary experiences per week on the trampoline may activate the sweat glands, but are unlikely to develop an understanding of motion and rhythm, or contribute to physical fitness.

Teachers who are fortunate in having equipment and regular periods for physical education, can console themselves that they have just one major problem to confront. Canadian learning materials are not abundant. Information Canada and the National Film Board have provided more instructional material than all private publishers combined. Essentially, the latter concentrate on books about sporting heroes and not on items to assist active participation. The ghost-written first-person account outdistances the guidebook by a wide margin. Moreover, hockey seems to hold a strange fascination for publishers. Judging by the titles available, Canada is composed of young titans on skates, whose motto is "five minutes for fighting" and whose coat of arms is emblazoned with a "Dave Shultz rampant" and an "Yvon Cournoyer couchant".

A limited sampling of hero-oriented material has been listed to indicate what is available. There is a place in the school program for reading about the great figures in sport, particularly if these can be integrated into the reading/literature and/or social studies curricula (e.g. Jack Ludwig's *Hockey Night in Moscow* (Toronto: McClelland, 1972), an excellent book by any standard; and professional quarterback, Frank Cosentino's scholarly history of the Canadian Football League). Recalling the heydays of Ned Hanlan (sculling), Tom Longboat (long-distance running), Marilyn Bell (marathon swimming), the Edmonton Grads (women's basketball), Louis Cyr (weightlifting), Barbara Ann Scott (figure skating), and Lionel Conacher (versatile competitor in many sports), illustrates diversity of excellence and can stimulate student interest. It is in making the leap from armchair reading to active participation that school efforts must be concentrated.

♦ ♦ ♦ ♦

How-to Books on Sports

La Pêche au Québec, Michel Chamberland (Homme, 1969), $3.00.

The Art of Angling, Tiny Bennett (Prentice, 1970), $8.90.

Get Wet: Aquatic Activities, (Information Canada, 1964), $1.50 pa.

Basketball: Coach's Manual, (Information Canada, 1972), $1.00 pa.

Family Camping, (Information Canada, 1968), 75¢ pa.

Canoe Canada: The Most Comprehensive Guide to Canoeing in Canada, N. Nickels (Van Nostrand, 1976), $9.95 pa.

Ernie Richardson's Curling, Mark Mulvoy and Ernie Richardson (McClelland, 1973), $4.75 pa.

Hiking Near Vancouver, Dougald MacDonald (Mitchell, 1971), $3.95 pa.

Howie Meeker's Hockey Basics, Howie Meeker (Prentice, 1973), $3.95 pa.

Hockey: Coach's Manual, Dept. of National Defence (Information Canada, 1974), $1.25 pa.

Beginning Hockey, (Information Canada) 25¢ pa.

How to Play Better Hockey, (Information Canada, 1972), 50¢ pa.

Hockey: The Right Start, Larivière (Holt, 1973), $1.75.

Goal Tending, Jacques Plante (Collier-Macmillan, 1972), $2.95 pa.

Box Lacrosse: The Fastest Game on Two Feet, J.D. Hinkson (Dent, 1974), $4.75 pa.

The Saddle Horse, (Information Canada, 1973), $1.00 pa.

Sailing: From Armchair to Sea Legs, Peter Sulman and David Terhune (Burns, 1973), $4.95 pa. A beginners' handbook.

All About Sailing: A Handbook for Juniors, Mario Brunet (Greey de Pencier, 1975), $4.95 pa.

All About Boating in Canada 1975, Tom Taylor (Clarke, Irwin, 1975), $2.95 pa.

Pleasure Craft Guide Book, (Information Canada), 50¢ pa.

Cross Country Skiing Handbook, Edward R. Baldwin (Modern Canadian Library, 1972), $3.95 pa.

Skating for Beginners, (Griffin), $8.15.

Soccer: Coach's Manual, (Information Canada, 1974), $1.35 pa.

Soccer: A Guide for Adult Coaches and Young Players, Redmond (LeBel Enterprises), $3.95 pa.

J'apprends à nager, Régent Lacoursière (Homme), $4.00.

Volleyball: Coach's Manual, (Information Canada, 1963), $1.00 pa.

How to Play Better Volleyball, (Information Canada, 1975), $1.00 pa.

Shape Up! Progressive Fitness for Practical People, Vic Sanders (McGraw, 1975), $6.95.

Titles from a series of illustrated handbooks for children and adults, Colban, $2.00 each pa.

> *Cross Country Skiing; Lacrosse; Field Hockey; The Game of Soccer; The Game of Table Tennis; Softball; Swimming; Tennis; Volleyball.*

Camping (filmstrip). col, N.F.B. set of 4, $5.00 each.

Introduction to Badminton (filmstrip). N.F.B., $5.00.

Lacrosse: The Canadian Game (filmstrip). N.F.B., $5.00.

Figure Skating (filmstrip). N.F.B., set of 3, $4.00 each.

Skiing (filmstrip). N.F.B., set of 4, $4.00 each. Downhill skiing.

Basic Skills in Synchronized Swimming (super-8mm film loop). N.F.B., set of 10, $21.00 each.

Reading About Sports

Canada's Sporting Heroes, Doug Fisher and S.F. Wise (General, 1974), $14.95. Over 170 biographies; the best available reference.

Games of Fear and Winning: Sports with an Inside View, Jack Ludwig (Doubleday, 1976), $8.95. The author is one of Canada's most accomplished authors.

Canadian Football: The Pigskin Preacher, Ted Sommerville (Sportbook, 1974), $9.95.

The Queen's Plate, Trent Frayne (McClelland, 1971), $4.95 pa.

Garney Henley: A Gentleman and a Tiger, 2nd ed., Robert F. Nielson (Potlatch, 1973), $3.95 pa. Biography of the Hamilton Tiger Cat football player.

Hockey Night in Moscow, Jack Ludwig (McClelland, 1972), $6.95. The best available account of the 1972 Team Canada-U.S.S.R. hockey series.

Hockey Night in Canada, Foster Hewitt (McGraw, 1970), $6.95.

Brian McFarlane's Hockey Annual, Brian McFarlane (Clarke, Irwin, 1975), $5.75. Stories, biographies, statistics, tips, and routines for young players.

Affiches

Affiches 'Grand Soleil', une série d'affiches illustrant les sports et les activités de plein air. Au recto, on retrouve l'illustration, au verso, tout ce qu'il faut connaître sur une activité sportive: historique, caractèristiques, conditions de pratique, organismes compétants et une bibliographie audio-scripto-visuelle. Série Complète, 46 affiches, 25½″ x 37½″, $30.00.

> Série A, *Sports de combat*—escrime, boxe, judo, lutte olympique, $3.00.

Série B, *Sports de raquette*—badminton, squash, tennis sur table, tennis, $3.00.

Série C, *Athlétisme*—courses: vitesse et relais; obstacles: demi-fond et fond; $2.25.

Série D, *Athlétisme*—lancers: poids, disque, marteau, javelot, $3.00.

Série E, *Athlétisme*—sauts: hauteur, longeur, triple saut, perche, $3.00.

Série F, *Sports Aquatiques*—nage synchronisée, natation, plongeon, water polo, $3.00.

Série G—*Sports Nautiques*—aviron, canoë-kyak (eau vive), canoë-kyak (plat), voile, ski nautique, $3.75.

Série H, *Sports de Neige*—ski alpin, ski nordique, saut a ski, $2.25.

Série I, *Sports de Glace*—patinage de vitesse, patinage artistique, $2.25.

Série J, *Sports de Ballon*—basket-ball, volley-ball, handball olympique, soccer (football), $3.00.

Série K, *Sports Divers*—halterophilie, cyclisme, sports equestres olympiques, crosse, gymnastique, $3.75.

For Teachers and Parents

For the Love of Sport: A Guide for Parents of Young Athletes, Renate Wilson (J.J. Douglas, 1975), $5.95 pa. A comprehensive book on many aspects of sport: coaching, the pressures of winning and losing, handicapped people, women, equipment, expenses.

A History of Physical Education in Canada, Frank Cosentino and M.L. Howell (General, 1971), $3.95 pa.

Periodicals

Action Sports, Canadian Periodical Publishers' Association. Monthly, $2.50.

All About Boating, Canadian Periodical Publishers' Association. Quarterly, $2.95.

Sports, Fitness and Recreation, Canadian Periodical Publishers' Association. Monthly, $6.00. Information on the improvement of physical fitness, coaching, training, and athletic skills.

Chapter 21

PHYSICS

Chalk River, Ontario is symbolic of the study of Canadian Physics. This centre of nuclear research is nestled amid the hills on the banks of the Ottawa River, 130 miles north of the nation's capital. Somewhat removed from public view, work has progressed there for over thirty years on problems ranging from the production of the Cobalt 60 isotope for cancer treatment to the use of nuclear reactors for the production of energy. Canadian Physics learning materials are even further hidden away. As with the other physical sciences (see chapters on Biology-Botany, Chemistry), the development of this field of learning in Canada is almost totally ignored in textbooks and other materials. To belabour the point would be repetitive. In short:

> Canada's development in science and medicine has been retarded by proximity to the United States. We have often been willing to have our science "second hand", and many Canadian subsidiaries of American companies have done no original research themselves, depending blindly instead on the development program of the parent company.
> Careless, Brown, *The Canadians 1867-1967*
> (Toronto: Macmillan, 1967, p. 547)

Research in physics, as far as Canadian youth is concerned, does not exist. That is the message either actually or inadvertently conveyed by the foreign learning materials commonly used. The contributions made by Ernest Rutherford at McGill, J.H.L. Johnstone at Dalhousie, R.W. Boyle at the University of Alberta, and E.E. Burton at the University of Toronto, to take a representative, nation-wide sample, goes unnoticed.

To be sure, research in theoretical and experimental physics is in the international domain. Only a fool would argue for a parochial, "let's seal up the borders of Canada" approach to study in this or

205

any other area. But how is anyone to develop awareness, let alone understanding, of the demonstrable potential Canada has in science if, as a society, we are infinitely willing to hide our lights under prairie bushels? Is it not practical when studying light, electricity, acoustics, or the Stark effect, to incorporate some reference to the valuable work done through the government-sponsored National Research Council, or at various universities from the University of British Columbia in the west to Laval and Dalhousie in the east? Perhaps Canada is forever consigned to the role conveniently portrayed by the voyage of the American supertanker *Manhattan* through the Northwest Passage. When problems arose, the C.C.G.S. (Canadian Coast Guard Ship) *John A. Macdonald* with Captain Fournier in charge was on hand to help. Study, plodding, solid support, just like the unsung part played by Canadians in another Manhattan Project—the splitting of the atom leading to the tests at Los Alamos, New Mexico. Working jointly with French, American, and British support, Canadian physicists established the first heavy water pile with a neutron density greater than any other pile. The significance of this work was obviously not lost in the community of science, even if little attention has been paid to it in learning materials.

In reply to the anticipated argument that, "it really doesn't matter—the University of Saskatchewan in Saskatoon, or Case-Western Reserve University at Cleveland are really one and the same in terms of their complementary efforts; the laboratories at Cavendish (Great Britain), Moscow (U.S.S.R.) and Hamilton, Ontario, are primarily colourful variations in the one spectrum", it can be replied that it does matter considerably. For a student in the early years of high school whose future career in physics depends on knowledge of what research is being done, where, and by whom, an understanding of Canadian opportunities is of some moment, and especially so if there is concern for enhancing scientific developments at home rather than being resigned to a subservient branch-plant mentality.

Medals need not be struck, nor lists of trivial facts forced upon students, to encourage an appreciation of past and present accomplishments. Anyone can benefit by examining the varied and remarkable career of Ernest Rutherford (later Lord Rutherford), a native of New Zealand who spent nine of his most productive years establishing the department of physics at McGill University in Montreal. Among his contributions were: observation of the first spontaneous transmission of an element; initial observations on recoil atoms; extensive investigations into thorium and associated elements; discovery of radium A, B, C, D, and E and establishment of their properties; determination of the ratio of charge to mass for alpha particles. For comparison purposes the career of J.C. McLennan, Rutherford's counterpart at the University of Toronto, can be studied. His research group in atomic spectroscopy led to the discovery of the auroral line. He was the first physicist in North America to bring about the liquefaction of helium which, in turn, led to the study of physics phenomena at low temperatures. Work completed with his pupil E.H. Burton in 1901-1903 constituted some of the earliest proofs of the existence of cosmic rays. Students of Burton were subsequently to do important research on the electron microscope. In Atlantic Canada, J.H.L. Johnstone and G.H. Henderson of Dalhousie University in Halifax, together with R.W. Boyle from Toronto, worked on the problem of demagnetizing magnetic mines—a vital wartime contribution. Their work led to the development of an energized cable which could be looped around each ship—commonly known as a "degaussing belt". And then there is the research of J.A. Gray into the field of X- and gamma ray absorption . . . and so on through the efforts of university laboratories at Queens (Kingston, Ontario); McMaster (Hamilton, Ontario); Western (London, Ontario); and l'université de Montréal.

No, Canada is not bereft of a scientific heritage or a community of scholars. It only seems that way when the bibliography of available Canadiana is perused. Perhaps for our grandchildren the following list will be expanded.

◆ ◆ ◆ ◆

Physics: A Human Endeavor (teaching program). Holt, six units, $3.25 each pa. Each book contains 100 pages of text plus 60 pages of experiments, activities, notes on the NFB Film Loop series, and bibliography. Titles:
   Motion; Motion in the Heavens; Energy and the Conservation Laws; The Nature of Light and Sound; Electricity; The New Physics.

A series of super-8 film loops, N.F.B. can be used in conjunction with the Physics: A Human Endeavor Program, Holt; 49 titles.

Physics (super-8 film loop). N.F.B., set of 16, $16.00 each.
   Titles include *Measurement of Very High Speed; Types of Motion; Uniform Motion in a Straight Line; Displacement; Free Fall.*

Chapter 22

POLITICAL SCIENCE

Canadian education literature is replete with the pious dogma of democracy. The following passages are typical of the cant of curriculum handbooks, programs of study, and government-initiated inquiries:

... make each person aware of and value the rights of and responsibilities of citizenship by making him conscious of his past and present, as well as the past and present of the Canadian nation, and by creating in him a lasting concern for its future.

... developing in him lasting political awareness.

... encouraging him to analyze and develop an understanding of political and socio-economic issues.

... stimulating active participation in democratic electoral processes.
>
> *Survey of Education* (Department of Education, Yellowknife, NWT., 1972, pp. 11-12)

With a more elaborate flourish the authors of the 1968 Ontario Royal Commission on Education opened their discourse on philosophy with "The Search for Truth in a Democratic Society."

Democracy implies the freedom to think, to dissent and to bring about change in a lawful manner in the interest of all. It is a flexible, responsive form of government, difficult to describe in fixed terms. Democracy does not arise as a result of imposed or structured political practices, but as a dynamic, liberating force, nurtured by the people themselves. It can thrive and flourish only when its citizens are free to search continually for new ideas, models, and theories. . . .
>
> *Living and Learning* (Ontario Department of Education, 1968, p. 21)

Further space obviously need not be consumed to illustrate the point. The persevering reader may, however, want to consult the *Alberta Commission on Educational Planning* published in 1972 for more elaboration.

The quality of platitudes and jargon need not detain us. Neither is a precise definition of "democracy" now germane. What is pertinent is a pragmatic evaluation of the teaching of Canadian democratic processes, as this is most likely to be performed through the medium of political science. Again, there is a remarkable absence of materials to assist teachers, and those that can be found are weakened by their blandness. Anything that might arouse teacher-student interest has been skillfully neutered in most instances. Students can scarcely be faulted if they find textbook political science a tepid, even hypocritical experience. While providing an historical framework within which student inquiry can be developed is defensible, a merciless and mirthless attack on every British-Canadian parliamentary act from 1215 onwards is not to be undertaken with relish.

This need not be the case. At the high school level every individual should have the opportunity to pursue such alternatives as:

1.   "You Can't Tell the Players without a Scorecard". The political arena can be crowded. Among the contending teams are the perennial favorites Liberals, (Grits, Rouges) and Progressive Conservatives (Tories, Bleus). In third place is the New Democratic Party, while well down in the standings are the Créditiste and Social Credit. Outsiders trying to gain league admittance include the Communist Party of Canada (Marxist-Leninist), the Rhinocerous Party from Quebec, and the Garden Party of Prince Edward Island. Future generations of voters need time not only to learn to identify the parties, but to disassemble and reconstruct party platforms if they are ever to understand the various planks. Knowing the national party stance on various issues leads logically to regional and provincial study. Using periodicals and television, students can try to figure out if an Alberta Progressive Conservative is the same as, or different from, a Manitoba N.D.P. member. Similar match-ups can be developed between a Newfoundland Liberal (when Joseph Smallwood was premier) and a B.C. Social Creditor (under the Bennetts—father or son). Equally instructive, if more exacting, is the determination of what is being said in various parts of the country by any one politician. Does a Liberal speaking in Montreal on transportation policy say the same thing in Saskatoon, or does an N.D.P. man from Vancouver speak the same language in Oshawa? The possibilities are infinite.

2.   "The Art of the Possible." Understanding how governments operate at all levels of the system is taxing. Textbook versions are simply that. What goes on in practice can be strikingly different from the theory. As cases in point, students should examine the roles of party bagmen, the ward-heelers of civic politics, the patronage of party politics, and the government by Prime Minister's Office fiat of recent times. Development of a cynical indifference is not the objective of such exercises. On the contrary, an awareness of how any system operates creates a much healthier attitude than shielding students from realities with sophomoric sermons on the topic of parliamentary government.

3.   From "Old To-Morrow" to "P.E.T." An informative, entertaining way to understand and sense the politics of a particular time is via the political biography. Sir John A. Macdonald and the National Policy are less dry, if not quite intoxicating, when read within the context of his daily life. Similarly, authors Richard Gwyn and Peter Newman, who have written biographies of Joseph Smallwood and John Diefenbaker respectively, bring a dash of controversy into their writing which creates human interest rather than hero worship. Autobiographical material may have the same commendable quality if the writer does not take himself too seriously. Behind the scenes revelations are welcome as they give that rare, first-person close-up on how events actually transpire. The anonymous worlds of the diplomat and the career civil servant become a little more comprehensible when elevated from the textbook to the level of diaries and memoirs.

4.   Pacific Scandal, Conscription, Byng-King . . . such political issues can grab the attention, especially if studied within a broad social framework. All too seldom are political decisions studied in context. One of the most popular blunders is the "here are the causes—these are the results" approach to teaching political science. An increasing supply of materials which provide many, often conflicting, points of view, helps to destroy this oversimplified method of understanding the origin and resolution of political issues. Important, too, are extreme interpretations of events (i.e. extreme in the sense that the views do not reflect the established philosophy of compromise). Relatively little known publishing firms (e.g. Progress Books and N.C. Press) are making their own distinctive contributions which add a provocative dimension to this area of learning.

5.   ". . . there exists an urgent need for a critical appraisal of democracy in Canada." Those words from an essay entitled "Some

Obstacles to Democracy in Quebec" (*Canadian Journal of Economics and Political Science,* vol. xxiv, no. 3, August, 1958, p. 297) were written by Pierre Elliott Trudeau. His concern must be shared by Canadians generally today. Democracy, as he pointed out, rests on a "flimsy" structure.

> . . . democracy will continue to be thwarted in Canada so long as one-third of the people hardly believe in it—and that because to no small extent the remaining two-thirds provide them with ample opportunity for distrusting it. (*Ibid*)

The accuracy of the comment is still valid. Not only have relationships among the two founding peoples shown less than marked improvement, but feelings of frustration, separation, and alienation are increasingly expressed from diverse sources. Political unrest cuts across ethnic, racial, cultural, regional, and generation lines, defying ready identification or classification. Political science curricula available to every senior high student will not alone remedy the situation. They may contribute to improved understanding. Focusing on major problems and employing multi-language materials are valid approaches. Combining with sociology, economics, law, and history materials can broaden and deepen awareness. Strident calls for national unity are as barren as they are illogical in an interdependent world society. Improved political awareness, leading to increased individual participation, is a question of privilege in any house or society.

N.B. See also Chapter 6—Business Education, Chapter 10— Economics, Chapter 16—Law, Chapter 25—Social Studies, and Chapter 26—Sociology.

◆ ◆ ◆ ◆

General Reference

Democratic Government in Canada, 4th ed. Robert M. Dawson (U.T.P., 1971), $2.95 pa.

How We Are Governed, Ricker and Saywell (Clarke, Irwin), $2.50 pa.

The Canadian Political Process, rev. ed., Orest Kruhlak, Richard Schultz and S.J. Pobihushchy (Holt, 1973), $7.95 pa.

The Parliament of Canada, rev. ed., George Hambleton (McGraw, 1951), $5.65.

Politics are People: An Illustrated Guide to Canadian Elections, ed. Moyra Tooke (Griffin, 1974), $5.95.

Bureaucracy in Canadian Government, Kernaghan (Methuen), $4.90.

Follow the Leader (cassette tape). 30 min, C.B.C. Learning Systems, set of 3, $24.00. These tapes deal with the form, functions, and facts of Parliament.

Political Parties

Canadian Political Parties, Engleman and Schwartz (Prentice, 1975), $7.50. Origin, character and impact of political parties.

The Dynasty: The Rise and Fall of Social Credit in Alberta. John Barr (McClelland, 1974), $12.50.

Social Credit Handbook, William Rose (McClelland, 1968), $2.95 pa.

N.D.P.: The Dream of Power, Morton (Hakkert, 1974), $3.95 pa.

The Dilemma of Canadian Socialism: The C.C.F. in Ontario, G.L. Caplan (McClelland, 1973), $3.95 pa.

The Anatomy of a Party: The National C.C.F. 1932-1961, Walter Young (U.T.P., 1969), $3.75 pa.

The Power and the Tories: Ontario Politics 1943 to the Present, Jonathan Manthorpe (Macmillan, 1974), $12.95.

The Rise of a Third Party: A Study in Crisis Politics, Maurice Pinard (McGill, 1971), $6.00 pa. A study of the growth and development of the Creditiste party in Quebec.

Réflexions sur la politique au Québec, André Bernard and others (P.U.Q.) $2.50 br.

The Progressive Party in Canada, William L. Morton (U.T.P., 1967), $3.50 pa.

The Swastika and the Maple Leaf: Fascist Movements in Canada in the Thirties, Lita-Rose Betcherman (Fitzhenry and Whiteside, 1975), $9.95.

Provincial Parties

The Provincial Political Systems: Comparative Essays, D. Bellamy, J. Pammett and D. Rowat (Methuen, 1976), $8.50 pa. Reference for senior students.

Municipal Politics

A Citizen's Guide to City Politics, James Lorimer (James Lorimer, 1972), $4.95.

The Real World of City Politics, James Lorimer (James Lorimer, 1970), $3.95 pa.

Up Against City Hall, John Sewell (James Lorimer, 1972), $3.95 pa.

Power to Make it Happen, Donald R. Keating (Green Tree, 1975), $3.95 pa. Mass-based community organizing.

Biographical

The Backbencher, Gordon Aiken (McClelland, 1974), $8.95. The former M.P. from Parry Sound-Muskoka provides an insight into the life of a backbencher in parliament.

Memoirs of a Bird in a Gilded Cage, Judy LaMarsh (Simon & Schuster, 1970), $1.25 pa. Judy La Marsh give her views of political life.

Political Warriors: Recollections of a Social Democrat, Lloyd Stinson (Queenston, 1975), $3.95 pa. A personal account of experiences in the Winnipeg City Council and in the Manitoba legislature.

Tim Buck: A Conscience for Canada, Oscar Ryan (Progress, 1975), $4.95 pa. The best-known leader of the communist party in Canada.

Smallwood: The Unlikely Revolutionary, Richard Gwyn (McClelland, 1972), $4.95 pa.

The Wonderful World of W.A.C. Bennett, Ronald B. Worley (McClelland, 1971), $10.00. Biography of the former premier of British Columbia.

The Things that Are Caesar's: Memoirs of a Canadian Public Servant, Arnold Heeney (U.T.P., 1972), $12.50.

The Siren Years, Charles Ritchie (Macmillan, 1974), $10.95. The diary of the years 1937-1945 recorded by Charles Ritchie, formerly Canadian High Commissioner in London.

"I Never Say Anything Provocative": Witticisms, Anecdotes and Reflections by Canada's Most Outspoken Politician, John George Diefenbaker, ed. Margaret Wente (Peter Martin, 1975), $3.95 pa.

Coroner, Morton Shulman (Fitzhenry and Whiteside, 1975), $8.95. Autobiographical account of experience in Ontario political life.

Political Interpretations

Gentlemen, Players and Politicians, Dalton Camp (McClelland, 1970), $12.00. The former national president of the Progressive

Conservative Party provides an analysis of the Diefenbaker-Stanfield years, in particular.

The Distemper of Our Times, Peter C. Newman (McClelland, 1968), $1.50 pa. A controversial examination of the Diefenbaker-Pearson years.

Minority Men in a Majority Setting, Christopher Beattie (McClelland, 1975), $4.95 pa. The civil service and its influence.

Shrug: Trudeau in Power, Walter Stewart (New, 1971), $1.75 pa. A study of Trudeau's first term of office.

Working Papers on Canadian Politics, John Meisel (McGill-Queen's, 1975), $6.00 pa. A valuable resource item for obtaining information on the federal election campaigns of 1968-1972 in particular.

The Canadian Political Nationality, Donald V. Smiley (Methuen, 1967), $2.25 pa. An analysis of politics from 1939 to the 1950s.

Political Issues

The Unfinished Revolt: Some Views on Western Independence, ed. John Barr and Owen Anderson (McClelland, 1971), $4.95 pa. Western separatist aspirations.

Federalism and the French Canadian Society, Pierre Elliott Trudeau (Macmillan, 1968), $2.50 pa. Trudeau's views prior to becoming a Liberal party member.

The New Romans, ed. Al Purdy (Hurtig, 1968), $2.95 pa. A collection of views on U.S.-Canada relations.

The Tar Sands: Syncrude and the Politics of Oil, Larry Pratt (Hurtig, 1975), $3.95 pa. The Athabaska tar sands are the focus for this study of corporate-government involvement and collusion.

Bleeding Hearts . . . Bleeding Country, Dennis Smith (Hurtig, 1971), $2.95 pa. The 'October Crisis' of 1970.

White Niggers of America, Pierre Vallières (McClelland, 1971), $3.95 pa. The place of French-Canadians in society.

Quebec/Canada and the October Crisis, ed. Dan Daniels (Black Rose, 1973), $2.25 pa.

Le monde ouvrier au Québec, André E. Leblanc and others (P.U.Q.), $7.00. Bibliography.

The Genocide Machine in Canada: The Pacification of the North, Robert Davis and Mark Zannis (Black Rose, 1973), $2.95 pa.

Le travailleur québécois et le syndicalisme, Richard Desrosiers et Denis Heroux (P.U.M.), $3.00 pa.

Canada and Radical Social Change, ed. D.I. Roussapoulos (Black Rose, 1973), $2.95 pa.

The Politics of the Canadian Public School, ed. George Martell (James Lorimer, 1974), $4.95 pa. A collection of articles on the political aspects of the school system and the teacher-government confrontations in Quebec, British Columbia, and Ontario.

The Politics of Education, Frank MacKinnon (U.T.P., 1960), $3.25 pa.

Canadian-American Relations (kit). Clarke Irwin, $6.50. Senior high.

Titles from the series Canadian Dimension Kits, Canadian Dimension. Essays and folders on current topics.

> *New Left and Youth Revolt,* $2.00; *Canadian Nationalism and Independence,* $2.00; *Quebec, part 1, The 1960s,* $2.00; *Quebec, part 2, October 1970,* $1.00; *Canadian Foreign Policy,* $1.50; *Native People,* $1.50.

Periodicals

The Quarterly of Canadian Studies, Canadian Periodical Publishers' Association. Quarterly, $6.00. History and political science.

Journal of Canadian Studies, Canadian Periodical Publishers' Association. Quarterly, $6.00. History, politics, literature, society and the arts.

The Last Post, Canadian Periodical Publishers' Association. 8 issues annually, $5.00. Political comment.

The Canadian Forum, Canadian Periodical Publishers' Association. 10 issues annually, students, $5.00, regular subscribers, $7.50. Political comment, poetry, short stories, and reviews.

The Independencer, Committee for an Independent Canada. 6 issues annually, $5.00.

Canadian Review, Box 8316, Alta Vista Terminal, Ottawa, K1G 3H8. 6 issues annually for 2 years, $6.50. Political comment, fiction, reviews.

Chapter 23

READING

With the possible exceptions of prompt and regular school attendance and washing behind the ears, nothing in current primary and
elementary school practice surpasses the fascination that reading
exerts on the minds of educators. It is the subject of paramount
importance, particularly in the early years of a child's education.
The unspoken wisdom of the age has it that if you cannot read,
you cannot learn. Only when the skills of reading have been mastered
can the door to knowledge be unlocked.

An examination of reading philosophy, methodology, and materials,
as these have evolved in the twentieth century, suggests the need for
thoughtful attention and consideration.

In 1904 the *Royal Readers* were published in Halifax. This was
one of the earliest attempts at developing a reading series in Canada,
following in the wake of the original American endeavour, the *Mc-
Guffey Readers* of 1879. The preface to the *Royal Readers* provides
a quality of insight that makes the reader hunger for a simpler age.

Good reading is more readily acquired by practice than by precept.

The more children read, they will read the more fluently, intel-
ligently and gracefully; and children can only be induced to read
much by giving them subjects to read about, in which they will
naturally feel interested, and by so treating these subjects as to
render them attractive.

The lessons are designed so to interest young people as to induce
them to read, not as task-work merely, but for the pleasure of the
thing.

They (i.e. reading materials) avoid as much as possible that dull
solidity which so much tends to make school hours a weariness to
the young.

The numerous illustrations afford an important aid . . .

216

The interest of children is far more readily quickened through
the eye than through the understanding; it is through the eye that
the understanding itself is most quickly reached.

(*The Royal Readers,* Halifax, A.&W. MacKinlay,
1904, p. iii)

The brevity of the foregoing information is striking. Prior to the
advent of the science of education and the subsequent proliferation
of colleges, faculties, departments, and institutes of educational research (with the attendant subject specialization) it was feasible to
provide teachers with two pages of introductory information on the
topic of reading. The remaining 192 pages in Volume III of the *Royal
Readers* encompassed material now referred to as language arts—
reading, grammar, pronunciation. Evidently, high expectations were
then held for the teacher's competency. A quick browse through either
college of education course descriptions or publishers' catalogues
will indicate the remarkable progress that has been made in the inter-
vening seven decades. What was once seen as a matter of exquisite
simplicity has grown into a subject of notorious complexity. No
reputable educational institution today, be it primary school or a
post graduate university faculty, would feel complete without an
arsenal of word attack skills, eye-ear discrimination devices, and
reading machines for the war against illiteracy. Nor would publishers
feel comfortable with less than a battalion of front line equipment:
core/basal readers; supplementary "leisure" reading materials;
teacher's handbooks; student workbooks; multi-media kits. . . .
Illiteracy, like poverty, should have gone down to defeat some years
ago, given the extensive attention it has received on all sides. But the
victory has yet to be achieved. Reading difficulties persist, a fact
which justifies the continuing search for solutions.

Let us examine more closely the philosophy of reading expressed
at the turn of the century, and make comparisons with current practice.

1. "Good reading is more readily acquired by practice than precept."
Linger momentarily over those two words "practice/precept". Among
the various synonyms for "precept" are: instruction, recipe, rule,
canon, formula. In the classrooms of the 1970s it would be heresy to
suggest that the "recipes" be abolished and replaced by "subjects to
read about in which they (i.e. children) will naturally feel interested. . . ." The multitude of reading formulae have been canonized
by teacher education institutions and, subsequently, the faith has

been reaffirmed through the "Gospel according to Ginn" (or any other major publishing firm). Children today are instructed in reading skills. Any practice will come from access to the school library during free reading periods, or the availability of materials in the home. More damning, what children have to read and what they may enjoy reading, often are poles apart. Anyone who has attempted to come to grips with the sparkling narrative of life on "Cherry Street" or travels along "Open Highways" can attest to the discrepancy between textbook prose and stimulating writing. It is little wonder that students are likely to be less than enthusiastic about the rules of reading embedded in their learning materials.

2. "Interesting, attractive" materials deserves special consideration from a Canadian viewpoint. The bibliography at the end of this chapter speaks for itself. Canadian children have relatively little opportunity to read about their own country. In her book, *The Republic of Childhood: A Critical Guide to Canadian Children's Literature in English* (Toronto: Oxford, 1967, pp. 9-11), Sheila Egoff has categorized the situation well: "The most striking thing about Canadian children's books is their paucity."

In the approximately 225 years since the first book was published in New France, less than four thousand Canadian children's books have been published. In round figures, the national average has been twenty titles per year. Ignoring questions of quality, if every Canadian item published since the mid 1700s could be collected, these could be shelved nicely in one standard classroom. L.F. Ashley drew reference to this situation in his study, *Children's Reading and the 1970's* (Toronto: McClelland, 1972). Among the students surveyed regarding their reading habits and preferences, roughly one child in twenty selected stories about Canada as their first choice. (p. 28). And little wonder. The materials employed in Canadian schools, libraries, and Faculty of Education courses, are essentially American. A hypothetical situation can be used to illustrate the realities.

The undergraduate teacher education student is instructed in how to teach reading through the use of American models, utilizing American textbooks and other materials, and possibly drawing upon the experience of an American or American-educated professor. Having completed the course, the teacher in the Canadian classroom is scarcely in a position to orient the reading program to Canada, much less the particular region of the country in which he or she happens to be working.

The problem is magnified when it is realized that "Canadianized" American textbooks have a monopoly in the reading market. The reading series probably incorporates a scanty selection of items authored by Canadians. This consitutes primarily the local content. Everything else bears little or no relationship to this country. The end result? The child who wishes to read Canadian material may do so in "library" or some other designated time period—assuming that Canadiana can be distinguished in the library collection.

3. " . . . not as task-work merely, but for the pleasure of the thing." Surely, there must be a mistake. The author of the *Royal Readers* was not suggesting that reading could be enjoyable? Most informed educators now know the fallacy of that approach. Reading is a discipline and as such is to be pursued with rigorous, regular attention. Otherwise, it would not be necessary to schedule faithfully the major portion of a young child's learning life around language arts, reading, or whatever convenient label comes to mind. Moreover, reading groups have to be established; the series has to be covered; the workbook pages have to be completed. In a word, the "rituals" have to be performed. It would be blasphemous to advocate any real change in this methodology. Except for isolated instances influenced by the British Infant and Nursery schools, reading has evolved into a cult whose supporters would make the original Puritans flinch. Avoiding the "dull solidity" which makes school attendance "a weariness" is the sort of terminology which many school administrators would now associate with the radical left. "How, in heaven's name, are the 252 cards in the controlled reading kit to be completed, if pleasure is permitted to permeate the high interest—low vocabulary reading group?"

4. " . . . Illustrations afford an important aid. . . ." If colourful illustrations are the goal, then current materials are superior to those of three generations ago. Advances in technology (colour process work, lithography) have made it possible to produce books and related items of the most lavish, if expensive, design. Black and white engravings can hardly be mentioned in the same breath. However, it is the content of the illustrations that must be emphasized. Pictures can be incorporated in such a way as to supplement the printed word. The child who has experienced problems with the text can learn from the illustrations alone. The feeling inherent in the prose or poetry is often more adequately conveyed through artistic interpretation. Conversely, space-filling illustrations which have little if anything to do with the substance of the material should be avoided.

Too few present publishing efforts use illustrations for purposes other than merchandizing. Swatches of colour and judicious spacing of illustrations may sell books. They do not necessarily help a child to become interested in either reading or artistic excellence.

5. "...It is through the eye that the understanding itself is most quickly reached." The reference here is to pictures rather than words. Approximately two decades before the motion picture industry entered public awareness, and over a half century prior to the ready accessibility of television, educators of a distant age were aware of the primacy of pictures over print for developing understanding. It is dizzying to speculate on what the same people might have thought about reading practices in the mass media age. The print-oriented classrooms of today should be influenced by Ashley's comment:

> ... of every one hundred children passing through our schools, only five will maintain regular reading habits; ninety-five will not, and the majority of these will probably become passive devotees of mass mediocrity.
> [Ashley, p. 1]

Mmm! Is it possible that some of the time and expense concentrated on reading skills might be better spent on helping children to acquire basic literacy through television? It is probable that for many students learning how to discriminate, evaluate, and interpret visual imagery is a more realistic life-skill than one more waltz through book X in the "Let's Get It Together" reading recipe.

What Can Be Done? Becoming familiar with the names of the more fertile writers of children's literature is helpful. Minimally, it would then be possible to keep an eye open for their material. A representative cross section, with examples of their writing, includes:

> Kay Hill, Indian legends of the Maritimes and historical material (an award-winning biography of John Cabot: *And Tomorrow The Stars*).

> Dennis Lee, poetry and nonsense verse (*Alligator Pie*).

> Lucy Maud Montgomery, creator of the *Anne of Green Gables* series.

> Farley Mowat, light hearted (*The Dog Who Wouldn't Be*) and adventurous material (*Lost in the Barrens*).

> Ann Blades, material based on her experiences in the Pacific north-west (*Mary of Mile 18*).

> Christie Harris, possibly the best known writer of children's material in British Columbia (*The Raven's Cry*).

James Houston, books of Inuit (*Tiktaliktak*) or Indian origin (*Eagle Mask*).

Emily Hearn, writer and co-editor of the Nelson and Sons (Canada) Ltd. Language Development Program (*Hockey Cards and Hopscotch*).

Kerry Wood, Alberta author of books in the Great Stories of Canada series (*The Map Maker: the story of David Thompson*).

Lyn Cook, books with varied Canadian locales (*The Secret of Willow Castle*).

Barbara Bondar, author and editor of the Fitzhenry and Whiteside *Zap* series.

Bill Straiton and Len Norris, humorous text by Straiton coupled with cartoon-type illustrations by Norris (*The Winkle Pickers*).

Similarly, it is relatively easy to keep an eye on the catalogues of specific publishing firms whose efforts deserve greater attention by educational authorities than they often receive. Tundra Books of Montreal is an outstanding example. In recent years its publications have merited numerous awards for their illustrations and design; for example, *A Prairie Boys Winter* by William Kurelek (Montreal: Tundra, 1973). Canadian Women's Educational Press is equally deserving of greater consideration. Their efforts in publishing non-sexist literature include *Mandy and the Flying Map*. Among the major firms, Macmillan provides a substantial listing.

Related to awareness of the publishing companies is the question of editorial competency. Particularly is this relevant when considering textbook series. John McInnes of Nelson and Sons (Canada) Ltd. ranks with the best in this respect, as in *Nelson Venture Books*. Carol Martin of Peter Martin Associates must be recognized for her contributions to the excellence of that firm's efforts; for example, *Wildlife Discovery Series*. Oxford University Press has published some of the most attractive items currently available, in large measure due to the efforts of its editorial staff (for example, *The Wind Has Wings: Poems From Canada*). The well deserved success of *The Canadian Children's Annual,* Potlatch Publications, reflects the editorial ability of Robert Nielsen.

One valuable indicator of the quality of books being produced is the annual awards lists of organizations such as the Canadian Association of Children's Librarians. Consultation with that list through C.A.C.L. publications, *Quill and Quire,* or the *Annual Year Book* of the *World Book Encyclopedia* (refer to section on Canada; sub-section on children's literature) is helpful.

Recommending materials to assist teachers and parents in making selections is simultaneously simple and difficult. There are a few essential references: Sheila Egoff's *Republic of Childhood,* Irma McDonough's *Canadian Books for Children/Livres Canadiens Pour Enfants,* an annual subscription to *Quill and Quire,* and/or *Books in Canada* and *Canadian Materials.* However, there is obviously room in this area for even more information. Publishers' catalogues are not in themselves sufficient. Furthermore, the larger the company the more elaborate the advertising, which leaves the independent publishers with good materials with too few customers. Educational budgets directed to the latter could alleviate this situation. To do so will require the availability of more information for teachers and administrators. If better informational networks can be established throughout Canada, it will then rest squarely with the education profession to make changes in their philosophy and methodology of teaching reading. Any or all of the following books are too valuable to relegate to the position of an afterthought while the latest thing in reading workbooks is being consumed.

[N.B. See Chapter 15—*Indian—Inuit—Metis,* Chapter 11—*English,* Chapter 13—*French,* and Chapter 17—*Literature* for further references.]

♦ ♦ ♦ ♦

Individual Titles—Grades 1-3

Alligator Pie, Dennis Lee (Macmillan, 1974), $5.95. Poetry.

Nicholas Knock and Other People, Dennis Lee (Macmillan, 1974), $5.95. Poetry.

Wiggle to the Laundromat, Dennis Lee (New, 1970), $5.00. Poetry.

Calico Pie/Calico Jam/Calico Drum, Veighey (McGraw, 1968), $2.75 each.

An Illustrated Comic Alphabet, A.F. Howard-Gibbon (Oxford, 1966), $6.50. The earliest known Canadian picture book completed in 1859 at Sarnia, Ont.

How the Pelican Got its Baggy Beak, Joey Hildes (Peguis, 1974), $1.95 pa. Story by a 10-year-old author-illustrator.

The Adventures of Mickey, Taggy, Puppo and Cico and How They Discover Toronto, Kati (Canadian Stage, 1974), $1.95 pa.

Patrick the Diesel, Kendall McDonald (Peguis, 1974), $1.25 pa. Story by a 9-year-old author-illustrator.

Nico et Niski visitent le Manitoba, (Landry), $1.50 pa. An activity book in French with crossword, cut-outs, and pages to colour.

Snails, Slugs, Spiders and Bugs, Trudy Rising (McClelland, 1975), $6.95.

Pouf: The Moth/La mite, Peter Angeles (Tundra, 1975), $1.00 pa. Bilingual.

Bufo: The Toad/Le crapaud, Marla Stevenson (Tundra, 1975), $1.00 pa. Bilingual.

There are Trolls, John F. Greene (Peguis, 1975), $1.60 pa.

The Little Magic Fiddler, Lyn Cook (Macmillan, 1951), $3.95. A story about a Winnipeg Ukrainian girl.

Bonnie McSmithers, You're Driving Me Dithers, Sue Anne Alderson (Tree Frog, 1975), $2.95 pa.

Alphonse Has an Accident, Susan Hiebert (Peguis, 1974), $4.00.

Bo, the Constrictor that Couldn't, Patti Stren (Green Tree, 1975), $3.25 pa.

The Forest Is My Kingdom, Carruthers (Oxford, 1958). An Indian boy who wishes to become a painter. $4.50.

Little Wood Duck, Wildssmith (Oxford 1973). $9.00.

Boggeley Marsh, Stan Beadnell (Western Producer, 1969), $3.95. An illustrated story of the animal characters of a typical marsh.

At the End of the Garden, Marion Stavrakov (Mitchell, 1967), 95¢ pa.

How the Kookaburra Got his Laugh, Aviva Layton (McClelland, 1975), $4.25.

Rainsploosh: An Empty Book, Merilyn Read (Borealis, 1975), $4.95 pa. Story of a raindrop.

Adventure at Moon Bay Towers, Marian Engel (Clarke, Irwin, 1974), $3.95.

Titles from *Before We are Six* (Canadian Women's Educational Press), $1.75 pa. each. Themes include one parent families, death, separation, day care, handicaps, culture.

   The Grunk, Doug Jamieson (1974).

   Irene's Idea, Bernice Geoffroy (1975).

   The Last Visit, Doug Jamieson (1977).

Minoo's Family, Sue Hefferman (1974.

Families Grow in Different Ways, Barbara B. Parrish (1973).

When I Visit Daddy or Daddy Visits Me, Susan W. Gustar (1973).

Titles written by children from Kids Can Press:

Harriet and the Great Bike Robbery, $2.25; *I'm a Child of the City,* 95¢ ; *Yak le Yak,* $1.95; *Julie News,* $1.95; *The Mush-rooming House,* $1.95; *The Peanut Plan,* $2.25; *The Double Mirror,* $1.25; *The Green Harpy at the Corner Store,* $2.75; *The Sandwich,* $2.25. The story of a little Italian boy. *Strange Street,* $1.75. Sam learns about life in his street

Non-Sexist Books

She Shoots, She Scores, Heather Kellerhals-Stewart (Canadian Women's Educational Press, 1975), 95¢ pa.

Mumbles and Snits, Beverley Allinson (Canadian Women's Educational Press, 1975), $3.00. pa.

The Travels of Ms. Beaver, Rosemary Allison (Canadian Women's Educational Press, 1973), $1.25 pa. The story of a hitch-hiking beaver.

Stone Soup, Allan Sutterfield and Carol Pasternak (Canadian Women's Educational Press, 1975), $3.00 pa. Toronto-based story on the theme of a French folk tale.

Mandy and the Flying Map, Beverley Allinson (Canadian Women's Educational Press, 1973), $2.00 pa. An insight into the life of an independent girl.

I Climb Mountains, Barbara Taylor (Canadian Women's Educational Press, 1975), $3.00 pa.

Fresh Fish and Chips, Jan Andrews (Canadian Women's Educational Press, 1973), $2.00 pa. A mother sets out with rod and line to catch a strange assortment of exotic sea creatures.

The Makwa Books from Peguis, $1.50 each: *A Little Mouse; Here I Go; The Bang Book; Jack and Jet; The New Baby; Grandmother Knows; Helping Mother; The Snare.*

Grades 4-6

A Wishing Star, Bess Kaplan (Queenston, 1975), $2.95. A novel about a Jewish girl growing up in the north end of Winnipeg.

The Incredible Journey, Sheila Burnford (General, 1973), $1.25 pa.

Adventures into Unknowns, David Maclagan (Hurtig, 1972), $4.95. Five adventure stories for ages 9-12; full colour drawings.

Night of the Sasquatch, Edward James Ashlee (Holt, 1973), $3.25.

Red Horse of the West, Isabel M. Reekie (Holt, 1972), $3.50.

Robber's Roost, Carol F. Barton (Holt, 1972), $3.25.

Judy and the Secret Moons of Korea, Audrey McKim (Hurtig, 1970), $4.50.

The Secret World of Og, Pierre Berton (McClelland, 1962), $1.10 pa.

The Dog Who Wouldn't Be, Farley Mowat (McClelland, 1957), $7.95.

The Twelfth Mile, Ernest G. Perrault (Doubleday, 1972), $6.50. An adventure story set in Vancouver.

No Word for Good-bye, John Craig (Peter Martin, 1969), $2.95 pa. Friendship and adventure—an Indian and a white boy in the Lake-of-the-Woods country of Northern Ontario.

Jacob Two-Two Meets the Hooded Fang, Mordecai Richler (McClelland, 1975), $5.95. Governor General's Award for children's literature.

Shantymen of Cache Lake, Bill Freeman (James Lorimer, 1975), $4.95 pa. Canada Council Children's Literature Award.

A Boy of Taché, Ann Blades (Tundra, 1973), $5.95. An Indian boy on a reserve in Taché, B.C. joins his parents on a spring beaver hunt.

Canadian Wonder Tales, Cyrus Macmillan (Clarke, Irwin, 1974), $14.70. Anthology of French-Indian tales first published in 1918-1922.

Sky Man on the Totem Pole, Christie Harris (McClelland, 1975), $6.95. B.C. setting.

The Princess of Tomboso, Frank Newfeld (Oxford, 1960), $3.95 pa. An illustrated French Canadian folk tale.

The Golden Phoenix and Other French Canadian Fairy Tales, Marius Barbeau and Michael Hornyansky (Oxford, 1958), $7.95. Winner of the C.A.C.L. Book of the Year Award.

The Magic Fiddler and Other Legends of French Canada, Claude Aubry (Peter Martin, 1968), $3.95 pa.

The Talking Cat and Other Stories of French Canada, Carlson (Fitzhenry and Whiteside, 1974), $6.00).

Rebel on the Trail, Lyn Cook (Macmillan, 1953), 25¢. Historical story of the rebellion of 1837.

Mary of Mile 18, Ann Blades (Tundra, 1971), $5.95. A story written and illustrated by a teacher and her students from a farming community in northern B.C.; winner of the C.A.C.L. Book of the Year award in 1972.

Panther, R. Haig-Brown (Collins, 1967), 95¢ pa. Winner of the C.A.C.L. Book of the Year Award.

Beautiful Joe, Marshall Saunders (McClelland, 1934), $2.49. The classic Canadian dog story.

The Year of the Horse, Walker (Fitzhenry and Whiteside, 1975), $8.25. A humorous story for upper elementary-junior high students.

Stand in the Wind, Little (Fitzhenry and Whiteside, 1975), $6.50. Story of four young girls and their visit to a summer cabin.

La Biche Miraculeuse. Une légende hongroise/The Miraculous Hind: An Hungarian Legend. Elizabeth Cleaver (Holt, 1973), $10.95. A beautifully illustrated story available in French and English editions.

The Wind has Wings: Poems from Canada, Ed. M.A. Downie and Barbara Robertson; illus. E. Cleaver (Oxford, 1968), $7.50.

All About Us—Nous Autres, comp. Betty Nickerson (Content, 1973), $1.75 pa. Paintings, poems, stories by young Canadians.

It's Not Always a Game, ed. Russ Huzzard (All about Us, 1974), $4.95 pa. Bilingual poetry by young writers.

Tigers of the Snow, James MacNeil and Glen Sorestad (Nelson, 1972), $3.50. Eighteen short stories.

Titles from the Great Stories of Canada series, Macmillan, $2.95 each: *The Great Chief, Maskepetoon: Warrior of the Crees; Adventures from the Bay: Men of the Hudson's Bay Company; Runner of the Woods: The story of Young Radisson; The First Canadian: The Story of Champlain; The Queen's Cowboy: James MacLeod of the Mounties; The Map Maker: The Story of David Thompson.*

Junior High

Lumberjack, William Kurelek (Tundra, 1974), $7.95. Life in lumber camps of Northern Ontario and Quebec; 25 full colour illustrations.

A Prairie Boy's Winter, William Kurelek (Tundra, 1973), $7.95. Winner of the 1974 C.A.C.L. award for the best illustrated book.

Raven's Cry, Christie Harris (McClelland, 1966), $2.49.

Secret in Stalakum Wild, Christie Harris (McClelland, 1972), $3.95.

A Child in a Prison Camp, Shizuye Takashima (Tundra, 1971), $7.95. The author's experiences in a Japanese internment camp in World War II; winner of the C.A.C.L. award for the best illustrated book of 1972.

The Secret of Willow Castle, Lyn Cook (Macmillan, 1966), $4.25. A young girl's adventures in Napanee, Ont. in 1834.

Hockey Fever in Goganne Falls, R.J. Childerhose (Macmillan, 1973), $5.95.

River of Stars, Jean Mackenzie (McClelland, 1971), $5.95.

The Christmas Wolf, Claude Aubry (McClelland, 1965), $3.50. English or French editions.

Owls in the Family, Farley Mowat (McClelland, 1961), $1.95 pa.

Spectacles, Raskin (Griffin), $1.10 pa.

The Muskie Hood, Cohen (Griffin), $1.10 pa.

Harry the Wild Horse, Clymer (Griffin), $1.10 pa.

The Artist's Workshop, George Wallace (Holt, 1971), $4.25.

Sailing Ships, George Wallace (Holt, 1972), $4.25.

The Artist's Zoo, George Wallace (Holt, 1970), $4.25.

Voyage into Danger: Adventures in the Queen Charlotte Islands, Ted Ashlee (Holt, 1970), $4.35.

Textbook series

Reading Through Phonics, Dent, 5 workbooks, 95¢ each.

Developing Comprehension in Reading series, Dent, Books 3A and 3B, $3.75 each. Reading skills, grade 3.

Starting Points in Reading, Ginn, Level A, 2 books, $3.95 each. Teacher's handbooks, $5.75 each. A program to reinforce and extend reading skills acquired in grade 1-3; opportunities to integrate reading with art, natural and physical sciences, and social studies.

Titles from the Nelson Language Development Reading Program, Nelson, Grades 4-6; includes storybooks, $3.25 each, workbooks $1.25 each, and teacher's handbooks $3.60 each. *Driftwood and Dandelions; Hockey Cards and Hopscotch; Northern Lights and Fireflies; Kites and Cartwheels; Sleeping Bags and Flying Machines; Toboggans and Turtlenecks.*

Titles from the Zap series, Fitzhenry and Whiteside, $2.60 each, pa. Teacher's manual, $3.95 pa. Stories, poems, puzzles, games and informative selections related to the theme of each book; grades 1-3. Titles: *Eating; Flying; Hockey; Magic.*

Titles from the Colours series, Longman. Anthologies of literary selections with source books, $2.10 each pa. and skills books $1.75 each pa.; upper elementary.
> *Brown is the Back of a Toad,* $4.25 pa. Teacher's manual, $1.95 pa.
> *Yellow is a Lemon Tart,* $4.50 pa.

Voyager, Copp Clark. Grade 4-6; basal text, resource book, workbook, and teacher's guidebook for each grade.

Nunnybag Stories, Gage, Books 1-5, ages 6-9, $2.80 each.

Rubaboo Stories, Gage, Books 1-5, ages 10-12, $2.80 each.

Nelson Venture Books, Nelson. Grade 1-3; 50 paperbacks.
> Level one, part A, 10 titles, $15.95.
> Level one, part B, 10 titles $15.95.
> Combined levels A & B, 20 titles, $29.90.
> Individual titles, $1.50 each. Teacher's handbook, $1.60.

Supplementary Materials

Thinklab: A Reading Motivator (kit). SRA, $49.50. Grade 4–adult. Four copies of 125 cards dealing with object manipulation, perception, creative insight, perceiving image patterns, and logical analysis.

Pandora's Box: Prize-Winning Canadian Student Poetry (kit). Canadabooks, $13.50. One hundred award-winning poems printed in large type on coloured posters; recording by Cedric Smith included.

Individualized Reading Skills Program (teaching program). SRA, $20.70. Grades 3-8; four textbooks, record cards, answer keys.

Design for Reading (teaching program). SRA, 2 student textbooks, $8.00 each. Teacher's handbooks, $1.00 each, Grades 7-9.

High Interest/Low Vocabulary Series

Titles from the Time Out series, Dent $1.85 each. Junior high. *Big Cat; Hang On; Landslide.*

Titles from the Passport to Reading series, Macmillan:
> *Anchors Aweigh,* $3.40. Reading level grade 2; interest level grade 6.
> *Over the Horizon,* $3.40. Reading level grade 4; interest level grade 7.
> *Outward Bound,* $3.50. Reading level grade 5; interest level grade 8.
> *Into Orbit,* $4.25. Reading level grade 6, interest level grade 9.

Full Flight, $4.25. Reading level grade 7; interest level grade 10. Teacher's handbooks, $2.50 each.

Titles from the Hockey Action series, Maclean-Hunter, $3.00 each. Teacher's handbook, $1.50. Eight paperback novels relating the hockey career of Dave Brodie from high school to professional. Reading range, grade 3-8. *Puck Hog; The Championship; Training Camp; Rookie under Fire; Hockey Powerhouse; Battle for the Cup; Brodie turns Pro; Playoff Pressure.*

Titles from the series Pine Mountain adventures, Maclean-Hunter, $2.50 each. Eight paperbacks relating the adventures of Barbara Manning who lives with her family in a ski lodge; reading range, grades 4-6. *Skiing Sabotage; Mountain Mishap; Devil's Chute; Mysterious Rescue; End of a Legend; Cruel Contestant; Who's Guilty; Coach or Champion.*

Titles from the series Checkmate, Mathuen, $1.80 each. A paper-back series by Leslie McFarlane, author of the Hardy Boys books; grade 5 ability level. *Squeeze Play; The Spider Lake Mystery; The Dynamite Flynns; The Agent of the Falcon; Breakaway; Snow Hawk.*

Titles from the series the Robb Family Adventures, Dent. Interest, 8-14 years, reading levels as noted. *The Chase,* 1.5, $2.00; *Pine Island Adventure,* 1.7, $2.00; *Niagara Rescue,* 2.0, $2.00; *Dangerous Waters,* 2.5, $2.25; *Winter Rescue,* 2.7, $2.35; *Avalanche,* 3.0, $2.35; *Stolen Secrets,* 3.2, $2.35; *Trapped!,* 3.5, $2.35.

Titles from the Canadian Paperbacks series, Scholastic.
Grades 1-3. Nine books including, *How the Chipmunk Got its Stripes; Giant Dinosaurs; Amanda Grows Up; In My Backyard.* Set, $9.70.
Grades 4-6. Twenty-three books including *Dan Patch; The Forgotten World of ULOC; It Happened in Canada; Sketco the Raven.* Set, $22.60.
Grades 7-12. Eight books including *Megan; Hockey in my Blood; Two against the North; Season of Burnt Grass.* Set, $7.70.

Books for Teachers

The Republic of Childhood, Sheila Egoff (Oxford, 1975), $6.95. A critical guide to Canadian children's literature.

Children's Reading and the '70s, L.F. Ashley (McClelland, 1972), $5.25. The reading habits of children between 4-7; the effects of television on reading tastes.

Profiles, ed. Irma McDonough (Canadian Library Association, 1971), $6.00 pa. Biographies of 44 authors of children's literature.

Children's Literature: A Guide to Criticism, ed. Whitaker (Athabaskan), $2.50 pa.

Periodicals

Canadian Children's Magazine, Box 469, Ganges, B.C. V0S 1E0. A new and badly needed item in this barren area of publishing. Write for subscription information.

Canadian Children's Literature: A Journal of Criticism and Review, Canadian Periodical Publishers' Association. Quarterly, $9.00.

Ahoy: An Atlantic Magazine for Children, Ahoy, Box 3380, Halifax South Postal Office, Halifax, N.S. B3J 3J1. Write for subscription.

Watch for *Magook,* a children's magazine forthcoming from McClelland.

Chapter 24

SCIENCE

Anyone who has thumbed the toy section of a mail order catalogue, or who has had occasion to browse through the toy department of a large store may well stand agape at the exciting variety
of science materials and apparatus available to the child. Equally,
anyone who has viewed the teaching of science in schools may well
stand aghast. The discrepancy is prodigious. Science for children
between the ages of five and fourteen is commonly non-existent
or token, and almost exclusively textbook-workbook oriented. In
the senior grades only the minority in the academic stream will have
an opportunity to explore the real thing: chemistry, physics, biology,
and possibly zoology. And this in an era of human development
often referred to as the age of science and technology, when most
students take for granted the latest space spectacular, synthetically
prepared foods, the intricacies of multi-speed bicycles, and the relative merits of rotary and V-8 automobile engines. Science, it would
seem, is everywhere except in the classroom.

Lampooning, as opposed to lambasting, the quality of science instruction may be the more effective means of bringing about changes.
Circular 15 of the Ontario Ministry of Education (1974) can be an
unwitting accomplice. Among its recommended materials for Canadian pupils is the mistress of the science classroom—*Sally Sunflower*.
It is she—"Sally who grew from a seed to a large sunflower", who
undoubtedly stalks the legions of pickle jars arrayed on the window
ledges of the nation's elementary classrooms. For many young
sprouts, growing a bean plant in crumpled blotting paper or a potato
in a Mason jar is the sum of their science involvement in the early
school years. For variation, children may read a *Trip With Twinkle*
("In this fantasy a young girl learns some facts about the sun, moon,
and planets") or *Fun on a Wild River* (". . . a family's hazardous
river passage and a climb up steep rock cliffs to band a young eagle. . .

231

a sense of contentment as the family gathers for an evening meal").

Over a decade ago Marshall McLuhan criticized this discrepancy between the world and the school. His comments of 1965 bear repetition:

> We haven't really cottoned on to the fact that our children work furiously processing data in an electrically structured information world; and when these children enter a classroom—elementary school—they encounter a situation that is very bewildering to them. The youngster today, stepping out of his nursery or TV environment, goes to school and enters a world where the information is scarce, but is ordered and structured by fragmented, classified patterns, subjects, schedules. He is utterly bewildered because he comes out of this integral and complex world of electric information and goes into this nineteenth century world of classified information that still characterizes the educational establishment. . . . The young today are baffled because of the extraordinary gap between these two worlds.
>
> McLuhan, "Address at Vision '65," (In *Ekistics,* January 1967, p. 48)

Mark well the date of McLuhan's remarks. If there was evidence in support of his contentions in 1965, how much additional corroboration can be now assembled? The instantaneous transmission of ideas (including attitudes and values) via networks of global telecommunications brings the world to the doorstep of increasing numbers of people, including the very young child. From the earliest years of life, pre-school children acquire skills of extracting information from the media which has meaning for them. To do so implies the ability to absorb, analyze, discard, and apply information that is perceived to have meaning and utility. Whether or not the child can verbalize the processes of induction and/or deduction is not the salient consideration. What is important is that children raised in a mass-media environment enter the kindergarten classroom with "scientific" skills and understandings already refined to a remarkable degree. In educational parlance, they have learned how to formulate hypotheses, abstract data, and draw conclusions, all without the benefit of formal instruction. The scientific method, as this phrase is employed in teacher guidebooks, is an apparent strength of the five year old girl or boy.

Does the school conventionally build learning experiences on the basis of this obvious characteristic? Not usually. Aside from the employment of manipulative materials in the primary and kindergarten years, which permit open-ended experimentation by the child, science as a subject of learning must be preceded by the ability to read textbooks. The reliance on textbook-workbook approaches to learning almost everything, science included, is the American, and hence Canadian way. Contriving a curriculum that amounts to little more than reading pages and filling in the blanks becomes the over-riding objective. The weaknesses in this approach are not hidden. In the University of Alberta publication *Elements* (February 1971), the results of a study of popular elementary level science textbooks were reported. In this instance the researchers examined the level of reading ability required to comprehend the printed word in books developed for specific grade levels. It was concluded, as one example, that the grade two science materials required a grade four level of reading comprehension. After evaluating and reviewing three major textbook series the observation was made that "concrete experience"; that is, direct child participation and involvement was of greater benefit to students than reading about science. This does not mean that children should not read and write about science, but simply that science activities should be a priority.

For teachers who wish to transform their science instruction, major obstacles frequently stand in the way. School budgets, speci-fically at the early grade levels, are notorious for their preoccupation with print. Per capita pupil grants provide for purchasing the pro-vincially recommended textbook series and supplementary library resources, all of which fall into the category of printed and possibly audio-visual material. Essentially, money for buying learning mater-ials is available for reinforcing passive learning. Too seldom do educa-tional administrators allow available finances to be reallocated for items which demand direct child investigation and experimentation. Building a model windmill requiring knowledge of pulleys, levers, and wind resistance can bring delight and knowledge to the home-bound child on a rainy day. In the classroom available learning materials may dictate that reading and writing about "the making of a raindrop" is an easier alternative.

Admittedly, it is convenient to avoid involving kids in doing things. Six hours a day of the teacher telling and the immobile stu-dent absorbing at least keeps children under control. Roaming about the classroom, handling objects, upsetting apparatus, talking, even staring out the window could suggest an absence of learning—and a disregard for decorum. Behind the scenes, too, the tasks of the teacher are increased. If activities in science are to be pursued, the assembly of materials becomes considerably more exacting than if Chapter 5 is to be done today, followed by a film on Friday after-noon. A typical argument to overcome centres on the lack of avail-able items and space: "If only there was a well-stocked storeroom, perhaps a lab, but certainly an open area space, then science activities could be attempted." Attitudes of this kind are ingrained. In the last twenty-five years of North American progress, the myth of dependency has been established. Making do with what is immediately available has been replaced by the notion that if something cannot be constructed (e.g. science rooms), packaged (e.g. science kits), or merchandized by specialized agencies (e.g. science supply firms), then it is difficult, even impossible, for anything to be accomplished. Open-ended learning presumably has to be structured around manufactured items which in themselves, because of their structure, are a denial of the principle.

This pattern of circuitous thinking can only be broken when teacher education prepares Canadian teachers to work in other than "I tell—you listen" classroom situations. Particularly is this so from grade 4 up. Employing the senses of sight, touch, taste, hearing, and smell may very well pervade the learning methodology for the initial school years. By the fourth year children evidently are ready to discard upwards of three-fifths of their senses in order to expedite the gaining of information. Seeing—reading books and watching films, and hearing—listening to the teacher's voice, film sound tracks, and recorded information, become paramount in importance. Criticizing teachers for the perpetuation of this method is easy. They constitute a ready target, as an almost infinite array of editorials, letters to the editor, popular books, and magazine articles will attest. Too rarely is the brunt of the attack focused on colleges and faculties of education. The professor may well extol the virtues of activity-centred learning through assigned readings, term papers, and lectures, all of which are passive routines and in obvious conflict with the philosophy being conveyed. The novice junior high teacher is then expected to perform the miraculous feat of transforming the inert data of his lecture notes into a "live" classroom performance. This process of professional preparation is akin to preparing a lawyer for the courtroom solely through readings in jurisprudence, or a dentist through viewing pictures of a cavity. Teachers who have had little opportunity to observe, experiment, and practice teaching techniques, cannot be expected to undergo a form of metamorphosis once they become responsible for the education of young students. The demands of any teaching position can be heavy. Trying to improve dramatically the quality of science education without the benefit of practical experience is impossible.

The on-going developments of the British Nuffield Foundation should have greater influence on future directions in Canadian science education. Five basic principles can be isolated for consideration. Incorporation of these principles in teacher education courses could bring about a substantial conversion in terms of common practices.

1.
Children learn by sensory experience. To learn about something, a child must feel it, handle it, smell it, or taste it. Motor sensory experience is necessary and satisfying. Children must try out magnets, find out what will float, or see how a gear works. Films, books, radio, television, and verbal explanations can extend, but cannot replace, sensory appreciation. Children learn through concrete situations and practical inquiry.

2.
Each child is unique in himself. Each has his own particular feelings, needs, and reactions, and the school can in various ways compensate for limited experience. A wide range of learning opportunities can be offered and children encouraged to explore them fully.

3.
Children must be active and involved in order to understand and appreciate. Basic ideas essential to full understanding of the world are formed through practical experience. As a child explores his immediate surroundings he applies his knowledge to explore further and thus his horizons expand.

4.
Children need to talk, tell, discuss. Oral vocabulary goes hand-in-hand with interest and involvement. Any new stimulating experience motivates the use of language, first oral, then written.

5.
Children do not learn through passive absorption. Learning is an active process which Jean Piaget termed, "Living Learning". New understanding becomes part of what is already understood and in turn stimulates further inquiry.

Suppose that in each of the foregoing statements the words "teacher-education students" were substituted for "children". Consider the practical application of the meaning in each statement for the process of teacher preparation. Might not the utilization of these precepts in education courses more adequately equip tomorrow's teachers with the understandings, attitudes, and skills necessary for providing adequate science experiences for young students?

This may well be one curriculum area where the relative absence of Canadian learning materials is a mixed blessing. Whether Canadian or foreign in origin, the availability of more printed items in the science room can be expected to retard rather than accelerate the necessary changes in approaches to this subject.

N.B.   See Chapter 12—Environment.

♦   ♦   ♦   ♦

Series: Primary-Elementary

Elementary Science Curriculum Study (teaching program). Robert K. Crocker, McGraw, 1973. A program for grades 1-6 prepared at Memorial University, St. John's, Nfld. Materials are designed to encourage student investigation and experimentation. Apparatus kits, teacher's handbooks, and student textbooks are included. Sample titles:

> *Grade 1*
> Unit I— *Observing: The Use of the Senses*
> Unit II— *Classifying: Directly Observable Properties*
> Unit III— *Quantifying: Comparison of Objects in Relative Terms*
> Unit IV— *Classifying: Leaves, Twigs, Bark*
> Class Kit, $131.13 net.

Series: Elementary

Our Science Program (teaching program). Macmillan. Booklets on individual topics; each title sold in packages of 10 for $10.00. *Bicycles,* R.H. Horwood, 1969; *Mostly about Pigs,* R.H. Horwood, 1969; *String,* R.H. Horwood, 1969; *Watching the Weather Change,* J.A. Aikman, 1969; *Flights, Kites and Boomerangs,* R.W. Trueman, 1970; *Snow,* R.W. Trueman, 1973; *Trees,* R.H. Horwood, 1973; *Sound,* J.A. Aikman, 1975; *Simple Solutions,* R.W. Trueman, 1975.

Series: Elementary-Junior High

Science Activities, H.G. Hedges and others, Gage. Grades 4-8. A textbook series available in an Ontario, Prairie or Atlantic Canada edition.

Series: Junior-Senior High

Reading About Science, Holt, 1969-70. Book I, Gr. 7-8; Book II, Gr. 8-9; Book III, Gr. 9-10. $5.90 each. Readings about science and scientists in biology, chemistry, physical, and earth sciences; questions, photographs, drawings, and diagrams.

Titles from the Collier-Macmillan Science Studies series, Collier-Macmillan, 1974. $3.45 each pa.
> *Schoolyard and Beyond,* David A. Coburn; *The Living Community,* Rosemary Kelsch.

Searching for Structure, Donald H. Pike, Holt, 1973. $3.25 each; package of six, $17.95. Twenty books for students in grades 7-10; ideas, materials, and a suggested framework for developing a science program included.

Titles from the series Investigations in Science: Life and Environment, John Wiley, 1974. $3.50 each. pa. Grades 7-10. *Alphabet Jungle; Wings, Weights and Wheels; Bubbles to Batteries; Inside Story; Mini Things; Green Power.*

Individual Books

Explorations Scientifiques (Gage), *Premier livre et Deuxieme livre.* $6.95 each.

Weeple People, D.C. Gillespie (McGraw, 1970), $2.15 pa. Grades 1-3.

Colourweeples, D.C. Gillespie (McGraw, 1972), $2.95 pa. Grades 1-3. Teacher's handbook, $3.10.

Bicycles to Beaches, D.C. Gillespie and others (McGraw, 1972), $4.95. Grades 4-6. Teacher's edition, $4.50.

Foundations of Space Science, William Krynowsky and others (Holt, 1968), $7.45. Junior-high textbook which emphasizes the physics of space; laboratory activities included. Teacher's edition, $3.00.

Destination Moon (cassette tape). 30 min, C.B.C. Learning Systems, set of 3, $24.00. The past, present and future of lunar theories and exploration.

Science Labs I and II (kit). Scholar's Choice, $15.00 each. Organized sets of student activity cards on such topics as sound, plants, the universe, electricity, cells, rocks and minerals, and animals and their environment.

Science films, 16mm, English or French are available for purchase or rental from Moreland-Latchford.

For Teachers

Teachers, Children and Things, Clifford J. Anastasiou (Holt, 1971), $3.95. A philosophy of science education based on the work of Jean Piaget.

Teaching Science in Canadian Schools, Maynard Hallman and others (Holt, 1961), $7.25. A science program for grades 1-3.

Chapter 25

SOCIAL STUDIES

The length of this chapter is deceptive. A glance at the bibliography may suggest that a profusion of material exists. It would seem that only the incorporation of these items into the curriculum is required to reduce, if not eliminate, concern for "Canadian content." Canadian students are well served in developing an understanding of the geography and history of their country, it appears.

In reality, classrooms do not have access to a satisfactory selection of Canadian social studies materials. Keeping in mind that the materials listed are representative of the publishing marketplace, and that this is not an all-inclusive bibliography, close scrutiny of the items is recommended, with the following considerations in mind:

1. In the search for materials in all the subject areas mentioned in the various chapters, approximately one item in every four appeared to fall into the field of social studies. Initially, this seemed to be a good omen. Upon closer assessment, a pattern began to emerge.

Many relevant social studies books are trade, rather than school editions. Although senior high school students could benefit from exposure to such authors as James Laxer, Robert Chodos, and Ramsay Cook, their teachers are not often trained to search out and use these materials. Guidebooks and resource manuals which demonstrate the practical application of trade editions in the classroom are needed. (The few available are listed in the "Items for Teachers" section in the bibliography.) For primary, elementary and junior high students fewer sources exist. Finding material to suit their reading ability and interest levels is a continuing concern.

2. The influence of two central Canadian universities on historical research and writing has been substantial. The University of Toronto, dating back to the years of G.M. Wrong, History Department chairperson, and Queen's University in Kingston, from the time of Adam

238

Short, have influenced the interpretation of Canadian history. This is not to suggest that the efforts of either of these respectable institutions or their newer offspring should be censured. Without their contributions the supply of materials would be even more inadequate. But it is worth noting that through their influence the writing of history has largely taken place from a central Canadian perspective, with a distinct orientation eastward to Europe, Britain in particular. Referring to his undergraduate preparation in history at the University of Toronto in the 1909-1914 era, Arthur Lower described the situation as:

> I found my way through many tracts of European and English history, but I cannot recall whether I had any Canadian history or not. Probably not; it would not have been considered very important. *My First Seventy-five Years* (Toronto: Macmillan, 1967, p. 53)

The extent of the monopoly on historical research shared by a small number of Ontario universities is reflected in learning materials generally. A book supported by the 1967 Centennial Commission is instructive. *The Canadians, 1867-1967* (Toronto: Macmillan, 1967) contains selections written by twenty-four university scholars. Seventy per cent were written by people from University of Toronto or other central Ontario institutions. The fringes of Canada were represented by one University of British Columbia author and one historian from the University of New Brunswick. Two French Canadian writers from Laval and McGill gave a nod in the direction of furthering French-English awareness and mutual appreciation. Further evidence of this domination of the centre can be found in the title pages or indexes of any random selection of materials. If powerless to change this situation, teachers can be aware of the narrow focus characteristic of much historical writing. Finding useful regional, ethnic, or socio-economic perspectives is difficult. For the most part children today are provided only with materials of white, Anglo-Saxon, middle-class, and Ontario orientation. This is a serious limitation in a country with a scattered, multicultural population.

3. The standardized textbook model of Canadian history conjures up all the interest and excitement of a federal- provincial conference on freight rates. The content is lacking in controversy and the results are predictable, even pre-ordained. Perseverance, justice, and the Union Jack traditionally won out over the "primitive savages", and the French.

Fortunately, an alternative to this school of neutered textbook composition is open. Relatively little-known regional publishers have available materials which add flesh to skeletal historical outlines. The reminiscences of former Prince Edward Island Premier Walter Shaw (*Tell Me The Tales,* Square Deal) provide a down-east, homespun dimension to understanding Maritime life. On the prairies, a biography of an early black settler (*John Ware's Cow Country,* Saskatoon: Western Producer, 1974), preserves a story otherwise ignored in textbooks. The effort and time required to locate these resources is amply justified. Through their use future generations of students will be able to sample those events which lift Canadian history above the level of hard-driving men marching across the frontier to the tune of "Rosemarie".

4. History is a male preserve. Men write it and men live it—Laura Secord, her cow, and Nellie McClung notwithstanding. Conventional materials provide women with the domesticated look, in words and pictures. Stoking the hearth, seeing their men off to new adventures, and patiently awaiting their return are the themes of pioneer life. In the twentieth century, except for the interruption in the usual routine provided by the suffragettes, women gracefully returned to their role of supporting actresses. Until recently, it was impossible to puncture the myth of the weak, inferior woman waiting behind the scenes while the man went about making history. Learning materials ignored the contributions of women to both domestic and national life. Materials from women's collectives and feminist groups are becoming increasingly available. These have been tabulated separately and are particularly useful at the senior high levels.

For younger students little in the way of improvement on traditional items now exists.

5. Current Events information is difficult to locate, especially if attention is given to age and ability levels of students. One periodical, *Canada and the World,* (McLean-Hunter) prepared for high school students, is the sum total of publishing efforts in this regard. It is small wonder that elementary children have a greater awareness of the American presidency, the House of Representatives, and the C.I.A. than of Canadian affairs, when it is recognized that American periodicals often have their exclusive attention on a weekly basis. (e.g. *Weekly Reader,* Scholastic). One alternative to American magazines and the Associated Press (A.P.) interpretation of the world news is *Newslab* produced by General Publishing. Through this kit the daily newspaper can be thoroughly analyzed and evaluated. The latter process is important. Schools that subscribe to newspapers at

all undoubtedly rely heavily on the local press and not on papers of national stature such as the *Globe and Mail* and *Le Devoir*. There is a need for school authorities to make available current information which will convey the views of both English and French speaking Canadians. This information could then be supplemented by regional and local reports. Students in southern Canada seldom have the opportunity to familiarize themselves with day-to-day life north of the 60th parallel of latitude. Among major Canadian newspapers, the *Edmonton Journal* provides the only coverage of note. It could be beneficial to have access to the *News of the North* (Yellowknife) and *The Whitehorse Star* (Whitehorse, Yukon), particularly given the increased importance of petroleum and mineral developments in these areas.

6. The "pebble in the puddle" approach to geographic-historical understanding is the essence of the Local Studies Local History methodology and materials. Commencing with study of the local community, students can expand their understanding to the province, the region, the nation, and the international setting. Developing relationships in this manner is beneficial by itself. To do this successfully will make demands on environmental, political, social, economic, and artistic skills and resources. The interplay of the several disciplines is the most important, if unstated, goal in this approach.

Materials for this study must be obtained from a variety of sources.

- Museums, heritage foundations, archives, newspaper columns, and the unrecognized publishing contributions of local people comprise much of the best source material.
- Academic research studies in anthropology, archeology and geology should not be ignored.
- Universities throughout Canada often have their own presses and these are valuable sources of ideas and information.

To assist teachers in utilizing these resources, *Local History in Atlantic Canada* (Macmillan, 1974) is a source book of practical suggestions.

Although the references are localized, the essential themes for activities could be transposed to other areas as well. Historian Kenneth McNaught made reference to the changing demands that this approach to social studies would place on teachers:

It remains true, however, that a Canadian Studies Program will require for its conduct far more than the body of teachers who are at present trained in history. The problem then is to devise a method of integrating into the new program much of what was previously taught separately as well as a good deal of material that has not been ordinarily presented at all.

> McNaught, *A Little More For The Mind in Teaching For Tomorrow: A Symposium on Social Studies in Canada* (Toronto: Nelson, 1969)

The method can be local studies. Types of materials to look for are indicated on a province-by-province basis in the pages following.

7. There remains an overwhelming flaw in existing materials. Social studies should lead to improved international understanding. With a degree of optimism it is feasible to advocate a better quality of Canadian program. However, in extending the student's knowledge from Canada to the world community, the absence of resources is a major problem. The need is for international studies which can be related to Canadian experiences. To use a routine classroom example, an assignment is given to write a report on Brazil: its social development, trade, politics and foreign relations. The student is likely to turn to the handiest encyclopedia and reference materials, most of which have their origin in the United States. Upon completion of the report, it would be remarkable if the student knew very much about Canada vis-à-vis the Organization of American States, Canadian industrial involvement in Brazil (e.g. Brascan), or Canada's trade relations with Brazil.

Similar examples could be cited for literally every other country. *World Book, Comptons, Encyclopedia Britannica*, combined with Time-Life materials, do contribute useful information. It is in relating that information to Canada that the problem arises. Students are denied the chance to learn from and about other nations in a fashion relevant to their own country's history, policies, and practices. Canadian periodicals, C.B.C. resources, and material available through Information Canada bookstores partially help to overcome these woeful inadequacies. Most of these fragmentary materials could be used at the high school level. For young children, little material is currently available. From the Chanak Affair of 1922 to Lester B. Pearson's involvement in Suez in 1956, to official government reactions to the death of Salvador Allende in 1973, Canada's international affairs constitute a secret well-guarded from most students.

N.B. Cross referencing with the other chapters will be helpful, particularly on a provincial and/or regional basis.

General Reference

Atlases and Maps

The National Atlas of Canada/L'Atlas national du Canada, Dep't. of Energy, Mines and Resources (Macmillan, 1974), $56.00. The most comprehensive atlas available; 307 maps providing information on geography, economics, cultures, geology, agriculture, forestry, logging, fossil fuels, pipelines, primary metals, transportation.

Dent's Canadian Metric Atlas, H.E. Mindak (Dent, rev. 1975), $2.50.

Canadian Oxford Junior Atlas, ed. E.G. Pleva and Norman Barnard (Oxford, 1969), $2.75. Maps of the development of Canada since the 18th century; environ maps of major Canadian and American cities; maps of native peoples.

An Historical Atlas of Canada, rev. 3rd ed. D.G.G. Kerr (Nelson, 1975), $10.95.

Looking at Maps, Lillian J. Wonders and William C. Wonders (Longman, 1964), $1.95. An introduction to maps; reading, scale, geographical, and economic material.

Reading Topographic Maps, Harry Graham (Holt, 1968), $3.95. An introduction to map reading skills.

Topographic Map and Air Photo Interpretation, Emile D. Chevrier and D.F. Aitkens (Macmillan, 1970), $6.95 pa.

By Map and Compass, ed. C.A. Mustard (Macmillan, 1950), $1.75 pa.

Exploring Canada through Maps. (kit). Oxford, $35.00. Includes 52 illustrated skill cards, 20 slides; teacher's handbook; answer guide.

Where in the World: A Mini Map Pak (kit). Gage, $4.15. Nine illustrated cards to provide help in map making and map reading.

Simplified Political Map of Canada (map). 51" x 48", markable and cleanable, Scholar's Choice, $30.50.

Detailed Political Map of Canada (map). 50" x 36", markable and cleanable, Scholar's Choice, $30.70.

Wall Map Tablets (map). Scholar's Choice, set of 50 large outline maps, $6.40. Titles: Canada; The Maritimes; Newfoundland; N.W.T.; Ontario; The Prairie Provinces; Quebec; Southern Ontario.

Pictorial

Portraits of the Prime Ministers (print). col, 11" x 14", Dent, set of 15, $15.00.

The Canadian Diary 1862-1872 (diary). 11″ x 17″, EB, $16.50. One hundred leaves, engravings, and news reports.

Canada: A Visual History, D.G.G. Kerr and R.I.K. Davidson (Nelson, 1966), $6.95. Illustrated.

Canada and the Canadians, rev. ed. George Woodcock (Macmillan, 1973), $13.75. Illustrated.

Canada in Colour, Val Clery (Hounslow, 1972), $5.95.

Illustrated

This Land, These People: Visual Studies in Canadian Social and Economic History, David Meakin and Jeremy Vincent (Longman, 1973), $2.75.

Filmstrips

Titles from the series Social Science filmstrips, Scholar's Choice, $6.95 each. Set of 3, $20.85.
Royal Winter Fair; A Japanese Canadian Family; Forest Industries in B.C. Part 1, Logging; Newsprint in Quebec; Pulp and Paper Manufacturing in Newfoundland.

Titles from the filmstrip series Canada: A Nation Built on Trade, McIntyre Educational Media, set, $42.00:
Fur; Fish; Wheat; Timber; Minerals; A Survey.

Geography of Canada (filmstrip). col, EB, $7.00 each or set of 8, $48.00.

Overhead Transparencies

Titles from the series Canadian Study Transparencies, Scholar's Choice, $45.00 each. Each set contains ten transparencies with multiple overlays.
History: Canada Before 1800; World Explorers; Explorers of Canada; Canada and the Ice Age; Regions of Canada; Southern Ontario.

National Geography (overhead transparency). McIntyre Educational Media, set of 9 with 31 overlays, $59.00.

Regional Geography (overhead transparency). McIntyre Educational Media, set of 13 with 48 overlays, $99.00.

Urban Geography (overhead transparency). McIntyre Educational Media, set of 6 with 22 overlays, $39.00.

Microfilm

Maclean-Hunter has available
Maclean's Magazine 1911-1970, $20.00 per year.

Chatelaine Magazine 1928-1970, $20.00 per year.
Financial Post 1907-1970.

Microfiche

Canada and the World Magazine, 1973-74, Maclean-Hunter, $9.00 per year.

Recorded Tapes and Records

Titles from the series Canadian Public Figures on Tape, O.I.S.E., cassette or reel-to-reel, $7.00 each. Nine hour-long interviews with political leaders and a half-hour dialogue between J.W. Pickersgill and J.R. Smallwood about the problems facing Newfoundland at the time of Confederation. Titles:
  L.B. Pearson; J.G. Diefenbaker; T.C. Douglas; Walter Gordon; René Lévesque; M. Lamontagne; J.W. Pickersgill; Paul Martin; Judy LaMarsh; Dialogue—J.W. Pickersgill and J.R. Smallwood.

Century (record). C.B.C. Publications Branch, 2 albums, $5.00 each. The first one hundred years of Canadian life.

Kit

Ten Years in a Box (kit). O.I.S.E., in Ontario, $60.00; elsewhere, $120.00. A box of items relating to the depression years: Pictures, documents, recorded material.

Games

Canadian Events (game). Dundurn, $9.75. For 2-6 players, 10 years and up; association of major events in Canadian history with their dates and prominent participants.

Canadian Album (game). Dundurn, $9.75. For 2-6 players, 10 years and up; requires a general knowledge of Canadian history.

Confederation Game (game). Dundurn, $9.75. For 7-37 participants 16 years and up; through study of the Quebec Conference and the British North America Act, the object is to design a constitution.

Caucus: Canadian Politics in Action (game). Van Nostrand, $49.95. Additional party handbooks for $5.00 per package of 10. A simulation game based on the caucus of the party governing Canada; 16 to 46 high school students can play.

Across Canada Travel (game). Scholar's Choice, $20.00. A map of Canada constitutes the game board.

Stamps

A Postage Stamp History of Canada, Victor Seary (McGraw, 1972), $6.45.

Mosaic of Canada on Postage Stamps, Nick and Helma Mika (Hurtig, 1967), $9.95.

Canada's Postage Stamps, Douglas and Mary Patrick (McClelland, 1964), $10.00.

The Musson Stamp Dictionary, Douglas and Mary Patrick (General, 1972), $8.95. A complete book for the beginner.

Please refer to Chapter 4 on Art for additional items.

Reference Texts

A New History of Canada, (Saannes, 1973), 15 vol. $30.00. French or English; Grade 10 reading level.

Canadian Centenary Series McClelland, 18 vol. $14.95 each. From the year 1000 to the present time.

Encyclopédie du Québec, 2 vols (Homme), $6.00 each.

Canada's Illustrated Heritage, a sixteen-volume series forthcoming from McClelland in 1977.

Titles from the Canadian Reprint series, Hurtig:

The Discovery of the North-West Passage, R.M. M'Clure (Hurtig, 1969), $5.95. Originally published 1856.

Journey from Prince of Wales's Fort in Hudson's Bay to The Northern Ocean, Samuel Hearne (Hurtig, 1971), $20.00. First published 1795.

Peace River: A Canoe Voyage from Hudson's Bay to the Pacific, Archibald McDonald (Hurtig, 1970), $5.95. Originally published 1872.

Voyages from Montreal on the River St. Lawrence through the continent of North America, Alexander Mackenzie (Hurtig, 1971), $20.00. Originally published 1801.

Wanderings of an Artist, Paul Kane (Hurtig, 1967), $8.95. Paul Kane's experiences in Western Canada. Originally published 1859.

Titles from the History of Canada series, C.B.C. Publications Branch, $2.25 each pa.

The French Colonial Period; The British Colonial Period; Canada's First Half Century; The Modern Era, 1914-1967.

Challenge of Confrontation, Fraser Kelly and John Marshall (McClelland), $2.95 per set. A boxed set of six paperbacks on regional Canadian problems.

Titles from the Canadian Critical Issues series, O.I.S.E., $1.25 each:

The Right to Live and Die, 1973; *Crisis in Quebec,* 1973; *Native Survival,* 1973.

Titles from the Canadian Political Studies series by Barry Riddell and John Lynch, Maclean-Hunter, $3.45 each:
Urban Politics, 1972; *Issues Facing Political Parties,* 1972; *Ideology,* 1973; *Bureaucracy,* 1973; *Propaganda and Public Opinion,* 1973.

Titles from the Canadian Critical Issues series, General, $1.25 each:
Don't Teach That, 1972; *The Law and the Police,* 1972; *Rights of Youth,* 1972.

Local History

General References and Sources

Titles from the series Canadian Historic Sites, Information Canada, paper, illustrated.
Armstrong Mound: Rainy River, Ontario, $3.00.
Lower Fort Garry: Excavations 1965-76, $3.00.
Rocky Mountain House, Alberta, $3.00.
Signal Hill, Newfoundland, $3.00.
The Canals of Canada, $5.00.
Architectural Heritage of the Rideau Corridor, $5.00.
Battle of Queenston Heights, Fort George, $5.00.

Titles from the Coles Canadiana Collection, Coles. Paperback reprints of historical material.
Canadian Folk Life and Folklore, William Parker Greenough (Coles, 1971), $2.98. c 1897.

Narrative of Fugitive Slaves in Canada, Benjamin Drew (Coles, 1972), $5.10. c 1856.

Mounted Police Life in Canada, Burton Deane (Coles, 1973), $5.10.

The Ontario Reader: Fourth Book, (Coles, 1971), $2.50.

Peace River: A Canoe Voyage from Hudson's Bay to the Pacific, Archibald McDonald (Coles, 1971), $2.15. c 1872.

The Backwoods of Canada, Catherine Parr Traill (Coles, 1971) $4.50. c 1836.

Settlers and Rebels: Royal North West Mounted Police Reports, (Coles, 1973), $5.95.

Titles from the Mika Publications of Rare Canadiana, Mika. Reprints of historical material.

Kingston City Hall, Nick and Helma Mika (Mika, 1974), $2.00. A colourful portrait of the historic City Hall of Kingston, Ontario's oldest city and once the capital of Canada.

Historic Fort William, John R. Lumby (Mika, 1974), $10.00. An illustrated history of Fort William, now Thunder Bay, from fur trading post to the twentieth century. First published 1927.

Country Life in Canada, Caniff Haight (Mika, 1971), $12.00. Personal recollections of pioneer life, early transportation, taming a wilderness. First published 1885.

His Faults Lie Gently: The Incredible Sam Hughes, Alan R. Capon Hall (Mika, 1969), $4.50. Biography of Canada's controversial minister of the militia in World War I.

Friendly Persuasion: Canadian Advertising of Yesteryear, Nick and Helma Mika (Mika, 1974), $4.00. Reproductions of advertisements from daily and weekly Ontario newspapers from 1819 to the early 1900s.

Mosaic of Canada on Postage Stamps, Nick and Helma Mika (Mika, 1967), $15.00. Historic events, landmarks, people, industrial development, illustrated with Canadian postage stamps.

History of Prince Edward Island, Duncan Campbell (Mika, 1973), $12.50. First published 1875.

A History of Newfoundland, D.W. Prowse (Mika, 1973), $30.00. First published 1895.

Wooden Ships and Iron Men, F.W. Wallace (Mika, 1973), $15.00. The history of the square-rigged merchant marine; first published 1937.

History of Nova Scotia, Thomas Chandler Haliburton (Mika, 1973), 2 vols $15.00 each. First published 1829.

New Brunswick with a Brief Outline of Nova Scotia and Prince Edward Island, A. Monro (Mika, 1973), $15.00. General history of the 3 provinces.

The Chignecto Isthmus and its First Settlers, Stuart Trueman (Mika), $15.00.

From Chalk Dust to Hayseed, Helen Richards Campbell (Mika, 1975), $5.00. Recollections of an Ontario school teacher of the early 1900s.

Place Names and Places of Nova Scotia, Charles B. Ferguson (Mika, 1974), $30.00. More than 2300 names of places with their derivation and a brief history of each community.

Individual Materials

A Community Study for Primary Children, Vancouver Environ-mental Education Project (B.C. Teachers' Lesson Aid service), $1.70. Ideas for teachers.

Community Studies for Community Schools, Vancouver Environ-mental Education Project (B.C. Teachers' Lesson Aid Service), $2.00. Ideas and activities based upon a study conducted by Carnarvon Community School in Vancouver.

The Origin and Meaning of Place Names in Canada, G.H. Arm-strong (Macmillan, 1972), $10.95.

Heroic Beginnings, Donald Creighton (Macmillan, 1974), $14.95. An illustrated account of 60 historic sites and parks in Canada.

Glimpses of Canada, Marius Van Steen (Scholar's Choice, 1974), $2.40 pa. Collection of folklore, historical events, biographical sketches.

Living in Canada, rev. ed., Alex A. Cameron, M.Q. Innis and J.H. Richards (Clarke, Irwin, 1968), $5.25. Studies of different re-gions focusing on exploration, settlement, rivalries, pioneer life, the settlement of the west.

Nineteenth Century Pottery and Porcelain in Canada, Elizabeth Collard (McGill-Queen's, 1967), $25.00.

Eaton's 1901 Catalogue, (Musson, 1970) $3.98 pa. Reprint.

Dateline Canada, 2nd. ed., Robert Bowman (Holt, 1973), $7.65. Interesting events in history.

Fame in a Name (cassette tape). 30 min, C.B.C. Learning Systems, $8.00. The origin and history of Canadian place names.

Life in Early North America (print). Daniel R. Birch and others, Fitzhenry and Whiteside, 1974, $35.00. Teacher's handbook and 24 study prints focusing on areas of settlement.

Growth of a Nation (print). Daniel R. Birch and others (Fitzhenry and Whiteside), 1974, $43.00. Teacher's handbooks with 29 study prints.

Atlantic Canada

Basic Books for Teachers

Local History in Atlantic Canada, William B. Hamilton (Mac-millan, 1974), $4.95.

Local Studies, M. Frederickson (Atlantic Institute of Education, 1976), $1.00 pa.

Historical Essays on the Atlantic Provinces, George A. Rawlyk (McClelland, 1967), $3.95 pa.

Alden Nowlan's Maritimes (l.p. record). mono, C.B.C. Publications Branch, $5.00. Alden Nowlan reads his poetry and a short story based on his experiences in Nova Scotia and New Brunswick.

Les Acadiens, Emery Leblanc (Homme), $2.00.

The Acadians: Creation of a People, Naomi Griffiths (McGraw, 1973), Frontenac Libraries. $3.75 pa.

Inventaires sur les Acadiens (Acadie), $8.00. Ouvrage de référence d'une très grande valeur. Tous les endroits, en Amérique et en Europe où l'on peut trouver les documents concernant les Acadiens sont y cités.

Nova Scotia

The Neutral Yankees of Nova Scotia, John Bartlett Brebner (McClelland, 1969), $3.95 pa.

A Pocketful of Nova Scotia History: I. Joseph Howe (Petheric, 1973), $1.95 pa. A jackdaw-type collection.

Glimpses into Nova Scotia History, William Pope and Bruce Ferguson (Lancelot, 1975), $4.00.

Nova Scotia Sketchbook, L.B. Jenson (Petheric, 1970), $3.95. Sketches from around the province.

The Birds of Nova Scotia, Robie W. Tufts (Nova Scotia Museum, 1973), $15.00.

Trees of Nova Scotia, Saunders (Nova Scotia Dep't. of Lands and Forests), 75¢.

Collecting Minerals in Nova Scotia, Corbett (Nova Scotia Museum), 25¢.

Amphibians and Reptiles of Nova Scotia, Martin (Nova Scotia Museum), 25¢.

The Bottle Collector: Bottles Made and Used in Nova Scotia, Azor Vienneau (Petheric, 1969), $2.50 pa.

Nova Scotia Furniture, George MacLaren (Petheric, 1971), $2.00 pa.

A Guide to Some Domestic Pioneer Skills, Sparling (Nova Scotia Museum), $1.00 pa.

Antique Potteries of Nova Scotia, George Maclaren (Petheric), $2.00 pa.

Out of Old Nova Scotia Kitchens, Marie Nightengale (Nightengale, 1970), $5.25.

Folklore of Lunenburg County, Nova Scotia, Helen Creighton (McGraw), $8.95. A reprint of the 1950 folklore classic.

Seasoned Timbers: Historic Buildings, Heritage Trust of Nova Scotia (Petheric), 2 vols., $4.95 each.

Iron Roads: Railways of Nova Scotia, David E. Stephens (Lancelot, 1972), $2.00 pa.

The MacKay Motor Car; Nova Scotia's First Production Car, W.H. McCurdy (Petheric, 1967), $1.00 pa.

The Guysboro Railway: 1897-1939, Bruce MacDonald (Formac, 1973), $1.95 pa.

Men Against the Sea, Cyril Robinson (Lancelot, 1971), $2.95.

The Sinking of the "I'm Alone", Jan Patton (McClelland, 1973), package of 6, $5.96.

Phantom Ship, Roland H. Sherwood (Lancelot, 1975), $2.95 pa. Stories of the phantom vessel that sails the Northumberland Strait.

Davey's Pilots and the Sea Wolves, Catherine L. Brown (Petheric, 1975), $2.50 pa. Sea tales from the age of sail.

Lighthouses of Nova Scotia, David E. Stephens (Lancelot, 1973), $2.00 pa.

The History of the Nova Scotia Tartan, M. Major (Petheric, 1972), $1.00 pa.

Beyond the Atlantic Roar: A Study of the Nova Scotian Scots, D. Campbell and R.A. MacLean (McClelland, 1974), $4.95 pa.

Highland Settler: A Portrait of the Scottish Gael in Nova Scotia, Charles W. Dunn (U.T.P., 1953), $3.75.

Cape Breton Island, Pat and Jim Lotz (J.J. Douglas, 1974), $8.95.

Cape Breton Harbour, Edna Staebler (McClelland, 1972), $8.95.

Memoirs of a Cape Breton Doctor, C.L. MacMillan (McClelland, 1974), $7.95.

Cape Breton Anthology, Claribel Gesner (Lancelot, 1971), $1.00 pa.

The Girl from Loch Bras d'Or, Margaret MacPhail (Lancelot, 1973), $2.95.

Wood and Stone: Pictou, Nova Scotia, Lathem B. Jenson and the Pictou Heritage Society. (Petheric, 1972), $2.95. Sketches of buildings with text.

Pictou Pioneers, Roland H. Sherwood (Lancelot, 1973), $2.95 pa.

It Happened at Moose River, David E. Stephens (Lancelot, 1974), $2.00 pa. Gold mine disaster.

Ox Bells and Fireflies, Ernest Buckler (McClelland, 1974), $2.75 pa. Novel set in the Annapolis Valley.

Sable Island, Lyall Campbell (Lancelot, 1974), $2.95.

Joseph Howe of Nova Scotia, Bruce Ferguson (Lancelot, 1973), $2.95 pa.

Nova Scotia's Two Remarkable Giants, Phyllis Blakeley (Lancelot, 1970), $1.50.

The Life and Times of Angus L., John Hawkins (Lancelot, 1969), $3.95. A biography of a former Liberal Premier.

New Brunswick

An Intimate History of New Brunswick, Stuart Trueman (McClelland, 1970), $2.95.

New Brunswick: Story of Our Province, Neil Sutherland (Gage, 1965), $5.95. Elementary textbook.

Geographical Names of New Brunswick, Rayburn (Information Canada), $8.00. The stories behind over 4 000 names; wall map of New Brunswick included.

People and Places in New Brunswick, Wright (Lancelot), $2.25.

Antique Furniture by New Brunswick Craftsmen, Huia G. Ryder (McGraw, 1965), $4.95.

Regional Developments in North-East New Brunswick, Ralph Krueger (McClelland, 1975), $3.24 pa.

Ghosts, Pirates and Treasure Trove: The Phantoms that Haunt New Brunswick, Stuart Trueman (McClelland, 1975), $8.95.

The Sisters, Brewster (Oberon), $3.50 pa. A novel about growing up in New Brunswick in the 1930s and 1940s.

Prince Edward Island

Canada's Smallest Province, Frances Bolger (P.E.I. Heritage Foundation), $7.95.

Cornelius Howatt: Superstar, Baglole and Weale (P.E.I. Heritage Foundation, 1975), $3.00 pa. In 223 pages of wit and perception, the "Brothers and Sisters of Cornelius Howatt" make the point that "progress" and the "quality of life" on P.E.I. are not necessarily synonymous.

A People's History of P.E.I., Errol Sharpe (Steel Rail, 1976), $5.95 pa.

Folklore: Prince Edward Island, Ramsay (Square Deal, 1975), $3.95 pa.

Island Prose and Poetry: Centenary Collection, (P.E.I. Heritage Foundation), $2.00 pa.

Tell Me the Tales, Walter Shaw (Square Deal), $4.95. Autobiography of Walter Shaw, former premier of P.E.I.

Seaweeds of P.E.I., (P.E.I. Heritage Foundation), $2.75.

La cuisine acadienne, (P.E.I. Heritage Foundation), $3.00 pa.

Agriculture, Shipbuilding, Fisheries (kit). (P.E.I. Heritage Foundation), set of 3 jackdaw-type kits, $6.00.

Canadian Collector: Vol. VIII, No. 1, P.E.I. Heritage Foundation (periodical devoted to the centennial of P.E.I.), $2.00.

Newfoundland

Newfoundland: A Pictorial Record, Charles P. DeVolpi (Longman, 1972), $24.95. One hundred and eighty-one illustrations.

My Newfoundland, A.R. Scammell (Harvest, 1971), $2.50 pa. Stories, songs, poems.

The Oldest City: The Story of St. John's, Newfoundland, Paul O'Neil (Porcépic, 1975), $17.95.

"Complaints is Many and Various but the Odd Divil Likes It": Nineteenth Century Views of Newfoundland, Robert Moyles (Peter Martin, 1975), $12.00. Newspaper accounts, diary entries, and ship's logs provide the source information.

Newfoundland and Labrador, Leslie Harris (Dent, 1968), $3.90.

Labrador and Anticosti, Huard (Leméac), $12.50.

Woman of Labrador, Elizabeth Goudie (Peter Martin, 1973), $3.95 pa. Autobiography.

Wake of the Great Sealers, Farley Mowat and David Blackwood (McClelland, 1973), $16.95. A tribute to 19th and early 20th century sealers.

The Greatest Hunt in the World, George Allen England (Tundra, 1969), $5.95. A reprint of an illustrated account of the sealing industry of 50 years ago.

Captain Harry Thomasen: Forty Years at Sea, Andrew Horwood (Saannes, 1973), $6.50. A story of one man's life and the Port of Grand Bank.

By Great Waters: A Newfoundland-Labrador Anthology from the Year 1003 to the Present, ed. Peter Neary and Patrick O'Flaherty (U.T.P., 1974), $3.95 pa. Sixty-five items selected from literary and historical sources, portraying the development of the Newfoundland community.

Here the Tides Flow, E.J. Pratt (Macmillan, 1962), $2.00 pa.

The Chronicles of Uncle Mose, Russell (Breakwater, 1975), $3.95 pa. An anthology of penetrating glimpses into outport life.

Baffles of Wind and Tide, ed. Rose (Breakwater, 1975), $3.50. An anthology of prose, poetry and drama.

After the Locusts, Watts (Breakwater, 1975), $2.50. Poetry.

Point Lance in Transition: The Transformation of a Newfoundland Outport, John J. Manion (McClelland, 1976), $3.50 pa.

Through One More Window, Pitman (Breakwater), $2.50 pa. Poetry.

You May know them as Sea Urchins, Ma'am, Guy (Breakwater, 1975), $4.95 pa. An anthology of witty provocative writings.

The Latecomers (l.p. record). C.B.C. Publications Branch, $5.50. Pianist Glenn Gould's interpretation of Newfoundland.

Newfoundland (kit). Clarke, Irwin, $6.50. Jackdaw.

Quebec

Quebec: Society and Politics: Views from the Inside, ed. Dale Thomson (McClelland, 1973), $4.95 pa.

Contemporary Quebec: An Analytical Bibliography, Jacques Cotnam (McClelland, 1973), $2.95 pa.

Québec-Canada anglais, Michel Brunet (H.M.H., 1970), $4.75. Relationships between the two cultures are explored.

Le Québec: traditions et evolution (Gage, 1976). Two volumes of prose, poetry, newspaper articles, and illustrations. Each $4.90.

Québec, John R. Colombo; L. Hawke, trans; A. Tardif and C. Harris, photos; (Hounslow, 1973), $7.95. Eighty colour photographs of Montreal, Quebec, the Gaspé peninsula, and the countryside.

Pourquoi le fédéralisme, Gilles Lalande (H.M.H.), $4.50.

Le féderalisme et la société canadienne française, Pierre Elliott Trudeau (H.M.H., 1968), $4.95. Useful for understanding the early thinking of Pierre Elliott Trudeau.

The French Canadian Outlook, Mason Wade (McClelland, 1964), $1.95 pa.

Two Societies: Life in Mid-Nineteenth Century Quebec, R. Cole Harris (McClelland, 1976), $3.50 pa.

The Decolonization of Quebec, Sheilagh and Henry Milner (McClelland, 1973), $3.95 pa.

Titres d'un série de brochures, Arts, Vie et Sciences au Canada français, l'Editeur Officiel du Québec, $1.00 chacune, br.

  Panorama des lettres canadiennes françaises, Guy Sylvestre. English translation, *Literature in French Canada.*

  Le théâtre au Canada français, Jean Hamelin. English translation, *The Theatre in French Canada.*

  La peinture moderne au Canada français, Guy Viau. English translation, *Modern Painting in French Canada.*

  La vie des sciences au Canada français, Cyrias Ouellet. English translation, *The Sciences in French Canada.*

  L'essor des sciences sociales au Canada français, Jean-Charles Falardeau. English translation, *The Rise of the Social Sciences in French Canada.*

  La Renaissance des métiers d'art au Canada français, Laurent Lamy.

  Vingt ans de cinéma au Canada français, Robert Daudelin.

  Architecture contemporaine au Canada français, Claude Beaulieu.

The Beautiful Old Houses of Quebec, P. Roy Wilson (U.T.P., 1975), $12.50. The traditional architecture of Quebec in 49 pencil sketches.

Le drapeau québécois, Luc André Biron (Homme), $1.00. Retrace l'histoire des drapeaux, armoiries et emblèmes utilisés en Nouvelle-France et au Québec jusqu'à l'avènement du fleurdelise.

Le Québec tel quel, (Ed. Officiel, 1975), $2.50 br. Synthèse de l'activité du Québec dans ses branches principaux: politique, sociale, culturelle; précédée d'une brève présentation de l'histoire et du territoire.

The Bitter Thirties in Quebec, Evelyn Dumas (Black Rose, 1975), $3.95 pa. Several strikes of the 1930s are analyzed through oral history.

The Impertinences of Brother Anonymous, Jean-Paul Desbiens (Harvest, 1962), $1.95 pa. A basic reference for understanding the recent changes in Quebec society.

For Pity's Sake: The Return of Brother Anonymous, Jean-Paul Desbiens (Harvest, 1965), $2.00 pa.

The Quebec Revolution, Hugh Bingham Myers (Harvest, 1963), $1.95 pa.

Quebec: A Chronicle 1968-1972, ed. Rae Murphy and Mark Starowicz (James Lorimer, 1972), $2.50 pa. Development of a militant opposition and the rise of labour as a major political force.

Quebec in Question, Marcel Rioux (James Lorimer, 1971), $3.95 pa. An English translation of a book which views Quebec politics as a rational development arising from the interplay of historical forces.

Histoire de l'insurrection au Canada, Louis-Joseph Papineau (Leméac, 1968), $2.50 pa. Papineau's view of the 1837 uprising.

Henri Bourassa and French Canadian Nationalism, Casey Murrow (Harvest, 1968), $2.50 pa.

An Option for Quebec, René Lévesque (McClelland, 1968), $3.50 pa.

Canadiens et nous, Jacques de Roussan (Homme), $1.00.

Québec, une autre Amérique, Michel Régnier (Ed. Officiel, 1967), $15.00. Album, 130 photos noir et blanc et couleurs, textes poétiques.

La Guerre trilogy by Roch Carrier, Anansi, $3.95 each. Three novels offering insight into the social history of Quebec. *La Guerre, Yes Sir!,* 1970; *Floralie, Where are You?,* 1971; *Is it the Sun, Philibert?,* 1972.

La nation québecois (cassette tape). 60 min, C.B.C. Learning Systems, $15.00. On the historical roots and present goals of Québecois.

Ontario

Historical Essays on Upper Canada, J.K. Johnson (McClelland, 1975), $4.95 pa.

A Brief Review of the Settlement of Upper Canada, D. McLeod (Mika, 1971), $12.00. An account of sixty pioneer years; first published 1841.

Max Braithwaite's Ontario, Max Braithwaite (J.J. Douglas, 1974), $10.00.

The Scotch, John Kenneth Galbraith (General), $3.50 pa. Autobiographical account of the early Ontario years of the economist John Kenneth Galbraith.

The Gentle Pioneers, Audrey Morris (General, 1973), $1.50 pa. Account of Samuel Strickland, his sisters, Catharine Parr Traill and Susanna Moodie, and their husbands—a family of early pioneers and writers.

Gentlewoman in Upper Canada, Anna Langton (Clarke, Irwin, 1950), $1.95 pa. Life of a settler in the Peterborough area in the 1840s.

Roughing it in the Bush, Susanna Moodie (McClelland, 1962), $1.95. A literary classic.

The Furniture of Old Ontario, Philip Shackleton (Macmillan, 1973), $30.00. Six hundred black and white and ten colour plates.

Women's Costumes in Early Ontario, K.B. Brett (Royal Ontario Museum, 1965), $1.00.

Lighting the Pioneer Ontario Home, L.S. Russell (Royal Ontario Museum, 1966), $1.00 pa.

Shantymen of Cache Lake, Bill Freeman (James Lorimer, 1975), $4.95 pa. Illustrated recollections of the 1873 era in the Ottawa valley, ages 9-14.

Rural Roots: Pre-Confederation Buildings of the York Region of Ontario, Byers, Kennedy, McBurney and the Junior League of Ontario (U.T.P., 1976), $6.50 pa. in 1977. A useful research item.

Poverty Pockets: A Study of the Limestone Plains of Southern Ontario, R.G. Langman (McClelland, 1976), $3.25 pa.

Patterns of Settlement in Southern Ontario: Three Studies, R.G. Langman (McClelland, 1971), $2.75 pa.

Georgian Bay: The Sixth Great Lake, James P. Barry (Clarke, Irwin, 1971), $2.50 pa.

Pioneer Gardens at Black Creek Pioneer Village, Eustella Langdon (Holt, 1972), $3.95 pa.

Perspectives on Landscape and Settlement in Nineteenth Century Ontario, David Wood (McClelland, 1975), $4.95.

The Niagara Escarpment, W.M. Tovell (Royal Ontario Museum, 1965), $1.00.

Niagara Falls: Story of a River, W.M. Tovell (Royal Ontario Museum), 50¢.

The Brantford Pottery 1849-1903, Daniel Webster (Royal Ontario Museum, 1968), $3.00.

The William Eby Pottery, Conestoga, Ontario, 1855-1907, (Royal Ontario Museum, 1971), $3.50.

Methodist Point, W.A. Kenyon (Royal Ontario Museum, 1970), $1.50.

Dating Rock Art in the Canadian Shield Region, Selwyn Dewdney (Royal Ontario Museum, 1970), $3.50.

The Miller Site, W.A. Kenyon (Royal Ontario Museum, 1968), $6.00.

The Swan Lake Site / The Brock Street Burial, W.A. Kenyon and N.S. Cameron (Royal Ontario Museum, 1961), $1.00.

A History of the Toronto Islands, Island Public School Students (Coach House, 1972), $2.00 pa.

Toronto is for Kids: A Parents' and Kids' Resource and Idea Guidebook, Clarke and others (Greey de Pencier, 1976), $4.95 pa.

By the Sound of Her Whistle, John Craig (Peter Martin, 1966), $5.95 pa. Steam navigation and pioneer settlement along the Trent waterway.

Western Canada

An Illustrated History of Western Canada, Tony Cashman (Hurtig, 1971), $12.95. History of the four western provinces in photographs, drawings, and reproductions.

The Prairies: Selected Historical Sources, Kenneth Osborne (McClelland, 1969), $2.25 pa.

Historical Essays on the Prairie Provinces, ed. Donald Swainson (McClelland, 1970), $3.95 pa.

The Western Interior of Canada, John Warkentin (McClelland, 1964), $3.25 pa.

West to the Sea, J.W. Grant MacEwan and M. Foran (McGraw, 1968), $4.95. Development of the West from prehistoric to the present time.

Salt of the Earth, Heather Robertson (James Lorimer, 1974), $17.50. Homestead life between 1880 and 1914; letters, diaries, autobiographies, and 150 photographs.

How the Depression Hit the West, Jan Patton (McClelland, 1973), package of 6, $5.96.

Men Against the Desert, James H. Gray (Saannes, 1970), $7.95. The story of the struggle to restore productivity to the prairie soil after the drought of the 1930s.

It's all Free — on the Outside, Ann Henry (McClelland, 1975), $8.95. Sideshows and carnivals in the depression years in Western Canada.

Maps of the Prairie Provinces, ed. T. Wier and G.J. Matthews (Oxford, 1972), $35.00. Thirty-one pages of maps and 5 pages of text.

The Great Fur Land, H.M. Robinson (Coles, 1973), $8.95. Life and travel in the Hudson Bay Company's territories in the 19th century.

Hudson's Bay, Robert M. Ballantyne (Hurtig, 1971, $8.95. The waning years of the Company's activities in the Northwest Territories, first published 1848.

The Little White Schoolhouse, vol. I, John C. Charyk (Western Producer), $7.50. Prairie life of the early 1900s.

Pulse of the Community, vol. II, John C. Charyk (Western Producer), $10.00. A sequel to the above.

Titles by J. Grant MacEwan, Western Producer:
Power for Prairie Plows, 1971, $8.95; *Harvest of Bread,* 1969, $6.95; *Fifty Mighty Men,* 1974, $6.95; *And Mighty Women Too; Stories of Notable Western Canadian Women,* 1975, $5.00; *Blazing the Old Cattle Trail,* 1966, $6.95; *Eye Opener Bob,* 1974, $8.95; *John Ware's Cow Country,* 1974, $7.95.

The Rum Runners, Frank Wesley Anderson (Frontier, 1966), $1.25.

The Cypress Hills, Tom Primrose (Frontier, 1970), $1.25.

Wagon Roads North, Art Downs (Gray, 1969), $4.95.

Good Food Naturally, John B. Harrison (J.J. Douglas, 1972), $4.50.

Years of the Sasquatch, John W. Green (Cheam, 1970), $2.95.

I Saw Ogo Pogo, (Western Heritage), 75¢.

Janey Canuck in the West, Emily F. Murphy (McClelland, 1975), $4.50. An early feminist leader provides an account of women's roles in pioneer life.

The Opening of the West (print). col, E.B. set of 10, $19.90. Indian peoples, exploration and transportation, RCMP, Riel Rebellions, C.P.R.

A Picture Study of the Settlement of the West: Nation-making Documents, Saywell and Ricker (Burns, 1973), $3.00 pa. A collection of 25 prints.

Manitoba

Manitoba: Profile of a Province, K. Wilson (Peguis, 1975), $3.50 pa. A brief history for ages 10-13.

In the Beginning, Gwain Hamilton (Derkson, 1964), $6.95. A history of Manitoba.

Manitoba Past and Present, Denise Dawes (Peguis, 1971), $12.50.
A pictorial history of Manitoba up to the centennial of 1970; introduction and legends are bilingual.

Manitoba: A History, 2nd ed., William L. Morton (U.T.P., 1967),
$3.95 pa.

Manitoba: A People and a Province, Knight (Fitzhenry and Whiteside, 1976), $3.95 pa. Grades 4-6.

Pioneers of Manitoba, Robert Harvey (Western Producer, 1970),
$4.00. Illustrated biographical sketches of forty pioneers.

Pioneers and Early Citizens of Manitoba, Manitoba Library Association (Peguis, 1971), $9.50. Approximately 500 biographies
from early times to 1920.

The Red River Settlement, Alexander Ross (Hurtig, 1971), $8.95.
First published 1856.

Women of the Red River, W.J. Healy (Peguis, 1970), $5.50. Eleven biographies.

Early Buildings of Manitoba, Gillian Moir and Ione Thorkelsson
(Peguis, 1973), $12.50. Buildings from early times to the 1930s.
228 photographs and illustrations.

Outlaws of Manitoba, Frank Wesley Anderson (Frontier, 1972),
$1.75 pa.

Lake Winnipeg: Route of the Adventurers, C.B. Gill (Peguis, 1972),
$1.75 pa. Exploration and settlement of Manitoba and the role of
boats on Lake Winnipeg.

Speaking of Winnipeg, ed. John Parr (Queenston, 1975), $3.50
pa. Eleven Canadians look back on their formative years spent in
Winnipeg; Marshall McLuhan, Mitchell Sharp, Tom Easterbrook,
Grace MacInnis, John Hirsch, Margaret Laurence, Peter Stemkowski, Jack Ludwig, Duff Roblin, David Sector, Larry Zolf.

Winnipeg Architecture: 100 Years, William Paul Thompson
(Queenston, 1975), $3.50. Eighty photographs.

Beginnings: A Winnipeg Childhood, Dorothy Livesay (Peguis,
1973), $4.95 pa.

The Street Where I Live, Haas (McGraw), $8.95. Life in Winnipeg's North End during the Depression.

Cranberry Portage, Ruth and Jack Paterson (J.J. Douglas, 1974),
$3.95 pa. Life in a northern Manitoba boom town in the 1930s.

*Early Printing in the Red River Settlement 1859-1870 and its
Effects of the Riel Rebellion,* Bruce Peel (Peguis, 1974), $5.00
pa.

Memories Are Made of This, Melinda McCracken (James Lorimer, 1975), $7.95.

The Lonely Land, Sigurd F. Olson (McClelland, 1972), $6.95. The account of a canoe expedition down the Churchill river in northern Manitoba.

Churchill, Manitoba: Canada's Northern Gateway, Nan Shipley (Burns, 1974), $3.25 pa.

Saskatchewan

Saskatchewan: A People and a Province, W.L.R. Knight and D. C. Barnett (Fitzhenry and Whiteside, 1974), $3.95. Grade 4 students discover Saskatchewan through words, maps, graphs, diagrams, and photographs.

Saskatchewan: Sample Studies, John Newton and Les Richards (McClelland, 1971), $2.50 pa.

Regina's Terrible Tornado, Frank Wesley Anderson (Frontier, 1965), $1.75 pa.

Upon a Sagebrush Harp, Nell Parsons (Western Producer, 1969), $4.95. Memories of pioneer life in the early 1900s.

Sawbones Memorial, Sinclair Ross (McClelland, 1974), $7.95. Novel of the life of a country doctor in a small prairie town.

Prairie Storekeeper, D.E. MacIntyre (Peter Martin, 1970), $4.95. Life on the frontier in 1906.

Why Shoot the Teacher?, Max Braithwaite (McClelland, 1965), $6.95. A witty, often hilarious account of school teaching in the early years.

North to Cree Lake, Karras (General, 1970), $9.25. Recollections of life in northern Saskatchewan.

The Meadowlark Connection, Mitchell (Pile of Bones, 1976), $4.00 pa. A humorous, bawdy novel about the plot to destroy the world from a base of operations in Meadowlark, Sask.

Alberta

A History of Alberta, James G. MacGregor (Hurtig, 1972), $10.00.

Two Thousand Place Names of Alberta, Holmgrem and Holmgrem (Prairie Books, 1973, 2nd ed.), $7.95. The history behind place names.

The Lost Lemon Mine, Hugh A. Dempsey and Thomas Primrose (Frontier, 1963), $1.75 pa.

The Frank Slide Story, Frank Wesley Anderson (Frontier, 1961), $1.75.

Growing up in Minby, Person (Western Producer), $8.95. Life in an Alberta prairie town in the late 1920s.

The Incredible Roger's Pass, Frank Wesley Anderson (Frontier, 1965), $1.75.

Calgary: An Urban Study, Richard P. Baine (Clarke, Irwin, 1973), $4.25.

Stops of Interest in Alberta: Wild Rose Country, Fryer (Frontier), $1.75 pa. A guide to places of historical interest.

Peace Country Heritage, De C. Stacey (Western Producer, 1974), $8.95. The agricultural potential of this area of northern Alberta.

Alberta: A People and a Province, Knight (Fitzhenry and Whiteside, 1976), $3.95. Grades 4-6.

While Rivers Flow, Kate Colley (Western Producer, 1970), $5.95. An autobiographical account of the 1919-1940 period.

The Mountains and the Sky, Lorne Render (McClelland, 1974), $27.50. The history of the Glenbow Foundation.

Social Change in the Alberta Foothills, Patricia Sheehan (McClelland, 1975), $3.25.

Badlands, Robert Kroetsch (New, 1975), $4.95. A novel set in the Red Deer River area of Alberta.

British Columbia

British Columbia and Confederation, Shelton, G. W. ed. (Gray, 1967), $7.50.

British Columbia: An Introduction to Geographic Studies, J.V. Horwood (McClelland, 1966), $2.95 pa.

British Columbia in Books, Mary Lou Cuddy and James J. Scott (J.J. Douglas, 1974), $6.95. Nearly 1000 entries concerning books, pamphlets, periodicals about B.C.

Canada's Pacific Province: Selected Sources: British Columbia From Early Times, Patricia M. Johnson (McClelland, 1966), $2.25 pa.

Western Shores: Canada's Pacific Coast, Ted Spiegel (McClelland, 1975), $22.50.

British Columbia: One Hundred Years of Geographical Change, J. Lewis Robinson and Walter G. Hardwick (Talonbooks, 1973), $2.95 pa.

British Columbia Recreational Atlas, Department of Recreation and Conservation, B.C. (Belford), $5.95 pa. Index of 9 000 place names and landmarks; 96 pages of full colour maps.

Portraits of the Premiers: an Informal History of British Columbia, Sydney W. Jackman (Gray, 1969), $7.50. Biographies.

Cariboo Mileposts, Richard Wright (Mitchell, 1972), $3.75. Guide to the Cariboo Highway from Cache Creek to Barkerville.

British Columbia Coast Names, 1592-1906, John T. Walbran (J.J. Douglas, 1971), $15.00.

Wildlife of British Columbia, Tom Hunter (Foremost), $2.95 pa.

Ghost Towns of British Columbia, Bruce Ramsay (Mitchell, 1966), $7.50.

A Small and Charming World, John Frederic Gibson (Collins, 1972), $6.95. A sensitive and profound account of life in coastal Indian communities.

Vancouver Island: Portrait of a Past, Rodger Touchie (J.J. Douglas, 1974), $12.95.

Bella Coola, Cliff Kopas (Mitchell, 1970), $6.95. History of a B.C. coastal community.

Backwoods of British Columbia, Bryan, J. and J. (J.J. Douglas), $9.95 pa. Social and natural history of the interior.

B.C. Ghost Town Map (Western Heritage), $2.50 pa.

British Columbia Trails (Western Heritage), $2.50 pa.

A History of Terrace, Asante (J.J. Douglas), $4.25 pa.

Vancouver Island Railroads, Turner (J.J. Douglas), $14.95.

A History of Victoria, Harry Gregson (J.J. Douglas), $8.95.

History of Port Coquitlam (Western Heritage), $3.95.

Queen Charlotte Islands, Francis Poole (J.J. Douglas, 1972), $8.95. Experiences in searching for copper on the islands.

The Queen Charlotte Islands, 1774-1966, Kathleen E. Dalzell (Cove, 1973), $12.50. A well-illustrated history of the Haida Indian peoples and the explorer, missionary, pioneer era.

Whistle up the Inlet: The Union Steamship Story, Gerald Rushton (J.J. Douglas, 1974), $10.95. The steamships of the Pacific coast.

The Fraser, Bruce Hutchinson (Clarke, Irwin, 1950), $2.50. The part played by the Fraser River in B.C. history.

The Fraser Canyon: Valley of Death, ed. Linda Hall (Frontier, 1967), $1.75 pa.

Overland to Cariboo, Margaret McNaughton (J.J. Douglas, 1973), $7.95.

Cariboo Yarns (Western Heritage), $2.50 pa.

Halfway to the Goldfields: A History of Lillooet, L. Harris (J.J. Douglas), $10.95.

Wagon Road North, Art Downs (Foremost, 2nd rev. ed. 1973), $2.95 pa. The Cariboo Gold Rush and the settlement of the B.C. interior.

Logging: British Columbia's Logging History, Ed. Gould (Hancock, 1975), $14.95. Approximately 400 photographs enhance this comprehensive book.

Timber: History of the Forest Industry in British Columbia, G.W. Taylor (J.J. Douglas, 1975), $10.95.

Kamloops Cattlemen, Alex T. Bulman (Gray, 1972), $8.95. A record of the ranching industry in the B.C. interior.

Grass Beyond the Mountains, Richmond P. Hobson (McClelland, 1951), $6.95. The story of the discovery of the last cattle frontier in northern B.C.

The Newspapering Murrays, Georgina M. Keddell (Lillooet, 1974), $2.95 pa.

Barkerville: A Guide to the Fabulous Cariboo Gold Camp, Bruce Ramsay (Mitchell, 1974), $3.95.

Gold Panners' Manual, Garnett Basque (Stagecoach, 1975), $3.95 pa.

Trailblazer of the Canadian Rockies, Thomas Wilson (Glenbow, 1972), $2.00. The building of the Kicking Horse Pass railway route.

Stanley Park: An Island in the City, Barry Broadfoot and Ralph Bower (November, 1972), $2.95 pa.

The Town that Got Lost: Memories of a Boyhood spent in the B.C. Interior, Pete Louden (Gray, 1973), $7.50.

North with Peace River Jim, L.V. Kelly (Glenbow, 1972), $2.00. Personal recollections of an expedition to the B.C. Peace River country in 1910.

The Buffalo Head, Raymond Murray Patterson (Macmillan, 1972), $3.95. Personal adventures in the Rockies in the 1920s.

Kootenai Brown, His Life and Times, William Rodney (Gray, 1973), $2.95 pa.

Squire of Kootenay West, Hodgson (Hancock), $12.50. Biography of Bert Herridge, respected parliamentarian and leader of the opposition to the flooding of the Arrow Lakes in southern B.C.

A Pioneer Gentlewoman in British Columbia: The Recollections of Susan Allison, ed. Ormsby (U.B.C. Press, 1975). A valuable insight into life in the interior of B.C. in the late 19th century.

James Douglas: Father of British Columbia, Dorothy B. Smith (Oxford, 1971), $3.95.

Barkerville Poster (poster). Western Heritage, $1.50.

British Columbia Ghost Town Map (map). Western Heritage, $2.50 pa.

The Northern Territories

The Northland: Studies in the Yukon and Northwest Territories, John Wolforth (McClelland, 1969), $2.25 pa.

Canada's North, R.A.J. Phillips (Macmillan, 1967), $10.95.

La norde cité Canadienne, Hamelin (H.M.H.).

Canada's Changing North, William C. Wonders (McClelland, 1971), $3.95 pa.

The Arctic Circle, ed. William C. Wonders (Longman, 1975), $3.95 pa. Examination of distinctive features of northern development in circumpolar countries; senior high.

Northern Almanac, Donald Wood (Research Institute of Northern Canada, 1976), $10.00.

Up North: The Discovery and Mapping of the Canadian Arctic, (Royal Ontario Museum, 1958), 75¢.

The North; Le Nord, Wonders (U.T.P., 1972), $5.00 pa. Relatively technical information.

The Mighty Mackenzie, Lyn Hancock (Hancock, 1974), $3.95 pa. Pictorial account of a trip down the Mackenzie River; 200 photographs.

Another Way of Being: Photographs of Spence Bay, N.W.T., ed. Harris, Applebaum and Sugino (Impressions Photographic Society, 1976), $7.95 pa. Illustrations provide an understanding of one Arctic community today.

The Howling Arctic, Ray Price (Peter Martin, 1970), $3.95 pa. How the north has been exploited by white people.

The Past and Future Land: An Account of the Berger Inquiry into the Mackenzie Valley Pipeline, Martin O'Malley (Peter Martin, 1976), $8.95 pa. An excellent account of the issues, people, and testimonies heard before Judge Thomas R. Berger.

The Canadian North: Source of Wealth or Vanishing Heritage? B.W. Hodgins, J. Benidickson, R.P. Bowles, G.A. Rawlyk (Prentice-Hall, 1977), $3.75 pa. An anthology of comment, articles, addresses prepared for senior high students.

The Arctic Imperative: An Overview of the Energy Crisis, Richard Rohmer (McClelland, 1973), $3.95 pa. A call for renewed awareness and understanding in northern development.

Nunaga: My Land, My Country, Duncan Pryde (Hurtig, 1971), $8.95. Autobiography of a white man in the N.W.T.

Tiari and Atigi, Pat Carney (Mitchell, 1971), $5.95. Good for pictures of the Royal Family's visit to the N.W.T. in 1970.

Their Own Yukon, Cruikshank and Robb (Yukon Indian Cultural Education Society and Yukon Native Brotherhood, Yukon Press, Whitehorse, Yukon). Yukon history and life captured in the photographs of the Indian peoples; accompanying text provides an introduction to the native history of the territory.

Klondike, Pierre Berton (McClelland, 1972), $1.50 pa. The gold rush period is vividly described.

The Yukon Story, Walter R. Hamilton (Mitchell, 1964), $7.00. Story of the overland route to the Yukon from Ashcroft, B.C., during the gold rush.

Klondike Cattle Drive, Norman Lee (Mitchell, 1964), $2.95 pa. Story of an 1898 cattle drive involving 200 head of beef cattle.

I Married the Klondike, Laura Beatrice Berton (McClelland, 1972), $2.75 pa. Life in Dawson City at the turn of the century.

Nobody Here but Us: Pioneers of the North, M. Farrow (J.J. Douglas, 1975), $10.00. Biographical portraits based on interviews with old-timers of northern B.C. and the Yukon.

Jawbone: Yukon Memories, Dim Mack (J.J. Douglas, 1975), $5.95 pa. One woman's experiences, 1890-1920.

Nahanni, Norma West Linder and Hope Morritt (Nelson, Foster, 1975), $6.95. Autobiographical account of life in the south Mackenzie River area of the N.W.T.

Lutiapik, Betty Lee (McClelland, 1975), $10.00. Autobiography of a nurse in Arctic Canada in the late 1950s.

Yellowknife, Ray Price (Peter Martin, 1974), $3.95 pa. The settlement of the capital city of the N.W.T. by white people.

Arctic Fever, Wilkinson (Clarke, Irwin), $6.50. Various attempts to discover the Northwest Passage.

Arctic Breakthrough, Paul Nanton (Clarke, Irwin, 1970), $6.50. Sir John Franklin's search for the Northwest Passage.

Search for Franklin, Leslie H. Neatby (Hurtig, 1970), $7.95.

Ultimatum, Richard Rohmer (Clarke, Irwin, 1973), $7.25. A novel on the theme of the future of the North and of Canada.

The Snow Walker, Farley Mowat (McClelland, 1975), $8.95. A collection of stories with Arctic settings by Farley Mowat.

North Book, Jim Green (Blackfish, 1975), $4.95 pa. Poetry by a sensitive interpreter of life in the Arctic.

Education in the Canadian North: Three Reports 1971-72/Education nordique: trois rapports 1971-72, Gourdeau (Arctic Institute of North America), $3.00. English or French.

Nigger in a Parka (cassette tape). 60 min, C.B.C. Learning Systems, $15.00. Problems created by white people in the North.

Northern Adventures (cassette tape). 30 min, C.B.C. Learning Systems, $8.00. Insight into the lives of northern pioneers.

Individual History Books

Canada: A Modern Study, Ramsay Cook, John T. Saywell and John C. Ricker (Clarke, Irwin, 1972), $2.75 pa.

The Fur Trade in Canada, Harold Innis (U.T.P., 1956), $2.45 pa.

Canadian Identity, William L. Morton (U.T.P., 1972), $2.75 pa.

Path of Destiny, Thomas H. Raddall (Doubleday, 1957), $3.95 pa.

Century of Conflict, Joseph L. Rutledge (Doubleday, 1956), 95¢ pa.

The White and the Gold, Thomas Costain (Doubleday, 1954), 95¢ pa.

Ordeal by Fire, Ralph Allen (Doubleday, 1961), 95¢ pa.

Canada: This Land of Ours, Wiley and others (Ginn, 1970), $5.20 pa.

Dominion of the North, Donald Creighton (Macmillan, 1957), $4.95 pa.

Canada: An Outline History, Joseph Lower (McGraw, 1973), $3.50 pa.

Nation Making: Documents, eds. Saywell and Ricker (Burns, 1974), $3.00 pa.

A Source Book of Canadian History: Selected Documents and Personal Papers, J.H. Stewart Reid and others (Longman, 1964), $6.95.

Canadian History in Documents 1763-1966, J.M. Bliss (McGraw, 1966), $4.50 pa.

Nationalism and Internationalism: Selected Sources from 1844 to Modern Times, Joseph Lower (McClelland, 1969), $2.25 pa.

Self-Government: Selected Sources in the History of the Commonwealth, Arthur J. Lower (McClelland, 1968), $2.25 pa.

Today's World: Selected Sources from 1688 to Modern Times,
Joseph Lower (McClelland, 1966), $2.25 pa.

Decisive Decades, A.B. Hodgetts and J.D. Burns (Nelson, 1973),
$5.20. An analysis of Canadian history from 1890 to the present
for senior high students.

How Canada Got its Capital, Corkum (McClelland, 1976), $4.95 pa.
Upper elementary-junior high readers, illustrated.

Canadians in the Making, Arthur Lower (Longman, 1958), $6.25.

The Story of Canada's Flag, George Stanley (McGraw, 1965),
$4.05.

*Thrust and Counterthrust: The Genesis of the Canada-U.S.
Boundary,* H. George Klassen (Longman, 1965), $7.50.

Canada and the American Revolution, Gustave Lanctot (Clarke,
Irwin, 1967), $6.50.

Lord Durham's Report, ed. Gerald M. Craig (McClelland, 1963),
$2.25 pa. Written 1839.

Le rapport Durham, ed. Denis Bertrand et Albert Desbiens
(P.U.Q.), $2.50.

A Global History: 1870 to the Present, Walsh (McClelland, 1976),
$4.95 pa. A senior high text on events in China, Japan, the Third
World, Europe, and the Western World.

The Education of Canadians 1800-1967, Howard Adams (Harvest,
1968), $5.95. History of the years leading up to Confederation
which helped sow the seeds of separatism.

Individual Geography Texts

Canada: A New Geography, Ralph R. Kreuger and Raymond G.
Corder (Holt, 1969), $7.25.

Basic Geography, Irving C. Harris (Longman, 1965), $4.25.

Readings in Canadian Geography, ed. Robert M. Irving (Holt,
1972), $6.25.

A New Geography of Canada, Neville V. Scarpe and others (Gage,
1963), $7.50. Teacher's handbook, $2.55.

Studies in Canadian Economic Geography, E. Bruce Braund and
W.C. Blake (McGraw, 1969), $3.35.

Canada: Problems and Prospects, J. Wreford Watson (Longman,
1968), $4.95. A regional study of cultural geography.

Canada: This Land of Ours, William Wiley and others (Ginn, 1970),
$4.75 pa.

A Guide to Understanding Canada, James Peters and others (Guinness, 1968), $3.85 pa.

Canada: A Geographical Interpretation, ed. John Warkentin (Methuen, 1970), $9.50. A senior high text; also available in French, *Le Canada: une interpretation géographique,* $12.95.

Resources of the Canadian Shield, J. Lewis Robinson (Methuen, 1964), $2.95 pa. Senior high.

A Geography of Urban Places, ed. Frank Taylor, Philip Kettle and Robert Putnam (Methuen, 1970), $6.25 pa. Senior high.

Perspectives in Geography, (Macmillan), $58.00. Two kits on initial settlement and central place studies.

Process and Method in Canadian Geography, (Methuen, 1971), Water, $2.50 pa. Geomorphology, $6.65 pa.

Biography

The Macmillan Dictionary of Canadian Biography, William Stewart Wallace (Macmillan, 1963), $14.95.

George Dawson: The Little Giant, Joyce Barkerhouse (Clarke, Irwin, 1975), $7.50. Biography of the geographer after whom Dawson City, Yukon is named.

Titles from the series The Canadians, Fitzhenry and Whiteside, $1.95 each. Booklets on individuals from various walks of life, including *Allan Napier MacNab; Elizabeth Simcoe; Egerton Ryerson; Casimir Gzowski; Joseph Brant; William Hamilton Merrit; Timothy Eaton.*

Titles from the series Canadian Lives, Oxford, $3.50 each.
 James Douglas: Father of B.C.; John Strachan: Pastor and Politician; Alexander Mackenzie and the Northwest.

Colourful Canadians (cassette tape). 30 min, C.B.C. Learning Systems, $8.00. Little-known contributors to Canadian life.

Prime Ministers (some examples)

Macdonald: His Life and World, ed. P.B. Waite (McGraw, 1975), $12.95. Biography of Canada's first prime minister.

Robert Laird Borden, ed. Heath McQuarrie (McClelland, 1969), 2 vols, $3.95 each. Memoirs, first published in 1938.

Laurier, Joseph Schull (Macmillan, 1965), $4.95.

Arthur Meighen, Roger Graham (Clarke, Irwin) 2 vols, $7.50 and $8.00.

Louis St. Laurent, Dale Thompson (Macmillan, 1967), $11.95.

Trudeau, le paradoxe, Anthony Westell (Homme), $5.00.

Canada's Governors General, Cowan (Griffin, 1952), $9.25.

Provincial Premiers and Political Leaders

The True Face of Duplessis, Pierre Laporte (Harvest, 1974), $2.00.

Mitch Hepburn, Neil McKenty (McClelland, 1967), $8.95.

René Lévesque: Portrait of a Québécois, Jean Provencher (Gage, 1975), $8.75.

The Firebrand: William Lyon Mackenzie and the Rebellion in Upper Canada, William Kilbourn (Clarke, Irwin, 1956), $2.50 pa.

The Ballad of D'Arcy McGee, Josephine Phelan (Macmillan, 1967), $1.95 pa.

Notable Canadians

Bethune, Roderick Stewart (New, 1973), $8.60.

Docteur Bethune, Sydney Gordon and Ted Allen (Etincelle), $3.95.

The Scalpel, The Sword, Ted Allen and Sydney Gordon (McClelland, 1971), $4.95 pa.

Father Lacombe, James G. MacGregor (Hurtig, 1975), $10.00. Influential Roman Catholic priest of the last half of the nineteenth century.

Lady Lumberjack, Dorothea Mitchell (Mitchell, 1967), $1.95. Autobiography of a pioneer Ontario woman who wrote and co-produced the first amateur feature film made in Canada.

Brock Chisholm, Carl Dow (Harvest), $8.50. The first director-general of the World Health Organization.

Laura Secord: The Lady and the Legend, Ruth McKenzie (McClelland, 1971), $5.65.

Woman of the Paddle Song, Elizabeth Clutton-Brock (Copp, 1972), $4.95.

Vice Regal Cowboy, Cashman (Western Producer), $2.00. J.J. Bowlen, born in P.E.I., became Lieut. Governor of Alberta.

Ladners of Ladner, Leon Ladner (Mitchell, 1972), $3.95 pa. Biography of a Fraser Delta, B.C. family.

The Silence of the North, Olive Frederickson and Ben East (General, 1972), $6.95. Life story of a B.C. woman, Olive Frederickson.

Forty Years in Canada, Samuel B. Steele (McGraw, 1973),

$8.95. Autobiography of a career R.C.M.P. officer.

Deux innocents en Chine rouge, Pierre Elliott Trudeau et Jacques Hébert (Homme), $2.00.

The Unusual Canadian

The Outlaw of Megantic, Bernard Epps (McClelland, 1973), $5.98.

The Mad Trapper of Rat River, Dick North (Macmillan, 1972), $6.95. Albert Johnson, the hunt and the aftermath.

Current Issues

Critical Issues in Canadian Society, Carl F. Grindstaff and others (Holt, 1971), $5.95 pa.

Independence: The Canadian Challenge, ed. Abraham Rotstein and Gary Lax (McClelland, 1972), $3.95 pa. Essays on economic, cultural, and political independence.

Canadian Issues and Alternatives, ed. Robert J. Clarke (Macmillan, 1974), $7.95.

Canadian Perspectives, McCarthy (Holt, 1971), $2.95 pa.

In Search of Canada, ed. George Ronald (General, 1971), $1.75.

A North American Education, Clark Blaise (Doubleday, 1973), $1.75. A search for identity.

The Mackenzie Pipeline: Arctic Gas and Canadian Energy Policy, ed. Peter Pearse (McClelland, 1974), $4.95 pa.

Canada's Energy Crisis and *Energy Crisis Update,* James Laxer (James Lorimer, 1975), $3.95 and 95¢.

Vancouver Ltd., Donald Gutstein (James Lorimer, 1965), $5.95 pa. The power structure behind city government.

Canada and the United States, Kenneth S. McNaught and Ramsay Cook (Clarke, Irwin, 1963), $5.25.

The Final Plateau: The Betrayal of Our Senior Citizens, Daniel Jay Baum (Burns and MacEachern, 1974), $4.25 pa.

Outrage!: The Ordeal of Greenpeace III, David McTaggart (J.J. Douglas, 1973), $10.95.

Challenge of Confidence, Eric Kierans (McClelland, 1967), $2.95 pa. Canada and its relationship to the American economic empire.

Women's Rights

The Woman Suffrage Movement in Canada, Catherine C. Cleverdon (U.T.P., 1974), $5.95 pa.

Women in the Canadian Mosaic, ed. Gwen Matheson (Peter Martin, 1975), $5.95 pa. A collection of essays by noted women leaders.

Mother was not a Person, ed. Margaret Anderson (Black Rose, 1973), $3.95. A collection of writings on women's rights.

She Named it Canada Because That's What it Was Called, ed. Andrea Lebowits (James Lorimer, 1972), $1.00. Canadian history as perceived by a Vancouver women's collective.

Canadian Woman's Almanac, 1977 (Canadian Women's Educational Press, 1976), $3.95. An appointment calendar, illustrated.

Never Done (Canadian Women's Educational Press, 1974), $3.75. A story of women's participation in the development of Canada.

Women in Canada: 1965-1972: A Bibliography, Harrison (McMaster University Library Press), $2.00.

The Clear Spirit, ed. Mary Quayle Innis (U.T.P., 1966), $4.95 pa. Biographies of women.

The School of Femininity, Margaret Lawrence Greene (Musson, 1972), $3.49. The lives and works of feminists.

Wilderness Women, Jean Johnston (Peter Martin, 1973), $8.95. Biographies of eight women.

The Indomitable Lady Doctors, Carlotta Hacker (Clarke, Irwin, 1974), $8.50.

A Woman in a Man's World, Thérèse-Forget Casgrain (McClelland, 1972), $7.95. Memoirs of an outstanding feminist leader.

Anne Francis, Florence Bird (Clarke, Irwin, 1974), $8.95.

Women of British Columbia, Jan Gould (Hancock, 1975), $14.95. Diaries, letters, photographs, 400 illustrations.

On Being a Woman: The Modern Woman's Guide to Gynecology, W. Gifford-Jones (McClelland, 1973), $3.95 pa.

The Parlour Rebellion: Profiles in the Struggle for Women's Rights, Isabel Bassett (McClelland, 1975), $10.00. Biographical sketches of nine prominent Canadian feminists.

Girls will be Women/Femmes de demain, ed. Betty Nickerson. Words and pictures by Canadian girls ages seven to eighteen (All about Us/Nous autres Canada, 1975), $2.00 pa.

The Visible Woman (Women Teachers' Association of Ontario), 25¢ pa. A booklet on history, with a bibliography on women's rights.

The Women's Kit (kit). O.I.S.E., $57.50. Slides, filmstrips, records, photos, postcards, booklets, and posters.

The Visible Woman (film), and *A Matter of Choice* (film). Women Teachers' Association of Ontario.

R.C.M.P.

The Royal Canadian Mounted Police, Nora and William Kelly (Hurtig, 1973), $10.00. A history.

The Royal North-West Mounted Police, Ernest J. Chambers (Coles, 1972), $14.95. First published 1906.

Maintain the Right: The Early History of the North West Mounted Police, 1873-1900, Ronald Atkin (Macmillan, 1973), $12.50.

Wake the Prairie Echoes, Saskatchewan History and Folklore Society (Western Producer, 1974), $2.50. History of the R.C.M.P in poetry.

An Unauthorized History of the R.C.M.P., Lorne and Caroline Brown (James Lorimer, 1973), $2.50 pa.

Mountie, 1873-1973, Dean Charters (Collier-Macmillan, 1973), $7.95. History in photographs.

The Law Marches West, Sir Cecil E. Denny (Dent, 1972), $9.95. A first-hand account of the march from Dufferin, Manitoba, to the Rockies in 1874.

The R.C.M.P., Harwood Steele (Clarke, Irwin, 1968), $3.25. Jackdaw kit of documents, maps, posters.

Military

Canada's Soldiers, George F.G. Stanley (Macmillan, 1974), $14.95. Illustrated history.

The Last War Drum, Desmond Morton (Hakkert, 1972), $9.00. History of the Northwest Rebellion.

Canada and the First World War, John Swettenham (McGraw, 1973), $4.95.

Conscription, Hewlett (Maclean-Hunter, 1970), set of 6 for $7.50. The issue raised in 1942.

Gauntlet to Overlord, Ross Munro (Hurtig, 1972), $8.95. Governor General's Award-winning account of Canadian army campaigns of World War II; first published in 1945.

The Shame and the Glory, Terence Robertson (McClelland, 1967), 95¢ pa. The Dieppe campaign of World War II.

Canada's Nursing Sisters, G.W.L. Nicholson (Hakkert, 1975), $12.95. History of the nurses in the armed forces from the Riel Rebellion to the present day.

Ten Lost Years, Barry Broadfoot (General, 1975), $5.95 pa. Impressions of the Depression in words and pictures.

Six War Years 1939-1945, Barry Broadfoot (General, 1976), pa. Impressions in words and pictures of the World War II years.

Vimy (l.p. record). C.B.C. Publications Branch, set of 2, $5.00 each. Recollections of World War I veterans.

Humour

Charlie Farquharson's Histry of Canada, Don Harron (McGraw, 1972), $5.95.

The World of McNally, Ed McNally (Optimum, 1972), $12.50. A decade of history illustrated with cartoons.

The Day of the Glorious Revolution, Stanley Burke and Roy Peterson (James Lorimer, 1974), $4.95. A satirical look at the 'communicators' in society, including "Pierre Bulion" and "Réné Terrifique"; illustrated with cartoons.

Frog Fables and Beaver Tales, Stanley Burke and Roy Peterson (James Lorimer, 1973), $4.95. A satirical look at bilingual, bicultural relations, illustrated with cartoons.

Transportation

Transportation, Schreiner (McGraw, 1972), $3.95.

Railways of Canada, Helma and Nick Mika (McGraw, 1972), $8.95.

Railways of Canada, Robert F. Legget (J.J. Douglas, 1973), $10.00.

The C.P.R.: A Century of Corporate Welfare, Robert Chodos (James Lorimer, 1973), $4.95 pa.

History of the Canadian National Railways, Stevens (Collier-Macmillan, 1973), $14.25.

I'll Take the Train, Kenneth Liddell (Western Producer, 1966), $6.95. A light-hearted history of railroads.

Cars in Canada, Glenn Baechler and Hugh Durnford (McClelland, 1973), $25.00.

Iron Roads: Railways of Nova Scotia, David E. Stephens (Lancelot, 1972), $2.00 pa.

Goggles, Helmets and Airmail Stamps, Georgette Vachon (Clarke, Irwin, 1974), $8.50. A pictorial history of the early days of aviation.

Paddles and Wheels, Linda Grayson and J. Paul Grayson (Oxford, 1974), $3.95 pa. The effect of transportation on Canadian life.

Current Events

Learning from Newspapers, Hugh Partlow (Education Services Dept., Canadian Daily Newspaper Publisher Association, 1974), $3.00. Useful ideas for classroom use of newspapers.

Titles from the series Canadian History through the Press, Holt; Books providing coverage of a variety of historical topics from newspaper sources.
> *War of 1812,* $2.85; *Guibord Affair,* $3.00; *Winnipeg General Strike,* $3.00; *Confederation, 1854-1867,* $3.25; *Imperialism and Canada, 1895-1903,* $3.00.

China: An Introduction for Canadians, ed. Ray Wylie (Peter Martin, 1973), $3.95 pa. A useful handbook for senior high students.

Newslab I and II (kits). General, $59.95 each. For building current affairs study programs; each kit contains newsguide, study guide cards, record forms, teacher's guide.

Contemporary Issues on Tape (tape). O.I.S.E., cassette, $7.00 each or reel-to-reel, $7.75 each. Titles:
> *Canada and China; Canada's Foreign Relations 1867-1919; Canada's Foreign Relations 1919-1945; Canada's Foreign Relations 1945 to the Present; Diplomacy and Foreign Policy; Russia for Canadians.*

Primary Series

One World: New Dimensions in Canadian Social Studies (teaching program). Fitzhenry and Whiteside. A three-part program of pictorial materials with accompanying teacher handbooks, for use in oral language development, health, and science. Titles:
> Year I — How Families Live, $74.00. 87 pictures.
> Year II — Families and Communities, $78.00. 96 pictures.
> Year III — Interaction of Communities, $89.00. 50 pictures.

Titles from the series Canadian Community Studies, by Tom Smith and Allan Cunningham, Dent, 1973-74, $1.85 each.
> *All Aboard Mouse; A Ride for Samson; Hold a Shell to Your Ear; One Cold Day; No Home for Sandy.*

Primary-Elementary Series

Titles from the series Concepts—A Series in Canadian Studies, Griffin House. Basic information about selected Canadian events in kit form, including booklets, maps, documents, and filmstrips.
> *Land of Gold Land of Ice,* $9.50. Comparison study of

Columbus and Frobisher; *The Day of the Treaties: Life
and Times of Indian Peoples*, $5.95; *The Shape of Canada:
An Introduction to Canadian Geography*, $4.75; *Roads on
Water: History of Water Transportation*, $4.75; *Nestum Asa:
Indian Peoples and How they Lived with Their Environment*,
$5.00.

Social Studies Involvement Program (kit). 3 kits. SRA.

Elementary Series

Titles from the series Ginn Sample Studies of Canada, Ginn.
Twenty paperback booklets each portraying one geographically
significant facet of Canada. Set of five of one title, $5.00. Specimen
set of one of each title, $23.15. teacher's handbook included.
Making Steel in Hamilton, 1967; *A Forest Industry at Port
Alberni*, 1968; *Sardine Fishing and Canning in New Brunswick*, 1968; *Wheat Farming near Regina*, 1969; *Iron Mining
in Quebec-Labrador*, 1968; *An Arctic Settlement: Pangnirtung*, 1971; *The Nation's Capital*, 1971.
In French:
*Une exploitation forestière à Port Alberni; L'industrie de
la sardine au Nouveau-Brunswick; La culture de blé aux
abords de Regina.*

Titles from the series World Community Studies, Gage. Booklets
on selected regions of Canada and particular international com-
munities, $1.80 each. Multi-media kits are available.
Northern Canada (Frobisher Bay); *Australia* (Barwidgee);
Norway; Botswana (Serowe); *Trinidad; Brazil; Africa*
(Uturi Forest); *Israel* (Negev Desert).

Titles from the series Man in his World, Fitzhenry and Whiteside.
Nineteen booklets, $1.92 each. Filmstrips, $5.95, and teacher's
handbooks, 80¢, available for each title.
Understanding Communities, 1972; *Longhouse to Blast
Furnace: The Growth of an Industrial Community*, 1973;
China, 1972; *Japan*, 1972.

Communities in Action (teaching program). SRA. Community
life, past and present in picture-card format, coloured. Available
in French. *Communauté en marche*. Unit 1, $34.85. Bilingual
teacher's handbook, $2.50.

Elementary-Junior High Series

Titles from the Ryerson Social Science Series, McGraw. A textbook series focusing on contrasting values and attitudes.

Contact, 1971. $4.95 pa. Teacher's handbook, $1.05 pa.
Involvement, 1972. $3.95 pa. Teacher's handbook, $6.95.
Discovering, 1974. $4.75. Teacher's handbook, $7.95.

Titles from the series People and Places in Canada, Holt. Booklets on specific areas and communities, $1.50 each.

Crowsnest Pass: A Mining Community, 1971; *The Fishermen of Lunenburg,* rev. ed. 1972; *Flin Flon: A Northern Community,* 1968; *Home Oil, Calgary: Oil Exploration and Production,* 1971; *Opasquiak: The Pas Indian Reserve,* 1973.

Titles from the series Regional Studies of Canada, Gage. Nine booklets and teacher's handbook. Sample set $13.70. Teacher's handbook, $1.80.

British Columbia: Mountain Wonderland, 1970, $1.80; *Saskatchewan: Land of Far Horizons,* 1970, $1.65; *Southern Ontario: Workshop of the Nation,* 1970, $1.95; *Atlantic Provinces: Tidewater Lands,* 1970, $1.95; *North of Sixty: Canada's Advancing Frontier,* 1970, $1.35.

Titles from the series Studies in Canadian History, Ginn. Twenty booklets on selected historical events. Package of 5, $5.50. Teacher's handbook, $4.15.

Nomads of the Shield: The Ojibway Indians, 1970; *Life at Red River: 1830-1860,* 1971; *Shipbuilding in the Maritimes,* 1970; *The Seigneury of Longueuil,* 1971; *Fort York,* 1972; *The London and Port Stanley Railway: 1856,* 1972; *Ellen Elliott: A Pioneer,* 1972.

Titles from the series Collier-Macmillan History Program, Collier-Macmillan. Nine booklets, $2.70 each.

Two Streaks of Rust—The Building of the C.P.R.; New France; Pioneers in Upper Canada; The Fourth World and Indian Reality, 1974, $7.95; *The Canadian Indian: History since 1500,* 1971, $3.00; *Bayonets on the Street,* 1974, $2.00 pa.

Titles from the series Studies in Canadian History, Gage, $2.25 each. Teacher's handbook, 90¢.

Montreal: 1850-1870, 1971; *Early Days in Upper Canada,* 1972.

Titles from the series Nelson Canadian Studies, Nelson, $1.95 each

The Arctic: Canada's Last Frontier, 1973; *Canadian Patterns of Settlement,* 1973; *Canada: Land of Immigrants,* 1973; *Life in New France,* 1973; *Native Peoples of Canada,* 1975; *The Canadian Worker,* 1975.

Titles from the series Growth of a Nation, Fitzhenry and Whiteside, 1974, $2.95 each pa. The development of the Canadian nation with special emphasis on the West; grades 5-10.

> *Building of the Railway; Fur Trade; Gold Rush; North-West Mounted Police; Settlement of the West.*

Canadians All: A Collection of Biographies, Terry Angus and Shirley White (Methuen, 1975), $3.50 pa. Twenty biographies, grade 6 level; photographs, activities, and bibliographic information; includes J.H. Sissons (judge), Anna Swan (giantess), Celia Franca (ballerina), K.C. Irving (industrialist), Anne Murray (singer), Ferguson Jenkins (baseball player), Nellie McClung (feminist leader).

Titles from a series of Jackdaw kits, Griffin, $3.70 each. Documents, maps, newspaper clippings, illustrations all packaged in large envelopes.

> *Canada and the (American) Civil War; Laurier* (Canada's First French-Canadian Prime Minister); *Selkirk* (the settlement of the area which is now Manitoba); *1837: Mackenzie; The War of 1812.*

Junior-Senior High Series

Titles from the series Adventures in Canadian History, Burns and MacEachern, $1.50 each pa.

> *The Execution of Thomas Scott,* 1968; *Sir John A. Builds a Nation,* 1973; *First Lady of Upper Canada,* 1968; *Stand Fast, Craigellechie: The Building of the C.P.R., 1867-1885,* 1968.

Titles from the series Man on the Earth, Oxford, $1.95 each. Grade 6.

> *Resource Use in Canada,* 1974; *Inequalities within Canada,* 1974; *Power Blocks in Eurasia,* 1968; *Problems of Industrialization in Eurasia,* 1973; *Population Pressure in Indonesia,* 1973; *Teacher Resource Book.*

Titles from the series Man in Society, Maclean-Hunter, set of 6 of one title, $4.80.

> *Poverty,* 1971; *Minority Groups,* 1971; *Punishment and Rehabilitation,* 1972; *The Family,* 1972; *Labour and Management,* 1972; *Crime in Canada,* 1972.

Titles from the Canadian Issues series, Maclean-Hunter, set of 6, $4.80.

> *Separatism,* 1972; *Economic Nationalism,* 2nd. ed. !972; *Regional Disparity,* 1971; *The Law,* 1972, *Conscription.*

Titles from the series Foundations of Contemporary Canada, McClelland, $1.95 each. Senior high, developed by teachers in the

Canadian Studies Foundation Laurentian Project.
The Great Canadian Debate: Foreign Ownership; Canadians and their Environment; Technology and Change: The Crisis in Canadian Education; The Agrarian Myth in Canada.

Items for Teachers

Focus on Canadian Studies, ed. Edward H. Humphreys (O.I.S.E., 1970), $4.35. The use of various disciplines for teaching Canadian studies at the elementary and secondary grade levels.

What Culture? What Heritage?, Bernard Hodgetts (O.I.S.E., 1968), $3.50 pa. Available in English or French; report on the status of civic education in Canada.

National Consciousness and the Curriculum: The Canadian Case, ed. Milburn and Herbert (O.I.S.E., 1968), $2.95 pa. A collection of articles.

The History and Social Science Teacher, Canadian Periodical Publishers' Association. Quarterly, $8.00. Articles, book and audio-visual reviews.

The Two Histories (cassette tape). 30 min, C.B.C. Learning Systems, $8.00. French and English-speaking university students discuss the stereotyped history they were taught in school.

Periodicals

Canada and the World, Maclean-Hunter. Published 9 times from September to May. $2.00.

Heritage Canada, Canadian Periodical Publishers' Association. Quarterly, $2.00, students; others $5.00.

Canada: An Historical Magazine, Holt. Quarterly, $12.50. Senior high.

City Magazine, Canadian Periodical Publishers' Association. 8 issues annually, $7.00.

Canadian Antiques Collector, Canadian Periodical Publishers' Association. 6 issues annually, $9.00.

Alive Magazine, Canadian Periodical Publishers' Association. 12 issues annually, $5.00.

Golden West, Canadian Periodical Publishers' Association. Quarterly, $3.50.

Simgames, Canadian Periodical Publishers' Association. Quarterly, $2.00. Information on the use of simulation games.

Periodicals for Regional Historical Study and Current Events

B.C. Studies, University of British Columbia Press, Vancouver.

Alberta Historical Review, Historical Society of Alberta, 95 Holmwood Ave., N.W. Calgary, Alta.

Saskatchewan History, Saskatchewan Archives Office, University of Saskatchewan, Saskatoon, STN 0W0.

Ontario History, Ontario Historical Society, 40 Eglinton Ave. E., Toronto.

Newfoundland Quarterly, Creative Printers and Publishers, Box 967, St. John's, Newfoundland.

The Atlantic Advocate, Gleaner Bldg., Phoenix Square, Fredericton, N.B. Monthly, $5.00.

Axiom: Atlantic Canada's Magazine, Box 1525, Halifax, N.S. $3.00.

Acadiensis: Journal of the History of the Atlantic Region, Department of History, University of New Brunswick, Fredericton, N.B. 2 issues annually. $5.00.

Cape Breton Magazine, Wreck Cove, Cape Breton. 6 issues, $4.50, 12 issues, $8.50.

The Nova Scotia Historical Quarterly, Petheric Press, Halifax. Quarterly, $10.00.

News of the North, Box 68 Yellowknife, N.W.T. Weekly, $12.00.

North/Nord Magazine, Information Canada. 6 issues annually, $6.00. A bilingual periodical of present and past northern activities; beautifully illustrated.

Arctic in Colour, Box 2850, Yellowknife, N.W.T. X0E 1H0. Quarterly, $5.00. Full colour illustrations and topical articles make this periodical useful at all grade levels.

Periodicals of Women's Collectives

Québécoises—Deboutte!, 4319 St. Denis, Montreal. Monthly, $3.00.

Newsletter of Women's Place, Newfoundland Status of Women Council, Box 5021, St. John's Nfld.

Canadian Newsletter of Research on Women, c/o Margaret Eichler Dept. of Sociology, University of Waterloo, Waterloo, Ontario. 3 issues annually, $4.00.

The New Feminist, Box 597, Stn. A., Toronto 116. Monthly, students, $1.50; others $3.00.

Saskatoon Women's Lib Newspaper, 147-2nd Ave., S., Saskatoon, Sask. Monthly, $3.00.

Pedestal: Vancouver Women's Lib Newspaper, 130 W. Hastings St., Vancouver 3, B.C. Monthly, $3.00.

Chapter 26

SOCIOLOGY

The development of a sociology curriculum related to the realities of Canadian society would enhance the reputation and status of this subject. At the high school level the study of sociology has been of marked inconsequence. At the elementary-junior high level it is the amoeba of the curriculum, not easily identifiable in its own right, but finding an accessible host in the social studies curriculum. While teacher handbooks and curriculum publications do stress the importance of developing sociological understanding, in practice the effectiveness of current instruction is negligible.

To improve this situation, significant changes in teacher education and in the orientation of the curriculum are required.

Even if a course in sociology is included in the teacher's professional training, its effectiveness is likely to be severely limited. One familiar problem to be confronted has been described by Bryan Finnigan and Cy Gonick in *Making It: The Canadian Dream*.

It is not a happy commentary on the state of sociology in Canada to note that there are few interesting and readable Canadian sociology textbooks. Indeed, sociology is so new to Canada, and so American in tradition, that there are all too few sociology texts for any sociology courses. Canadian instructors of sociology are anxious about the lack of Canadian text material, if for no other reason than because the present vacuum could be filled with a sense of culture and identity among Canadian students of sociology.
Finnigan, B., Gonick, C., *Making It: The Canadian Dream* (Toronto: McClelland, 1972)

The problem of "all too few sociology texts" is compounded by university staffing procedures. The "Canadian instructors" referred to by Finnigan and Gonick are themselves scarce. The novice teacher's understanding of Canadian society is frequently provided by foreign-educated professors who are not familiar with the limited Canadian resources available.

282

If a Canadian sociologist is available, this by itself does not guarantee that the university student will be exposed to the realities of Canadian society. The American scholarship can be exchanged easily for an English-Canadian bourgeois mentality. The realization that a class struggle, compounded by ethnic diversity, has been, and is increasingly, a fact of Canadian life has yet to pervade most sociology classrooms. Any in-depth analysis of social class and power structures, as these factors influence and determine the decision-making process in government, business, and unions, is ignored.

Teachers who are products of this type of training are ill-equipped to do more than strengthen the proverbs inherent in the conventional social doctrine. Léandre Bergeron has isolated some of the common maxims which seem to be the revealed wisdom of many classroom experiences:

— The rich are richer than the others because they have worked harder. So they deserve the grand life they lead.

— Everyone can become rich like them.

— The middle class means everybody, or almost; it includes the labourer, the judge, the doctor, the janitor, the Prime Minister, the farmer, you, and me. If we worked a little harder and saved a little more, we could become very rich, but we stay where we are because we do not have the will, the courage, or the ability. However, we really should not complain because there are those who are poorer than we are.

— The poor are stupid and don't have the courage to work. Look at them: when you give them money they waste it in a tavern. They deserve their fate.

> Bergeron, L., *The History of Quebec: A Patriot's Handbook* (Toronto: N.C. Press, 1971, pp. 198, 199

At first glance, Bergeron's observations might appear to be too extreme and therefore of dubious value. Closer inspection of the education establishment, which has tolerated and perpetuated curricula inimical to any honest portrayal of Canadian life, will reveal otherwise. Middle class dominated bureaucracies in universities, government, and professional organizations have succeeded remarkably well in preserving the status quo through mindless sociology courses.

This process of teacher and subsequently student education must be abolished. In a society where one child in four suffers the misfortune of being born to families living below the poverty line,

teachers are needed who understand issues, who can explain the
implications to their students, and who will be in the vanguard of
social change. Teacher education must become a means of deepening awareness and understanding of social undercurrents. The fact
that over one and a half million children (1 657 017) presently are
destined to a life of poverty (*Poor Kids: A Report By The National
Council of Welfare On Children In Poverty In Canada,* Ottawa, 1975)
will not be eradicated through sociological study alone. Teachers
who are themselves prepared to comprehend the significance of
economic disparity, and who are confident in their ability to raise
questions of justice and equality, could form the nucleus of social
action.

Socio-economic undertanding must be complemented by comprehension of ethnicity and its implications for both national and international society. Significant improvement in present practice cannot
be expected until this dimension of sociology evolves from its present
embryonic state.

In the chapter following, "Ukrainians and Other Unknown Canadians", emphasis is placed on the pluralistic composition of society
outside of the English and French populations. Here the chronic
failure to provide teachers with an understanding of the two dominant charter groups is stressed. There are few opportunities to become familiar with their general sociological characteristics. English
Canadian teachers may be exposed to a potpourri of stereotypes ranging from the poetic imagery of William Henry Drummond ("Leetle
Bateese"), to the suppression of the people by the Roman Catholic.
church, down to the radicalization of the Québécois by the Front
de Libération du Québec. Conversely, for French Canadian teachers
the study of English Canada may be little more than a recital of
repression and exploitation. As perceived from within Québecois
society, the imperialist tendencies of English-speaking Canadians
know no limitations.

The need for teachers to be educated to destroy these obnoxious
generalities is obvious. To admit that Canadian education has failed
completely to prepare teachers who can use sociology as a means of
eliminating barriers of suspicion and racial hatred between English
and French peoples should prompt profound anxiety for the future
of Canada. Failing this admission on the part of educators, what
hope is there that future generations of children will not be indoctrinated to perpetuate the education atrocities of the past?

Sociological study could be an important means for uniting Canadians. Combining ethnic understanding with knowledge of social

class hierarchies would permit working class Québécois, their English Canadian counterparts, and native and immigrant peoples, to see themselves as sharing common concerns in their struggles against political-economic injustice. In this nationalistic sense the sociology classroom could become an important liberating influence.

The need for improvement in international understanding is equally great. Currently, the textbook interpretations applied to life in other societies are uniformly grim. With the possible exceptions of Britain and the United States, Canadian students are provided with only the most rudimentary understanding, especially of the non-white world. The reasons are clear. The American way of life is the yardstick used to measure progress and development in other societies. Learning materials present and reinforce this view. Thus, it becomes difficult to understand the influence of Fidel Castro on the life of Cubans while recognizing American hegemony in this hemisphere. Cuba is viewed as a questionable aberration in the American scheme of things—a cancer to be quarantined and watched with suspicion. (Exorcism may or may not be required.) The possibility that Cuban people may actually prefer their particular form of political-social organization to that of the United States is not even considered. Young children learn early that two alternatives are open: either the Cuban people do not know any better, or given enough time their society will eventually evolve into a replica of their northern neighbours. It would be unthinkable that any people would logically prefer to exist under a different social system. Suggestions that Canadians and Cubans might exchange ideas to the mutual advantage of both societies are unmentionable. Canadian sociological views of Cuba are non-existent, at least in textbooks.

The study of every other Central-South American, African, and Asian society is similarly restricted. It is preposterous that the sociological characteristics of China, the most populous country on earth, are either given only superficial consideration or are simply omitted. Generations of students are left with a vague awareness of millions of Chinese peasants going about their chores in the rice paddies. But then, China is a communist society. Presumably there would be little to learn from such a system.

Until now, India has provided the textbook counterpoint to China in the study of societies. India is part of the British tradition, and British political-economic structures are sound. India is democratic; the people are free and happy. The wheels of progress in India are restrained only because of questionable features inherent in the people themselves.

Children are quick to draw conclusions. Goodness and justice will prevail. It becomes obvious to them that, in the long term, the people of India will outstrip their Chinese neighbours, who have been victimized by the yoke of dictatorship.

If this example seems extreme, supporting evidence is to be found in provincially authorized textbooks throughout the country. Canadian students are pathetically unfamiliar with any honest portrayal of social systems, beliefs, and customs characteristic of humanity generally. The small amount of information available to them is customarily so hopelessly slanted or otherwise erroneous as to be useless. Superficial studies of happy little Pedro at work in the tin mines of Bolivia, stern Rabinovich trudging through a Soviet commune, or petite Heidi merrily skipping over a Swiss meadow to fetch a pail of milk, confirm the misgivings students have as to the authenticity of school experiences. Other peoples in other places are quaint. There is nothing to be learned and nothing to be understood that might affect positively the quality of life in Canada. The good life is here . . . until festering sores of non-white immigration traumatize the schools of Vancouver; Italians become visible and organized in Toronto; Arab-Jewish conflicts break out in Montreal; and United Empire Loyalist descendants grow nervous in the face of growing numbers of strangers in their particular valley of Canada.

Whether or not it is possible to shake or shock Canadian educators into action on this question of social understanding remains to be seen. Affluence in the staff room breeds complacency in the classroom. Educational authorities have not had a reputation for disturbing a somnolent atmosphere. Green Papers on Immigration, like Royal Commissions on Poverty, come and go. The indoctrination of prejudice has prevailed. Adopting vague approaches to the study of attitudes and values continues to disguise the failure of educational systems to do more than graduate young people who see the world through a prism—the diffusion of colours being essentially red, white, and blue. Sociology in the classroom, like much of Canadian society, has faithfully imitated the American model.

Materials listed here, coupled with those applicable from social studies, economics, business, counselling, and the fine arts, would constitute a step in the direction of improvement. If definitive, appropriate items are not abundant, with effort enough valid information can be assembled to combat the conventional inaccuracies. That much could be done in the immediate future.

N.B. References to the multi-ethnic peoples in Canadian society appear in the bibliography for the following chapter.

Basic Reference

The Vertical Mosaic, John Porter (U.T.P., 1965), $6.00 pa.

Perspective Canada, (Information Canada), $6.75. Annual, 300 pages of information, tables, statistics, and charts on health, education, work, cultural diversity, family formation, housing, and criminal justice, English or French.

The Canadian Style; Today and Yesterday in Love, Work, Play and Politics, Raymond Reid (Fitzhenry, available 1977).

Canada: A Sociological Profile, W.E. Mann (Copp, 1971), $5.75 pa.

The Canadian Family Tree, Information Canada (Queen's Printer, 1967), $3.00 pa. A study of the ethnic composition of the population.

La société canadienne-française, ed. Marcel Rioux and Yves Martin (H.M.H.), $7.95. An anthology of papers comprising an introduction to French Canadian sociology.

Le Québec en mutation, Suzanne Rocher (H.M.H.), $6.95. An analysis of social change in Quebec.

Making It: The Canadian Dream, ed. B.W. Finnigan and Cy Gonick (McClelland, 1972), $6.95 pa. A collection of essays on various aspects of Canadian society.

Canadians and Their Society, ed. Alan Skeach and Tony Smith (McClelland, 1973), $5.50 pa.

Canadian Social Structure, John Porter (McClelland, 1967), $2.95 pa.

French Canadian Society, vol. 1. Marcel Rioux and Yves Martin (McClelland, 1965), $4.50 pa.

Issues in Canadian Society: An Introduction to Sociology, D. Forcese and S. Richer (Prentice, 1975), $8.95 pa.

Studies in Canadian Social History, Michael Horn and Ronald Sabourin (McClelland, 1974), $6.95 pa.

Communities in Canada: Selected Sources, Leonard Marsh (McClelland, 1970), $2.95 pa.

Canadian Society: A Sociological Analysis, H. Hiller (Prentice, 1976). $5.00 pa. A reference item for senior students.

Prophecy and Protest: Social Movements in Twentieth Century Canada, Samuel Clark and others (Gage, 1975), $6.50 pa.

Socialization and Values in Canadian Society, ed. Robert M. Pike and Elia Zureik (McClelland, 1975), 2 vols. $4.95 each pa.
   Vol. 1: *Political Socialization.* Vol. 2: *Socialization, Social Stratification and Ethnicity.*

Titles from the McGraw-Hill, Ryerson series in Canadian Sociology, $4.95 each pa. Seven titles; resource information for teachers and senior high students.

Demographic Bases of Canadian Society, Warren B. Kalbach (McGraw, 1971), $7.50.

A Statistical Profile of Canadian Society, D. Kubat and D. Thornton (McGraw, 1975), $3.95 pa.

Ideological Perspectives on Canada, M. Patricia Marchak (McGraw, 1975), $4.95 pa.

Social Stratification: Canada, J. Curtis and W. Scott (McGraw, 1973), $8.50.

Social Mobility in Canada, Lorne Tepperman (McGraw, 1975), $4.95 pa.

Ethnic Group Relations in Canada, W. Isajiw (McGraw, 1977).

Social Change in Canada, Marsden (McGraw, 1977).

Canadian Studies: Self and Society, Ian R. Munro, Howard Doughty and Alan King (John Wiley, 1975), $8.70. A basic Canadian studies text for junior high.

Titles from the series Social Problems in Canada, Guidance Centre, University of Toronto, 85¢ each pa.

What About Poverty in Canada; One-Parent Families in Canada; Immigrants in Canada.

Quebec

Le Québec qui se fait, ed. Claude Ryan (H.M.H.), $5.50. A collection of papers dealing with the evolution of Quebec society in the 1960s with a view to future trends.

Le Québec d'aujourd'hui, ed. Jean-Luc Migue (H.M.H.), $5.95. A collection of papers dealing with current issues.

La jeunesse du Québec en révolution, Jacques Lazure (P.U.Q.) $2.50 pa. The youth of Quebec and their concerns vis-à-vis their society.

From Rural to Urban Living

The Urbanization of Sophia Firth, Sophia Firth (Peter Martin, 1974), $8.95. An autobiographical account of a woman whose family moved from Restigouche County, N.B., to the inner city of Toronto.

"There's No Better Place than Here": Social Change in Three Newfoundland communities, Ralph Matthews (Peter Martin, 1976), $3.95 pa. An examination of three outport communities

and people's reactions to the prospect of relocation and rapid social change.

Urban Problems

Urban Problems: A Canadian Reader, ed. Charles R. Bryfogle (Holt, 1975), $5.95. Articles on housing, transportation, pollution, social welfare, environment.

Urban Prospects, John Wolforth and Roger Leigh (McClelland, 1971), $3.50 pa.

Four Cities: Studies in Urban and Regional Planning, G. Peter Nixon and Maurice Campbell (McClelland, 1971), $2.25 pa.

Urban Development in South Central Ontario, Jacob Spelt (McClelland, 1972), $3.95 pa.

Metropolitan Problems: International Perspectives, ed. Simon Miles (Methuen, 1970), $10.00. A survey of problems as presented at a York University seminar.

Family

The Canadian Family, K. Ishwaren (Holt, 1976), $9.75 pa. A collection of papers on the family from ethnic and regional perspectives.

Welfare

The Failure of the Social Welfare System in Canada, Andrew D. Armitage (McClelland, 1975), $4.95 pa.

Poverty

The Poverty Wall, Ian Adams (McClelland, 1970), $2.95 pa. Controversial examination of Canadian poverty.

The Real Poverty Report, Ian Adams, William Cameron, Brian Hill, and Peter Penz (Hurtig, 1971), $2.95. Four ex-commissioners who took issue with findings and recommendations of the Royal Commission on Poverty.

The Anatomy of Poverty: The Condition of the Working Class in Montreal, 1897-1929, Terry Copp (McClelland, 1974), $3.95 pa.

Industrial Society

Industrialization and Society: Selected Sources, Gerald Walsh (McClelland, 1969), $2.50 pa.

Man in Industrial Society: An Inquiry, Gerald Walsh (McClelland, 1973), $2.95 pa.

Religion

The Comfortable Pew, Pierre Berton (McClelland, 1965), $2.50 pa.
An examination of religious practice in the 1960s.

Power Structures

The Smug Minority, Pierre Berton (McClelland, 1968), $2.50 pa.
The economic and political control exercised by the elite of Canadian society.

Communications

A Media Mosaic: Canadian Communications through a Critical Eye,
McDayter (Holt, 1971), $9.50. The impact of communications on
society.

The Future

Visions 2020: Fifty Canadians in Search of a Future, ed. Stephen
Clarkson (Hurtig, 1970), $2.95 pa. A look at Canadian life as it
might be in the next fifty years.

Education

Schoolbook: Perspectives on Education, Gerald Clift and J. Lia-
botix (Gage, 1971), $1.90 pa. Teacher's handbook, $1.90. A textbook on the past, present, and future of schools.

The Failure of Educational Reform in Canada, ed. Douglas Myers
(McClelland, 1973), $2.95 pa. An across-Canada collection of papers
on attempts to change existing educational practices.

Must Schools Fail?, ed. Niall Byrne and Jack Quarter (McClelland,
1972), $4.95. An anthology; note Section V, Cultural Diversity and
Education.

A Sociology of Canadian Education, Pat Hutcheon (Van Nostrand,
1975), $7.95. Useful as a reference to many problems of teaching
in contemporary society.

The Teacher and the City, ed. H. Symons (Methuen, 1971), $4.95 pa.
Suggestions for teaching in an urban environment prepared by a
group of British Columbia teachers.

Periodicals

Boreal, Canadian Periodical Publishers' Association. Quarterly,
$6.00. A tri-lingual, tri-cultural journal of northern Ontario.

Toronto Life, Canadian Periodical Publishers' Association. Monthly, $7.00. Various aspects of life in a major city.

Warpath, Canadian Periodical Publishers' Association. Quarterly, $3.00. "Canada's National Patriotic Quarterly of Cultural Struggle".

New Canada, Canadian Periodical Publishers' Association. Ten issues annually, $3.00. A Canadian liberation magazine which reports on working-class struggles and culture developments.

Content, Canadian Periodical Publishers' Association. Monthly, $5.00. Understanding the media, its control, and its influence.

Next Year Country, Canadian Periodical Publishers' Association. 6 issues annually, $4.00. A Saskatchewan news magazine focusing on government activities, labour problems, farmers' concerns.

Our Generation, Canadian Periodical Publishers' Association. Quarterly, $5.00. Reports of research into and analysis of social, economic, and political conditions in Canada and other countries.

Chapter 27

UKRAINIANS AND OTHER UNKNOWN CANADIANS

Interest in how the ethnic diversity and multicultural complexion of Canadian society should influence education practice is of very recent origin. Only in Canada's second century of development as a nation has the concept of a society composed of the peoples of many other societies, and enriched by their individual contributions, attracted attention. Traditionally, education has encouraged assimilation—a course of action completely at odds with the ideal of the Canadian mosaic. The classroom has been perceived as the purveyor of the attitudes and values of the dominant social class. In practice, schools have served the established social order as instruments of denigration of the culture and debasement of the language of minority groups. Both the written and unwritten curricula of schools throughout Canada reflect an ignorance of, and lack of concern for, the multi-cultural composition of society.

Before effective educational changes can be contemplated, two preliminary steps must be taken. The emerging pattern of ethnicity not only has to be recognized, but more importantly, it must become the cornerstone of educational planning. The 1971 Census data provides this portrait of Canadian society:

— Twenty-five per cent of the population traced their ethnic origins to non-British, non-French backgrounds.

— Seventy per cent of these people claim ethnic origin in one of seven groups: German, Italian, Ukrainian, Dutch, Scandinavian, native Indian and Inuit, and Polish.

— Between 1961 and 1971 the pattern of immigration has seen an increase in immigrants from Greece, Portugal, Asia, and the United States, and a decline in the proportion from Britain.

> *Perspective Canada* (Ottawa: Information Canada, 1974, pp. 257-284)

The Canadian Family Tree, (Ottawa: Information Canada, 1967), provides descriptive information complementary to the foregoing statistical analysis. Exclusive of the English/French populations forty-five ethnic groups are portrayed. This historical survey of growing ethnic diversity lends substance to the view that for far too long educators have ignored the obvious.

> Since 1945 about three million immigrants have taken up a new life in Canada. They represent some fifty ethnic groups, and are found throughout all of the provinces and territories, although main concentrations are in the larger cities, notably Toronto and Montreal.
>
> Today, nearly thirty per cent of Canada's population is of neither British nor French origin, which is evident in the fact that approximately 200 foreign-language publications are produced regularly in Canada in twenty-seven different languages.
>
> *The Canadian Family Tree* (p. 21)

The implications of these statements become more apparent when multi-culturalism is related directly to development of curriculum and learning materials. Joseph Katz, University of British Columbia curriculum authority, has provided a tidy summation in this respect.

> Every course of study in the school curriculum brings together bodies of knowledge from around the world, each item of which has been discovered or developed by someone from and influenced by a particular culture. Each of these contributions to knowledge can be culturally identified in the curriculum to the benefit of the student's intellectual appreciation, not only of the contribution itself, but of the culture that helped to create it.
>
> J. Katz, "Multi-Cultural Curricula" *(Education Canada,* September, 1974, p. 44)

Through interpretation of culture in this manner, the practical importance of the concept becomes clear. Each learning experience affords the opportunity to examine opinions, ideas, and feelings, sometimes identical, but frequently contrasting in nature. Each student is able to learn more about himself and to grow in his appreciation of others. Canadian society, representing as it does a microcosm of world cultures, lends itself readily to this type of study. The next step is to advance the student's understanding to the global community. The fact that curricula and learning resources have lagged behind the growth both of the multi-cultural society and the interdependency of humanity should now elicit an urgent response from the education system. The ever-widening cultural gap between schools and the public they serve must be closed.

A comprehensive plan, including the following ingredients, is needed:

1. The intimate relationship between language and culture has to be understood. It is the key to education opportunity. Children whose mother tongue is different from that of the teacher, must have opportunities to learn in their native language. Internationally, the importance of learning in the mother tongue has been established.

> The language of a society incorporates into its lexical level the categories that have been useful in its way of life; the language is itself a compendium of what the society regards as important.
>
> *Mother Tongue Practice in the Schools* (Paris: UNESCO, 1972, p. 14)

The first language not only transmits the culture of the individual, but as well provides the potential for acquiring bilingual competency. Linguists have recognized that within the first three years of life the acquisition of speech is virtually completed, while in the succeeding six years the child learns new words and recognizes the socially favoured pronunciation and grammatical forms. Most of the language development occurs incidentally within the home. By the time the child enters school he is linguistically capable of learning in his own language. Traditional teaching practices whereby the child is then required to erase from his mind everything he has learned in his mother tongue and commence the process of language replacement, cannot be justified on humanitarian or educational grounds. The learning progression from the known to the unknown is as pertinent to language as it is to other curriculum subjects.

2. The fear that multicultural recognition leads to the splitting of society into isolated republics, neighbourhoods, and ghettos has to be overcome. To the present time a garrison mentality has characterized much of Canadian society. People have withdrawn into their particular pockets. In the face of assimilation, no other course has been open to them.

History is instructive on this point. Consider two examples:

— A long standing feature of Canadian life has been the political and education policies designed to eradicate the languages and cultural identity of native peoples. The expectation has been that, given enough time, Indians and Inuit would disappear as distinctive members of society. They would meld into the prevalent social milieu.

— From the time of Lord Durham, a parallel expectation has been held out for the French population. Their particular acreage, be it located on the banks of the Miramichi in New Brunswick, in the Vancouver suburbs at Maillardville, or in Quebec itself, was only a small holding in the estate of Les Anglais. In generations to come these tenant farmers would see the errors of their ways and they too would merge into a homogeneous social order.

Not surprisingly, the one nation concept has not materialized for native, French, or other ethnic peoples. The threat of language deprivation and loss of cultural identity has caused substantial numbers of people to retreat, to regroup and find strength from within their own ethnic group. In effect, the assimilation policies and programs which were intended to prevent Balkanization have accomplished just the reverse. Society has been fractured, possibly irreparably. A national curriculum which supports and builds upon those things any people treasure most highly, their languages, beliefs, and traditions, must be implemented if this situation is to be rectified.

3. The value of existing cultural and language programming requires reassessment. It is commendable that provincial school officials have authorized languages other than English or French for instructional use and study purposes. Similarly, a social studies unit devoted to ethnic understanding should not be summarily dismissed. In fairness, the effectiveness of these minor additions to the on-going curriculum has to be questioned. The multicultural curriculum will not be realized by appending a course here and a festival of folk music there. These techniques are part of the band-aid philosophy which pronounces the basic good health of the education body while noting a minor abrasion here and there. A continuing application of temporary remedies can disguise the ravages of even terminal illness, for a time. Public reaction to proposed changes in the Immigration Act is one indication that a social malaise of suspicion and prejudice has reached an advanced stage. Major surgery on the curriculum is needed now.

An integrated curriculum encompassing the kindergarten to high school graduation years must be devised. Throughout the primary-elementary years the emphasis in each subject would be placed on how people communicate through languages, mathematics, the fine arts. . . . In junior high the influence of the environment on peoples, and the converse, would provide the common focus. High school students would study the development of local, national, and international social-economic systems by societies, working independently and cooperatively.

A cohesive curriculum which emphasizes the common as well as the unique characteristics of humanity will provide a sense of direction to the total educational program.

4. A philosophy which will influence the development of learning resources is required. The simple, conventional answer has been found in the publication of items which are supplementary to the authorized textbook. The narrow preoccupation of influential Canadian historians, noted previously in Chapter 25—Social Studies, is central to this issue. The implications of ethnicity will not be understood until the prevailing interpretation of Canadian history is revised. A social historical philosophy encompassing the characteristics and contributions of each ethnic group is needed as the basis upon which subsequent resources can be developed. The existing blank pages vis-à-vis non-British, non-French peoples demand attention. Canadian social history must become the means for comprehending not only the past, but as importantly, the significant issues besetting society now and in the foreseeable future. To know, for example, that the black heritage in Nova Scotia dates from the time of the construction of British Military fortifications in Halifax is a detail of little consequence. To recognize that from the arrival of the Maroons from Jamaica in the 1700s to the present time, black people have continually and consistently been relocated on inhospitable lands should raise questions of equality and social justice. In a like manner, current textbook descriptions of European peoples who came to Western Canada seeking religious freedom, creates and sustains the impression of a Canadian society which does not exist. A book such as David Flint's *The Hutterites: A Study in Prejudice* (Toronto: Oxford, 1975) will help students to learn from the experiences of people who chose to pursue their way of living despite political and social pressures. It should be firmly established that a reinterpretation of the past and present is not an exercise in establishing a sense of national guilt. Rather it should provide the opportunity for each student to comprehend the full range of human endeavour, what is praiseworthy and what is lamentable, in our collective customs and traditions. An educated person, capable of drawing upon the lessons of his individual heritage and willing to re-examine his assumptions in the light of the experiences and ideas of other peoples, should be the goal.

5. One dimension of the education of teachers for a multi-cultural society has received attention in some universities. Courses and programs designed to prepare Indian and Inuit teachers dot the map. The impetus primarily came from the University of Saskatchewan in

Saskatoon. In 1961 André Renaud conducted the first university-based summer session for the orientation and training of teachers in the North and on Indian reserves. This led to the gradual development of core courses in the Faculty of Education and of supporting classes in the Faculty of Arts for a major in Indian and Northern Education in the B.Ed. Degree of the Elementary Program. By 1968 a series of courses was developed at the graduate level for a Master's Degree program. Related endeavours have included the establishment of an Indian and Northern Curriculum Resources Centre and the publication of an important journal, *The Northian,* and equally valuable learning materials for the use of teachers and their students. Universities in other provinces have followed suit to the point where it is now feasible to screen teachers' applications on the basis of their exposure to this type of cross-cultural training.

Over a decade of experience in this specific area should provide the guidelines and evidence to support the development of a multi-cultural education program for all teachers. Renaud tentatively advanced this proposition in his 1971 Quance Lecture.

It is only a matter of time, we hope, before the Colleges of Education include cross-cultural content as part of the general programs for training all teachers.

> A. Renaud, *Education And The First Canadians*
> (Toronto: Gage, 1971, p. 55)

Today, it is practical and necessary to move beyond the perception of cultural understanding as part of a program. Social imperatives, nationally and internationally, create an exigency that cannot be denied. Interrelated courses in the following fields of learning must be made available.

— Linguistics: Teaching in the mother tongue and teaching English/French as second languages are invaluable skills in a pluralistic society. Not every teacher has the aptitude to acquire multilingual competency. Each ethnic group undoubtedly does have bilingual resource people. The opportunity for them to engage in specialized courses in methodology must be provided. Stringent academic qualifications which have heretofore excluded them from university training, and the closed-shop mentality of teachers' unions which deny access to the classroom, must be altered. There has to be room in universities and schools for the harnessing of the respective skills of teachers and community people to the advantage of the students.

— Cultural Studies: Considerable anthropological and sociological information is accessible. Masters' theses and Doctoral dissertations which analyze cultural attributes provide source material. The pressing need is not to accumulate additional evidence through surveys, contrastive studies, and opinion-sampling devices, but to use what is now known as a basis for action. This body of objective content can help to overcome teachers' deficiencies in understanding. It must be complemented by the contributions ethnic peoples themselves can make to comprehending their customs and traditions. In the university, as in the school, academic and community resources should not be construed as rival factions competing for attention. A two-way flow of information between the social scientist and the public has to be established if the future teacher is to benefit fully.

— Methodology: Teaching techniques must be appropriate to the society. The teacher-dominated classroom can be in conflict with the home environment. Children who are raised to learn through observation and actual experience find the adjustment difficult. The opposite is equally true. Chinese Canadians accustomed to the rigorous discipline of British-influenced schools in Hong Kong may find the degree of permissiveness tolerated in Canadian schools hard to understand. For other students, emphasis on the competitive nature of independent study stands in contrast to the preference for cooperative ventures. Each of these variations should provoke a thorough reassessment of how individual curriculum subjects can be best utilized.

In his analytical examination of attempts at developing a multicultural education system in the Northwest Territories, N.C. Bhattacharya made an observation which has national implications.

They (i.e. slogans, theories, half-measures) can be used as well-greased chutes to help generations of unconsulted children to slide into the cave of poverty, unemployment, and dependence. If an expensive program of formal education . . . cannot enable children to evade such a future, the whole exercise is almost pointless.

N.C. Bhattacharya, "Education In The Northwest Territories", *Alberta Journal of Educational Research*, (September, 1973, p. 252).

Current piece-meal experimentation, uncoordinated and with little follow-up and diffusion, will never bring about the major changes that are needed. Educators have to find a way to develop curricula, produce materials, and educate teachers in a manner that will build on cultures and identity, and at the same time, equip students with those understandings and skills necessary to function not only as members of their own societies but as citizens of the world community.

N.B. Cross referencing with Chapter 25—Social Studies, Chapter 26—Sociology, Chapter 13—French, and Chapter 15—Indian, Inuit, Métis, will provide additional coverage.

♦　♦　♦　♦

Culture

Cultures in Canada, Sproule, Thompson, Lethwig et al (Macmillan, (1976), $4.50 pa. A text for grades 9-11.

Culture and Nationality, Alfred G. Baily (McClelland, 1972), $4.50.

Canada: Unity in Diversity, Paul G. Cornell and others (Holt, 1967), $6.95. Also available in French.

Titles from the series Cultures and Communities, Holt. A series of monographs providing resource material.

Saint Pascal: Changing Social Structure of a French-Canadian Town, G.L. Gold (Holt, 1975), $3.50 pa.

Village in Crisis, K. Westhues and Peter R. Sinclair (Holt, 1974), $3.25 pa. Conflict and change in a small southern Ontario town, 1971-73.

We/They Class Pak (kit). Grolier, $19.95. Material for kit gleaned from newspaper items pertaining to cultures and ethnic groups.

Ethnic Groups

The Pageant of Canadian History, Peck (General, 1967), $7.50. A record of peoples of many racial origins who settled in Canada.

The Other Canadians: Profiles of Seven Minorities, Morris Davies and J. Krauter (Methuen, 1971), $3.55 pa. A senior high text which focuses on Indian, Inuit, Chinese, Japanese, black, Doukhobor, and Hutterite peoples.

Blacks

The Blacks in Canada, Robin W. Winks (McGill-Queen's, 1971), $20.00. A basic reference book on the history of the black people.

Black Canadians: A Long Line of Fighters, Headley Tulloch (N.C. Press, 1975), $3.95 pa.

The Blacks in New Brunswick, W.A. Spray (Brunswick, 1972), $2.50 pa.

Forgotten Canadians: The Blacks in Nova Scotia, Frances Henry (Longman, 1973), $2.95 pa.

Africville: The Life and Death of a Canadian Black Community, P.H. Clairmont and Dennis Magill (McClelland, 1974), $4.95 pa.

Born Black (film). 51 min, 16mm, b&w, International Tele-Film Enterprises, $395.00 or $50.00 rental per day. Experiences of black people in Canada.

Black Images, Canadian Periodical Publishers' Association. Quarterly, $7.00. Articles on Third World cultures and literary reviews.

Chinese

East Meets West: The Chinese in Canada, Francis C. Hardwick (Tantalus, 1975), $2.95 pa. Documents and graphics for high school students.

In the Sea of Sterile Mountains: The Chinese in British Columbia, James W. Morton (J.J. Douglas, 1974), $12.50.

Doukhobors

Tanya, E. Popoff (Mir, 1975) $9.45. An historical novel which pictures Doukhobor life, religion, and persecution in Canada.

Hutterites

The Hutterites: A Study in Prejudice, David Flint (Oxford, 1975), $5.95 pa.

East Indian

From Beyond the Western Horizon: Canadians from the Indian Subcontinent, Francis C. Hardwick (Tantalus, 1974), $2.50 pa. Documents and graphics.

Icelandic

Saga of New Iceland: Pictorial History of Icelandic Settlement in North America, Eric Wells and Thorn Cooke (Peguis, 1975), The years 1875-1925, including the settlement of Gimli, Manitoba.

Italians

Italian Canadians: The Italians in Transition (film). 26 min, 16mm, col, O.I.S.E., $200.00. A view of the problems faced by immigrant families—attitudes, values, schools.

Japanese

> *The Exodus of the Japanese,* Jan Patton (McClelland, 1973), $5.96 per package of 6.

Jews

> *The History of the Jews in Canada,* Benjamin Sack (Harvest, 1964), $8.50.

> *Raisins and Almonds,* Fredelle B. Maynard (General, 1973), $1.50 pa. A memoir of a Jewish individual's experience growing up on the prairies.

> *Jewish Dialogue,* Canadian Periodical Publishers' Association. 10 issues for 2½ years, $12.50.

Mennonites

> *Mennonites in Canada, 1786-1920; The History of a Separate People,* Frank H. Epp (Macmillan, 1974), $9.95.

> *A String of Amber,* Blodwen Davies (Mitchell, 1974), $8.50. An account of the arrival and settlement of Mennonite peoples in Western Canada.

> *Reflections on Our Heritage,* Abe Warkentin (Derksen, 1971), $7.95. The history of the first Mennonite migration to Manitoba.

Norwegians

> *Norwegian Settlers in Alberta,* Jan Harold (National Museum, 1974), 75¢.

> *The Cape Scott Story,* Lester R. Peterson (Mitchell, 1974), $3.95 pa. History of a remote Vancouver Island community settled by Norwegian people.

Ukrainians

> *Sons of the Soil,* 2nd ed. Illia Kiriak (Trident, 1973), 3 vols, $12.35 pa. Vol. 1, $4.25 pa. Vol. 2, $3.85 pa. Vol. 3, $4.25 pa. Novel about an early Ukrainian prairie settlement; printed in Ukrainian.

> *The Call of the Soil,* Honore Ewach (Trident, 1973), $2.50 pa. A short story written in Ukrainian describing life in Canada; includes a Ukrainian-English glossary and questions in English.

> *To the Promised Land: Ukrainians in Canada,* Francis C. Hardwick (Tantalus, 1972), $2.50 pa. Documents and graphics.

> *The Ukrainians in Canada: A Concise History of A Major Canadian Ethnic Group,* Ol'ha Woycenko (Trident, 1968), $10.00. English edition.

Neopalyma Kupyna and *Kolesnychenko,* Y. and S. Plachynda (Trident, 1970-71), 2 vols, $1.50 each.

Folk Narrative among Ukrainian-Canadians in Western Canada, Robert B. Klymasz (National Museum, 1973), $2.25 pa.

The Flying Ship and Other Ukrainian Folk Tales, Victoria Symchych and Olga Vesey (Holt, 1975), $8.95.

Zakhar Berkut, Franko (Trident). $3.00 pa. Ukrainian language.

Our Native Land That Is Not Ours. Kowalenka (Trident). $7.50 pa. Three volumes. Ukrainian language.

Glory of Past Ages, Lotosky (Trident). $2.50 pa. Ukrainian language.

Drama

Guest From The Steppes, Hrenchanka (Trident Press). $1.50 pa. A five-act play in the Ukrainian language.

Bright Stars, Hrenchenka (Trident Press). $1.00 pa. A five-act play in the Ukrainian language.

The Quest, Iwanko (Trident Press). $1.50 pa. A five-act play in the Ukrainian language.

For young readers

Escape From The Tatars and *Prodigal Son,* Chaykowsky (Trident Press). $1.50 pa.

History of the Ukraine, Dytyny (Trident Press). $3.95 pa.

Language

Ukrainska Mova (Holt, 1972). A beginner's course.
Activity kit, $10.00; Teacher's Text I, $24.95; Teacher's Text II, $23.95.

Ukrainska Rozmova, Holt, 1973. A follow-up course to the above.
Student's text, $6.50; Teacher's text I, $24.95; Teacher's text II, $23.95; Wall charts, $29.95.

Ukrainian by the Audio-Visual Method I (Teaching program). Marcel Didier. Twenty-five lessons.
Tapes, 25 5" tapes recorded at 7½ i.p.s., $145.00.
Filmstrips, 25 col and b&w, $135.00.
Teacher's handbook, $5.00.
Set of tests for 25 lessons, $2.00.
Student's picture book, $3.30.
Student's workbook, $3.30.

Ukrainian by the Audio-Visual Method II (Teaching program). Marcel Didier. Five lessons.

Filmstrips, 5 col and b&w, $32.50.
Tapes, 5 5" tapes recorded at 7½ i.p.s., $36.25.

Titles from a filmstrip series, The Ukrainians: Canadian Home-
steaders, E.T.H.O.S. Set, $24.50. Each set includes 2 filmstrips,
cassette tape, teacher's manual and reading script.
Set 1 *Hello Canada; Free Land*
Set 2 *Strangers to Canada; Prairie Homestead*

Grammar

Ukrainian Grammar, J.W. Stechishin (Trident, 1971), $6.50.
Textbook of Ukrainian grammar in English with Ukrainian-
English and English-Ukrainian vocabulary.

Periodical

The Ukrainian Canadian, Canadian Periodical Publishers' Association. Monthly, $5.00. In English; history, culture, heritage,
fine arts.

Immigration

Strangers within our Gates, J.S. Woodsworth (U.T.P., 1972),
$3.95 pa. The founder of the C.C.F. provides a view of the im-
migration which was a part of the settlement of the prairie
provinces.

Education of Immigrant Students: Issues and Answers, ed.
Aaron Wolfgang (O.I.S.E., 1975), $5.75 pa. A collection of 16
articles useful to teachers in any multi-lingual learning situation.

Immigrant Children and Canadian Schools, Mary Ashworth
(McClelland, 1975), $5.95 pa. A helpful resource for teachers.

Issues

The Race Question in Canada, André Siegfried and Frank H.
Underhill (McClelland, 1966), $2.95 pa.

The Anatomy of Racism, David Hughes and Evelyn Kallen (Harvest, 1973), $4.50 pa.

*The Harrowing of Eden: White Attitudes toward North Ameri-
can Natives,* J.E. Chamberlin (Fitzhenry and Whiteside, 1975),
$10.95.

White Man's Country: An Exercise in Canadian Prejudice, Ted
Ferguson (Doubleday, 1975), $8.95. The "Kamagata Maru" in-
cident of 1914 when a shipload of Punjabis was anchored off
Vancouver seeking entry to B.C.

Let the Niggers Burn!: Racism in Canada, ed. Dennis Forsythe (Black Rose, 1971), $2.45 pa. Essays on the problems faced by black immigrants to Canada; the riots at Sir George Williams University and the Caribbean sequel.

Canada's Third World (cassette tape). 30 min. C.B.C. Learning Systems, $8.00. Dispossessed peoples.

Chapter 28

VOCATIONAL

An alphabetical arrangement of curriculum subjects places vocational (technical/industrial arts) in the position of bringing up the rear—a place not far removed from its actual importance in education practice and planning. Two research studies of critical importance to the future development of Canadian education provide evidence in support of this contention.

The Reviews of National Policies for Education: Canada by the Organization for Economic Co-Operation and Development (Paris, 1976) provides an insight into educational policies as these are characteristic of all levels of the system, from elementary grades to post secondary learning opportunities. The report notes that in practice it is customary for practical courses to be viewed only as an "appendage", "a basement department", a receptacle for "weaker and less motivated" students who have, apparently, little or no academic potential. The instructional methodology characteristic of such courses amounts to little more than "busy work" in many instances. The course content is "not deep". The implications for students are clear. Basic vocational education of real value to young people is denied.

Although the verdict of the OECD examiners may be considered to be harsh the report does indicate where the emphasis on improvement must be placed. In this subject area, as in most others, schools which afford their students vocational instruction must integrate technical and humanistic materials in their goals in order to transmit the foundation of a new culture. There is the need to combine the practical with the theoretical, reflective approach to technology *and* a generous portion of liberal and fine arts and science.

An indication of how this lofty goal can be realized is to be found in *The Report of the Commission on Canadian Studies: To Know*

305

Ourselves by the Association of Universities and Colleges of Canada
(Ottawa, 1975). Admittedly, the focus of the Commission's attention was the university and not the school. However, echoes of its
findings and recommendations must be heard and heeded in junior-
senior high classrooms if students are to acquire a valid technical
education. In this respect, the observations on engineering could
accurately be applied to what transpires in the name of education in
multiple activity industrial arts laboratories and the vocational wings
of composite high schools.

> Engineering is often thought to be 'value free', but it is full
> of cultural implications. Engineering, like science in general,
> is international in scope and impact. This is particularly true
> of solutions to basic engineering problems. However, engineer-
> ing, especially the application of engineering theory, cannot
> be divorced from the culture of the country and society in
> which it is studied, taught or practised. (Ibid, pp. 197, 198)

In vocational education as elsewhere in the curriculum, the need for
vigorous and creative rethinking of aims and objectives within a
Canadian perspective is evident. Vocational students can be given
the chance to learn about our heritage in technology. The contributions of inventors, scientists, and engineers to Canada and the international community are of interest in themselves. More importantly,
many of these initiatives reflect the environmental influences of life
in a northern nation. The pioneer efforts of Armand Bombardier
(snowmobile), Abraham Gesner (kerosene), and Wallace Turnbull
(variable-pitch propeller) are just three examples of endeavours
which have influenced winter transportation, the petroleum industry,
and aviation here and abroad. In his conclusion to the book, *The
Inventors: Great Ideas in Canadian Enterprise* (Toronto: McClelland
and Stewart, 1967) J.J. Brown noted:

> I repeat that Canadians have made contributions to world
> science and technology out of all proportion to their small
> numbers.

Can not Canadian students be given the chance to know of these
contributions and to see the relationships between many of them
and our natural surroundings? Would it not then be feasible to plan
technical curricula which would prepare students for exploring and
solving problems that are related directly to present and future needs
of Canadian society?

The Report of the Commission on Canadian Studies provides ample suggestions. Among them are: road and building construction under Arctic conditions; waste disposal during winter climatic conditions; natural resources extraction; transportation technologies; energy requirements; architectural design in relationship to the physical setting. It was the belief of the Commissioners that:

> . . . all parts of the man-made environment in Canada—housing, urban development, transport systems and recreation areas, to name but a few—should be designed in the context of Canadian conditions. (Ibid, p. 190)

Surely such guidance will be heeded in the vocational courses of tomorrow. The possibilities for creating curricula and learning materials to fill this void are boundless as the following bibliography will attest. Here, too, a social purpose combined with a commitment to building anew are required.

◆　◆　◆　◆

General

General Shop Work, C.C. Ashcroft and J.A.G. Easton (Macmillan, 1959), $3.95. Grades 7-9.

Automotives

Automotive Mechanics and Technology, Tillman Steckner and Mervin J. McGriffin (Macmillan, 1975), $8.95.

Automotive transparencies (transparencies). General. Two col, 7½" x 9½", mounted and framed, 3 sets. Set A, $44.00. Set B, $38.00. Set C, $39.50. Topics included are : DC generator, alternator, carburator, valve lifters, wheel cylinders, steering gear, and cooling system.

Building construction

Building Construction Transparencies (transparencies). General. Col, 5 sets. Set A, *Structural framing details,* $49.40. Set B, *Roof framing,* 26.60. Set C, *Exterior finish,* $69.25. Set D, *Interior finish,* $77.00. Set E, *Stair building,* $33.00.

Drafting

New Basic Drafting, Davies and Skinner (General, rev. 1973), $4.95.

Electronics

Introductory Electricity, 2nd ed. Frank J. Long (General, 1964), $4.65.

Intermediate Electricity, 2nd ed. Frank J. Long (General, 1969), $5.45.

Electrical Experiments: A Laboratory Manual, Frank J. Long (General, 1968), $4.95.

Electrical and Electronic Technology, H.M. Brouwers (General, 1967), $8.95.

Machine Shop

Machine Shop Transparencies (transparencies). General. Col, 8 sets. Includes: Lathe— major parts; drill-press operations; thread terminology; grinder wheel; spur gear and rack; vernier caliper scale; nomenclature of milling cutter; die forming; electro-chemical machinery; blast furnace; tensile testing; introduction to hydraulics; piston drive systems.

Woodwork

Hand and Machine Woodwork, rev. ed. H.G. Miller (Macmillan, 1972), $4.50.

Mathematics

Math Lab for the Trades, Machine Shop (kit). General, $59.95. A kit designed to relate mathematics to the machine shop trades; 100 core cards; 50 trade application cards; student study books and teacher's handbook.

Periodical

The Canadian Log House, Canadian Periodical Publishers' Association. $3.50 each.

Films

Moreland-Latchford has available over eighty 16mm films on several aspects of industrial arts, vocational, and industrial education. Several are available in English or French. Films may be rented, purchased in sets, or purchased individually.

Chapter 29

RUMINATIONS AND PROJECTIONS

In 1953, one of the most widely acclaimed books in Canadian education was published, *So Little For The Mind: An Indictment of Canadian Education,* by Hilda Neatby (Toronto: Clarke, Irwin). One of her concerns then (and one of the major emphases in these pages) was the extent of foreign influence over the education of Canadian children. She concluded her skillful dissection of education at the mid-point of the twentieth century with these words:

> Surely a clear and precise statement of a Canadian philosophy of education based, not on an awkward synthesis of three or four mutually exclusive American schools of thought, but rather on a consideration of the essential values of western civilization, would be a worthy project. (Neatby, p. 334).

The "worthy project" has attracted indifferent attention. Throughout the 1960's, in particular, the need for a philosophy, a sense of purpose, was obscured. The loosened strings on the education purse permitted wide-scale experimentation with pre-packaged solutions. More money to prime the education pump was regarded as the key to improved effectiveness and efficiency. Education as a growth industry was the concept in vogue. Any doubts to the contrary were swamped in a tidal wave of sophisticated hardware and software, the bulk of which bore a foreign imprint.

Technicians to ease the change-over and implement the modifications were abundant also. If universities at Berkeley, California or Eugene, Oregon or Harvard itself, did not have the personnel to solve Canadian problems, then surely the branch plant offices of the American education fraternity, Phi Delta Kappa, knew of someone, somewhere in America, who did. Educational "change agents" were parachuted across the border and throughout the land. There were no ailments in Canada that an imported philosophical treatise could not cure. The transformation of education was imminent.

309

Times have changed. The balloon of rising expectations has been punctured. Economic uncertainty has spawned a school of social unrest. Reappraisal and retrenchment are now relevant. For educators a note of warning has been sounded. Behind the slogan, "Return to the Basics", lie two related misgivings. Has the investment in education been misplaced? Has public trust in professional educators been betrayed?

The total absence of a philosophical basis upon which all aspects of Canadian education could be developed is not reassuring. The "awkward synthesis" of a clutter of philosophies, psychologies, teaching strategies, resources, and technologies, noted by Neatby a quarter of a century ago, continues. An evaluation from outside the Canadian educational establishment, the 1975 *Examiners' Report of the Organization for Economic Cooperation and Development* made this telling observation: ". . . there is no clearly formulated concept of education policy set in the context of a comprehensive framework of general social policies." (OECD, Paris, November, 1976, p. 4)

Parent, teacher and student faith in their education system will be restored only when the continuing proponents of obscurantism are disarmed and the apostles of trivia are ignored.

The accomplishment of these objectives requires an inventory of Canadian resources. For purposes of illustration, the lessons learned in the tabulation of materials included in this book may be useful.

1. Educational Publishing. An unabashed partiality for Canadian-owned publishing has dominated much of the book. Quality Canadian materials are available, even if something close to blind dedication is needed to discover them. Secretary of State Hugh Faulkner touched on this problem in his address before the Conference on the State of English Language Publishing in Canada held at Trent University in January, 1975:

> One of our problems in Canada is that so many Canadians
> do not know and have no ready way of finding out, what is
> being written in this country and by whom.

Although the Secretary of State was referring to English language publishing in general, a few examples from the educational field will indicate the nature of the problem as it applies to classrooms and school libraries. Each of the following publishing firms has a limited listing of books which could be an asset to students throughout Canada.

McDonald House has published *Sunseeds for Children* ($1.25).

The Development Press has published *Understanding the Community,* a handbook for community educators.

Vesta Publications has published *Seaway Valley Short Stories.*

See Hear Now is a Toronto-based filmstrip production company. Their materials, including *The War of 1812, Women in Canada, The Great Depression, The Metric System, History of Labour, The Rise of Socialism, Cultural Mosaic, Library Science,* and a three-part Canadian literature series are available from Prentice-Hall, Canada, Limited.

Durndurn Press has available biographies of *Frances Anne Hopkins* and *John Flemming.* Another item to be published will be based upon the artistry of C.W. Jefferys.

Potlatch Publications has published the delightful *Canadian Children's Annual,* $6.95.

A. Klassen has published in two languages (English and German) *In The Fullness of Time,* a history of the Mennonite peoples in Russia prior to the 1917 revolution.

And there are many others with very good things to offer. But how can a busy teacher find them? In general, even if they have heard of the *Quill and Quire* publication, *Canadian Publishers Directory,* from which the foregoing examples were taken, teachers are unlikely to have the time to search the fine print for details.

With considerable justification Canadian publishers have made their plight known:

> The strongest market for Canadian titles is sales to schools, where Canadian books make up 32% of the business. However, only 3% of these books are produced by Canadian-owned publishers. This means that virtually the entire educational market is controlled by foreign-owned houses.
>
> *Quill and Quire,* 41, January, 1975, p. 1.

Once the attention of the public, including educators, is aroused, it is reasonable to ask why the dilemma of the publishing industry cannot be resolved, and information about the various products be made available. If publishers are concerned about their percentage of the market, then surely every avenue of cooperation and innovation should be explored—if the potential customer is ever to have the opportunity to purchase.

On the credit side of the ledger, several developments are underway which could improve the situation for the educational system. It need only be mentioned (one more time) that, positive as these ventures seem to be, Canada does consist of something more than downtown Toronto. Teachers from Kitimat to Random Island are equally deserving of being informed. From the addresses of the organizations that follow, the reader might get the impression that the stem of the maple leaf is planted at 59 Front St. East, Toronto!

Canadabooks: Books For Canadian Education currently represents forty-three small Canadian publishing houses, all of whom produce books that are suited to educational use. Through cooperation the widely-divergent publishers, who make up the Canadabooks membership, have coalesced into one sustained effort to gain access to the educational market. Their catalogue of over nine hundred annotated titles, organized into sixteen major subject categories, should be available in every school.

Canadian Book Information Centre, 59 Front St. East, Toronto, M5E 1B3 is a useful address if you are looking for books but are lacking information regarding the publisher, price, and availability.

Canadian Basic Books, 59 Front St., East, Toronto, M5E 1B3 has available a catalogue which lists approximately 900 books in 26 categories, which have sold well for their Canadian publishers.

The Canadian Periodical Publishers' Association has available *Great Canadian Magazines Magazine,* a catalogue of 130 periodicals available by subscription through the Association.

The Literary Press Group, 59 Front St., East, Toronto, M5E 1B3 represents seventeen presses which publish many of the major poets, novelists, dramatists, and critics currently writing in Canada. Their catalogue of approximately 500 titles is an essential reference, specifically in literature and fine arts curricula.

The Playwrights Co-op is a member of the Literary Press Group. However, it deserves special attention because of its contribution to the dramatic arts. The Co-op is the primary source of English Canadian plays, with more than 200 plays by 100 playwright members in print. Among its extensive catalogue listings are: *Inook and The Sun* by Henry Beissel; *Cyclone Jack,* based on the life of Indian marathon runner, Tom Longboat, by Carol Bolt; and *A Dream of Sky People* by Isabelle Foord. As well as providing information on each play produced by Co-op members, the catalogue lists dramas available from other publishers and provides concise biographical information on the playwrights. The *Bibliography of Canadian Theatre History, 1583-1975* by John

Ball and Richard Plant is one example of basic resource information available from this publisher.

The Canadian Library Association publishes valuable monographs (e.g. *Coloured Reproductions of Canadian Paintings Available For Purchase*) and is producing a much needed item, *Canadian Materials.* A thrice-yearly periodical, *Canadian Materials* provides annotated, current, critical, and evaluative bibliographies of material for elementary and secondary schools in all media formats.

By this stage, the reader is probably longing for a handy omnibus distributor of learning materials such as Scholar's Choice.

2. The French Fact. With the exception of Canadabooks, almost all of the previously cited organizations engaged in the promotion and distribution of materials confine themselves exclusively to English language publications. The title of the conference attended by the Secretary of State (". . . English language publishing") speaks for itself. Similarly with the Annual Conference of the Canadian Book Sellers Association held in Halifax in June, 1975. French language publishing seems to be an afterthought. Outside of Quebec, materials prepared by Québécois are seldom displayed or promoted. This situation must be altered. Publishers, retail outlets, cooperatives, and national organizations should work toward acquainting educational institutions with publications in both official languages. A guideline of sorts is provided by looking quickly at the evolution of retail book outlets in Canada. Within recent memory it has become commonplace to enter book stores and search the shelves for those labelled "Canadiana". Initially, the search was a national embarrassment. Only a small collection of Canadian titles could be found amid the excess of imports. Gradually the situation has improved. Increased public awareness leading to an expanding market has stimulated more extensive publishing. A similar development in the promotion of Acadien, Québecois, Manitobaine and Franco-Colombien contributions should follow. The initial step is to create an awareness. Pierre Tisseyre, president of Le Conseil Superieur du Livre (the Quebec equivalent of the Canadian Book Sellers Association) has defined the problem:

The thing we'd all really like is to have a distributor willing to distribute French books across English Canada.

Quill and Quire, 40, September, 1974, p. 6.

In the same interview M. Tisseyre noted the ultimate in Canadian irony:

> Perhaps there is an ironic commentary in the fact that Le Conseil Superieur de Livre has found a distributor to pump French Canadian books into a predominately English market in the United States, but not in Canada.

It will be beneficial if teachers now will avail themselves of resources such as:

> *Le livre canadien,* 4635, rue de Lorimier, Montréal, Québec, H2H 2B4. This useful periodical keeps its readers informed of the books published in French in Canada. The subscription fee is $5.00 annually.

> Bibliothèque Nationale du Québec is publishing a series of bibliographies. An initial release is entitled *La femme au Québec.*

> Prise de Parole, c/o Cambrian College, 1400 Barrydown Road, Station A, Sudbury, Ontario offers Franco-Ontarien authors a reading service; assistance in re-writing manuscripts; and publishing opportunities (e.g. the play *Les Communards* by C. Belcourt is available).

> Cedar House Publishing, Room #1, 4507 Rupert Street, Vancouver V5R 2J4 has published a bilingual book for young readers, *Adventures in Canada /Les aventures au Canada,* $3.50.

> Les Éditions Ferland, Québec has available *La ville française* by Alphonse Deveau, a history of the Acadian peoples of southwestern Nova Scotia, $3.00.

Resources like these are limited in terms of what is required. They will, in combination with the addresses provided in the Appendix, help to make a beginning. Much more is necessary.

3. Government Activities. The report *Canadian Studies in Canadian Schools* gives an insight into the degree of enthusiasm with which Departments of Education have approached the question of Canadian curricula and learning materials. This study, commissioned by the Council of Ministers of Education in the early 1970s, involved interviews with 450 students, teachers, administrators, and curriculum experts. From the data obtained, three approaches for improving the quality of Canadian studies were suggested:

> There *might* be more references to Canadians and Canadian events.

Specific aspects of Canadian life *might* be examined through short-term units.

Interdisciplinary studies, *some* based on Canadian themes, *might find a more prominent place in a school program.*

> *Canadian Publishers and Canadian Publishing*
> (Toronto: Queen's Printer, 1973, p. 226)

Although the bureaucrats are not about to be stampeded into action, a few exceptions can be exploited. The efforts of the Ontario Ministry of Education through its curriculum publications have been mentioned previously. In 1975, the Alberta Department of Education launched two significant projects. The Great Canadian Content Machine, a mobile display of Canadian materials, toured the schools and communities of that province. Subsequently, the book *Canadian Resources* was published and distributed. It contains an extensive listing of materials useful in two subject areas: language arts and social studies. It is available from the Director of Curriculum, Alberta Department of Education, Executive Building, Edmonton. In the long term, perhaps the more significant development was the Alberta Government's announced intention of providing loans for Alberta publishers. Grants may be forthcoming to assist authors and publishers to produce literary works and textbooks.

Officially, education is not a federal concern. However, the publication *Federal Government Publications Selected For High School Libraries* should not be overlooked. Available in French and English from Information Canada, it lists five hundred annotated titles of items published between January, 1967 and June, 1973, with a supplement to January, 1974.

4. The Education Profession. Resources for improving education are not lacking. Annually, the Canadian Education Association publishes the *C.E.A. Handbook/Le Ki-es-ki.* In the 1975 edition the department of education, school board, teacher education, university and college, federal government, and private officials who influence the course of Canadian education are listed in 135 pages of fine print. It is clear that Canada is not lacking in governing bodies or worthy groups. Putting all of the pieces together to benefit the children who are the subject of this attention is something of a challenge.

A practical starting point is indicated in the following recommendation:

We recommend that teacher-training institutions provide

special training in the evaluation of learning materials, and particularly in the selection of books for educational resource
centres (school libraries), giving special attention to such skills
as assessing the adequacy of presentation of Canadian points
of view. We further recommend that this special training aim at
providing insights into the writing and publishing processes
as well as into the principles of selection, with a view to encouraging wider participation, including experimental participation,
in the creative development of new Canadian learning materials.

> *Ontario Royal Commission on Book Publishing*
> (Toronto: Queen's Printer, 1973, p. 266)

The need for teacher education programs along these lines is enor-
mous. A coalition of concerned parties, drawn from the groups just
mentioned, should seize this opportunity with alacrity.

A catalogue of resources is of value if it becomes a platform for
future action. Through item-by-item documentation, a picture
emerges of what can be used to advantage. Perhaps less apparent
but of equal importance, the gaps in existing materials are revealed.
With a degree of optimism it is possible to foresee these omissions
reduced and eventually eliminated. An examination of citizen,
government, and publisher initiatives across Canada suggests that a
trend in this direction is already underway.

But will these material contributions make a difference in the
lives of Canadian students? Will Canadian education give to all
students access to their cultural heritage in all of its dimensions? If
these basic questions are to be resolved emphatically in the favour
of Canadian young people, then there must be a radical shift in the
thinking of educators. Equal educational opportunity is not the
equivalent of equal access to mere resources, whether buildings,
books, or B.Ed. degrees.

> Equal opportunity for all does not mean nominal equality,
> the same treatment for everyone, as many still believe today;
> it means making certain that each individual receives a suitable
> education at a pace and through methods adapted to his par-
> ticular person.
>
> > *Learning To Be: The World of Education To-*
> > *day and Tomorrow*; UNESCO (Toronto: O.I.S.E.,
> > 1973, p. 75)

To date Canadian children have been rejected as persons with their
own specific linguistic, cultural, social and environmental characteristics. Responsibility for drastically altering this situation rests with

concerned parents, teachers, and students. The cumbersome education goliath will not be circumvented or subverted with ease. Neither will a sling-shot full of ideas do more than stun momentarily the educational establishment. Public opinion combined with politicized teacher organizations will have to bring to bear concerted and sustained pressure.

The realization that one generation separates the pre-school child of today from the twenty-first century should create a sense of urgency for sweeping change. The education of students who are secure in their own sense of identity and who are prepared to live in that world hinges largely on the willingness of the education system to move with uncustomary rapidity. That much Canadian society has the right to expect.

♦ ♦ ♦ ♦

Basic Reference Materials

Encyclopedia Canadiana, (Grolier, 1972), $139.50. 10 vols. Revision of 1957 edition.

Biography

Dictionary of Canadian Biography (U.T.P.), $20.00 each. Volume I (1000 – 1700), 1966; Volume II (1701– 1740), 1969; Volume III (1741 – 1770), 1975; Volume X (1871 – 1880), 1972.
Who's Who in Canada (General, 1975), $47.50.

Quotations

Colombo's Canadian Quotations, ed. John Robert Colombo (Hurtig, 1974), $15.00. Six thousand quotations from 2500 contributors; a topic and a keyword index of 20 000 entries included.

Finding Books

Canadian Books in Print, ed. Martha Pluscauskas (U.T.P., annual). Author and Title Index, $25.00. Subject Guide, $25.00. Lists in-print titles of most English-Canadian publishers.

Repertoire de l'édition au Quebec, (Édi-Quebec, annual), Lists in-print titles for most Quebec publishers.

Canadian Book Review Annual, ed. Dean Tudor, Nancy Tudor and Linda Biesenthal (Peter Martin, 1976), $27.50. Two-hundred-word reviews of all Canadian trade titles published on 1975, including 1975 reprints of books published before 1966, selected federal and provincial government publications, and English translations of French Canadian titles.

Canadian Fiction: An Annotated Bibliography, ed. Margery Fee and Ruth Cawker (Peter Martin, 1976), $8.95 pa. All in-print fiction titles by Canadians published to the end of 1974, including Quebec novels in translation and critical and biographical studies,   are listed with brief annotations.

Canadian Books for Children/Livres canadiens pour enfants, ed. Irma McDonough (U.T.P., 1976), $7.50 pa. An annotated subject catalogue of 1200 books and magazines in both French and English languages.

Canada Since 1867: A Bibliographical Guide, ed. J.L. Granatstein and Paul Stevens (Hakkert, 1974), $3.50 pa. Over 2000 entries.

Needed Canadian Textbooks, Paul Robinson (Atlantic Institute of Education, 1976), $1.00 pa. A digest of tips and shortcuts for locating materials.

Quill and Quire, Greey de Pencier. Monthly, $12.00. The best available periodical for keeping informed on Canadian publishing.

Books Canada, Canadian Review of Books. Monthly, $9.95. A useful book review periodical.

The Association of Canadian Publishers, 59 Front St. East, Toronto M5E 1B3, is a useful address for locating the lesser known Canadian publishers.

In Review, Ontario Provincial Library Service. Free within Ontario; elsewhere, 3 years, $10.00. Make cheques payable to the Treasurer of Ontario and mail to Ministry of Culture and Recreation, Provincial Library Service, Parliament Buildings, Queen's Park, Toronto, Ontario, M7A 2R7.

Canadian Materials, Canadian Library Association. Tri-annual, $5.00.

Canadian Reader, Readers' Club of Canada. Monthly. Free to members. To others, $8.00 a year.

Finding Magazines

Canadian Periodicals for Schools, Canadian Periodical for Schools.

Finding Films

The Handbook of Canadian Film, 2nd ed. Eleanor Beattie (Peter Martin 1977), $5.95 pa. History, biographies, a guide to sources and resources for Canadian films. Two useful addresses for locating information on feature film production:

Société de developpement de l'Industrie Cinématographique Canadienne, C.P. 71, Tour de la Bourse, 800 Place Victoria, Suite 2220, Montreal 115, P.Q.

Canadian Film Development Corporation, Store 18, Lothian Mews, 96 Bloor Street West, Toronto 5, Ontario.

Finding Games

Thinking Games, Carl Bereiter and Valerie Anderson (O.I.S.E., 1975), 2 vols, $3.25 each. Vol. 1 has 54 games for ages 5-8; Vol. 2 has 64 games for ages 8-12.

Parker Brothers, Box 600, Concord, Ontario. L4K 1B7.

House of Games, Bramalea, Ontario.

Canadian Literature

CANLIT is an independent non-profit research corporation which provides information and materials of value to any course on Canadian literature. A free newsletter is available by writing to Box 1551, Peterborough, Ontario.

Finding Scholarly Periodicals

The Periodicals Department, University of Toronto Press, has available 21 items of value to senior high school students and teachers. Among them are:

The Canadian Geographer. Quarterly, $15.00.

Canadian Journal of Economics. Quarterly, $15.00.

Canadian Journal of Linguistics. Bi-annual, $10.00.

Science Forum. Bi-monthly, $10.00.

Appendix

Publishers and Distributors

Acadie
Les Éditions d'Acadie Ltée.
120 rue Victoria
C.P. 2006
Moncton, N.B. E1C 8H7

All about us/Nous autres
All about us/Nous autres
Box 1985
Ottawa

Anglican Book Centre
Anglican Book Centre
600 Jarvis Street
Toronto

Aquila
Les Editions Aquila Ltée.
3785 Côte de Liesse
Montréal H4N 2N5

Athabascan
Athabascan Publishing Company
3009-105 Street
Edmonton Alta.

Atlantic Institute of Education
Atlantic Institute of Education
5244 South Street
Halifax, Nova Scotia

Beauchemin
La Librairie Beauchemin Ltée
450 Ave. Beaumont
Montreal H3N 1T8

Belford
Belford Book Distributing
11 Boulton Ave.
Toronto M4M 2J4

Bell
Bell Books
612 Herald Bldg.
206-7th Avenue, S.W.
Calgary, Alta. T2P 0W7

Berandol Music
Berandol Music
11 St. Joseph St.
Toronto M4Y 1J8

Bien Public
c/o Les Éditions de l'Homme Ltée.
955 rue Amherst
Montreal H2L 3K4

Blackfish
Blackfish Press
1851 Moore Ave.
Burnaby, B.C.

Black Rose
Black Rose Books
3934 rue St.-Urbain
Montreal G9K 9A5

Book Centre
Book Centre Inc.
1149 Beaulac St.
Montreal L3R 1H1

Book Society
Book Society of Canada
Box 200
Agincourt, Ont. M1S 3B6

Borealis
Borealis Press Ltd.
9 Ashburn Dr.
Ottawa K2E 6N4

Boy Scouts of Canada
Boy Scouts of Canada
1345 Baseline Road
P.O. Box 5151, Postal Stn. "F"
Ottawa

Brandon University Press
Brandon University Press
Brandon, Man.

Breakwater
Breakwater Books
Box 52 Site C
Portugal Cove, Nfld.

British Columbia Teachers' Federation,
    Lesson Aid Service
105-2235 Burrard St.
Vancouver, B.C. V6J 1H9

Brunswick

Brunswick Press
74 Cliffe St.
Fredericton, N.B.

Burns and MacEachern
Burns and MacEachern Ltd.
62 Railside Road
Don Mills, Ont. M3A 1A6

C.B.C. Learning Systems
Box 500, Terminal A
Toronto M5W 1E6

C.B.C. Publications Branch
C.B.C. Publications Branch
Box 500, Terminal A
Toronto M5W 1E6

C.P.P.
Centre de Psychologie et de Pedagogie
260 ouest, rue Faillon
Montréal H2R 2U7

Canada Studies Foundation
252 Bloor St. W.
Toronto M5S 1V5

Canadabooks
Books for Canadian Education
59 Front St. E., 2nd Floor
Toronto M5E 1B3

Canadian Books for Children
Book and Periodical Development
    Council
Box 6428, Stn. A
Toronto M5W 1X3

Canadian Daily Newspaper Publishers
    Association
Suite 206, 250 Bloor St. E.
Toronto M4W 1E7

Canadian Dimension
Canadian Dimension
Box 1413
Winnipeg, Man.

Canadian Education Association
252 Bloor St. W.
Toronto M5S 1V5

Canadian F.D.S. Audiovisual
185 Spadina Ave.
Toronto M5T 2C6

Canadian Library Association

Canadian Library Association
151 Sparks St.
Ottawa K1P 5E3

Canadian Materials
Box 190, Stn. O
Toronto M4A 2N3

Canadian Nature Federation
46 Elgin St.
Ottawa K1P 5K6

Canadian Periodical Publishers' Association
3 Church St. Suite 407
Toronto M5E 1M2

Canadian Periodicals for Schools
Ontario Library Association
2397 A Bloor St. W.
Toronto

Canadian Remainder Sales
366 Adelaide St. E.
Toronto M5A 1K1

Canadian Review of Books
6 Charles St. E.
Toronto M4Y 1T2

Canadian Stage
Canadian Stage and Art Productions
52 Avenue Rd.
Toronto

Canadian Womens' Educational Press
Canadian Womens' Educational Press
280 Bloor St. W. No. 305
Toronto M5S 1W1

Cedar
Cedar House Publishing
Rm. 1, 4507 Rupert St.
Vancouver V5R 214

Cheam
Cheam Publishers
P.O. Box 99
Agassiz, B.C. V0M 1A0

Cinemedia,
Box 332
Agincourt, Ont. M1S 3B9

Clarke, Irwin
Clarke, Irwin and Co. Ltd.
Clarwin House

791 St. Clair Ave. W.
Toronto M6C 1B8

Coach House
Coach House Press
401 Huron St.
Toronto M5S 2G5

Colban
Colban
Suite 380, 151 Bloor St. W.
Toronto M5S 1S4

Coles
Coles Publishing Co. Ltd.
90 Ronson Dr.
Rexdale, Ont. M9W 1C1

Collier-Macmillan
Collier-Macmillan Canada Ltd.
539 Collier-Macmillan Dr.
Cambridge, Ont.

Collins
William Collins and Sons Ltd.
100 Lesmill Rd.
Don Mills, Ont. M3B 2T5

Communique: Canadian Studies
The Association of Canadian Community Colleges
1750 Finch Ave. E.
Willowdale, Ont. M2N 5T7

Content
Content Publishing Ltd.
Suite 404, 1411 Crescent St.
Montreal 107

Co-operative Book Centre of Canada, Ltd.
66 Northline Rd.
Toronto M4B 3E6

Copp Clark
Copp Clark Publishing Co. Ltd.
517 Wellington St. W.
Toronto M5V 1G1

Cove
Cove Press
2125 Seal Cove Circle
Prince Rupert, B.C. V8J 2G4

Coyoti Prints
Box 6000
Williams Lake, B.C.

Crawley Films
19 Fairmont Ave.
Ottawa K1Y 3B5

Dent
J.M. Dent and Sons (Canada) Ltd.
100 Scarsdale Road
Don Mills, Ont. M3B 2R8

Derksen
Derksen Printers
Box 1209
Steinback, Man.

Development Press
Box 1016
Oakville, Ont.

Didier   see *Marcel Didier*

Doubleday
Doubleday Canada Ltd.
105 Bond St.
Toronto M5B 1Y3

Douglas   see *J.J. Douglas*

Dundurn
Dundurn Press
Box 245
Station "F"
Toronto M4Y 2L5

E.B.
Encyclopedia Britannica
151 Bloor St. W.
Toronto M5S 1T1

E.T.H.O.S.
Canadian Producers of Sound Film
   Strips Programs
2250 Midland Ave., Unit #9
Scarborough, Ont. M1P 3E6

Ed. Officiel
L'Editeur Officiel du Québec
675 est, Boul. Saint-Cyrille
Québec, P.Q. G1R 4Y7

Edi-Québec,
Edi-Québec
436 est, rue Sherbrooke
Montréal H2L 1J6

Les Editions d'Acadie   see *Acadie*

Editions Aquila, Ltée.   see *Aquila*

Les Editions du Bien public   see *Bien public*

Les Editions de l'Etincelle, Enr.   see *Etincelle*

Les Editions Ferland   *see Ferland*

Les Editions de l'Homme Ltée,   see *Homme*

Les Editions Hurtubise-H.M.H. Ltée.
see H.M.H.

Les Editions Leméac Inc. see *Leméac*

Les Editions Pedagogia see Pedagogia

Les Editions Québecoise   see Québec-oise

Educational Research Institute of
British Columbia
1237 Burrard St.
Vancouver V2J 1B2

Encyclopedia Britannica Ltd. see *EB*

Etincelle
Les Editions de l'Etincelle Enr.
C.P. 702
Montréal 154

Fiddlehead
Fiddlehead Books
c/o Saannes Publications Ltd.
1293 Gerrard St. E.
Toronto M4L 1Y8

Fitzhenry and Whiteside
Fitzhenry and Whiteside Ltd.
150 Lesmill Rd.
Don Mills, Ont. M3B 2T5

Foremost
Foremost Publishing Co.
P.O. Box 900, Postal Stn. "A"
Surrey, B.C.

Formac
Formac Ltd.
Box 111
Antigonish, N.S.

Frontier
Frontier Publishing Ltd.
27247 Fraser Highway, Box 519
Aldergrove, B.C. V0X 1A0

G.L.C.
G.L.C. Education Materials and Ser-vices Ltd.
115 Nugget
Agincourt, Ont. M1S 3B1

Gage
Gage Publishing Ltd.
P.O. Box 5000
164 Commander Blvd.
Agincourt, Ont. M1S 3C7

General
General Publishing Co. Ltd.
30 Lesmill Rd.
Don Mills, Ont. M3B 2T6

Ginn
Ginn and Co. Educational Publications
3771 Victoria Park Ave.
Scarborough, Ont. M1W 2P9

Glenbow
Glenbow Foundation
9 Ave & 1st St. S.E.
Calgary, Alta.

Graydonald
Graydonald Graphics
1070 Groveland Rd.
West Vancouver, B.C. V75 1Z4

Gray
Gray's Publishing Ltd.
P.O. Box 2160
Sidney, B.C. V8L 3S6

Green Tree
Green Tree Publishing Co. Ltd.
70 Bathurst St.
Toronto M5V 2P5

Greey de Pencier
Greey de Pencier Publications Ltd.
59 Front St. E.
Toronto M5E 1B3

Grolier
Grolier Ltd.
200 University Ave.
Toronto M5H 3E2

Griffin
Griffin House
461 King St. W.
Toronto M5V 1K7

Grosset
Grosset Publishing
c/o George McLeod Ltd.
73 Bathurst St.
Toronto M5V 2P8

Guidance Centre, University of
*   Toronto*
Guidance Centre, University of Toronto
100 Yonge St.
Toronto M4W 2K8

Guinness
Guinness Publishing
P.O. Box 46205
Vancouver V6R 4G5

H.M.H.
Les Editions Hurtubise-H.M.H. Ltée.
380 ouest, rue Craig
Montréal H2Y 1J9

Hakkert
Hakkert Ltd.
554 Spadina Cr.
Toronto M5F 2J9

Hancock
Hancock House Ltd.
3215 Island View Rd.
Saanichton, B.C.

Harvest
Harvest House Ltd.
4795 St. Catherine St. W.
Montreal H3Z 2B9

Heath
D.C. Heath Canada Ltd.
Suite 1408, 100 Adelaide St. W.
Toronto M5H 1S9

Highway Book Shop
Highway Book Shop
Cobalt, Ont. P0J 1C0

Holt
Holt, Rinehart and Winston of Canada Ltd.
55 Horner Ave.
Toronto M8Z 4X6

Homme
Les Éditions de l'Homme Ltée.
955 rue Amherst
Montréal H2L 3K4

Hounslow
Hounslow Press
124 Parkview Ave.
Willowdale, Ont. M2N 3Y5

Hurtig
Hurtig Publishers
10560-105 Street
Edmonton, Alta. T5H 2W7

Impressions Photographic Society
Box 5, Stn. B
Toronto M5T 2T2

Information Canada is now:
Publishing Centre
Supply and Services Canada
270 Albert St.
Ottawa K1A 0S9

Int'l Self-Counsel, see *Self-Counsel*
   Int'l.
International Tele-Film Enterprises
47 Densley Ave.
Toronto M6M 5A8

James Lorimer
James Lorimer
c/o Belford Book Distributing
11 Boulton Ave.
Toronto M4M 2J4

J.J. Douglas
J.J. Douglas Publishing Co.
1875 Welch St.
North Vancouver V7P 1B7

Kids Can
Kids Can Press
Box 5974, Stn. A
Toronto

Klassen
A. Klassen
174 Lydia St.
Kitchener, Ont.

Lancelot
Lancelot Press Ltd.
Box 2020
Windsor, N.S.

Landry
La Librairie Landry
180 Blvd. Provencher
St. Boniface, Man. R2H 0G3

Lebel Enterprises
10624-84 Avenue
Edmonton, Alta. T6E 2H6

Leméac
Les Editions Leméac Ltée.
5111 rue Durocher
Outremont, Montréal H2V 3X7

La Librairie Beauchemin   see *Beauchemin*

La Librairie Landry   see *Landry*

Lillooet
Lillooet Publishers
P.O. Box 100
Lillooet, B.C.

Les Livres Toundra   see *Toundra*

Longman
Longman Canada Ltd.
55 Barber Greene Rd.
Don Mills, Ont. M3C 2A1

Lorimer   see *James Lorimer*

Maclean-Hunter
Maclean-Hunter Ltd.
481 University Ave.
Toronto M5W 1A7

Macmillan
Macmillan Company of Canada Ltd.
70 Bond St.
Toronto M5B 1X3

McClelland
McClelland and Stewart Ltd.
25 Hollinger Rd.
Toronto M4B 3G2

McDonald
McDonald House
125 Davenport Rd.
Toronto

McGill-Queen's
McGill-Queen's University Press
Purvis Hall
1021 Pine Ave. W.
Montreal H3A 1AZ

McGraw
McGraw-Hill Ryerson, Ltd.
330 Progress Ave.
Scarborough, Ont. M1P 2Z5

McIntyre Educational Media Ltd.
86 St. Regis Crescent, North
Downsview, Ont. M3J 1Z3

Manitoba Indian Brotherhood
600-191 Lumbard Ave.
Winnipeg, Man. R3B 0X1

Marcel Didier
Marcel Didier (Canada) Ltd.
1422 ave. McGill College
Montreal H3A 1Z6

Marie Nightengale
Marie Nightengale
1050 Greenwood Ave.
Halifax, N.S. B3H 3L2

Memorial University Press
Memorial University Press
Memorial University
St. John's, Nfld.

Methuen
Methuen Publications
2330 Midland Ave.
Agincourt, Ont. M15 1P7

Metro Toronto News Co.
120 Sinott Rd.
Scarborough, Ont. M1L 4N1

Mika
Mika Publishing Co.
200 Stanley Ave.
Belleville, Ont. K8N 5B2

Mir
Mir Publication Society
Grand Forks, B.C.

Mitchell
Mitchell Press Ltd.
Box 6000
Vancouver V6B 4B9

Moreland-Latchford Ltd.
299 Queen St. W.
Toronto 133

Musson
Musson Book Co.
30 Lesmill Rd.
Don Mills, Ont. M3B 2T6

N.C. Press
N.C. Press Ltd.

Box 4010, Stn. A
Toronto M5W 1H8

N.F.B.
National Film Board of Canada
Box 6100
Montreal
(or regional office nearest you)

National Gallery of Canada
Ottawa

Natural Science of Canada
c/o McClelland and Stewart Ltd.
25 Hollinger Rd.
Toronto M4B 3G2

Nelson
Thomas Nelson and Sons (Canada) Ltd.
81 Curlew Dr.
Don Mills, Ont. M3A 2R1

Nelson, Foster
Nelson, Foster and Scott Ltd.
299 Yorkland Blvd.
Willowdale, Ont. M2J 1S9

New Brunswick Museum,
277 Douglas Ave.
St. John, N.B.

New Canadian Publications
2003 Yonge St.
Toronto 7

New Leaf
New Leaf Publications
80 Richmond St. E.
Toronto M5C 9Z9

New
New Press
30 Lesmill Rd.
Don Mills, Ont. M3B 2T6

Nova Scotia Dept. of Lands and Forests
1740 Granville St.
Halifax, N.S.

Nova Scotia Gov't. Book Store
Barrington St.
Halifax, N.S.

Nova Scotia Human Rights Commission
c/o Lord Nelson Hotel

South Park St.
Halifax, N.S.

Nova Scotia Museum
1747 Summer St.
Halifax, N.S.

November
November House Publishers
1004 Hamilton St.
Vancouver 3

Oberon
Oberon Press
555 Maple Lane
Ottawa K1M 0N7

O.I.S.E.
Ontario Institute for Studies in Education
Publications and Sales
252 Bloor St. W.
Toronto M5S 1V6

Oxford
Oxford University Press
70 Wynford Dr.
Don Mills, Ont. M3C 1J7

P.U.L.
Les Presses de l'université Laval
Avenue de la médecine
Cité universitaire, Sainte-Foy
C.P. 2477, Québec G1K 7R4

P.U.M.
Les Presses de l'université de Montréal
C.P. 6128, Montréal H3T 1J7

P.U.Q.
Les presses de l'université du Québec
3465 rue Durocher
Montréal 130

Pagurian
Pagurian Press Ltd.
335 Bay St.
Suite 603
Toronto M5H 2R3

Pedagogia
Les Éditions Pedagogia Inc.
192 est rue Dorchester
Québec 2, P.Q.

Peguis
Peguis Publishers

462 Hargrave St.
Winnipeg, Man. R3A 0X5

Penguin
Penguin Books Canada Ltd.
41 Steelcase Rd. W.
Markham, Ont.

Peter Martin
Peter Martin Associates Limited
280 Bloor St. W.
Toronto M5S 1W1

Petheric
Petheric Press Ltd.
1663 Market St.
Box 1102
Halifax, N.S.

Philatelic Service Philatelique
Postes Canada Post
Ottawa K1A 0B5

Pile of Bones
Pile of Bones Publishing Co.
University of Saskatchewan
Regina, Sask.

Pitman
Sir Isaac Pitman (Canada) Ltd.
517 Wellington St. W.
Toronto M5V 1G1

Playwrights' Co-op
Playwrights' Co-op
8 York St. 6th Floor
Toronto M5J 1R2

Porcépic
Press Porcépic
70 Main St.
Erin, Ont. N0B 1T0

Potlatch
Potlatch Publications
35 Dalewood Cres.
Hamilton, Ont. L8S 4B5

Prentice
Prentice-Hall of Canada Ltd.
1870 Birchmount Rd.
Scarborough, Ont. M1P 2J7

Prince Edward Island Heritage Foundation
2 Kent St., Box 922
Charlottetown, P.E.I.

Prise de Parole
Prise de Parole
c/o Cambrian College
1400 Barrydown Rd. Stn. A
Sudbury, Ont.

Progress
Progress Books
487 Adelaide St. W.
Toronto M5V 1T4

Québécoise
Editions de la Québécoise
Centre de diffusion de la poésie
    Canadienne
1773 rue St. Denis
Montréal H2X 3K4

Queenston
Queenston House
102 Queenston St.
Winnipeg, Man. R3N 0W5

Random House
Random House of Canada Ltd.
5390 Ambler Dr.
Mississauga, Ont. L4W 1Y7

Readers' Club of Canada
35 Britain St.
Toronto M5A 1R7

Research Institute of Northern Canada
Box 188
Yellowknife, N.W.T. X0E 1H0

Royal Ontario Museum
Royal Ontario Museum, c/o Publications
100 Queen's Park
Toronto M5S 2C6

SRA
Science Research Associates (Canada)
    Ltd.
707 Gordon Baker Rd.
Willowdale, Ont. M2H 3B4

Saannes
Saannes Publications Ltd.
1293 Gerrard St. E.
Toronto M4L 1Y8

Scholars' Choice
Scholars' Choice Ltd.

50 Ballantyne Ave.
Stratford, Ont. N5A 6T9

Scholastic
Scholastic Book Services
123 Newkirk Rd.
Richmond Hill, Ont. L4C 3G5

Self Counsel Int'l.
Self Counsel Press International
306 West 25th St.
North Vancouver, B.C.

Simon and Pierre
Simon and Pierre Publishers
Box 280, Adelaide St. Postal Stn.
Toronto M5C 1J0

Simon and Schuster
Simon and Schuster of Canada Ltd.
330 Steelcase Rd.
Markham, Ont. L3R 2M1

H.H. Simpson Ltd.
38 University Ave.
Box 636
Charlottetown, P.E.I.

Harry Smith and Sons
520 King St. W.
Toronto

Sono Nis
Sono Nis Press
4565 Church St.
Delta, B.C. V4K 2K9

Square Deal
Square Deal Publications
Charlottetown, P.E.I.

Stagecoach
Stagecoach Publishing Co.
Attn. T.W. Paterson
Fir Grove Acres
R.R. #2
Cobble Hill, B.C. V0R 1L0

Steel Rail Publishing
P.O. Box 6813, Station A
Toronto M5W 1X6

Talonbooks
Talonbooks
201-1019 East Cordova
Vancouver, B.C. V6A 1M8

Tantalus
Tantalus Research Ltd.
Box 34248
2405 Pine St.
Vancouver V6J 4N8

Tecumseh
Tecumseh Press
8 Mohawk Cres.
Ottawa K1H 7G6

Toronto Star
1 Yonge Street
Toronto M5E 1E6

Toundra
Les Livres Toundra
1500 St. Catherine St. W.
Montréal 107

Tree Frog
Tree Frog Press
10717—106 Avenue
Edmonton, Alta.

Trident
Trident Press Ltd.
840 Main St.
Winnipeg, Man.

Tundra
Tundra Books of Montreal
1374 Sherbrooke St. W.
Suite 17
Montreal H3G 1J6

U.T.P.
University of Toronto Press
Front Campus
University of Toronto
Toronto M5S 1A6

University of Alberta Press
University of Alberta Press
326 Assiniboia Hall
University of Alberta
Edmonton, Alta. T6G 2E1

University of British Columbia Press
University of British Columbia Press
2075 Westbrook Pl.
Vancouver V6T 1W5

University of Manitoba Press
University of Manitoba Press
Administration Building

University of Manitoba
Winnipeg, Man. R3T 2N2

University of Ottawa Press
University of Ottawa Press
65 Hastey Ave.
University of Ottawa
Ottawa K1N 6N5

Van Nostrand
Van Nostrand Reinhold Ltd.
1410 Birchmount Rd.
Scarborough, Ont. M1P 2E7

Vancouver Environmental Education
  Project (V.E.E.P.)
Lesson Aids Service
see British Columbia Teachers' Federation

Vesta
Vesta Publications
Box 1641
Cornwall, Ont.

Viking Films Ltd.
524 Denison St.
Markham, Ont. L3R 1B8

Visual Education Centre
115 Berkeley St.
Toronto

Waterloo Music Company
Waterloo Music Company
Box 250
Waterloo, Ont.

Western Fish and Game
Western Fish and Game
P.O. Box 303
West Vancouver, B.C.

Western Heritage
Western Heritage Supply Ltd.
Box 399
27247 Fraser Highway
Aldegrove, B.C. V0X 1A0

Western Producer
Western Producer Book Service
446 2nd Avenue N.
Saskatoon, Sask. S7K 2C4

Wiley
John Wiley and Sons Canada Ltd.
22 Worcester Rd.
Rexdale, Ont. M9W 1L1

Women Teachers' Association of
    Ontario
1260 Bay St., 3rd Floor
Toronto M5R 2B8

Yorkminster
Yorkminster Publishing
57 Yorkminster Rd.
Willowdale, Ont. M2P 1M4